Introduction to Austrian and European Legal History in its Global Context

Second, completely revised Edition

by

Thomas Olechowski

Translated by

Ramon Pils

Vienna 2025

facultas

To Miriam

Bibliografische Information der Deutschen Nationalbibliothek

Die Deutsche Nationalbibliothek verzeichnet diese Publikation in der Deutschen Nationalbibliografie; detaillierte bibliografische Daten sind im Internet über http://dnb.d-nb.de abrufbar.

Facultas.wuv Universitätsverlag, Stolberggasse 26, A-1050 Wien

Satz: Thomas Olechowski
Printed in Austria

ISBN 978-3-7089-2628-5

Preface to the Second Edition

The first edition of this textbook was completed before the launch of the International Legal Studies programme. We had no idea where the journey would take us, so I simply gave selected chapters of my German textbook for translation. The second edition is a thorough revision of the material and will hopefully better serve the needs of the new programme. Most noticeable is the new structure with its eight parts; most important, however, are the many asides to developments in the Middle East, the Americas, and other parts of the world which were significant for the development of European law.

Despite these additions, the textbook remains focused on European legal history, with a particular emphasis on Austria. It does not aspire to be a global legal history. A work deserving of that title would need to be written by someone with not only an extensive knowledge of diverse legal cultures but also a deep familiarity with legal developments across all continents—qualifications I do not claim to possess. My only viable approach to global legal history is to view the distant past through the lens of my own country's experience, just as the past can only be interpreted meaningfully from the standpoint of the present. For this reason, the title of this textbook makes no claim to global coverage. Its purpose is not to present a universal legal history, but rather to situate Austrian and European legal history within a broader global context.

The sections on international law in this textbook have been significantly expanded for this edition. The chapters on constitutional law have also been revised and extended, particularly in relation to the development of public law jurisdiction and fundamental rights. Given the inclusion of new material on Jewish and Islamic law, it seemed appropriate to offer a more comprehensive discussion of freedom of religion. In addition, the fundamental right to equality and, in this context, gender equality were also addressed. As a result, greater emphasis was placed also on the development of marriage law.

I received substantial support in preparing this edition. My one-year stay as a visiting scholar and visiting professor at Stanford University in 2024/25 afforded me valuable insights into legal history beyond Europe. Regarding aspects of religious legal history, I am indebted to Professor STEFAN SCHIMA for numerous helpful suggestions. I would like to thank ELKE MARIA PANI, Mag. BARTOSZ BUCHMAN, Dr. RICHARD LEIN, and KATHARINA LENZ for their assistance with the graphics, maps, and indexes. Finally, I would like to thank Mag. RAMON PILS, Dip.Trans., who kindly translated the new material.

Stanford, June 2025 THOMAS OLECHOWSKI

Preface to the First Edition

With the beginning of the winter semester 2021/22, degree programmes in International Legal Studies (LLB/LLM) will be introduced at the University of Vienna alongside the traditional Law programme. Like the latter, they will offer a preparatory academic education for the legal professions but, in addition, will also provide a more profound introduction to the international aspects of the law. As part of this programme, the module "European and Global Legal History" will be offered in English. This course will also be more internationally oriented than its counterpart in the existing Law programme but will retain much of the content of the traditional course "Legal and Constitutional History of the Modern Era".

This book covers what could be described as the overlap of both courses, i.e. those aspects of legal history that are taught both in the existing Law programme and in the new programme in International Legal Studies. It is a translation of the relevant chapters from my book "Rechtsgeschichte. Einführung in die historischen Grundlagen des Rechts", which appeared for the first time in 2006 and most recently in its fifth edition in 2019, all with the same publisher as this book. Some minor adaptations and updates have been included in the English edition. It does not cover all of the material of the new course; for any new content that will be added, regarding non-European and global aspects of the law, in particular, additional resources will be made available.

Conversely, this book does not cover the entire content of the older course. This is because, if the number of course units remains the same, the addition of new content will only be possible at the expense of other things that used to be taught in the past. It is therefore with a heavy heart that I have decided to omit, in particular, a history of Austrian private law, at least of the kind that Werner Ogris, Ursula Flossmann, and other Austrian legal historians have taught for decades, and that I myself continue to teach as part of the Law programme at the University of Vienna. [...]

I was very fortunate to have found a qualified translator in Mag. Ramon Pils, Dip.Trans., who was previously also a researcher and lecturer at the Institute of Legal and Constitutional History at the University of Vienna, and who was not least for this reason able to master the translation of complex legal and/or historical concepts. I would like to express my heartfelt thanks to him for his work. I would also like to thank Mag. Carmen Kleinszig, Dr. Stefan Wedrac, Martin Krall, Mia Krieghofer, and Milena Lepir for their very valuable help in developing this book. My sincere thanks also go out to the publisher, facultas, and Mr. Peter Wittmann, in particular, whose support for this project has made it possible to make this book available to our students in time for their first semester.

I dedicate this book to my wife.

Vienna, Summer 2021 Thomas Olechowski

Table of Contents

List of Tables and Maps

List of Abbreviations

ABGB	Allgemeines bürgerliches Gesetzbuch (General Civil Code of Austria)
AD	anno Domini
ALR	Allgemeines Landrecht für die Preußischen Staaten (Prussian General State Laws)
BC	before Christ
BGB	Bürgerliches Gesetzbuch (German Civil Code)
B-VG	Bundes-Verfassungsgesetz (Federal Constitutional Law)
BZÖ	Bündnis Zukunft Österreich (Alliance for the Future of Austria)
CC	Code Civil
CCC	Constitutio Criminalis Carolina
CCTh	Constitutio Criminalis Theresiana
CDU	Christian Democratic Union
CFR	Charter of Fundamental Rights
CMBC	Codex Maximilianeus Bavaricus Civilis
COMECON	Council for Mutual Economic Assistance
CPSU	Communist Party of the Soviet Union
CSCE	Conference on Security and Co-operation in Europe
CFSP	Common Foreign and Security Policy
CTher	Codex Theresianus
ČSR	Czechoslovakia
ČSSR	Czechoslovak Socialist Republic
D	Digest
EAEC	European Atomic Energy Community
EC	European Community
ECHR	European Convention on Human Rights
ECJ	European Court of Justice
ECSC	European Coal and Steel Community
ECtHR	European Court of Human Rights
EEA	European Economic Area
EEC	European Economic Community
EMU	Economic and Monetary Union
EPC	European Political Cooperation
EU	European Union
FPÖ	Freiheitliche Partei Österreichs (Freedom Party of Austria)
FRG	Federal Republic of Germany
GDR	German Democratic Republic
GG	Grundgesetz (German Basic Law)
Kg	King
KPD	Kommunistische Partei Deutschlands (German Communist Party)
KPÖ	Kommunistische Partei Österreichs (Communist Party of Austria)

KwEG	Kriegswirtschaftliches Ermächtigungsgesetz (War Economy Enabling Act)
NS	Nationalsozialismus (National Socialism)
NSDAP	Nationalsozialistische Deutsche Arbeiterpartei (National Socialist German Workers' Party)
ÖVP	Österreichische Volkspartei (Austrian People's Party)
PNF	Partito Nazionale Fascista
SEA	Single European Act
SED	Sozialistische Einheitspartei Deutschlands (Socialist Unity Party of Germany)
SPD	Sozialdemokratische Partei Deutschlands (Social Democratic Party of Germany)
SPÖ	Sozialdemokratische (Sozialistische) Partei Österreichs (Social Democratic / Socialist Party of Austria)
StGB	Strafgesetzbuch (Criminal Code)
TEU	Treaty on European Union
TFEU	Treaty on the Functioning of the European Union
UK	United Kingdom of Great Britain and (Northern) Ireland
USSR	Union of Soviet Socialist Republics
VdU	Verband der Unabhängigen (Association of Independents)
WGGB	Westgalizisches Gesetzbuch (Civil Code for Western Galicia)

Introduction

A The Purpose of Legal History

0001 **Legal history** is an interdisciplinary academic endeavour that belongs to both the legal and historical disciplines. It is relevant to jurisprudence not least because it facilitates a better understanding of the legal system that is currently in place.

➢ The law, in its historical development, reflects the values of a civilisation. The purpose of legal history is to reveal the ideological, social, economic, and other political factors that "lead to the development of the law as the life-conditioning order of every community" (HEINRICH MITTEIS).

➢ Thereby, legal history provides a deeper insight into the law and sheds light on the conditions of its mutability. To what extent legal history can make a concrete contribution to legal policy is widely debated and ultimately leads to the more general question of the extent to which humans can learn from their history at all. Whatever the case, legal history can help to prevent the "delusion that the development of a legal order will always lead, almost automatically, to a higher degree of perfection. The opposite is the case: no era and no legal order is free of challenges and the risk of relapse" (WERNER OGRIS).

➢ The prerequisite for legal history as it is defined here is, of course, that the law "can be understood as a historical phenomenon at all" (MICHAEL STOLLEIS). Legal history thus sets out from a specific concept of the law. Determining this concept is not the task of legal historical *research*; rather, legal history must *choose* the concept of the law that seems most *useful* for it to be able to pursue its tasks. It is therefore a matter of definition and not open to falsification.

0002 This textbook is based on the insights of the **Vienna School of Legal Theory** (the "pure theory of law"), which tells us that the law is a "regulatory system which is created by humans for humans and is generally effective, and which may apply organised coercion" (ROBERT WALTER).

➢ Legal history studies the law as an interpretative framework for human behaviour; many events only make sense when they are understood as reactions to legal norms. Therefore, it makes sense to focus only on law that was indeed "lived" (i.e. effective). This does not mean that all of its norms were consistently followed, but there had to be at least the "chance" of "coercion being applied by a staff of people in order to bring about compliance or avenge violation" (MAX WEBER).

➢ This definition of the law is confined to positive law, i.e. norms posited by humans. However, there has also always been an assumption that, apart from positive law, there is also a legal order that cannot be influenced by humans. This order has been called *natural law* (⇨ par. 2321). Since this idea had an impact on the development of positive law, it is considered a driving force of positive law and thus, to a certain extent, also an object of legal historical research.

➢ This definition also disregards the notion of justice (which is otherwise often used to define positive law), not only because, in the author's opinion, this can only ever be a subjective standard, but also because even legal systems that all "civilised nations" (cf. Article 7 ECHR) would perceive as unjust can, at least temporarily, achieve effectiveness (as evidenced by the example of National Socialist law, for instance), and legal scholars are also interested in understanding such legal systems.

0003 As HANS KELSEN has shown, all legal systems that are deemed valid are also interrelated. This textbook is based on the notion of a *universal international legal order* from which the various partial legal orders either directly or indirectly derive their validity. These partial orders include, in particular, **states and religious communities**.

➢ This means that a state is nothing more and nothing less than a (partial) legal order. The modern state is characterised by the fact that its legal order is relatively centralised and covers a relatively well-defined territory and group of people, which is conventionally described as the triad "state power – state territory – state people" (according to GEORG JELLINEK and others). Note, however, that this *three-element doctrine*, as a product of modern jurisprudence, is of limited use in relation to the partial legal orders of earlier periods. Whether one should also refer to these older entities as "states" or use a different term (for instance "regimes of normativity" or "feudal state of personal association" in the context of medieval feudal structures) depends on whether one wants to emphasise their resemblance or dissimilarity to modern states.

➢ A state that derives its existence directly from general international law is a *sovereign state*. Sovereign entities in this sense would be, for example, the Republic of Austria and the Federal Republic of Germany, but not their Länder. State theory up to the 20th century had been based on a sharp distinction between national and international law, with sovereignty acting as the dividing membrane between them. Therefore, only sovereign states could be subjects of international law (with a few exceptions); the legal relationships of individuals, on the other hand, were a matter for the respective states alone. More recent developments in international law and especially also in European law have increasingly called this dividing line into question.

➢ The difference between religious communities and states is that the coercion exercised by the former consists primarily in the granting or withholding of spiritual salvation (hierocratic coercion). The Catholic Church, in particular, likened itself to a state well into the 20th century. Since the Second Vatican Council, it has no longer embraced this view, but with the *Codex Iuris Canonici* of 1983, it has once again given itself a constitution that resembles that of a state, namely of an absolute monarchy. The law of a religious community can be derived either from the legal order of a state or directly from the international legal order; in the latter case, it is also sovereign (e.g. the legal order of the Holy See).

0004 This textbook focuses on the historical foundations of the legal order applicable in present-day **Austria**, which, however, can only be properly understood if they are embedded in the European context. On the other hand, many European tendencies can be demonstrated by using Austria as an example, which makes this textbook also an introduction to **European legal history**. By contrast, global or non-European legal developments are addressed only intermittently and in limited depth.

➤ The name "Austria" (in German: *Österreich*) originally referred only to the territory that emerged in the High Middle Ages (a duchy after 1156 and an archduchy after 1453) and was divided in the Late Middle Ages into "Austria above the Enns River" (from 1918 on: Upper Austria, in German: *Oberösterreich*) and "Austria below the Enns River" (from 1918 on: Lower Austria, in German: *Niederösterreich*, ⇨ par. 2106).

➤ In 1282, the Habsburgs were enfeoffed with the land of Austria (⇨ par. 2111) and henceforth used "Austria" as the name of their dynasty (Spanish: *Casa de Austria*, French: *Maison d'Autriche*), which is why subsequently all other Habsburg lands were also referred to as "Austrian"; in the 19th century, the name "Austria" was used for the Habsburg-ruled state as a whole (⇨ par. 3116).

➤ The republic founded in 1918 was initially called "German-Austria" (*Deutschösterreich*) and only adopted the name "Austria" following the Treaty of Saint Germain in 1919 (⇨ par. 6110).

➤ The conceptual history of the name "Austria" demonstrates that an "Austrian legal history" does not deal with a stable geographical area and therefore demands a focus on larger geographical contexts.

➤ The term "Europe" needs to be understood in cultural-geographical terms and thus also does not have a stable meaning throughout the ages. In relation to the period from about the middle of the 8th to the middle of the 20th century, it can be defined as that part of Eurasia whose civilisations developed from the basis of Greco-Roman antiquity and were shaped to a greater extent by Christianity than by the other two Abrahamic world religions (Judaism, Islam).

➤ Given the secularisation of European society in the 20th century, a direct reference to religions does not seem useful for a definition of contemporary Europe. Instead, it can be defined as the collective of states that have signed the European Convention on Human Rights (ECHR) and have thereby – for whatever reason – committed themselves to the values on which it is based.

0005 This textbook is organised into **eight periods**. Each period is introduced with a discussion of general political, constitutional, and international developments. This is followed by a more detailed description of the fundamental structures of state, church, economy, and society. The third and final part of each period addresses the characteristics of legislation and jurisprudence during that timespan.

➤ Periodization is always a necessary evil: it is necessary to organise the wealth of individual developments and to be able to holistically consider and evaluate a given period. On the other hand, it is all too easy to view the epochs in isolation and to neglect certain continuities across epochal boundaries. Numerous reference arrows (⇨) have therefore been added to help point out connections that could otherwise easily be overlooked.

➤ There is no generally accepted method of periodisation. The "classical" tripartite division of European history into antiquity (to c. 500 AD), the Middle Ages (c. 500–1500), and modern times (from c. 1500 to the present), which has been commonplace since around 1700, is only of limited use for our purposes. Nevertheless, the creation of the Corpus Iuris Civilis in 533/534 and the reception of learned law around 1500 are seminal events for us too, in the truest sense of the word, marking the boundaries between antiquity and the Middle Ages on the one hand, and between the Middle Ages and the modern era on the other.

➤ Apart from that, this textbook is primarily oriented towards the turning points in Austrian legal history, which can be seen as representative of the development of law in Europe, even though many developments occurred later in Austria than in other parts of Europe. Therefore, the periods of absolutism and natural law, which in the case of Austria can be relatively accurately defined as the years 1618–1848, are treated as a single period, as are the period of constitutionalism and the Historical School of Law, which, with regard to Austria, covers the years 1848–1918. It goes without saying that these dates are in no way adequate for describing developments outside Europe. The end of the Second World War in 1945, on the other hand, represents a turning point that has been significant for the entire world.

➤ The last epoch, starting in 1945, is called "contemporary legal history". It should be noted, however, that the term "contemporary history" describes the epoch of people still living; the moment at which contemporary history begins is therefore shifting and can never be fixed to a single point in time.

B Sources and Methods

0006 The term "**source**" in legal usage can have (at least) two different meanings. A *source of law* is every entity from which law emanates. In the context of legal historical methodology, however, the term "source" is used mainly to refer to a *source of legal cognition*. Thus defined, a source is anything that can provide us with knowledge about a (current or past) law.

➤ Sources of law include primarily the *legislator* as the source of statutory law (which today dominates the continental European legal systems) and the *judge* as the source of judicial law (primarily in Anglo-American legal systems). In some legal systems (Islamic law, for example), *jurisprudence* itself can also be a source of law. The oldest source of law, however, is custom *(usus)* grounded in the conviction that one is acting lawfully *(opinio iuris)*. This is the origin of customary law; today it is only of secondary importance in the states of Europe, whereas, for example, international law is still strongly based on customary law.

➢ In principle, a source of legal cognition can be anything "with which man has come into contact" (KARL BRUNNER). For most works in legal history, however, *written* sources are by far the most important sources of legal cognition. They can be categorised in terms of form into manuscripts (e.g. a medieval law book or a letter), inscriptions (e.g. on a building or a tomb), printed texts (e.g. the Imperial Law Gazette for the Austrian Empire) and electronic data (e.g. the Rechtsinformationssystem des Bundes [Austrian Federal Legal Information System, www.ris.bka.gv.at]).

➢ *Non-written* sources of legal cognition are, for example, buildings, monuments, paintings, insignia (e.g. crowns or wands of office), official attire, but also instruments used for torture or executions, coats of arms, seals, flags, coins, etc. Audiovisual sources (sound and image recordings) and oral tradition also fall into this category.

0007 Legal historians pose specific research questions to these sources and try to answer them using both historical and legal **methods**.

➢ Every legally relevant event consists of an act that can be perceived by the senses (for instance: somebody kills another person) and its legal meaning (here: it is murder/it is the execution of a death sentence). Whether and under what circumstances (when? where? who? in what way? etc.) this act took place needs to be established using historiographical methods. This process involves examining the sources to assess their external characteristics (e.g. their age, origin, etc.) in order to evaluate their validity. Then their content is established and placed in a context with other sources with the aim of reconstructing the historic events. Unlike the judge, the (legal) historian is not obliged to accept any given chain of events as facts but can locate his or her findings on a "scale of certainty" (CLEMENS JABLONER), which ranges from the greatest possible probability to vague presumption.

➢ Legal methods, on the other hand, need to be applied to determine the legal significance of these acts. But whereas the judge, when passing a sentence, has to draw on a specific legal system and explore the "objective meaning" of the relevant norms, the legal historian is interested in the meaning that contemporaries ascribed to this act, in order to be able to understand their actions. To achieve this, it is sometimes necessary to compare several contradictory contemporary legal opinions and to analyse the motivation and conclusiveness of the contemporary arguments (discourse analysis). However, there would be no point in accepting any of these contemporary opinions – or even one's own analysis of the historic law – as "objectively correct".

➢ *The subject of legal history is thus not the law itself, but the thoughts, words, and actions related to the law of people in the past.*

➢ For many types of sources, their own special disciplines have developed, such as diplomatics (the study of ancient documents), palaeography (the study of ancient scripts), or heraldry (the study of coats of arms). Depending on the circumstances, it may be necessary to draw on other academic disciplines and their methods in order to gain a better understanding of the text or facts in question. These may include philology, ethnology, or economics, among others.

0008 **Sub-disciplines** of legal history are the history of legal dogmas, the history of "law in action", the history of ideas in law, and the history of law-making.

➢ Legal dogmas are legal doctrines; legal dogmatics is therefore that branch of jurisprudence which investigates the content of the currently applicable law. The *history of legal doctrine* examines how the content of a legal system, or the statements of contemporaries about it, have changed over time. Its methods are very similar to those of the legal doctrine of the period in question (but taking into account the aspects mentioned in par. 0007).

➢ The study of "law in action" requires a completely different set of methods; here, the focus is on the extent to which law was "actually lived", and this is studied by evaluating individual legal acts (court rulings, contracts, wills) according to qualitative and quantitative criteria (in the latter case, by using statistical methods). Apart from important social-historical insights, the main concern in this context is the effectiveness of general legal norms.

➢ The history of ideas in law examines how legal scholars of past times conducted their work and the ideas that they developed in the process. Here, too, the interpretation of legal texts, which must be placed in their (legal) historical context, is of paramount importance.

➢ A properly pursued approach to the history of law-making should integrate all of these methods and thereby explain how the law developed from one stage to the next.

Prologue

Archaic Legal Culture

1001 In archaic (primordial) societies, the law was only vaguely distinguished from other regulatory systems such as customs, morals, and religion. It was **customary law**; conscious legislation or a scholarly approach were not part of it.

➢ Customary law is law that is *not consciously posited* but "lives" in the consciousness of the legal community and manifests through continuous practice. Nevertheless, customary law is also, albeit unconsciously, posited, positive law.

➢ Determining at which stage in human development the law emerged as a regulatory system is difficult. In any case, the question depends on what we understand by "law". According to our definition of law (⇨ par. 0002), we will most likely need to refer to the time when certain individuals (e.g. tribal chiefs, or all adult males, sometimes the entire population as a unit) gained the authority to ensure compliance with particular norms and, if necessary, to use coercion to enforce them.

➢ However, the same norms were also enforced through other mechanisms, mainly social and religious sanctions. The insight that there is law on the one hand and custom, religion, and morals on the other probably only emerged when these normative systems began to diverge in terms of their content, for instance, when a legally permissible action appeared morally reprehensible.

1002 In the absence of written sources, only very limited conclusions can be drawn about the **substance and nature of archaic law**.

➢ Germanistic legal history in the 19th century sought to identify and reconstruct a primordial Germanic law. Today, this endeavour has not only been abandoned as futile, but most scholars even doubt whether a common Germanic law ever existed.

➢ Since the law was passed down only orally, it depended on the memory of the people who applied it and was, therefore, subject to constant change. In the absence of a unifying central law-making authority, customary law fragmented across the different legal circles in which it existed.

➢ In their efforts to reconstruct Germanic law, legal historians inappropriately drew on written sources from later periods, but sometimes also only projected back their own wishful thinking. Legal history continues to struggle with the consequences of this misguided practice.

➢ Despite this, there has recently been a renewed interest in archaic law, this time that of the Celts. The reconstruction of Celtic law, however, is likely to encounter similar problems as that of Germanic law.

Part I

Antiquity

A Developments

1101 The oldest farming cultures that developed writing originated in an area that stretches in the shape of a crescent from Egypt via Palestine and Syria to Mesopotamia (Iraq) and is known as the **"Fertile Crescent"** (to distinguish it from the surrounding deserts). From the 6th century BC onwards, these countries were subjugated by the Persian kings, whose empire at its peak stretched from Libya to the Indus and probably comprised more than 40 per cent of the world's population.

➢ Agriculture and animal husbandry probably developed for the first time on the banks of the Nile as early as the 5th or 6th millennium BC. In the 4th millennium BC, Egyptians developed hieroglyphic writing. Traditional historiography attributes the political unification of Egypt to a *pharaoh* named MENES (around 3000 BC?), which has been put into question by more recent research. Egypt was conquered by the Persians for the first time in 525 BC but was able to free itself again before definitly falling under Persian rule in 341 BC.

➢ Mesopotamia, the land between the two rivers Euphrates and Tigris, was home to various states (Sumerian, Assyrian, Babylonian Kingdom, and others). A little later than Egypt, the Mesopotamian peoples also developed their writing system, the cuneiform script. The oldest peace treaty in cuneiform script which has come down to us was concluded between the city-states of Ebla in Syria and Abarsal in Mesopotamia around 2350 BC. In 539 BC, the whole of Mesopotamia became part of the Persian Empire.

➢ The Bible – which is a central document of faith for Judaism and Christianity to this day, but highly unreliable as a historical source (⇨ par. 1302) – refers to the alternating dependencies of the people of Israel on Egypt on the one hand and the Mesopotamian kingdoms on the other, between which there were also phases of their own statehood (Kings DAVID and SOLOMON, around 1000 BC). The exile of the Jewish upper class to Babylon in 597–539 BC was of decisive importance, especially as only a smaller part of the Jewish people returned to Israel after the Persian conquest of Babylon, while the majority remained dispersed (*diaspora*). It was probably only at this time that monotheism, and Jerusalem as the singular place of worship, became established.

➢ North of Israel, the seafaring Phoenicians (Punics) formed a number of city-states, e.g. Beirut, Sidon, and Tyre. From the 2nd millennium BC, they founded new cities ("colonies") throughout the Mediterranean, most notably Carthage (near modern-day Tunis) in the 9th century BC. After the

Phoenician motherland came under Persian rule, Carthage itself formed an empire, which at its peak in the 4th century achieved supremacy in the western Mediterranean, but was destroyed by Rome in three so-called Punic Wars (264–146 BC).

1102 A number of city-states (*poleïs*, singular: *polis*) emerged in the area of **Greece**, in particular Athens, Sparta, Corinth, and Thebes, which were able together to successfully fend off an attempted conquest by Persia (5th century BC), but did not form a unified state. In a similar way to the Punics, the Greeks also founded a number of colonies (*apoikía*) throughout the Mediterranean.

➤ Like most *poleïs*, Athens was originally ruled by a king (*basileús*), as Greek mythology still reminds us (THESEUS!). However, the monarchy was probably abolished as early as in the 7th century BC and first one, then a plurality of temporarily elected rulers (*archons*) became the head of state.

➤ Around 570 BC, the archon SOLON disempowered the old aristocratic families and created a *timocratic constitution* for Athens, i.e. a state in which each citizen had a different degree of political participation rights depending on their financial power.

➤ Under PERIKLES, around 450 BC, the Athenian political system was further developed towards the participation of as many citizens as possible (non-participation in political life was considered disgraceful!). It was later called "Athenian democracy" and became the paradigm for the discourse on democracy over the next two and a half millennia, although it corresponded neither to the contemporary (⇨ par. 1203) nor to the modern concept of democracy (⇨ par. 6201).

➤ In Athens, legislation was enacted by the people's assembly (*ekklēsía*), in which all adult male citizens who had completed their military service were entitled to vote. Children, women, freemen without citizenship (*metoíkō*), and slaves, thus around 80% of the population, were excluded from the political process. Of the remaining c. 40,000 eligible voters, only c. 6,000 actually came together, which only made it possible to hold popular assemblies in a public space (*agorá*) or other location.

➤ Athens emerged from the Greco-Persian Wars as the leading naval power in Greece and joined forces with other cities to form the Delian League. It was opposed by the land power Sparta and the Peloponnesian League led by it, which defeated the Delian League in the Peloponnesian War (431–404 BC), marking the beginning of Athens' political decline.

1103 In 338 BC, King PHILIP II of Macedon succeeded in gaining hegemony over almost all of Greece. His son ALEXANDER III "the Great" quickly conquered the Persian Empire and expanded it even further. Shortly after his death (323 BC), it disintegrated into several successor states, the so-called *Diadochi empires*. ALEXANDER's conquests achieved lasting significance because the Diadochi empires succeeded in merging Greek and Oriental culture into **Hellenism**.

➢ After his victory over Thebes and Athens in 338 BC, PHILIP II founded the League of Corinth, in which he granted autonomy to the Greek city-states, which nevertheless remained dependent on him.

➢ The fusion of Greek and Oriental cultures was explicitly sought by ALEXANDER, among other things through the founding of cities (e.g. Alexandria in Egypt). Soon after his death, battles broke out between his generals.

➢ ALEXANDER's general SELEUCUS was initially able to claim more than half of ALEXANDER's Empire for himself and his dynasty, but later the territory of this *Seleucid Empire* was reduced to Syria and Palestine. It was subjugated by Rome in 63 BC. The general PTOLEMY gained control of Egypt and founded the *Ptolemaic Empire*, which was the last of the Diadochi empires to be incorporated into the Roman Empire in 30 BC. Macedon itself was defeated by Rome already in 146 BC, which meant that Greece also became dependent on Rome and in 27 BC a Roman province.

➢ Persia (Iran) was able to free itself from the rule of the Diadochi in 250 BC, but the Hellenistic legacy remained alive there as well as in states further east (Greco-Bactrian Kingdom in Central Asia, Indo-Greek Kingdom, and others).

1104 Much like Athens, the city of Rome also disposed of its monarchy at the turn of the 6th century BC. The **Roman Republic** rapidly expanded, unifying all of Italy by 275 BC, and eventually establishing hegemony over the entire Mediterranean world through its victories over Carthage (⇨ par. 1101) and the Diadochi empires (⇨ par. 1103).

➢ Note: The word *res publica* ("public affairs") in Roman times referred to the state as such. It was only with NICCOLÒ MACHIAVELLI (*Il principe*, 1513) that the term "republic", in the study of political systems, came to specifically denote a non-monarchy. Nevertheless, in historiography it is common to refer to the Roman Empire as a "republic" only between the fall of the last king (allegedly 509 BC) and the establishment of the principate (27 BC).

➢ The details of the early history of Rome, which are shrouded in myth, are difficult to reconstruct. It is likely that the city of Rome, situated on the border with Etruria, was ruled by Etruscan kings around 509 BC, i.e. kings perceived as foreigners. Whether the removal of this foreign rule went hand in hand with the removal of the monarchical form of government as such and the establishment of a system of power-sharing between several people remains uncertain.

➢ What is more likely is that after the end of the kingship, a *praetor maximus* was initially appointed as the highest-ranking official, and only later, colleagues of equal rank were placed at his side. From around 450 BC, supreme power (*imperium*) was divided between two consules with equal rights; from 367 BC at the latest, they were joined by a *praetor urbanus*, who exercised jurisdiction over Roman citizens. In 242 BC, a *praetor peregrinus* was appointed for legal cases between Romans and foreigners.

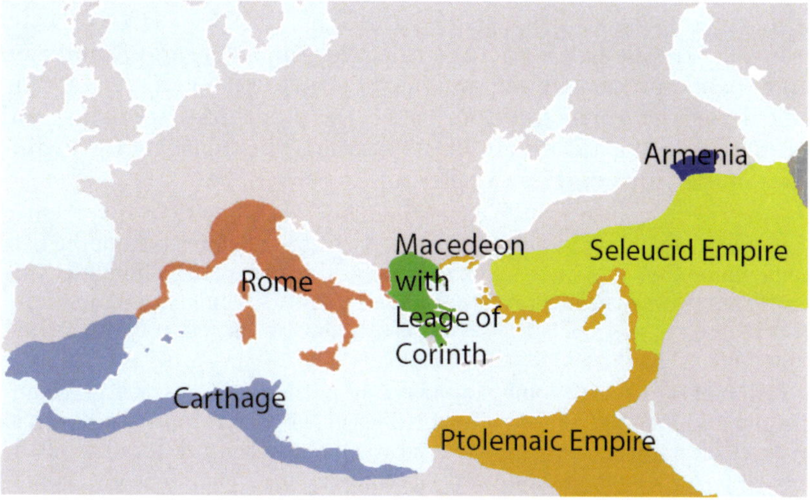

Map 1: Europe and the Mediterranean region in 244 BC

Source: Own drawing, using a map from https://de.wikipedia.org/wiki/R%C3%B6misches_Reich#/media/Datei:Roman_Republic_Empire_map.gif

➢ Initially, legislation was enacted by popular assemblies of all adult male citizens (but see also ⇨ par. 6205). Political power was actually concentrated in the hands of a few families, the *patricians*, who met in the Senate and held the offices of *consul* or *praetor* and other magistracies. Soon after the abolition of the monarchy, the "struggle of the orders" broke out, in which the common people (*plebeians*) gradually achieved participatory rights. In particular, they alone elected the *tribunus*, who could object to all acts of the patrician magistrates (later referred to as the right of veto).

➢ Gradually, the magistracies themselves became accessible to plebeians (fully in 367 BC). From 287 BC, Plebeian resolutions (*plebiscites*) had the force of law. As a result, the patricians lost almost all their privileges, and a new aristocracy emerged in line with the new balance of power.

➢ The Italian cities were initially only loosely connected to Rome on the basis of apparent equality. By contrast, conquered countries outside Italy were established as provinces under a governor (often a former *consul*), which were also legally dependent on Rome. The first province was Sicily in 241 BC, followed by Spain in 197 BC.

➢ While the population of Rome had originally been predominantly agrarian, after the defeat of Carthage, the economy became based on large estates (*latifundia*), which were worked by slaves. Around the same time, the system of universal conscription gave way to a professional army. The establishment of a great empire brought with it many economic and social changes and plunged the Roman Republic into a deep crisis.

1105 After a century of civil wars (133–30 BC), GAIUS CAESAR OCTAVIANUS was able to establish autocratic rule over the *Imperium Romanum* and – while preserving the republican structures – gained a monarchical position (*principate*) in 27 BC as *Imperator*, *Augustus*, and *princeps senatus* (first man of the senate), thus marking the beginning of the **imperial era in Rome**.

➢ The title *Imperator* (military commander) is the source of the English word "emperor", while the German word "Kaiser" is derived from the personal name CAESAR, which was adopted by all emperors. The honorary title *Augustus* (the illustrious one) was also used by all Roman emperors (until 1806 AD, ⇨ par. 3116). Nowadays, it is usually only used to refer to the first title holder, OCTAVIANUS (27 BC–14 AD).

➢ Even before 27 BC, some politicians, in particular AUGUSTUS' great-uncle and adoptive father GAIUS IULIUS CAESAR (as *dictator*, 46–44 BC), had at least temporarily held absolute power, yet a formal restoration of the kingship was almost unanimously rejected.

➢ Accordingly, after the end of the civil wars, AUGUSTUS restored the republican structures and rejected both the royal title and all special powers. His power was based primarily on the *tribunicia potesta*, which was separate from the office of *tribunus* and to which he was still entitled, and which gave him the right to veto decisions by magistrates, as well as on his rule over half of all provinces, including supreme command over a large part of the Roman army. Alongside this, the Senate, *consules*, *praetors*, and other magistrate positions continued unchanged.

➢ The problem of succession to the throne remained unresolved; only a few families managed to maintain a hereditary claim to the throne. Often, the emperors were installed in office by troops loyal to them and then had to assert themselves against rivals. They rarely died a natural death.

➢ In 58–50 BC, CAESAR conquered Gaul (roughly present-day France, Belgium, Switzerland, and the area of Germany west of the Rhine); after the conquest of Egypt by AUGUSTUS in 30 BC (⇨ par. 1103), the entire Mediterranean world was Roman. Soon after that, the Roman Empire was extended to the Danube, incorporating most of present-day Austria (establishment of the province of Noricum in 41 AD). In 43 AD, the conquest of Britain began. With the conquest of Mesopotamia in 116 AD (which, however, soon fell back to Iran), the *Imperium Romanum* had reached its greatest territorial extent.

➢ Judea had been able to shake off Seleucid rule in 165 BC (⇨ par. 1204). In 63 BC, it was initially only loosely attached to the Roman Empire and only gradually transformed into a province. A Jewish revolt against Roman rule that began in 66 AD was bloodily suppressed; the Temple was destroyed in 70 AD and Jews were forbidden from entering Jerusalem.

➢ In 212 AD, the *Constitutio Antoniniana* granted Roman citizenship to all free citizens of the empire. This reinforced a trend that had already set in earlier, whereby the dominant position of the city of Rome within the empire gradually declined.

1106 A far-reaching **reform of the empire** was carried out by Emperor DIOCLETIAN (284–305). However, it could only temporarily resolve the previous crises in the empire. The long-term significance of the administrative reorganisation of the empire was that it provided the basis for the emergence of two largely independent entities, the Western Roman and the Eastern Roman Empires.

➢ With DIOCLETIAN's reform of the empire, the Senate was completely stripped of its power and the rule of the emperor, who had himself worshipped as *dominus et deus* (lord and god), became manifest. This is why the period from 284 is referred to as the *Dominate*.

➢ The reform provided for a collegial government of the empire by two *Augusti* of equal rank, along with a succession arrangement (by co-option), which, however, did not prevail. After first (324–337) CONSTANTINE I the Great and ultimately (394–395) THEODOSIUS I the Great had again held sole rule, the empire finally disintegrated into a Latin-dominated West and a Greek-dominated East. The capital of the Eastern Roman Empire was Constantinople (Byzantium, now Istanbul), founded in 330, which is why it is also referred to as the *Byzantine Empire*.

➢ In addition to the (disempowered) Roman Senate, an (equally powerless) Senate was established in Constantinople, and the consules and praetores were also divided between the two capitals.

➢ The border between East and West Rome followed a relatively straight line from north to south through the Strait of Otranto. To this day, it can still be recognised as the border between the Roman Catholic Church and Latin script on one side, and the Greek Orthodox Church and Greek/Cyrillic script, on the other.

1107 While the Western Roman Empire soon collapsed, the **Byzantine Empire** (*Eastern Roman Empire*) persisted through the period of migrations and almost until the end of the Middle Ages (until 1453, ⇨ par. 2114).

➢ Starting in the 3rd century, but especially after the Huns invaded Europe in 375, there were extensive migratory movements, particularly of Germanic tribes, and waves of immigration into the Roman Empire. There they were settled as *foederati* in various regions and retained their power structures, so that the emperors only had loose suzerainty over largely independent communities. These so-called "tribes" were neither ethnically nor biologically homogeneous; these phenomena were merely of a legal-historical nature.

➢ The end of the Western Roman Empire did not result from a sudden upheaval but was an intermediate step in a gradual development in which the Roman central power increasingly lost ground to the Germanic princes. Although the last Western Roman emperor was overthrown in 476, a consul remained in office in Rome until 534. The Roman Senate probably continued to exist until the 7th century.

➢ The Eastern Roman emperor JUSTINIAN I (527–565) sought to restore the *Imperium Romanum* and destroyed the Germanic kingdoms in Italy and North Africa in 534/555, thereby politically unifying most of the Mediterranean world one last time. But most of these territories were soon lost again (⇨ par. 2102; par. 2103), the city of Rome itself finally in 756 (⇨ par. 2104).

➢ Internally, JUSTINIAN I sought to renew his empire by emphasising its ancient heritage, but it was during or shortly after his reign that the language of administration was changed from Latin to Greek. Nonetheless, the inhabitants of the Eastern Roman Empire continued to call themselves Romans (*Rhōmaîoi*).

➢ Thus, Byzantium became an important custodian of the legacy of the ancient *Imperium Romanum*. However, the closure of PLATO's Academy of Athens, founded in the 4th century BC, by JUSTINIAN I in 529 AD signalled the end of the ancient world itself.

B Structures

1201 Even the oldest societies known to us through written sources were characterized by a **double inequality**, on the one hand based on gender and on the other on the basis of class. Probably as soon as humans ceased to be nomadic hunters and began to settle in one place, the estates of farmers (peasants), craftsmen, warriors and priests emerged. The inequality of humans found its most extreme expression in the phenomenon of *slavery*.

➢ Almost all ancient societies were characterized by the subordination of women to their husbands or fathers. The head of the family (in Rome: *pater familias*) had comprehensive personal authority over his wife(s) and children and could represent them in legal transactions and in court. However, the extent of this subordination varied considerably. There were also instances in which a woman was not subject to the authority of any man (*sui iuris*). Priestesses enjoyed a particularly respected position.

➢ The origin of the estate system lies in the differentiation of society into certain vocations. However, these vocational groups soon became estates based on birth, in that membership of a particular estate was determined by descent, and it was not possible, or only with difficulty, to change to another estate.

➢ Slavery existed in all societies as far back as we can see. However, this state of bondage could have different dimensions. Although the Code of Hammurabi (⇨ par. 1301) already contained some rules on the keeping of slaves, it was only Roman law that created a comprehensive slave law and contrasted freeborn and freedmen as "persons" (legal subjects) with slaves as "things" (legal objects).

➢ The actual living conditions of slaves varied considerably. While agricultural or mining labourers, for example, had to perform hard physical labour, often under inhumane conditions that significantly shortened their lifespan, slaves who worked as domestic staff or even physicians and teachers sometimes had a better life than many free people. Thus, slavery in the

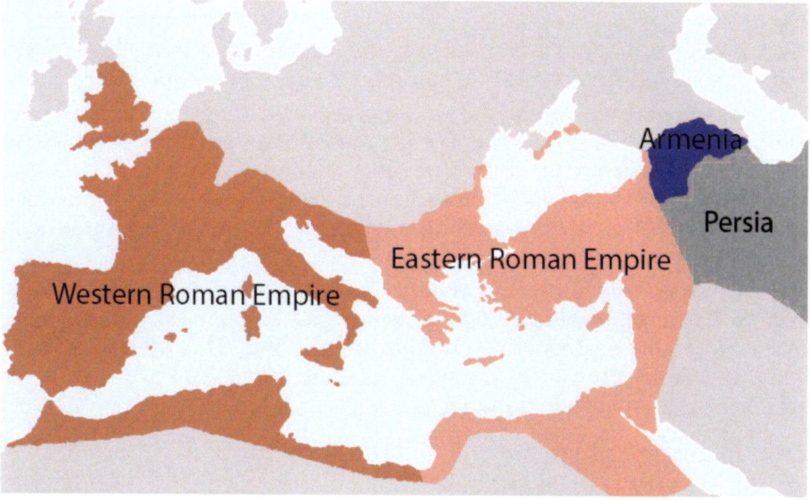

Map 2: Europe and the Mediterranean region in 405 AD
Source: Own drawing, using a map from https://de.wikipedia.org/wiki/R%C3%B6misches_Reich#/media/Datei:Roman_Republic_Empire_map.gif
Copyright: https://creativecommons.org/licenses/by-sa/3.0 (CC BY-SA 3.0)

ancient world is not the same as the offence of "slavery" prohibited today in Article 4 ECHR 1950 and § 104 Austrian Criminal Code 1974.

➢ Also, the real importance of slavery was relatively limited until about the 2nd century BC. In fact, both the construction of the pyramids and the rowing of galleys in ancient times were mainly done not by slaves, but by free workers. With Rome's victory over Carthage in the Second Punic War in 202 BC, the proportion of slaves in society increased significantly, with its peak during the Principate.

➢ In addition to capture in war, inability to pay debts could also result in slavery. Most slaves, however, were already enslaved when they were born to enslaved women. Their release was possible, but freedmen did not enjoy full legal equality with those born free.

➢ The impoverishment of large segments of the population in Late Antiquity led to a decline in the importance of slavery from the 3rd century AD onwards, and it was replaced by other forms of personal dependency. With this in mind, it can be said that the medieval estate system (⇨ par. 2201) was already beginning to take shape in Late Antiquity.

1202 As society became more differentiated, it also became more hierarchical; **legally organised communities** developed, typically headed, at least initially, by a king or, rarely, a queen.

➢ Whether it is justified to call these hierarchically organised communities "states" has already been addressed in ⇨ par. 0003. It is also a matter of debate whether these communities emerged from family groups (clans), to which "proto-state" characteristics were often attributed in the academic literature, or whether they arose in partial overcoming of family structures.

The driving factors for the emergence of the ancient kingdoms were probably primarily economic pressures (e.g. the shared use of scarce resources) and the need for protection from common enemies or natural forces.

➢ Like the head of a family, the king was the head of his kingdom. He was military leader, judge, and priest, with these three functions constituting "an indivisible whole, like different sides of the same crystal" (THEODOR MOMMSEN). It was only later that the king also acted as a legislator. As such he did not seek to create the law, but to safeguard the God-given, immutable order (⇨ par. 1301).

➢ Sparta was ruled jointly by two kings, who came from two different families. In Carthage, leadership was vested in two annually elected *shophets* with equal rights, just like the two *consules* in Rome. The principles of annuity and collegiality were intended to limit power and are thus early evidence of rational state thinking.

1203 Even in ancient times, we encounter a wide range of different **systems of rule**. In his book *Politiká* (c. 330 BC), ARISTOTLE categorised these schematically into three "good" and three "bad" types; in reality, these ideal types rarely existed in pure form.

➢ In this conception, a *monarchía* is a system in which a single person rules with a view to the common interest. If the ruler has only his own interests at heart, it is a *tyrannís*.

➢ The rule of a few individuals with a view to the common interest is an *aristokratía* (literally: rule of the best), if it is for their own benefit, an *oligarchia*.

➢ A government of the many with a view to the common interest ARISTOTLE called a *politeía*. He contrasted this with the *dēmokratía* as an unfavourable form of rule, with a view to the needy but not to the common interest.

➢ ARISTOTLE's conception shaped the theory of the state for thousands of years. What emerged in particular was a shift in the meaning of democracy, especially since from around the 17th century AD, this term was seen in a positive light, while the word *politeía* was forgotten. The word *ochlokratía* (from *ochlos* – crowd) was introduced into the theory of the state to denote the rule of the mob – roughly what ARISTOTLE meant by *dēmokratía*.

➢ Most of the real states of the ancient world followed a mixed system. Notably, the Roman consules were seen as a monarchical element, the Senate as an aristocratic element and the popular assemblies as a democratic element.

1204 The secular rule was inextricably linked with the **sacral sphere**. The king or emperor was not only a priest, but often enjoyed divine worship himself. The various pagan, polytheistic cults of antiquity could coexist. By contrast, monotheistic religions, such as *Judaism* and *Christianity* in particular, which strictly rejected the worship of other gods (Ex 20:3), challenged the traditional systems of worship and rule and were therefore persecuted by the state.

➤ Where kingship had been abolished, a special person with royal dignity was usually entrusted with the priestly duties of the former king In Athens, this was the *archon basileús,* who also exercised some judicial powers. In contrast, the *rex sacrorum* in Rome was kept away from all political power; not even the other priests were under his authority. Rather, the leadership of Roman priesthood was the responsibility of the *pontifex maximus*, an office that was always exercised by the emperor himself during the imperial period (until the adoption of Christianity), thus reuniting supreme political and priestly functions in one hand

➤ Usually, defeated peoples adopted the gods of the victors (since these had proven to be more powerful than their own). However, the Romans in particular also adopted foreign cults (Isis, Mithras, among others) or tried to equate foreign gods with their own (*interpretatio Romana*, e.g. Zeus = Jupiter, Teutates = Mars, Odin = Mercurius).

➤ The attempt of the Seleucid kings to identify the one God of the Jews with Zeus in the sense of an *interpretatio Graeca*, however, led to a revolt of the Jewish people in 168 BC (*Maccabean revolt*), as a result of which they were able to permanently escape Seleucid rule and establish a theocratic state, i.e. one supported primarily by priests, for some 100 years (⇨ par. 1105). During the Roman rule over Judea, phases of religious autonomy alternated with bloody acts of repression, which ultimately ended with the complete dispersion of the Jewish people. Adhering to their faith allowed the Jews to preserve their identity in the diaspora, but made them outsiders in society.

➤ Christianity, which goes back to JESUS CHRIST, originated around 30 AD as a Jewish sect that was in conflict with the Jewish leadership from the very beginning. Whether they formally banned Christians from attending synagogues around 95 AD, as has long been assumed, is questioned by recent research. More significant is the fact that the Apostolic Council as early as 48 AD allowed the baptism of non-Jews (pagans). Thus, Christianity increasingly broke away from its Jewish roots and gained a large following among pagans, especially slaves and the poorest strata of society.

➤ From the Roman perspective, Christianity had become a far greater disruptive influence than Judaism, and the refusal to worship the emperor as a god made it a serious problem, which is why persecutions of Christians soon began. These reached their climax under DIOCLETIAN in around 303. Not least because these persecutions were unable to curb the influx of converts to Christianity, the persecutory measures were ended under Emperor CONSTANTINE I, and Christianity came to be tolerated throughout the empire in 311/313.

1205 Under the rule of Emperor THEODOSIUS I the Great (379–395), Christianity became the **state religion** of the Roman Empire, and the creed formulated at the Ecumenical Council of Nicaea in 325 (*Nicaenum*) was made binding on all subjects (C I, 1). The emperor's claim to divine worship was transformed into a supremacy over the church, which was now reorganised into a state institution.

➢ For example, bishops came to be regarded as imperial officials, and their jurisdictions (still referred to as dioceses today) were set up in analogy to the dioceses of the Roman Empire. The supreme authority of the emperor was particularly evident in the leadership of the ecumenical councils (general church assemblies).

➢ At the Council of Nicaea in 325 and several subsequent councils (notably the Council of Chalcedon in 451), an attempt was made to understand the Christian doctrine, which had arisen from Jewish tradition, through the prism of Greek philosophy. JESUS CHRIST was considered by the majority of the councils' participants to be consubstantial (*homooúsios*) with the Almighty Father; in his person, two natures are united, he is "truly God and truly man, without confusion". The Father, the Son and the Holy Spirit are the three persons of the divine Trinity. According to this teaching, God is triune, but only one God.

➢ Those who did not want to accept these beliefs (dogmas) were threatened with persecution. This applied less to the pagans, of whom there were no longer a great many, than to the followers of dissenting Christian doctrines, such as Arianism (widespread among the Germanic peoples), Nestorianism (widespread in Asia as far as China) and Coptic Orthodoxy (dominant in Egypt). Whether these persecutions, as well as their rejection of the imperial church doctrine on the nature of CHRIST, facilitated the later conversion of many Nestorian and Coptic Christians to Islam – where JESUS is seen as a prophet, not as God –, or at least their acceptance of the new rulers, is a matter of scholarly dispute.

C Legislation and Jurisprudence

1. Ancient Oriental Law

1301 The oldest written civilisations also produced the first **legal records**, both of individual legal acts (e.g. contracts) and of general norms. However, the sources are not complete enough to allow modern research to reliably paint an overall picture of the legal systems of ancient Egypt or ancient Babylon – although attempts have been made.

➢ The oldest known legal record is the Code of Ur-nammu (23rd/21st centuries BC), which has only survived in copies. More famous is the *Code of Hammurabi*, named after King HAMMURABI of Babylon (around 1750 BC). It has survived in the form of a 2.5-metre-high black stone stele, which is on display today at the Louvre in Paris.

➢ This stele is engraved with 292 legal maxims in cuneiform script. They govern individual circumstances in a very detailed way (*casuistics*; in contrast to abstractly formulated *general clauses*, which are completely absent there, ⇨ par. 1304). Like many modern laws, they are in the form of conditional sentences (e.g. no. 196: "If a man put out the eye of another man, his eye shall be put out."). The modernity of the language is in stark contrast to the legal implications, which would be considered very harsh by today's standards. However, the latter are to be seen in a contemporary context; at the time, they served primarily to prevent excessive revenge.

➢ In an introductory paragraph, HAMMURABI explains that he was commissioned by the god Marduk to pass the laws so that "the strong would not harm the weak". With this divine legitimisation, the legal norms that followed the introduction were made unassailable.

➢ Nevertheless, it is doubtful whether the Code of Hammurabi is a genuine law in the modern sense of the word, i.e. an order by the ruler deliberately intended to create new, general norms. It is more likely to be a record of existing customary law, where the recording may well have provided an opportunity to clarify individual disputed questions. It is also conceivable, though unproven, that it may have been used in legal education.

➢ Although a large number of contracts and wills recorded on papyrus or other writing material have been preserved from Egypt, there is no collection of laws comparable to the Code of Hammurabi. It is therefore even more difficult to describe ancient Egyptian law than Babylonian law.

1302 Of the multitude of ancient oriental laws, **biblical law** stands out. Through Judaism and Christianity, it has also shaped modern law and – with all due caution – also allows conclusions to be drawn about other legal systems of the Fertile Crescent, especially since it is far better researched than all these other laws combined.

➢ The Bible is a collection of various types of texts (narrative, didactic, and normative texts as well as prayers and songs), written between the 12th century BC and the 1st century AD. Which of these were to be considered canonical (= belonging to the Bible) and thus sacred became established only gradually and at different times within the individual religious communities. The Hebrew Bible (*Tanakh*) roughly corresponds to the first part of the Christian Bible, also known as the *Old Testament*, while the other part, the *New Testament*, explicitly relates to JESUS CHRIST. In this context, the word "testament" refers to the two covenants that, according to Christian belief, God first made with the people of Israel and then with all of humanity.

➢ While the *Tanakh* is almost entirely written in Hebrew, the other parts of the Old Testament and the New Testament are written mainly in Greek, which was the main language of communication in the Mediterranean region at the time. There are a large number of traditions, but – not least because of strict rules for copying – only relatively minor deviations between them.

➢ The most important part of the Hebrew Bible is the *Torah* ("the law"), which, according to Jewish and Christian lore, MOSES received directly from God and which, in addition to the myths of the origin of the people of Israel, contains a wealth of legal rules. They include precepts pertaining to the relationship between individuals and the Almighty (*mitzvot bein adam lamakom*) and precepts pertaining to interpersonal relations (*mitzvot bein adam lehaveiro*), which are closely intertwined.

➢ The core of the Torah are the Ten Commandments with three precepts pertaining to the relationship with the Almighty and seven precepts pertaining to interpersonal relations (Ex 20:2–17; repeated in Deut 5:6–21). These are not formulated as conditional sentences, but as unconditional imperatives (e.g. "thou shalt not murder").

➢ A comparison of Biblical law with other laws of the Fertile Crescent reveals many parallels (for example, the above-cited legal maxim no. 196 of the Code of Hammurabi is found almost word-for-word in Ex 21:24). However, it is often unclear whether and in what way one legal system influenced the other; a mere reference to the different ages of the legal sources can easily lead to false conclusions.

➢ Outside of the Bible, further legal rules ("oral Torah"; *Mishnah*) arose through custom and jurisprudence. They were first recorded in the *Jerusalem Talmud* in about 400 AD and in the *Babylonian Talmud* in about 500 AD.

2. Greek, Roman, and Byzantine law

1303 There was no such thing as common **Greek law**; instead, the individual poleïs developed legal systems that differed widely from one another. We know about these systems to a very varying extent.

➢ The evidence is best for Athens, whose legal system was recorded from the 7th century onwards; around 410 BC these legal texts were collected by the *Anagrapheis*.

➢ An archaeological discovery of great importance in 1880 AD was the *Gortyn Code*, a monumental inscription from the 5th century BC that had originally been attached to a public building in the city of Gortyn on Crete. As a result, this local law has also been the subject of quite thorough research. For other Greek laws, our knowledge is sometimes extremely patchy.

➢ Compared to the influence of Greek culture on Roman culture in other areas, the influence of Greek law on Roman law is surprisingly small (but cf. the Twelve Tables legislation, ⇨ par. 1304). In court, each party would speak for themselves; there were no professional lawyers. Those who could afford it would commission a *logograph* to write a speech that the party would then learn by heart and present in court. However, these speeches required more rhetorical than legal skills; the kind of legal scholarship that flourished in Rome was absent in Greece.

1304 **Roman law** was characterised by precise terminology and a specific way of reasoning. Both aspects have shaped continental European law – and many other legal systems outside Europe – to this day. The establishment of a highly developed jurisprudence is one of the most important contributions of ancient Rome to European culture. For all the details, see the textbooks on Roman Law.

➢ Soon after the outbreak of the Struggle of the Orders (⇨ par. 1104), around 450 BC, a Roman delegation was sent to Athens to record the laws of SOLON (⇨ par 1102), which were considered exemplary. This endeavour resulted in the erection of initially ten, then twelve bronze tablets in the Forum Romanum. They contained procedural law, civil law, criminal law, and sacral law. While the tablets themselves were probably destroyed soon afterwards as a result of military conflicts, their content was in classical times repeatedly cited and regarded as authoritative.

➢ Important laws from later periods were, for example, the *lex Aquilia* (286 BC), which contained provisions on tort law (with very broadly formulated general clauses; cf. the comments on the Code of Hammurabi, ⇨ par. 1301), or the *lex Iulia de maritandis ordinibus* (18 BC) and the *lex Papia Poppaea* (9 AD), which reformed marriage law.

➢ Although statutory law existed, Roman law was primarily jurisprudential law, i.e. law created by jurists. The first legal experts were priests, later also secular nobles, who cultivated *iurisprudentia* out of interest and inclination. But not until the 2nd century AD did professional jurists became increasingly important for the further development of the law.

➢ In their daily work, the jurists' main role was to provide expert opinions (*consilia* or *responsa*) in civil proceedings, both for the parties to the case and for the *praetor*, the official in charge of administering justice, who was usually not trained in the law. Jurisprudential law was therefore primarily case law; there were only few systematic accounts, such as the textbook (*Institutiones*) of GAIUS from the 2nd century AD.

➢ The perfection, peak, and decline of Roman law essentially coincided with the fate of the Roman state. The classical age of jurisprudence with the two schools of the Sabinians and Proculians began in the 1st century, peaked in the 2nd century, and enjoyed a late period in the 3rd century AD.

➢ From the late 3rd century onwards, the law of the empire, which had been shaken by civil wars and Germanic invasions, was characterised by many simplifications (hence the, now controversial, designation "vulgar law"). Since the number of legal writings had become overwhelming, the *lex citationum* 426 established that (only) the writings of five classical jurists (PAPINIANUS, PAULUS, GAIUS, ULPIANUS, and MODESTINUS) would be authoritative.

➢ During the same period, the decrees of the emperor (*constitutiones*) gained in importance and were collected a short time later, in 438, in the *Codex Theodosianus*.

1305 In the Eastern Roman Empire, classical jurisprudence was revived in the 5th century at the law schools of Beirut and Constantinople (*classicism*). Under Emperor JUSTINIAN I (⇨ par. 1107), the law was comprehensively documented in the **Corpus Iuris Civilis** (known under this name only from the 13th century).

➢ The most important part of the *Corpus Iuris Civilis* (from today's point of view) was the Digest (*Pandects*), a systematic collection of writings by the classical jurists. They did not contain abstract legal principles but solutions to individual problems. Thus, the Digest has to a certain extent the character of a casebook. Thematically, it dealt primarily with private law (45 out of the 50 books).

➢ In the Digest, ULPIANUS and PAULUS were the most widely represented jurists. The texts were shortened and revised (*interpolated*) to enable their use for practical purposes. The compilation work was carried out by a commission headed by the jurist TRIBONIAN. Contradictions within the jurists' writings were often resolved by the emperor himself.

➢ At the same time, the imperial *Constitutiones* were collected in a new codex (*Codex Iustinianus*, first version published in 529, revised second version in 534); in addition to private law, it also contained public law.

➢ The third part of the *Corpus Iuris Civilis* was an authorised textbook, the *Institutiones* (*Iustiniani*), which was published together with the Digest in 533.

1306 The development of Byzantine law after 534 increasingly took place in the Greek language and became the basis of modern **Greek law**.

➢ Even the statutes of JUSTINIAN I after 534 have largely survived only in Greek. These *Novellae* were collected by private individuals and supplemented the *Corpus Iuris Civilis*.

➢ Byzantine law was again revised in 907 with the Greek-language *Basilika* ("Imperial Books"), which was subsequently expanded by adding scholarly glosses and commentaries (cf. the parallel to Upper Italian legistics, ⇨ par. 2319). In 1345, an abridged version was published as the *Hexabiblos* ("Six Books"). It also remained in force during Turkish rule (15th–19th centuries) and, after its end, remained the basis of Greek private law until the entry into effect of the Greek Civil Code in 1946.

Part II

Middle Ages and Early Modern Era

A Developments

1. The Arab Empire (622–1258)

2101 Islam teaches that the Prophet MUHAMMAD, who was born in Mecca in Arabia, received a series of revelations from God (*Allāh*) from around the year 12 before the beginning of the Islamic calendar. This calendar itself begins with the emigration (*hejra*) of MUHAMMAD from Mecca to Medina (622 AD). There he became the religious and political leader of an ever-growing community (*ummah*). His troops conquered Mecca and the whole of Arabia and led the Arabs to monotheism. The revelations of God were collected in the Qur'an (⇨ par. 2302). Under his successors, the Caliphs, the Arab Empire and with it the new religion, **Islam**, spread rapidly throughout the Near East, North Africa, and parts of southern Europe.

➢ The dispute over the succession after MUHAMMAD's death in the 10th year of the *hejra* (632 AD) resulted in a split among Muslims that continues to this day. The cousin and son-in-law of the Prophet, ʿALĪ IBN ABĪ TĀLIB, was recognised as the leader (*Imam*) by only a minority (the *schīʿat ʿAlī*, Party of ALI) which developed into Shia Islam. The majority recognised MUHAMMAD's father-in-law ABŪ BAKR as the prophet's successor (*caliph*); today's Sunna Islam goes back to them. It was only in the 35th year of the *hejra* (656 AD) that ʿALĪ was universally recognised as the (fourth) caliph; his assassination five years later led to the definitive split between Sunna Islam and Shia Islam.

➢ In the sphere of Sunni Islam, the Umayyad dynasty now succeeded in making the caliphate hereditary in their family. They continued the expansionist policy of the first four caliphs (the so-called *Rashidun caliphs*), who had already conquered Palestine and Syria, Egypt, Mesopotamia, and Iran, so that the Umayyad caliphate, with its centre in Damascus, at its greatest extent at the beginning of the 8th century, stretched from Spain and North Africa to the Caucasus and India.

➢ In 750, the Umayyads were overthrown by the Abbasid dynasty, who made Baghdad the centre of their empire. However, a member of the Umayyads escaped to Spain, where he and his descendants established an independent rule and, from 929, also took up the title of caliph again (*Caliphate of Córdoba*, until 1031).

➤ The Shiite Muslims are themselves split into a number of different groups. The largest group is Twelver Shi'ism. According to its teachings, ʿALĪ was followed by another eleven imams. The twelfth imam did not die, but lives in occultation and will return as *Mahdi* on Judgment Day (this is also explicitly stated in Art. 5 of the Iranian constitution of 1979, ⇨ par. 8123).

2102 As successors to the Prophet, the caliphs claimed both political and religious leadership over all Muslims; there was no separation of the secular and religious spheres. The **Arab Empire** ruled by the caliphs incorporated the cultural legacies of both the ancient Mediterranean and Persia, continuing them in the spirit of Islam. The blossoming of art and science was contrasted by a gradual political decline from the 10th century onwards; a growing number of peripheral areas became independent and only nominally recognised the caliph as their supreme leader. The conquest of Baghdad by the Mongols in 1258 effectively marked the end of the caliphate.

➤ While the Muslim conquerors forced the polytheists they had subjugated to convert to Islam, they initially showed relative tolerance towards Christians (who in many countries, such as Egypt, would long remain the majority population) and Jews. As "protected persons" (*dhimmi*), they were allowed to continue practising their religions with certain restrictions. However, they were gradually excluded from higher offices, which was associated with social disadvantages, and had to pay a special poll tax (to compensate for the fact that they were not usually drafted into the military).

➤ In 969, the Shiite Fatimids conquered Egypt and established their own caliphate, which at times also gained control over Palestine and Mecca. In contrast to previous Muslim rulers, the Fatimids became increasingly intolerant towards other religions; in 1009, the Church of the Holy Sepulchre in Jerusalem was destroyed.

➤ The accounts of the plight of Christians in the Holy Land were among the factors that led to the Crusades (⇨ par. 2109). Their temporary success (especially the conquest of Jerusalem in 1099) was due in no small part to the disunity of the Islamic world. In 1171, the Fatimids were overthrown by the Sunni Kurd SALADIN, and Egypt was at least formally re-united with Arabia. In 1187, SALADIN regained Jerusalem; in 1303, the crusaders lost their last possessions in Palestine.

➤ Prior to these events, the Islamic world had already been deeply shaken by the Mongol conquest of Baghdad in 1258; a large number of independent Muslim states emerged. A member of the Abbasid dynasty was able to flee to Egypt, where the dynasty (retaining the title of caliph but without any political power) continued to reside until 1517 (⇨ par. 2119).

3. The European Early and High Middle Ages (486–1214)

2103 From the 5th century on, the Germanic lords established their own kingdoms in the territory of the defunct Western Roman Empire, adopting both Christianity and some aspects of the administrative structures of the *Imperium Romanum*. The most prominent of these kingdoms was the **Frankish Empire**, which at its height under CHARLEMAGNE (768–814) encompassed practically the whole of Central Europe. After his death, the Frankish empire disintegrated. In a lengthy process of division in the 9th and 10th centuries, two new states were formed: West Francia and East Francia. The former developed into *France*, the latter into *Germany*.

➢ CLOVIS I (481–511) is considered the founder of the Frankish Empire. He gained control over northern Gaul in 486 and converted to Catholic Christianity in 496.

➢ Earlier, the Visigoths had already established a kingdom in southern Gaul. In 507, the Franks drove them into Spain. There, the previously Arian Visigoths converted to Catholicism in 589, which facilitated their integration with the Romano-Iberian population (⇨ par. 1205). In 711, the Arabs destroyed the Visigoth kingdom and conquered the Iberian Peninsula; a further advance of the Arabs in Europe was fought back by the Franks.

➢ In Italy, the Ostrogoths established a kingdom that was destroyed by the Byzantine Empire in 552/555. In 568, the Lombards invaded Italy and conquered the northern and central parts of the peninsula. The Lombard kingdom was conquered by CHARLEMAGNE in 774; Southern Italy still remained under Byzantine rule.

➢ The largest of the British Isles was settled by Angles and Saxons, which gave rise to the Kingdom of England in the 11th century. The Saxons who had remained on the mainland (the area of present-day Lower Saxony) were subjugated by CHARLEMAGNE in 772–802 and forcibly Christianised.

➢ Slavs migrated to the areas abandoned by the Germanic tribes, including present-day Austria. From the 7th century onwards, the Alpine Slavs became dependent on the Bavarians migrating from the north and west; both groups were incorporated into the Frankish Empire. The deposition of the last Bavarian Duke TASSILO III by CHARLEMAGNE took place in 788. While most of what is now Austria henceforth shared the fate of Bavaria, present-day Vorarlberg – as well as what is now south-western Germany and German-speaking Switzerland – was settled by Alemanni. They had already been subjugated by CLOVIS around 496 and incorporated into the Frankish Empire.

➢ Under the descendants of CHARLEMAGNE (the Carolingians), the Frankish Empire was repeatedly partitioned; however, this did not compromise the idea of the unity of the empire. Only over time did the separation turn out to be irreversible. From 888 onwards, non-Carolingians also attained kingship in parts of the empire, thereby breaking the dynastic bond.

➢ One reason for the disintegration of the Frankish Empire was the permanent threat from the Normans in the north, the Magyars in the east, and the Arabs in the south and west. These peoples also established their own states over time: the Normans in Normandy; the Magyars in the Pannonian Plain; and the Arabs in Spain, in Sicily and southern Italy.

2104 The Frankish kings entered into a close alliance with the pope, who at that time established his primacy over the Western Church. An important consequence of this development was the **coronation** in 800 of CHARLEMAGNE as **emperor** by the pope, (re-)establishing the tradition of the Western Roman Empire until the 19th century.

➢ After the fall of the Western Roman Empire in 476, the Eastern Roman (Byzantine) emperor had initially claimed the sole right to the imperial title and thus also supremacy over the Germanic kings, but he was unable to assert this claim.

➢ Instead, a power vacuum arose – particularly in Italy, where the Bishop of Rome (known as the *pope* since the 4th century) intervened to impose order and then claimed sovereignty over Italy himself. Battling the Lombards, he entered into a close alliance with the Franks and was granted secular rule over all of central Italy from Rome to Ravenna in 756. This *Papal State* existed until 1870 (⇨ par. 4119).

➢ The legal significance of CHARLEMAGNE's coronation in 800 was disputed. After initial hesitation, Byzantium acknowledged CHARLEMAGNE's emperorship in 812, and from then on, two emperors of equal status ruled in East and West. CHARLEMAGNE's coronation was therefore generally understood as the re-establishment of the Western Roman Empire (*renovatio imperii*).

➢ With the disintegration of the Frankish Empire, the imperial crown also temporarily lost some of its significance; it usually fell to the king who was currently in control of Italy.

2105 Under OTTO I the Great (936–73), the German kings attained a hegemonic position over the Christian Occident. OTTO united (northern) Italy with Germany and was crowned Roman Emperor in 962, thereby establishing the **Holy Roman Empire** (*Sacrum Imperium Romanum; Roman-German Empire*). From then on, German kings regularly claimed the right to be crowned as emperors by the pope.

➢ In order to receive the imperial crown, every German king had to travel to Rome at least once during his reign, which diverted the monarch's political powers for a considerable time and gave the pope great political weight. Nevertheless, almost every German king of the High Middle Ages undertook this journey to Rome.

➢ With the imperial title, the idea of world domination, or at least domination of all Christianity, handed down from late antiquity, continued to persist, but in reality, it could not be asserted, if only because a second emperor ruled in Byzantium (the "two-emperors-problem"). It was rather a primacy of honour of the Roman-German emperor over the other kings of the Occident, which, under powerful rulers (OTTO I, HENRY VI), could at least provide the legal title for hegemonic claims in Europe.

➢ The coronation of the Roman emperors is distinct from the coronation of the German kings, which in the Middle Ages usually took place in Aachen (⇨ par. 2117). From 1033, the Holy Roman Empire consisted of three kingdoms ruled by the Roman-German Emperor: Germany, (Northern) Italy, and Arelat (located in what is now south-east France/western Switzerland). With his coronation in Aachen, the German king also gained sovereignty over these two countries; a separate coronation in Italy or in Arelat was uncommon.

➢ The heartland of the Holy Roman Empire, the German Kingdom, was originally structured along tribal lines (Franks, Saxons, Bavarians, Swabians/Alemanni), each ruled by a duke. From the 12th century onwards, it was reorganised into a union of (territorially defined) lands. The first such territory was the Duchy of Austria under the Babenberg dynasty in 1156 (⇨ par. 2106). The Duchy of Bohemia, which was settled mainly by Czechs but also by many Germans from the 13th century onwards, was elevated to a kingdom in 1198 but remained a fiefdom of the Holy Roman Emperor.

➢ Many territories were not ruled by a secular but by an ecclesiastical prince; for instance, Salzburg was ruled by its archbishop. The dispute over the right to appoint bishops (*Investiture Controversy*, 1075–1122) resulted in the first major crisis for the emperor's political power (⇨ par. 2223).

➢ The royal throne was not subject to hereditary succession; instead, any new accession to the throne required the consent of the princes. However, in the period in which the kings had an abundance of power, the crown usually remained with a dynasty until its male line died out and then passed to descendants of daughters of the respective dynasty: Ottonians 919–1024; Salians 1024–1125; Hohenstaufen 1138–1208/1212–54.

➢ The election of the Swabian Hohenstaufen as German kings in 1138 was contested by the Welfs, who ruled in Bavaria and Saxony, which led to serious crises. An attempt at reconciliation in 1156 between the Hohenstaufen Emperor FREDERICK I "Barbarossa" (1152–90) and the Welf Duke HENRY "the Lion" was short-lived; in 1180, HENRY was stripped of his fiefs due to his renewed opposition to the emperor (⇨ par. 2209).

➢ Under Barbarossa's son Emperor HENRY VI, imperial power reached its final peak (conquest of Sicily and an oath of allegiance by the King of England, both in 1194), but his plan to transform the empire into a hereditary monarchy failed. When, after his death in 1198, a Hohenstaufen was elected by one faction of the electoral college and a Welf by another, this double election plunged the empire into its most serious crisis to that point (⇨ par. 2107, par. 2110).

2106 With the support of their close relatives, the Hohenstaufen, the **House of Babenberg** was able to transform the march of Austria into a duchy in 1156. They also acquired a second duchy, Styria, in 1192, which was henceforth linked to the land of Austria in a dynastic union.

➢ After his victory over the Hungarians in 955, OTTO I the Great had established a march on the eastern border of the empire, which was enfeoffed to LEOPOLD I of the House of Babenberg in 976. The oldest known document that refers to this march as *ostarrîchi* dates from 996; the Latin version *Austria* first appeared in 1147.

➢ Although the Austrian margraves were legally subordinate to the Bavarian dukes, they subsequently succeeded in establishing a largely independent rule based on their margravial (especially military and judicial) powers.

➢ In the course of the Welf/Hohenstaufen conflict, the Babenbergs replaced the Welfs as rulers of Bavaria in 1139 and were thus themselves elevated to the rank of dukes. Following the reconciliation between the Welfs and the Hohenstaufen in 1156 (⇨ par. 2105), the Babenberg Duke HENRY "Jasomirgott" (1141–76) was forced to give up Bavaria in favour of the Welfs. However, Austria was separated from Bavaria at this time as an independent duchy and granted several privileges (*Privilegium minus:* limits to the duties of providing troops to the emperor and attending the Reichstag, increased judicial sovereignty, etc.).

➢ After the Welf HENRY the Lion was permanently overthrown in 1180, Styria also became an independent duchy under OTTOKAR IV of Traungau. The latter appointed the Babenbergs as heirs to his extensive allodial possessions in Styria in an inheritance contract (documented in the *Georgenberg Compact* 1186). Thus, after the death of OTTOKAR IV in 1192, Emperor HENRY VI formally enfeoffed the Babenbergs with Styria.

2107 In contrast to the powerful position held by the German kings, the **French king** was initially characterised by a lack of power. In 1066, Duke WILLIAM "the Conqueror" of Normandy conquered the **Kingdom of England**, which meant that a vassal of the French king also became the king of a sovereign state. This unusual constellation gave rise to a series of conflicts.

➢ In France, there was initially also no hereditary claim to the throne. However, the Capetian dynasty, which ruled from 987 onwards, succeeded in transferring the crown from father to son twelve times in a row, thereby firmly establishing the hereditary nature of the crown. After the direct line of the Capetian dynasty had died out in 1328, the crown could be passed on to the Capetian collateral lines of Valois (1328–1589, ⇨ par. 2112) and Bourbon (1589–1792 and 1814–48, ⇨ par. 2118).

➢ The high aspirations of the French kings, who, like their German counterparts, saw themselves as the successors of CHARLEMAGNE, contrasted with their actual political power base, which in the High Middle Ages barely extended beyond the areas around Orléans and Paris, while the rest of France was firmly in the hands of powerful vassals.

➢ The Norman kings of England also saw themselves primarily as French princes after 1066 and steadily increased their possessions in mainland France; the "Anglo-Norman" King HENRY II of England (1154–89) ruled over more than half of the French kingdom and also initiated the subjugation of Ireland. The House of Plantagenet, which he founded, ruled in England until 1485.

➢ The ambitions of the House of Plantagenet, which was linked through marriage to the Welfs, ultimately resulted in conflict with the Hohenstaufen emperors. In 1192, the English King RICHARD I "Lionheart" (1189–99) fell into German captivity, from which he was only released in 1194 upon paying a high ransom and accepting England in fief from Emperor HENRY VI. Back in England, RICHARD I soon cast off this vassalage and, after the death

Map 3: Europe and the Mediterranean region in 1097
Source: Own drawing, using a map from https://commons.wikimedia.org/wiki/File:Blank_map_of_Europe_1097.svg and https://de.wikipedia.org/wiki/R%C3%B6misches_Reich#/media/Datei:Roman_Republic_Empire_map.gif

of HENRY VI in 1198, helped the Welf OTTO IV to establish a German rival kingdom against the Hohenstaufen as an act of revenge.

2108 The Magyars settled in the Pannonian Plain in the 10th century and f ounded the Kingdom of **Hungary**, which encompassed all the peoples living within the Carpathian Arc. In the year 1000, King STEPHEN I "the Saint" (997–1038) became a Christian.

➢ In 906, the Magyars, from the Ural region, destroyed the Great Moravian State on the Danube and March and subsequently advanced deep into Western Europe; they were not defeated until 955 by OTTO I the Great, after which they retreated to the Pannonian Plain.

➢ The Crown of Saint Stephen, named after STEPHEN I, which he received from the pope on the occasion of his conversion to Christianity in 1000, henceforth served as the symbol of the Hungarian kingdom, with which every legitimate king had to be crowned.

➢ In 1102, Croatia was united with Hungary in a personal union and from then on shared Hungary's fate until 1918.

2109 The **crusades** to the Holy Land (1095–1303) brought no lasting territorial gains for the Christians, but in the **Reconquista** (722–1492), they were able to reconquer the Iberian Peninsula from the Muslims. Europe's close contact with the (culturally far superior)

Arab world led to flourishing trade relations and a significant transfer of knowledge (Arabic numerals, the reception of ARISTOTLE's philosophy through the work of Arab scholars, etc.).

➢ Since the destruction of the Visigoth kingdom by the Arabs in 711, only the far north of Spain had remained Christian, while most of the peninsula constituted the Caliphate of Córdoba from 929 (⇨ par. 2101). It disintegrated into several Muslim petty kingdoms in 1031, which had to assert their independence against both the Christians and their North African brothers in faith.

➢ Christian efforts to reconquer Spain (*Reconquista*) began as early as 722. Several Christian kingdoms emerged (especially Castile, Aragon, Portugal), which in numerous wars subjugated almost the entire peninsula until the end of the 13th century. Only the extreme south – the Kingdom of Granada – remained under Muslim rule until 1492.

➢ The fight against the "infidels" had thus been long established as the central mission of Western chivalry when, from 1095, the popes called for crusades to the Holy Land, where the Byzantine Empire had until then tried on its own to regain the territories it had lost to the Muslims from the 7th century onwards (⇨ par. 2101). The "Latin" (i.e. Catholic) crusader armies managed to conquer a few areas but were unable to keep them permanently (⇨ par. 2102).

➢ Byzantium initially profited from the crusades, but in 1204, it was itself conquered and looted by crusaders, who established a "Latin Empire" in its territory. This event in particular made the split between the Greek Orthodox and Roman Catholic Churches irreversible. The main beneficiary of the conquest of Constantinople was Venice, which became the dominant sea power in the eastern Mediterranean.

➢ At the beginning of the 11th century, the Normans conquered Southern Italy, which had been partly Arab and partly Byzantine. They established a modern state (the "Kingdom of Sicily"), which also included the Neapolitan mainland. In 1194, the Roman-German Emperor HENRY VI conquered this kingdom, but the popes blocked the legal incorporation of Sicily into the Roman-German Empire, which effectively saved the Papal States from being encircled by the Empire and also prevented the unification of Italy.

➢ In later times, crusades were also launched against other non-Christian or "heretical" (⇨ par. 2113) targets, especially into the pagan Baltic region, where the Teutonic Order of Knights formed its own state in the 13th century. The Knights Hospitaller, who had been expelled from the Holy Land, conquered the until then Byzantine island of Rhodes in 1306/10, where they ruled until 1522 (⇨ par. 2119).

3. The Late Middle Ages (1214–1492)

2110 Under Emperor FREDERICK II (1212–50), the **Holy Roman Empire** flourished once again, but his death marked the beginning of a period of decline. As the weaker party in the power struggle against the pope, the German ruler was unable to maintain his supremacy over other European monarchs and also lost many domestic powers to the German princes.

➤ Even FREDERICK II had only been able to prevail against the rival Emperor OTTO IV from the House of Welf (1198–1218) with the help of armed forces from France (Battle of Bouvines 1214, ⇨ par. 2112). He was opposed by the popes not only because of his affection for Arab culture and science but also because – like his father HENRY VI – he ruled over both Imperial Italy and Sicily and thus once again had the papacy in his grip from both the north and the south.

➤ In 1246, the Babenbergs died out, and Emperor FREDERICK II seized their territories. For some time, he considered elevating them to a kingdom *(Regnum Austriae)*, but this did not materialise. His own death in 1250 caused a new power vacuum throughout Central Europe, as the princes were unable to agree on a new German king.

➤ Although – or even because – several kings subsequently often ruled at the same time, their rule was so ineffective that the period 1250–73 came to be known as a kingless period (*"interregnum"*). It was not until the election of RUDOLF I of Habsburg as German king (1273–91) that the gravest ills in the empire came to an end. However, RUDOLF was unable to attain the level of power formerly held by the Hohenstaufen dynasty.

➤ Due to their weak position in the empire, the German kings of the Late Middle Ages focused on strengthening and increasing their own hereditary territories, which they held as princes of the empire (*dynastic power politics*). The electoral college sought to counter this strategy and elected kings from different dynasties (mainly Habsburgs, Luxembourgs, and Wittelsbachs) to prevent any of them from becoming too powerful.

➤ Coronations of emperors were rare during this period. Emperor LOUIS IV "the Bavarian" from the house of Wittelsbach (1314–47) attempted to detach the imperial title from the coronation by the pope and to link it directly to the election as German king (*constitutio licet iuris* 1338), but this failed.

➤ Gradually, a circle of seven imperial princes crystallised who claimed the right to elect the king for themselves alone (the electoral princes). The electoral law and procedure were thoroughly regulated in 1356 by Emperor CHARLES IV from the House of Luxembourg (1347–78) in the *Golden Bull*. Membership in the electoral college was linked to the rule over a specific ecclesiastical (Mainz, Cologne, Trier) or secular (Bohemia, Rhenish Palatinate, Saxony, Brandenburg) electorate; the Golden Bull contained special succession rules and privileges for the electorates that made them largely independent of the empire.

2111 Over time, the **Habsburgs** were able to gain such a strong position that the electors could no longer deny them the kingship and from 1438 onwards regularly elected them as German kings (until 1740/1806, ⇨ par. 3110). However, German kingship was never made hereditary, and the election always remained a political issue.

➤ During the German Interregnum, OTTOKAR II of Bohemia had acquired the former Babenberg territories of Austria and Styria, as well as Carinthia and Carniola (in present-day Slovenia), thereby creating a power bloc stretching from the Sudetes to the Adriatic Sea. However, his efforts to have these acquisitions recognised under imperial law were unsuccessful.

➢ After RUDOLF I had been elected German king, he demanded that OTTOKAR II surrender these illicitly acquired territories. He was able to enforce his claim by military force and in 1282 enfeoffed his sons with Austria, Styria, and Carniola. With this enfeoffment in 1282, the dynasty, which originated in the Alemannic region and had its ancestral seat in present-day Switzerland (Habsburg castle in Aargau), became one of the most powerful families of the empire and took on the name "House of Austria". Accordingly, the countries they ruled were also called "Austrian" (in the sense of belonging to the Habsburgs).

➢ RUDOLF I enfeoffed Carinthia to his comrade-in-arms MAYNARD II of Gorizia-Tyrol in 1286 and also gave him Carniola as a pledge to pay off his debts. The counts of Tyrol, who until then had only been indirectly subjected to the king (namely through their direct liege lords, the bishops of Brixen and Trento), were thus elevated to the status of imperial princes. They were able to retain this status when the Habsburgs annexed Carinthia and Carniola in 1335, following the extinction of the male line of the Maynardins.

➢ Unlike in Carinthia, the Tyrolean estates allowed female succession, which is why the daughter of the last Maynardin, MARGARET "Maultasch" (1335–63), was able to inherit her father's position. The Luxembourgs, Wittelsbachs, and Habsburgs tried, in turn, to gain the rule over Tyrol, until it finally fell to the Habsburgs in 1363.

➢ The increased political influence of the Habsburgs on the one hand and their exclusion from the circle of electors (⇨ par. 2110) on the other prompted the Austrian Duke RUDOLF IV "the Founder" (1358–65) to unilaterally lay claim to certain privileges and to justify them by falsifying older documents, including the Privilegium minus (*Privilegium maius* 1358/59). However, Emperor CHARLES IV forced him to renounce those claims.

➢ The Habsburgs also suffered a setback in the Alemannic region, where in 1291 the three territories of Uri, Schwyz, and Unterwalden, which were under the direct authority of the emperor, had united to form a confederation that was primarily directed against the Habsburgs' efforts to increase their powers; later, other territories joined as well. In their struggle against the *Swiss Confederation*, most of the Habsburgs' ancestral lands were lost, including Habsburg castle itself in 1415.

➢ In 1453, the Habsburg Emperor FREDERICK III declared the forgeries of 1358/59 to be valid; the Habsburgs henceforth held the title of "Archduke of Austria" and enjoyed a series of privileges that further strengthened their dominion over their hereditary lands.

2112 The **King of France** was able to successively increase his political power and reduce the sphere of influence of the **King of England** within France.

➢ In the Battle of Bouvines in 1214 (⇨ par. 2110), PHILIP II of France (1180–1223) settled both the Anglo-French conflict and the dispute over the German throne between the Hohenstaufen FREDERICK II and the Welf

OTTO IV, which was the first time that the King of France directly influenced German domestic affairs. After 1214, the English King JOHN "Lackland" (1199–1216) could only retain a few provinces in southern France. In a weak position, he was forced by his English vassals to sign the *Magna Charta* in 1215, which permanently limited the monarch's power and led to the establishment of the English Parliament (⇨ par. 2218).

➢ The burgeoning French crown came increasingly into conflict with the popes. PHILIP IV (1285–1314) not only succeeded in maintaining his position through a united effort of the French estates (1302: first assembly of the *états généraux*; ⇨ par. 2218), but also forced the pope to relocate his court into the sphere of French influence ("Babylonian captivity" of the popes in Avignon 1309–76).

➢ When the Capetian collateral line of Valois ascended the French throne in 1328 (until 1589, ⇨ par. 2118), competing claims by the House of Plantagenet led to the so-called *Hundred Years' War* with England (1339–1453). After some initial success by the English, the "Maid of Orleans" JOAN OF ARC led the French army to victory. England lost virtually all its possessions on the mainland.

➢ In the course of the Hundred Years' War, the mighty Burgundian state emerged from German and French fiefdoms, extending along almost the entire Franco-German border; it was a constant threat to the French kingdom even after the war with England had ended.

2113 The crises of the imperial and papal powers on the one hand and economic changes and epidemics on the other led to **religious and national unrest** as well as the persecution of heretics, Jews, and (alleged) "witches".

➢ The German word *"Ketzer"*, meaning "heretic", comes from the sect of the Cathars in southern France. By destroying this (Christian!) religious community in a formal crusade in 1226, the French king was able to strengthen his power in southern France, which until then had been marginal.

➢ In 1376, the popes returned to Rome (⇨ par. 2112), whereupon a counter-papacy was established in Avignon. This schism in the Church led to a temporary decline in papal power and several councils, of which only the Council of Constance (1414–18) succeeded in ending the "Western Schism".

➢ Meanwhile, the attempts at religious reform by the Prague theology professor JAN HUS combined with Czech nationalist concerns. In 1415, HUS was executed as a heretic at the Council of Constance, and his followers were brutally persecuted (*Hussite Wars* 1419–34).

➢ Jews and "witches" were held responsible for the outbreak of the Black Death in 1347/48, which killed more than 50 percent of the European population. Persecutions (pogroms), mass executions, and expulsions ensued.

2114 After the decline of the Holy Roman Empire and of Constantinople, Western European influence also became noticeable in **East-Central Europe** and **Italy**.

➤ The Byzantine Empire was restored in 1261 but could not regain its former position as a leading power. In 1453, the Turks conquered Constantinople, which meant the definitive end for Byzantium.

➤ After the death of the Hohenstaufen Emperor FREDERICK II in 1250, the French Prince CHARLES I of Anjou conquered Sicily (including Naples), which until then had been ruled by the Hohenstaufen dynasty. CHARLES founded his own kingdom there, which initially succeeded in gaining hegemony over the whole of Italy but from 1282 ("Sicilian Vespers") became involved in a conflict over Naples-Sicily with the Spanish House of Aragon. After the Anjous had died out in 1435, Naples-Sicily was eventually annexed to Aragon (or, later, Spain).

➤ A collateral line of the House of Anjou ascended the Hungarian and Croatian throne in 1301 and the Polish one in 1370, making the empire of King LOUIS I the Great of Anjou (1342–82) stretch from the Adriatic to the Baltic and Black Seas. Following his death, this Hungarian-Polish empire disintegrated.

➤ Hungary and Croatia then entered into a personal union with Bohemia, which lasted – with interruptions and under changing dynasties, eventually the Habsburgs – until 1918.

➤ In 1386, Poland formed a personal union with Lithuania; in 1569, the two countries were legally united to form a "Republic of Nobles" (*Rzeczpospolita szlachecka*). Political power lay with the parliament (*Sejm*); the king was elected by the parliament from 1572 onward and had only limited powers.

4. The Early Modern Era (1492–1618)

2115 The transition from the Middle Ages to the modern era is marked by a series of scientific, political, economic, and artistic events at the turn of the 15th to the 16th century, with which European culture changed forever. Among the most significant of these was the voyage of CHRISTOFORO COLOMBO to the Americas in 1492, which led to the **conquest of America and the subjugation of their indigenous peoples** by the kingdoms of Western Europe.

➤ Portuguese seafarers had begun exploring the African coast in the early 15th century in search of a sea route to India, which was first reached by sea in 1498. In the process, some islands and cities in Africa and Asia were also conquered. Long-distance trade led to an economic boom in Portugal.

➤ Following the marriage of ISABEL I of Castile (1474–1504) and FERRANDO II of Aragón (1479–1516) in 1469, both countries had been politically united as the "Kingdom of Spain", even though constitutional unity was only achieved in 1714 through the merger of their respective *Cortes*, the assemblies of their estates (⇨ par. 3104). Together, the two monarchs brought the Reconquista (⇨ par. 2109) to a successful conclusion in 1492,

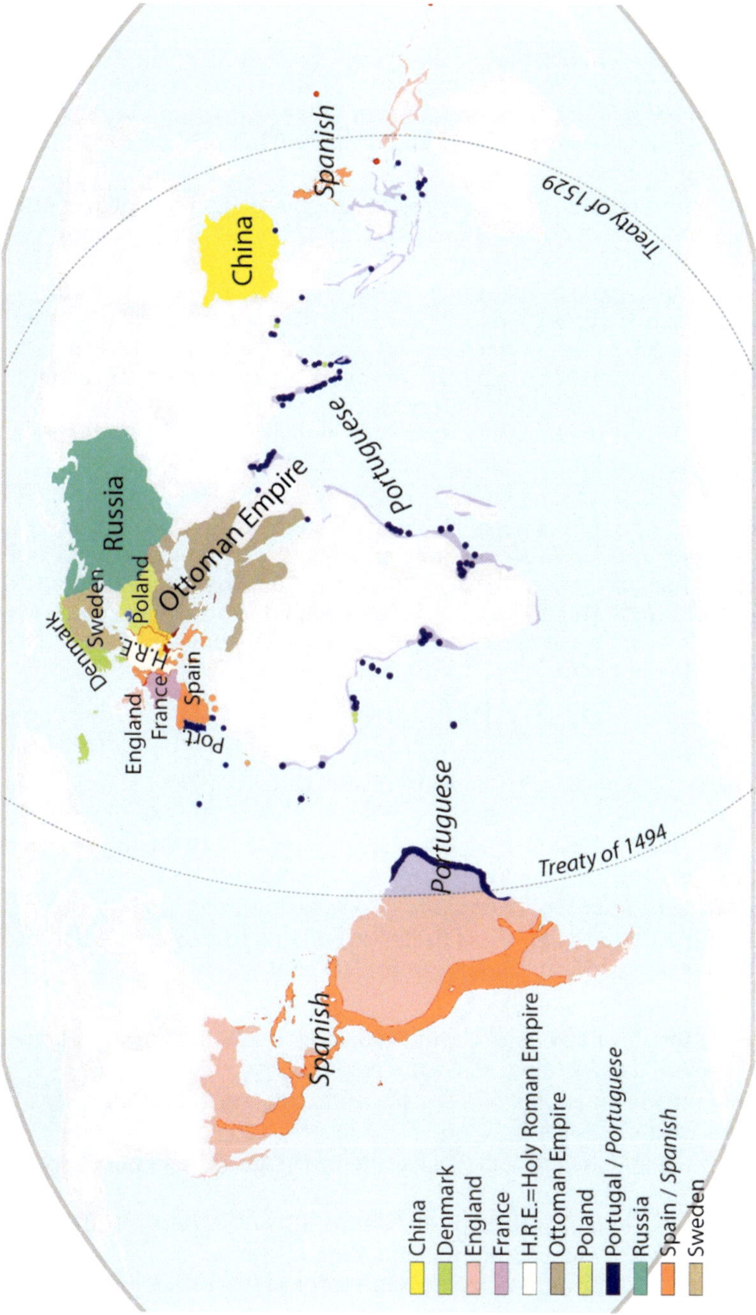

Map 4: The Europeanisation of the world in 1580

Only major powers and other colonial powers are shown in color. Source: https://upload.wikimedia.org/wikipedia/commons/a/ad/Philip_II%27s_realms_in_1598.png (modified). Copyright: https://creativecommons.org/licenses/by-sa/3.0 (CC BY-SA 3.0) which also resulted in the expulsion of all Muslims and Jews from Spain. On the same occasion, they commissioned COLOMBO to sail to India via the western route. He never reached his destination, but on 12 October 1492, he landed in America.

➢ The conquest of America (*Conquista*) can be seen as a seamless continuation of the Reconquista, in that it accommodated the continuing expansionist desires of Spain and the missionary zeal of its clergy. Within a very short time, Spain brought huge areas under its control and destroyed the Aztec empire in present-day Mexico in 1521, as well as the South American Inca empire in 1532. Wars and introduced diseases led to a massive decline in the population of the native Americans, who were subjected to economic exploitation by the European conquerors, often forcibly Christianised and largely robbed of their independent cultural development. Soon after, the importation of slaves from Africa also began.

➢ The competing colonial interests of Portugal and Spain were provisionally settled in 1493 with a papal ruling that became the basis for the Treaty of Tordesillas in 1494. According to this, all land west of 46° 37' west latitude (according to modern measurement) was to belong to Spain, and all land east of it to Portugal. This border line enabled Portugal to establish a colony in Brazil a little later. In 1529, it was complemented by a second dividing line in the Pacific.

2116 About the same time, the **Habsburgs** succeeded in establishing a dynastic empire where "the sun never set". The legal bases for these territorial acquisitions were mostly marriage articles, but coincidence played at least as great a role as the arranged marriages. Moreover, it was always also necessary to be able to sustain the acquisitions by military means. The equally common expression *bella gerant alii, tu felix Austria, nube* ("Wars may be waged by others, you, happy Austria, marry") is therefore misleading. Specifically, the Habsburgs acquired in the 15th and 16th centuries:

➢ 1. the Burgundian state (1477; ⇨ par. 2112);

➢ 2. the united Kingdoms of Castile and Aragon (Spain with its annexed territories in Italy and colonies in America, 1504/16);

➢ 3. the united Kingdoms of Bohemia and Hungary with their annexed territories (1526; ⇨ par. 3105);

➢ 4. the Kingdom of Portugal with its colonies in Africa, Asia, and America (1580).

➢ The Habsburg monarch CHARLES V (1516/19–56), by virtue of his dual position as Holy Roman Emperor and King of Spain, enjoyed unprecedented power, but the numerous problems associated with his roles drained his strength.

➢ In 1521/22, CHARLES V ceded the Austrian hereditary lands, i.e. the territories that had already belonged to Habsburg in the Middle Ages, to his brother FERDINAND I, who also became King of Bohemia and Hungary in 1526. However, the latter territory was, for the most part, lost to the Turks in 1529/41; only a narrow rim in the north and west of Hungary (approximately present-day Slovakia and Burgenland) remained with the Habsburgs.

➢ A Spanish line of the House of Habsburg descended from CHARLES V and a German line from FERDINAND I; they remained closely connected through intermarriage (and incest!). The title of emperor passed to the German line in 1556, but the Spanish line remained politically dominant. With the acquisition of Portugal in 1580, the Spanish Habsburgs were at the zenith of their power.

➢ By the end of the 16th century, it was evident that Spain had overstretched itself and was no longer able to assert its position, particularly in the face of the growing colonial ambitions of France and England. This increasing weakness was particularly evident in the Netherlands, which, as part of Burgundy, had been ruled by the Habsburgs since 1477. In 1579, the northern (Protestant) Netherlands declared itself independent (which was not recognised by Spain until 1648); only the southern (Catholic) Netherlands (present-day Belgium and Luxembourg) remained Spanish.

2117 In the Holy Roman Empire, an extensive **Imperial Reform** took place under Emperor MAXIMILIAN I (1493–1519), which, however, was soon overshadowed by the **Protestant Reformation**. The conflicts between Catholics and Protestants were temporarily ended by the Religious Peace of Augsburg in 1555.

➢ The Imperial Reform of 1495 created the *Imperial Diet (Reichstag)* as an institutional assembly of the imperial princes (⇨ par. 2217) and the *Imperial Chamber Court* (*Reichskammergericht*, ⇨ par. 2322), whose members were appointed in equal numbers by the Reichstag and the emperor, respectively. The emperor/king was left with only limited powers. These were enumerated exhaustively in *electoral capitulations* (binding promises to the electors); most of them he could only exercise jointly with the Reichstag *(iura Caesarea comitialia)*.

➢ From 1508 onwards, the German kings refrained from letting themselves be crowned as emperors by the pope, but with papal approval held the title of "Elected Roman Emperor". The last coronation of a Roman-German emperor by the pope took place in 1530 (CHARLES V). The coronation of the German king (which in modern times took place in Frankfurt) was now regarded as the coronation of an emperor, and in the minds of contemporaries, the terms "German king" and "Roman emperor" became blurred.

➢ The notion of a supranational nature of the Holy Roman Empire, which still prevailed in the Middle Ages, had faded due to the decline in the emperor's actual importance. The empire turned into a state of the Germans, which from the 15th century onwards was also expressed in the state name: "Holy Roman Empire of the German Nation".

➢ Northern Italy formally remained part of the empire, but the German kings had almost entirely abandoned their policies in regard to Italian affairs. The Italian princes were not represented at the Imperial Diet, and Italy became the object of French and Spanish power struggles.

➢ During the Reformation period, a large number of new denominations emerged whose causes only partially overlapped (⇨ par. 2225). Emperor

Charles V initially tried to forcibly suppress the new theology; the term "protestants" for the followers of the new doctrines, which is still in use today, is reminiscent of the protest they raised in 1529 against Charles V's attempt to withdraw previously made concessions.

➤ Eventually, Charles V. failed due to the opposition of the imperial princes who sympathised with the protestants. In the Religious Peace of Augsburg in 1555, the confessional unity of the empire was abandoned, and the princes of the empire were free to choose their own confession as well as to determine that of their subjects (principle of *cuius regio, eius religio*).

2118 In both **England** and **France**, confessional conflicts arose that were linked to matters of dynasty and succession to the throne and resulted in religious wars. While France remained Catholic, the Reformation prevailed in England.

➤ The English King Henry VIII (1509–47) of the House of Tudor broke with the Catholic Church because the pope would not annul his marriage to a Spanish princess who until then had not borne him any sons. In 1534, Henry VIII issued the Act of Supremacy and declared himself the head of the English Church after having unilaterally annulled his marriage in 1533 and married an English noblewoman, Anne Boleyn.

➤ Every male English adult had to swear an oath of allegiance to this Act, and those who refused were liable to prosecution and execution (a fate that befell the former Lord Chancellor Thomas More, who was beheaded in 1535).

➤ When Elizabeth I (1558–1603), a daughter of Henry VIII from his marriage to Anne Boleyn, ascended the English throne, the Catholics did not acknowledge her because of her (from the Catholic point of view) illegitimate descent; instead, they regarded the Scottish Queen Mary I Stuart (1542–67), a grandniece of Henry VIII, as the rightful Queen of England.

➤ When Mary Stuart was forced to flee to England in 1568 to escape a revolt by Scottish nobles, she was taken prisoner by Elizabeth and executed in 1587. After Elizabeth's death in 1603, Mary Stuart's son, James VI of Scotland (1567–1625), became King of England as James I, thus uniting Scotland with England in a personal union.

➤ In France, the Protestant House of Bourbon was to inherit the throne after the imminent extinction of the ruling Valois (⇨ par. 2112), which the French Catholic nobility tried to prevent. An attempt to reconcile the two parties through a marriage of the Protestant heir to the throne to a Catholic king's daughter in 1572 ended in the St. Bartholomew's Day massacre with some 20,000 Huguenots murdered.

➤ With Henry IV (1589–1610), the House of Bourbon ascended the French throne (until 1792/1848, ⇨ par. 3114, par. 4101). To gain broad acceptance, Henry converted to Catholicism in 1593, but also granted the Protestants tolerance in the Edict of Nantes of 1598.

➤ Following the Spanish example, both England and France established colonies in America – initially in the Caribbean, but then mainly in North America. The English colony of Virginia was founded in 1607, followed by the French colony of Nouvelle-France (Canada) in 1608.

2119 The Turkish sultans from the Ottoman dynasty subjugated the Balkans, southern Ukraine, and most of Hungary **(Ottoman Empire)**. Following the conquest of Constantinople in 1453, they claimed imperial rank, which, however, was initially not recognised in Europe. The ideological successor to Constantinople on the Christian Orthodox side was the Russian tsar.

➢ Turkic peoples had migrated to Anatolia from the 11th century onwards and had overthrown the local Byzantine rule in 1071 (which was one of the reasons for the Crusades, ⇨ par. 2109). After the Turkish "Sultanate of Rum" (= Rome!) was crushed by the Mongols in 1243, a gradual revival began under the Ottoman dynasty; by the 15th century, all of Anatolia was under Ottoman rule.

➢ The Ottomans' advance in the Balkans began as early as the 14th century. In 1389, the Serbs were defeated in the Battle of Kosovo. It was not until 1529 that the Turks' advance in Europe ended as a result of the failed (first) siege of Vienna.

➢ In a parallel development, the Ottomans subjugated almost the entire Arab world in the Near East and North Africa. In 1517, they deposed the last caliph in Cairo (⇨ par. 2102), which allowed them to later also claim this title and thus spiritual supremacy over all Muslims.

➢ As a result of the aforementioned conquests, a large part of the Mediterranean was also under Ottoman rule (which indirectly contributed to the boom in Atlantic trade). In 1522, the Ottoman fleet conquered Rhodes, whereupon the Knights Hospitaller, who had previously ruled there (⇨ par. 2109), received the island of Malta from CHARLES V (for which they are still known today as the "Knights of Malta", ⇨ par. 3118).

➢ After the fall of Constantinople in 1453 (⇨ par. 2114), many leaders of the Orthodox Church fled to the court of the Moscow Grand Prince IVAN III the Great (1462–1505). The latter took the title of "tsar" (from Caesar) in 1478, having previously married the niece of the last Byzantine emperor to underline the then-emerging theory of Moscow as the "Third Rome".

B Structures

1. General Remarks

2201 Despite promises to the contrary (cf. e.g. in the Bible: Gal 3:28; in the Qur'an: Surah 49:10), neither the Christianisation of Europe nor the Islamisation of the Near East and North Africa resulted in the immediate legal equality of all believers, let alone all people. In fact, both the **sytem of estates** and the **subordination of women to men** remained in place as fundamental principles, even if some details underwent changes. The Early Middle Ages saw a partial loosening of the estate system, in which both upward and downward mobility were possible more easily than before. However, the new structures soon solidified again, and the principle of "birth estates" prevailed (⇨ par. 1201).

➢ Slavery was not completely abolished in Europe, but the enslavement of Christians was frowned upon. It therefore retained its significance, for example, in the Mediterranean region (enslavement of Muslims by Christians and vice versa) but became completely obsolete in Central Europe. In most cases, personal bondage, in particular that of agricultural labourers, was transformed into serfdom. Although the serf was completely subjugated to his master, he was nevertheless recognised as a person, which is why, for example, he could – unlike a slave – marry with his lord's consent. Similar conditions applied to the serfs (*'abd*) in the Islamic world.

➢ The system of estates also underwent significant changes by the establishment of the *knighthood*. Knights were initially personally unfree, mounted warriors of a prince, who in the course of the Middle Ages advanced to the estate of the (lower) nobility (cf. the etymological connection between the word knight and the German word *Knecht* [servant]). Their Islamic equivalent were the *mamluks*, slave-soldiers who could sometimes achieve considerable political influence.

➢ Christianity extended the principle already existing in ancient Greece and Rome that a man could have only one primary wife, to absolute monogamy, so that all forms of secondary marriage (the so-called *Friedelehe;* concubinage) and all extramarital sexual intercourse were frowned upon. While this created an essential prerequisite for the later equality of men and women, it had devastating consequences for children born out of wedlock, who were now considered "illegitimate" and were therefore worse off.

➢ Although Islam retained the practice of polygamy that was widespread in the Arab world, it limited the number of wives to the number for which the husband could adequately provide, and to a maximum of four (Surah 4:3). Polyandry, which also existed in Arabia, was made illegal.

➢ The nature and extent of a woman's subjugation to her husband varied greatly between the estates and over time. Noblewomen and peasant women enjoyed a comparatively high degree of independence, while bourgeois women were usually very much subject to the authority of their husbands. A comparatively liberal period in the late Middle Ages was followed by increased subjugation of women in the early modern period, not least as a result of the reception of learned law (⇨ par. 2322).

➢ The consolidation of the system of estates was reinforced in particular by the principle of *equal birth*: a defendant could only be judged by his peers, and a marriage could only be contracted between persons from the same estate. Different solutions existed for children born of parents from different estates (which rarely occurred due to the principle of *equal birth*); usually the child assumed the lesser estate.

2202 In Europe, **Feudalism** dominated the entire Middle Ages and the early modern period and continued to have an impact into the 19th century. Feudalism is a state, economic, and social order that binds political and sovereign rights directly to economic power. It typically occurs in societies with poor infrastructure that cannot establish a central rule.

➢ "Economic power" in an agrarian society was synonymous with large-scale land ownership. The feudal lords were landlords. With the advent of the Industrial Revolution in the 18th and 19th centuries, feudalism lost its economic basis; its political significance had already steadily declined from the 17th century onward.

➢ Modern legal categories ("private law" vs. "public law") are not applicable to the feudal legal order. Rather, the essence of feudalism is precisely the combination of such elements.

➢ The concept of feudalism used here is significantly broader than the one usually employed in English-language scholarship, which usually confines it to the feudal pyramid (⇨ par. 2209). It is, however, narrower than that of Marxist historical theory, which sees in feudalism a universal phenomenon that necessarily ensues from the ancient slave-owning society (⇨ par. 4314)

➢ This is not to overlook the fact that similar structures also emerged under similar conditions in other parts of the world. For example, the Arab system of *iqta'*, and also the Japanese political system between the 12th century and the Meiji Revolution in 1867/68 (⇨ par. 4122) despite all their differences, also showed some remarkable parallels to the European feudal system.

2203 European feudalism emerged in the Frankish Empire (6th–9th century) and was based on both Gallo-Roman and Germanic **roots**. Its development was a consequence of the Frankish "land seizure" during the migration period.

➢ In late antiquity, feudal structures developed in the form of the *patrocinium*: a person in economic distress placed himself under the protection of a more powerful person (*patron*), but thereby forfeited part of his personal freedom.

➢ Their Germanic roots can be found in the allegiance of free men to a noble lord, originally for the purpose of war and later on a permanent basis. This was not associated with a diminution of the former's personal freedom, however.

➢ The territories conquered by the Franks in the course of the continued expansion of their empire initially fell to the king, who gifted them to his followers. Since, according to Germanic law, gifts obligated the recipient to make equivalent counter-gifts, which was not feasible in this case, the recipients were indebted to the king and thus bound to their lord.

➢ The legal form of the gift was reduced to a lease (*precarium*, *beneficium*) in the 8th century, which left the "ownership" with the lessor but granted the lessee the practically unlimited use of the land.

2. Manorialism

2204 For the **peasantry**, feudalism took the form of manorialism, which became the way of life for the majority of the European population for around 1,000 years. The peasants (*"villeins"*) were dependent on the landlord in terms of personal and property rights, as well as political authority.

➢ Manorialism emerged in the Early Middle Ages from both Germanic and Roman legal roots. While there had already been many different types of rule over the land and its people, what was new about the manorial system was that the leasing of land became an essential feature of the nobility's rule over its subjects.

➢ Both secular and ecclesiastical nobles, as well as monasteries or towns, could act as landlords. The ecclesiastical landlords (rightfully?) enjoyed a better reputation among the peasants than the secular ones.

➢ Princes or kings were only occasionally also landlords; such territories were called *"Kammergut"* in German (e.g., the *"Salzkammergut"* in present-day Upper Austria).

2205 The organisation of the manorial system varied from region to region. The main focus was usually on the landlord's household with the **demesne** held by the lord himself. Then there was also **tenured land**, which was leased to and cultivated by the peasants. In addition, there were usually also other types of land, e.g. woodland or peat cutting areas, which were used jointly (cooperatively) by all members of the manor, including its lord.

➢ The tenured land was cultivated by the peasants themselves, but they had to pay duties (in kind) to their landlord (crops, livestock), which were recorded in a special register, the *urbarium*. The peasant's claim to the tenured land was hereditary and – with the consent of the lord – usually also transferable; he thus appeared to other peasants of the same manor as the owner of the land ("inward ownership"). As the landlord could only exercise full ownership of the tenured land together with the peasant concerned, the glossators developed the theory of *divided ownership*.

➢ The demesne was cultivated on the landlord's account by unfree serfs together with the villeins, who had to provide manual labour as part of their duties, usually using their own tools and sometimes also their work animals.

➢ In Central Europe, including Upper and Lower Austria, Styria, and Carinthia, the tenured land held by the villeins was prevalent. Demesnes as well as free property of the peasants existed but had only limited significance. The peasants were personally dependent on their landlord (needing his permission if they wanted to marry and or leave the manor) but not completely subjugated to him.

➢ In Eastern and East-Central Europe, such as in Bohemia and Hungary (which also included present-day Burgenland), the manorial system developed in another direction; there, the economic interests of the demesne prevailed. The peasants became mere labourers with hardly any land of their own; their personal legal status was characterised by serfdom, i.e. an extremely reduced legal capacity which could extend to a deprivation of virtually all their legal rights.

➢ In some regions, such as Salzburg, Tyrol, and Vorarlberg, manorialism hardly developed at all. The free peasantry maintained its independence and even had political rights. At the diets they were represented in the curia of the "*Täler und Gerichte*" ("valleys and courts", ⇨ par. 2216).

2206 In the manors, a distinct legal circle, the *lex familiae*, developed. The landlord or his deputy (the *"Meier"*) acted as the judge; the manorial community acted as lawmen and actively participated in the law-making process at the manor. In modern times, this originally relatively cooperative relationship became increasingly unilateral (**patrimonial jurisdiction**).

➢ Patrimonial jurisdiction included all (from a present-day perspective) private law matters, a wide variety of administrative matters ("*policey*") as well as lower-level criminal cases. In serious criminal cases ("blood jurisdiction"), the patrimonial courts supported the judiciary of the prince. The majority of the population therefore hardly ever came into contact with the prince's judiciary (until the 18th century).

➢ However, the *lex familiae* was not only the law of the villeins and serfs. The landlord also had the manorial court as his ordinary place of jurisdiction whenever matters of the manor were concerned. This also reflects the initial cooperative element of the manorial system. Only in modern times did the lord of the manor exercise the patrimonial jurisdiction unilaterally. The peasants were now dependent on him not only in terms of their personal and property rights but also in terms of his political authority.

➢ The *lex familiae* was recorded in rural *Weistümer* (⇨ par. 2311).

2207 In the modern era, the situation of the peasants initially became much worse. Peasant uprisings caused by agricultural crises were put down, and the serfs and villeins were excluded from any participation in the legal life of the manor. From the 17th century onwards, however, the state sought to improve the legal situation of the peasants. This **peasant protection legislation** resulted on the one hand from an effort to improve their economic performance, but on the other hand also from an attempt to establish direct contact between the state and its subjects.

➢ Peasant wars against the landlords and the prince of their territory occurred in the Habsburg lands, especially in 1524–26. They were closely linked to the religious reformation that happened at the same time; however, the peasants' high expectations were disappointed. The attempt by the Tyrolean peasants under their leader MICHAEL GEISSMAYR to establish a "peasant republic" in 1525 was particularly radical. Once the peasants' uprisings had been suppressed, the governance of the manors became increasingly unilateral.

➢ Based on the *ius commune* (⇨ par. 2322), attempts were often made to deprive the peasants of their *right in rem* to the land and to turn them into mere agricultural labourers on the demesnes. It was not until 1654 that this practice was stopped through a ban on the conversion of tenured land into demesnes.

➢ In 1748, MARIA THERESA established district offices (*"Kreisämter"*) that would exercise state control over the patrimonial courts. Through "robot patents", which were issued for the individual hereditary lands (not for Hungary) from 1771 onwards, compulsory labour on the demesnes was limited to a maximum of three days per week.

➢ From the 17th century onwards, attempts were also made to regulate the duties paid by the peasants to the landlords. The Tax Patent of 1785 and the Tax and Urbarial Patent of 1789, issued by JOSEPH II, were particularly radical, as they limited the duties that were due to the state and the landlords to an overall maximum of 30 percent of the yield. The latter patent had to be revoked by LEOPOLD II in 1791.

2208 The complete **abolition of manorialism** only took place in the 19th century. In Prussia, the land was divided between landlords and peasants; the Austrian peasants received free ownership of the land while the expropriated landlords were compensated in money. In a parallel development, the patrimonial jurisdiction was brought under state control.

➢ In 1807, the personal dependencies of the Prussian peasants were abolished, and in 1811 it was decided to abolish the manorial system as such (STEIN-HARDENBERG reforms). However, the land cessions led to the economic ruin of many peasants, as the land they retained was often not sufficient to support them; in many cases it was also sold back to the nobility, and a rural exodus ensued.

➢ During the revolution of 1848, the Austrian Reichstag, in response to a motion by its member HANS KUDLICH, decided to abolish the patrimonial jurisdiction and free the peasants from the obligations tied to the land. This decision was upheld despite the defeat of the revolution; the detailed provisions were laid out in a patent of 4 March 1849, which was issued together with the March Constitution of 1849.

➢ While the obligations that had their roots in a merely personal dependency were abolished without compensation, the landlords were compensated for the lost *rights in rem* according to an estimate of the payments that would have been due over a period of 20 years, of which one third was to be paid by the peasant and another by the state, while the last third was to be borne by the landlord himself.

➢ The peasants were given 20 years to pay their contributions into designated land relief funds; the former landlords did not receive cash but interest-bearing bonds. Compared to the Prussian model, this procedure was much easier on the peasants but still had devastating consequences in some cases.

3. The feudal pyramid

2209 The feudal system of the **nobility** showed some similarities to but also differences from the manorial system. It also consisted of a personal (*vassalage*) and a property-based element (*beneficium*); however, it did not restrict the personal freedom of the vassal.

Table 1: The Feudal Pyramid

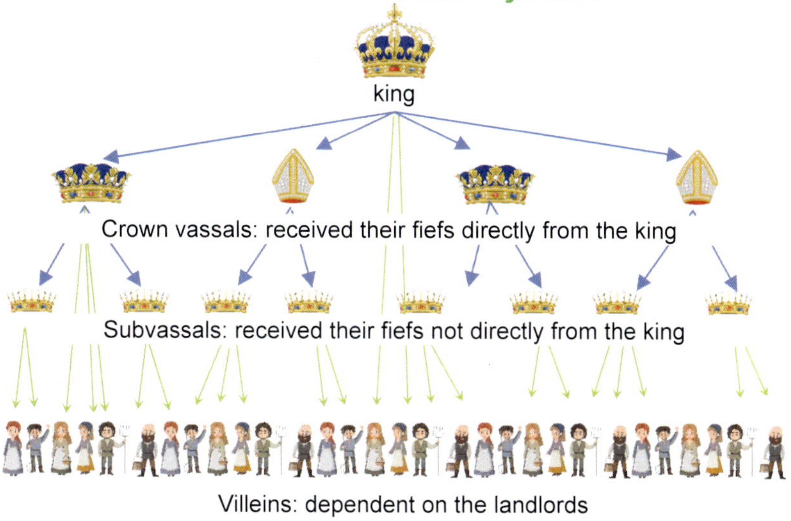

Source: Own drawing, using elements from https://commons.wikimedia.org and https://img.freepik.com/. Copyright: https://creativecommons.org/licenses/by-sa/3.0 (CC BY-SA 3.0). Blue arrows indicate feudal, green arrows indicate manorial relationships.

➢ The feudal lord provided his vassals with goods ("benefices"); in return, they took an oath of fealty, in which they pledged loyalty to their lord and promised to perform certain services. Vassals were noblemen; hence, their services could not be of a menial nature. They consisted especially of *consilium* (advice) and *auxilium* (assistance in arms) for the feudal lord. The duty to attend the lord's court for certain occasions and the duty to render military service developed out of this.

➢ The vassal's promise of loyalty was paralleled by a promise of protection by the lord. Breach of trust by the vassal ("felony") led to the revocation of the fief. This was the case, for example, in the lawsuit of the Hohenstaufen Emperor FREDERICK I "Barbarossa" against the Welf Duke HENRY the Lion in 1180, which led to the seizure of his duchies of Saxony and Bavaria (⇨ par. 2105). However, a breach of duty by the feudal lord could also have consequences (court case, feud).

➢ The feudal relationship was initially a purely personal one that ended with the death of either the feudal lord or the vassal. Over time, however, the fiefs became hereditary, i.e. certain persons (especially sons, sometimes also other male or, more rarely, female relatives) were entitled to be enfeoffed with the same fief. From the feudal lord's perspective, this resulted in *mandatory enfeoffment*.

➢ Not least in order to avoid fiefs becoming hereditary, many fiefs were not granted to secular but to ecclesiastical princes, who could not have children with inheritance rights. The reason for this was *celibacy*, the prohibition of marriage for clerics, which first emerged from the 4th century onwards and was generally enforced in 1139 (⇨ par. 2222)

2210 The object of enfeoffment was usually land; over time, political offices also came to be granted as fiefs. This led to a feudalisation of the state (**feudal state**). With the inclusion of the ecclesiastical principalities in the feudal system by the Concordat of Worms in 1122 (⇨ par. 2223), the feudalisation process in the Holy Roman Empire reached its peak.

➢ The initially still significant enfeoffment of movable property (hence the shared root of the English word *fief* and the German *Vieh* [cattle]) gradually became less important.

➢ With the advent of the money economy, monetary fiefs emerged (especially in Western Europe), where the vassal received an annuity instead of land. This made the personal element of the feudal relationship more prominent again.

➢ The most important form of enfeoffment, however, was the enfeoffment with land. While in Germany there was still a considerable amount of property that was outside the feudal system (*allod*), England and France were almost completely feudalised. In these two countries, there was a legal presumption that, in case of doubt, the disputed land was not an allod but a fief (*"nulle terre sans seigneur"*).

➢ The enfeoffment with land not only made it the vassal's property (as we would understand it today in a private law sense) but also included the political rule over this land and the people who lived on it. Conversely, the enfeoffment with an ecclesiastical or political office (*officium*, for instance a county, i.e. a court district) also included the granting of land (*beneficium*), from the proceeds of which the vassal covered his expenditures (but not a salary, as there was no money economy!).

➢ Certain sovereign rights, called *iura regalia*, could also be granted as fiefs: for example, the right to levy customs duties or certain taxes (tied to mining or salt rights, the "protection" of Jews, etc.).

➢ Altogether, this resulted in the local authorities becoming identical with the large landowners. Especially because of the inheritability of their position, they no longer saw themselves as holders of originally royal offices but as holders of their own personal rights. They also did not distinguish between their office on the one hand and private property on the other.

➢ Feudalism, which dominated the entire (agrarian) economic life, thus also became the foundation of the state and, through the vassals' obligation to render military assistance, also of the military system.

2211 The vassals could pass on the fiefs that they had received to their own vassals, who could do likewise, etc. Thus, a multi-layered organism emerged, which in medieval German law books, such as the *Sachsenspiegel* (Ldr I 3 § 2), was called the *"Heerschildordnung"*; in modern literature it is also called the **"feudal pyramid"**.

➢ At the top of this pyramid was the king, and below him were the crown vassals, who had received their fiefs directly from the king. Their own vassals, the subvassals, were only indirectly linked to the king.

➢ An essential factor in the subsequent development was the fact that the German king could only have direct relations with the crown vassals, i.e.

with a relatively small number of people. The subvassals were *mediatised*, and hence the king became alienated from them. He sought to counter this trend by splitting larger crown fiefdoms into several smaller ones (e.g. Saxony and Bavaria in 1180).

➢ In the Norman legal circle, on the other hand, a feudal pyramid developed in which the supreme feudal lord could also enter into direct legal relations with his subvassals, in that the oath of fealty of the subvassals to their immediate lords was modified by a reservation of loyalty in favour of the supreme feudal lord. The latter was thus *dominus ligius ante omnes*.

➢ In this regard, the Norman feudal system – introduced by the Normans in England and Sicily and adopted by PHILIP II "Augustus" in France – had the effect of strengthening the kingship, whereas the German feudal system had the effect of weakening it.

2212 In modern times, the feudal system lost its political function with the rise of the absolutist bureaucratic state and gradually declined; however, it was not formally **abolished** until the 19th century.

➢ This loss of practical significance was contrasted by legal perfection. The study of feudal law was called *feudistics*. In the course of the wave of codifications in Austria under FRANCIS II/I, a draft of an Austrian feudal code was drawn up in 1806, but it did not come into effect.

➢ With the dissolution of the Holy Roman Empire in 1806, the feudal relationship between the emperor and the imperial princes came to an end. In the individual territories, on the other hand, the feudal system was only gradually abolished; the fiefs were converted into free property, usually of the former vassal (*allodification*). In Austria, a law to abolish the feudal bond was passed in 1862 and gradually implemented over the years that followed.

➢ In England, the feudal system was abolished during the English Revolution in 1649/1660 (⇨ par. 3102), but some remnants have survived until today. The French feudal system, on the other hand, was completely abandoned in the French Revolution of 1789.

4. The towns

2213 The special legal position of the towns compared to other communities resulted from special **town privileges**, which were either granted to them by the town's lord or which the townspeople gave themselves (in a revolutionary act), and which granted the respective town a certain special position, which was, as a rule, a privileged one.

➢ In imperial towns (e.g. Aachen, Frankfurt am Main), the king himself was the town's lord; other towns were ruled either by the prince of the respective territory (e.g. Vienna, Salzburg) or another lord (e.g. Sankt Pölten, Hartberg). The imperial towns in particular had a great deal of freedom, so that the king's rule over the town was only a nominal one.

➢ From the 11th century onwards, some towns, especially those that were ruled by a bishop (e.g. Cologne, Strasbourg), were able to free themselves from this rule and adopt their own *statutes*. These *free towns* were later largely given equal status to the imperial towns.

➢ The municipal administration was usually entrusted to a town council and a mayor, who were elected by the urban upper class, the patricians.

➢ Not all the inhabitants of a town were also burghers; rather, town life was characterised by a colourful coexistence of various social classes and estates. This ranged from merchants and craftsmen to the many clerics (members of religious orders, secular priests), as well as municipal workers and domestic servants. The urban underclass included day labourers, hangmen, actors, beggars, prostitutes, etc.

➢ The Jews, who were segregated in ghettos, as well as the members of the universities (which included not only professors and students but also other persons working for the university, such as book printers, as well as their families, ⇨ par. 2316) each formed a separate legal circle within the town; they were therefore not, or only to a limited extent, governed by the municipal bodies.

2214 The **political significance** of the towns varied. While the Late Middle Ages in particular were a period of prosperity, many towns in modern times became increasingly dependent on the princes, who were seeking to establish an absolutist system.

➢ The might of the towns was particularly evident in alliances such as the Hanseatic League, which brought together up to 300 towns in northern Germany and in the North and Baltic Sea regions. The League was formed in the 12th century to pursue common economic interests, but it was also an important political force that at times even waged war. From the 15th century onwards, the Hanseatic League gradually lost importance but was never formally dissolved; many towns (e.g. Hamburg, Bremen, Lübeck) still call themselves "Hanseatic" today.

5. The dualistic state of estates

2215 The dualistic state of estates was a type of state that emerged from feudalism and in which the state power was **shared between two bodies**. One was an individual (the monarch or prince), the other a collegiate body (the assembly of the estates).

➢ Early traces of this development were already present in the feudal system, especially the duty of the vassal to provide advice to his lord (⇨ par. 2209). This obligation to attend the lord's court gradually developed into a right to participate in decision-making.

➢ However, not all estates were directly linked to the prince through feudal relationships; other persons, e.g. subvassals, but also persons or institutions that enjoyed a special protective relationship, could acquire an estate status. In this respect, the dualistic state of estates went beyond the legal relationships of the feudal system.

➢ In contrast to the feudal system, in which the individual vassals were only linked to their lord but not to each other, the estates in the state of estates met in an assembly, where estates of the same type joined together in curiae.

➤ Since the dualistic state of estates was based almost entirely on personal ties and characterised by a colourful coexistence of different powers, it differed significantly from the modern state, with its stable institutions (authorities) and its central state control in the hands of a government; legal historians speak of a "feudal state of personal association".

2216 At the level of the individual territories, the dualism consisted of the **prince** on the one hand and the **diet** on the other. This system was recognised under imperial law in the 13th century and underwent a process of consolidation until the end of the Middle Ages.

➤ During the High Middle Ages, individual princes (dukes, counts, and sometimes also ecclesiastical princes such as bishops) succeeded in accumulating a bundle of sovereign rights (fiefs such as judicial rights, *iura regalia*, the lordship of manors and towns, etc.) within a certain territory and thereby achieved political dominance. This *dominium territoriale* was eventually recognised under imperial law in 1220/32.

➤ At the same time, it was determined that territorial laws could not be enacted by the prince alone, but rather only with the consent of the (other) "great of the land" (*meliores et maiores terrae*), which referred to the estates (*sententia de iure statuum terr[a]e* 1231).

➤ The composition of the estates varied from region to region. Usually, the ecclesiastical (*prelates*) and the secular nobility were represented in the diet, the latter sometimes divided into high and lower nobility (lords and knights). Furthermore, towns and markets where the prince himself was the town lord also had a seat and vote in the diet.

➤ The diets of Austria above the Enns and below the Enns, for example, were divided into these four curiae (prelates–lords–knights–towns). In Tyrol and Salzburg, on the other hand, there was only one single curia for the secular nobility, but there, the free peasants, i.e. those who did not belong to a manor, were also represented (curia of the "valleys and courts").

➤ The estates did not see themselves as representatives of the people, but usually only pursued their own interests. The majority of the population (especially the peasants living in manorial communities) was therefore excluded from political decision-making.

2217 At the imperial level, the princes themselves formed assemblies to interact with the king/emperor. From 1495 onwards, the estates of the German empire were represented in the **Reichstag**.

➤ The medieval precursors of the Reichstag were the royal court assemblies on the one hand and the assemblies of princes (without the king present) on the other. As a result of the reform of the empire in 1495, which established an Imperial Chamber Court, the court assemblies largely lost their previous judicial functions; the Reichstag, together with the king, was mainly responsible for legislation. The obligation of the crown vassals to attend the royal court had evolved into the right of the princes of the empire to attend the Reichstag.

➢ The Reichstag was divided into three curiae: The *college of electors* for the prince-electors; the *college of the princes of the empire* for the other ecclesiastical and secular princes; and the *college of the free and imperial towns* (⇨ par. 2213). Larger estates of the empire had a vote for themselves ("virile votes"); smaller estates had to share a vote between them ("curiate votes").

➢ Only the emperor had the right to propose laws to the Reichstag; these were then discussed separately in each of the curiae. An *"imperial agreement"* was only reached if both the college of electors and the council of princes, and from 1648 also the college of towns, approved the proposal.

➢ In religious matters, the division into curiae was abandoned from 1648 in favour of a division into confessionally composed bodies (*corpus Catholicorum, corpus Evangelicorum*). A unanimous agreement (*amicabilis compositio*) between these two corpora was required (IPO Article V § 52).

➢ The prerequisite for membership in the Reichstag was imperial immediacy, i.e. the prince needed to be under the direct authority of the emperor. In order to attain this status, Prince JOHANN ADAM OF LIECHTENSTEIN, who owned a significant amount of property in Lower Austria, Bohemia, and Moravia but had not previously been able to obtain imperial immediacy, acquired the small dominions of Vaduz and Schellenberg (which were under the immediate authority of the emperor) in 1699/1712. This is how the Principality of Liechtenstein was established.

➢ However, imperial immediacy alone was not sufficient to acquire membership in the Reichstag; it had to be formally granted by the Reichstag itself. Thus, for example, the imperial knights and villages, which were also directly subordinate to the emperor, were not represented.

➢ In 1495, it was decided that the Reichstag would henceforth be convened annually; in reality, however, there were repeated breaks of several years. The Reichstag that convened in Regensburg in 1663 stretched out over a long time and eventually became the "Perpetual Reichstag", which sat permanently until 1806. The princes of the empire, who had originally attended in person, sent their envoys, while the emperor was represented by a principal commissioner.

2218 The assemblies of the estates in France (***états généraux***), England (**Houses of Parliament**), and Hungary (***Országgyűlés***) were also divided into curiae. However, the original three-tier system of ecclesiastical nobility – secular nobility – towns, which initially prevailed everywhere, remained in place only in France (until 1789); elsewhere, significant modifications took place.

➢ The French Estates-General (*états généraux*) were convened from 1302 onwards. The first estate comprised the ecclesiastical, the second the secular crown vassals, and the third the royal towns. As early as 1302, and increasingly so later on, the *états généraux* were also joined by estates that were only mediately linked to the king (subvassals, towns of territorial princes); cf. what has been said about French feudal law above (⇨ par. 2211). The *états généraux* thus represented a much larger group of people than the German Reichstag (which represented only the immediate princes and towns), but had less real political power than the latter.

➤ The assembly of the English crown vassals acquired a very powerful position. It dates back to the "Magna Charta" from 125 and was called "parliament" from the 13th century onwards. In the 14th century, the gentry (lower nobility) and the representatives of the towns joined together to form the House of Commons, while the peers (high nobility) and the clergy constituted the House of Lords. In principle, this two-tier structure of the British Parliament is still in place today (⇨ par. 4209).

➤ The Hungarian diet dates back to the "Golden Bull" of King ANDREW II from 1222; it initially comprised the high nobility and the clergy, from 1267 also representatives of the lower nobility and from 1402 also of the royal towns. Much like in England, the Hungarian diet in 1608 was divided into two chambers: one for the high nobility and the clergy (*magnates' table*); and one for the lower nobility and the towns (*table of representatives*).

2219 In the 17th century, absolutism replaced the dualism of the estates in France and in the German territories (⇨ par. 3202). At the imperial level, however, the Roman-German Empire preserved the dualistic system until its end in 1806. The contemporary ***"Reichspublizistik"*** (the discipline concerned with the study of the public law of the empire) was unable to place the empire within the framework of modern constitutional systems and considered it to be an anachronistic structure.

➤ The dualistic structure of the empire had been a source of controversy among jurists even before 1648. Theories about its nature ranged from monarchy (THEODOR REINKINGK 1619) and aristocracy (JEAN BODIN 1576) to a *"mixtum ex Monarchia et Aristocratia"* (JOHANNES LIMNAEUS 1629).

➤ Following the Peace of Westphalia, the relationship between the emperor and the estates of the empire had become so complex that SAMUEL PUFENDORF (⇨ par. 3303), in his *De statu imperii Germanici* (*The Present State of Germany*), published in 1667 under the pseudonym "SEVERINUS DE MONZAMBANO", did not want to describe the empire as a "limited monarchy" or a "federation of states". Instead, he called it an "irregular entity that resembles a monster" (*"irregulare corpus monstro simile"*).

➤ However, it would be wrong to deny the empire the character of a state after 1648, as legal historians did for a long time. The imperial authorities, such as the Imperial Aulic Council, the Imperial Chamber Court, etc., continued to function very effectively until 1806, and the emperor's supreme authority was certainly felt in the empire, at least by the lesser estates of the empire.

2220 The concept of a state of estates was obscured by absolutism but not completely eliminated; this only occurred in the 19th century, with the advent of constitutionalism. The "historical" doctrine of constitutional law brought it back to life (albeit with significant modifications) as a possible alternative to constitutionalism (**neo-corporative system**), but it did not prove sustainable in the long run.

Table 2: Estate-based vs. neo-corporative systems

Tyrolean Diet until 1848	Lower Austrian Diet from 1861
Bishops and Prelates (ecclesiastical nobility)	Bishops of Vienna and St. Pölten, Rector of Vienna University
Lords and Knights (secular nobility)	Large Landowners
Bourgeoisie	Towns; Chambers of Commerce and Trade
Peasantry	Rural communities

➢ The neo-corporative system was adopted, in particular, by the Austrian diets from their reactivation in 1861 until the fall of the monarchy in 1918, as well as by the Reichsrat until 1907. The new curial structure was based on the old organisation of the estates but also adapted to the changed socio-economic conditions.

➢ The new structure consisted of (1) the curia of the large landowners (*de facto* the successor of the curia of the secular nobility; called "noble large landownership" in Tyrol), (2) the towns and markets, (3) the chambers of commerce and trade (a concession to the economically prospering bourgeoisie), and (4) the rural communities (as the successor of the "valleys and courts", but in contrast to these now established in all crown lands). As in the past, bishops and now also university rectors had virile votes, i.e. they had a seat and vote in the diets by virtue of their office.

➢ A new problem of the 19th century, also for the concept of estates, was the new estate of the workers. Proposals for the creation of chambers of labour, which would have had their own voting rights analogous to those of the chambers of commerce and trade, were not realised; instead, a general electoral body was created in 1896 (⇨ par. 4212).

6. State – Church – Society

2221 The **unity of state, Church, and society** was characteristic of the European Middle Ages. Although state and Church were perceived as two independent regulatory systems (⇨ par. 0003), they were intertwined in many ways through functions and personal identities and in principle covered the entire society. In simplified terms, their functions were distributed as follows:

➢ The tasks of the Church were not limited to pastoral care and liturgy (celebration of mass, dispensation of sacraments, etc.); rather, it was also responsible for the entire sphere of education (cathedral and monastery schools, maintenance and ongoing development of libraries, ⇨ par. 2316) as well as the sphere of social welfare (poor relief, healthcare, orphanages).

➢ Not least for this reason, the responsibilities of the secular power were limited. It was primarily responsible for keeping the peace internally as well as externally. This entailed the administration of civil and criminal justice on the one hand and warfare on the other. Apart from these core functions, the secular power also had a few additional tasks, some of which resulted from the former, such as the collection of taxes and levies (*iura regalia*, ⇨ par. 0).

➢ The boundaries between the ecclesiastical and secular powers were not clearly defined and varied (e.g. in marriage law); the demands for regulation raised by the Church, which were sometimes quite far-reaching, could in reality only be realised to a certain extent.

➢ Still, the relationship between the state and the Church was for the most part characterised not by competition but by cooperation; for instance, the Church availed itself of the "secular arm" (*bracchium saeculare*) to enforce the judgements passed by the ecclesiastical courts.

2222 The state and Church also complemented each other such that the **secular rule was legitimised by the Church,** and the king or emperor was sometimes even attributed a spiritual role in society. The latter, in turn, also bestowed secular powers (*temporalia*) on ecclesiastical dignitaries, which they then exercised in addition to their spiritual powers (*spiritualia*).

➢ The medieval sacral kingship had its roots primarily in the Germanic kingship, which (as in most other archaic societies) combined priestly, judicial, and military functions.

➢ The second root can be found in the late Roman emperors, who also always held the position of pontifex maximus (⇨ par. 1204) and, after the adoption of Christianity, also ruled over the Church, which remained the case in the Eastern Roman (Byzantine) Empire until its fall in 1453 (⇨ par. 1205). Western historians have called this phenomenon (derogatorily and probably also misleadingly) *Caesaropapism*.

➢ Thirdly, ideas from Judaism also contributed to the medieval rulers' ideal because of the Bible. There were images of DAVID and SOLOMON (⇨ par. 1101) on the Roman-German imperial crown!

➢ The coronations of kings and emperors in Western Europe from the 5th century onwards usually took place as part of a church service; in the Middle Ages, they came to be regarded as sacraments. Whether this made the monarch a cleric (deacon) or whether he remained a layman was a matter of dispute.

➢ The *investiture* of ecclesiastical dignitaries (bishops, abbots) by kings or other secular authorities took place in the context of a church system in which the founder of a church was also entitled to appoint a person of his choice.

➢ Overall, this resulted in the king appointing persons of his trust as bishops in order to be able to endow them with the *temporalia* that went with this position. This system is known as the "Ottonian imperial church system" after Emperor OTTO I, who granted a particularly large number of counties and regalia to clerics (⇨ par. 2209).

2223 The **investiture controversy** brought about a turning point in this development, as it liberated the Church from the grip of secular power. In contrast to the "Caesaropapism" of the Byzantine emperors and the caliphs in the Islamic world, who also claimed both spiritual and secular power, the pope was able to establish himself as the spiritual head of the Christian West alongside the emperor.

➢ As the successor of the Apostle PETER, the Bishop of Rome has always enjoyed a certain "primacy of honour" in the Church. Since the 5th century, he has held the title of pontifex maximus previously held by the Roman emperors (⇨ par. 1204). However, a legal superiority over the other bishops only emerged over centuries, through a policy of the popes that aimed to constantly expand their legal positions, which was by no means free of setbacks. The bishops of Constantinople, in particular, did not want to recognise this primacy of the pope; this was the main reason for the split into a Roman Catholic Western Church and a Greek Orthodox Eastern Church (with definitive effect from the 11th century).

➢ The Cluniac reform movement, which developed in the 10th century in the Burgundian monastery of Cluny, opposed the involvement of the Church in secular affairs and rejected the investiture of clerics by the kings, who were now regarded as "laymen" (*lay investiture*), as well as the purchase of offices (*simony*, cf. Acts 8:18).

➢ When Pope GREGORY VII (1073–85) raised the Cluniac demands with the German and French kings, the investiture controversy ensued, which was resolved in France by the Council of Troyes in 1107 and in Germany by the Concordat of Worms in 1122. Under these agreements, the bishops would no longer be appointed by the king but elected by the clergy and the people. The elected bishop was to be enfeoffed with the *temporalia* by the king, while the *spiritualia* were passed on through the sacramental ordination to the episcopate.

➢ The papacy emerged triumphant from the investiture controversy, as it was able to increasingly assert its claim to dominance over the Latin Church and also gained more influence over the election of the bishops. The *Sachsenspiegel* (Ldr I 1) regarded the papal and imperial powers as two supreme, God-given powers (symbolised by two swords) that were of equal rank (*coordinating two swords doctrine*).

➤ The 13th century has been described as the "century of the popes"; in the course of the conflict between the papacy and the rising French kingship (⇨ par. 2112), Pope BONIFACE VIII even claimed supremacy over all secular powers in 1302 (*subordinating two swords doctrine*).

➤ However, the decline of the papacy in the 14th century (captivity of the popes in Avignon 1309–76, the Western Schism 1378–1415) resulted in a universal crisis of the Church, which once again enabled the secular power to strengthen its influence at the expense of the former; the emperor's position in this dichotomy was now filled by the princes.

➤ In the hereditary lands of the Habsburgs, FREDERICK III (1424–93) succeeded in securing a right of nomination (*nominatio regia*) for all Austrian bishops. The main difference from an investiture (as it had been carried out until 1122) was that the nominee merely received a *ius ad rem* to the episcopate and also required a canonical investiture. Thus, the Austrian rulers were able to influence the appointment of bishops until 1918 (⇨ par. 6223).

2224 The only significant religious minority in Christian society were the **Jews**. They lived separately from the Christians and were under the protection of the king and/or the princes. Nonetheless, there were recurring instances of pogroms against Jews.

➤ The relations between Jews and Christians were regulated by laws on Jews, which must not be confused with Jewish law (⇨ par. 2315). The laws on Jews were unilaterally imposed by the (Christian) emperor or prince, for instance an edict concerning the Jews by Emperor FREDERICK I in 1157. In addition, there were a number of princely or otherwise regional legal regulations concerning Jews, for example one in Austria in 1244. Ecclesiastical council decrees also had universal significance for the relationship between Christians and Jews, in particular that of the Fourth Lateran Council in 1215.

➤ The main aim of the law on Jews was to separate the Jews from the Christian population. They were forced to live in a ghetto and wear special clothing (e.g. in Vienna from 1267 a yellow "Jews' hat", and in Portugal from 1492 a six-pointed star). Among other things, they were forbidden to marry Christians, to employ Christian servants, and in most cases to own property outside the ghetto (which meant that they were largely excluded from agriculture). Jews were also typically denied access to public office.

➤ Instead, Jews were usually only allowed to engage in minor commercial activities (such as dealing in junk goods), sometimes also in certain trades and manufacturing, but mainly in the lending business, which was of particular importance given that Christians were prohibited from charging interest. A further problematic provision in FREDERICK I's 1157 edict was that Jews only had to return goods purchased from a thief to the rightful owner if they were reimbursed for the purchase price, as this ultimately encouraged the dealing in stolen goods. All of this ultimately led to the Jews being pushed further and further to the margins of society.

➤ Apart from a few exceptions (bankers, purveyors to the court, etc.), the situation of the Jews remained precarious and oppressive. Religious zeal, commercial competition, prejudice on the part of the Christian churches and the arbitrary actions of the authorities often led to the persecution and expulsion of the Jews. This was the case with the Visigoths in Spain in 589, then in particular from 1096 in connection with the Crusades, and in the late Middle Ages following the outbreak of the plague in 1348, for which the Jews were blamed.

➢ Initially the king, and then also the princes, provided a certain degree of protection to the Jews, for which the latter had to pay a levy, which represented an important source of income for the rulers (*Judenregal*). However, the actual value of this protection varied. It failed completely, for example, when the Jewish community of Vienna was annihilated in 1421, with over 200 Jews losing their lives.

➢ The conversion of Jews to Christianity (often through force and violence) in theory ended the discrimination against them according to the law on Jews. However, mass conversions, as occurred in Spain from the 15th century (a consequence of the Reconquista, ⇨ par. 2115), sometimes led to racist legislation against the converts (known in Spain as *Marranos*).

2225 The confessional unity of the Christian Occident was broken in modern times by the **Reformation**, from which the Protestant churches emerged, as well as by the **Counter-Reformation** carried out by the Catholic Church.

➢ At the end of the Middle Ages, the Catholic Church was plunged into more and more crises, giving rise to a multitude of reform movements with sometimes very different agendas. The most important were the followers of MARTIN LUTHERS, the "Lutherans" (Augsburg Confession) and the followers of JEAN CALVIN, the "Calvinists" (Helvetic Confession). They differ from the Catholic Church in particular in that they believe that salvation can be attained not through one's own good works, but only through faith (*sola fide*) and the grace of God (*sola gratia*). They recognize no source of faith beyond the Bible (*sola scriptura*) and reject all veneration of saints (*solus Christus*).

➢ Of the Protestant reformers' other positions, their rejection of papal primacy was especially significant. Monarchs and princes who embraced the Reformation, such as HENRY VIII of England (⇨ par. 2118), also took personal control of their state church, which further increased their political power.

➢ To end the crisis of faith, the Pope convened an Ecumenical Council. However, this Council of Trent (1545–63) only led to the rejection of the new teachings, thus permanently cementing the schism. The Council initiated a comprehensive reform of the Catholic Church and the re-catholicisation of areas that had already become Protestant ("Counter-Reformation"). The main driving force behind this movement was the Jesuit Order ("Society of Jesus"), founded in 1534, which came to exert considerable influence on education in Catholic countries, and thus also on censorship.

➢ In most European states, either the Catholic or the Protestant church was declared the state church (⇨ par. 2118). The Peace of Augsburg of 1555, on the other hand, led to a confessional split within the Holy Roman Empire. While the individual territories had to follow the religion of their respective prince ("cuius regio, eius et religio" – whose land, his religion), the emperor – although he remained Catholic himself – had to remain confessionally neutral in his function as head of the empire.

➤ The Peace of Augsburg gave subjects who did not want to accept the religion of their prince the right to emigrate. Although this *ius emigrationis* can be described as the oldest fundamental right of all, the severe (not only economic but also legal) hardships associated with it need to be emphasised: for example, emigration was usually only allowed upon payment of an additional tax (usually 10% of one's assets or three times the annual poll tax); only rarely were emigrants allowed to take their minor children with them.

➤ In the Habsburg hereditary lands, the princes made use of their religious authority in different ways: in 1568, MAXIMILIAN II (1564–76) granted the nobility and knights of Austria below the Enns, and in 1571 also their subjects, religious freedom; FERDINAND II (1590/1619–37), on the other hand, vigorously pursued the re-catholicisation of the Habsburg lands, which had already largely become Protestant, from 1598 onwards (*ius reformandi*). His attempt to extend the Counter-Reformation to Bohemia as well triggered the Thirty Years' War (1618–48), but ultimately proved successful.

➤ The *ius reformandi* was by and large confirmed in the Peace of Westphalia of 1648 (which ended the Thirty Years War, ⇨ par. 3103) and remained in force until the end of the Holy Roman Empire in 1806. As late as 1731, the Prince-Archbishop of Salzburg forced some 20,000 Protestants to emigrate. Those who survived the hardships settled mainly in Prussia and Holland, with some making their way to North America.

C Legislation and Jurisprudence

1. Sharīʿa and Fiqh

2301 The **Sharīʿa** is a binding normative order for all Muslims, and in Muslim countries, to some extent, also for non-Muslims. From a European perspective, it contains legal norms, ethical norms and religious commandments, and thus governs all areas of life. One particular feature of the Sharīʿa is that it divides human actions into categories that are sometimes foreign to Western legal systems.

➤ The Sharīʿa not only distinguishes between actions that are compulsory or obligatory (*farḍ* or *wājib*) and those that are forbidden (*ḥarām/maḥzūr*). Rather, some actions are "recommended" (*mustaḥabb/mandūb*) or "disliked" (*makrūh*). While there is no penalty for refraining from a recommended action, performing it will be rewarded; vice versa this also applies to disliked actions. Actions that do not fall into either of these categories, but are considered "neutral", are referred to as *mubāḥ/halal.*

➢ These categories are used not only for actions but also for objects, in which case certain human behavioural rules in relation to these objects are implied. For example, *ḥarām* foods are foods that Muslims are not allowed to eat. The Kaʿba in Mecca, the central shrine of Islam, is also considered ḥarām because it must not be treated in a dishonorable manner.

2302 The primary and generally accepted **sources of Sharīʿa** are the Qur'an (⇨ par. 2101) and the *Sunnah*, the traditions and practices handed down from the life of the Prophet MUHAMMAD in *ḥadīths*. One's own mental effort (*Ijtihād*) is also considered a source of law. With regard to other sources, Sunni and Shia Muslims disagree.

➢ The Qur'an consists of 114 surahs that were collected by Caliph ʿUTHMĀN around 650, many of which contain legal norms. According to Islamic belief, they were revealed to MUHAMMAD directly by God, which is why their wording is beyond dispute.

➢ From the 8th century onwards, the traditions and practices of MUHAMMAD (the *Sunnah*), which had previously only been handed down orally, were collected in *ḥadīths*. The significance of the individual hadiths is determined primarily by the chains of tradition through which they can be traced back to the Prophet himself.

➢ The Qur'an and the Sunnah were never the sole sources of law. Rather, the Sharīʿa in Arabia was based on the existing Arab customary law, and in the conquered territories on the local traditions (and thus in large areas also on Roman-Byzantine law), which were gradually transformed in line with Islam. Thus, different regional forms of Sharīʿa have always existed. The caliphs sought to harmonise the law, but a comprehensive collection of the Sharīʿa, which would probably have had a binding character, was never realised, despite being proposed as early as 757 by IBN AL-MUQAFFAʿ.

➢ Two schools of thought emerged early on: the "people of reason" endeavoured to rationally penetrate the Sharīʿa through logical argumentation. The "people of tradition", on the other hand, rejected any further development of the law and tried to strictly follow the Prophet's Sunnah.

➢ The book *ar-Risāla* ("message"), written around 800 by MUHAMMAD IBN IDRĪS AŠ-ŠĀFIʿĪ, became fundamental to the doctrine of the sources of Sharīʿa. It succeeded in combining the teachings of the "people of tradition" and the "people of reason". Based on this, Sunni Islam regards not only the Qur'an and the Sunnah of MUHAMMAD as sources, but also the consensus of the legal scholars (*Ijmāʿ*). Shia Islam rejects Ijmāʿ as a source of law, but recognises the Sunnah of the Imams, i.e. their traditions and practices, as such.

2303 From the 8th century onwards, the different approaches to the sources gave rise to various schools of law (*Madhāhib*, singular *Madhāb*) in both Sunni Islam and Shia Islam, which still exist today. Islamic legal scholarship is called **fiqh**.

➢ The oldest school of law is the *Māliki* school, which goes back to MĀLIK IBN ANNAS, a legal scholar living in Medina in the 8th century who wrote the first manual of Islamic law. Today it is predominant mainly in North Africa and the Persian Gulf.

➢ ABŪ HANĪFA of Kufa in Mesopotamia, a contemporary of MĀLIK, founded the *Hanafi* school, which enjoyed official status under the Abbasids and is still the most widespread school of law today; in Austria, it was initially the only one recognised (⇨ par. 6224). It gives the judge more room for discretion than the Māliki school: if the interpretation of the sources and analogy cannot provide a solution, the judge's own discretion (*istihsān*) will prevail.

➢ At the turn of the 9th century, the aforementioned AŠ-ŠĀFI'Ī, a student of MALIK, was active in Mecca, Baghdad and Egypt and founded the *Šāfi'ī school*. This school flourished in Egypt between the Abbasid and Ottoman periods. Today, it is still predominant in parts of Egypt, Yemen, Kurdistan and Indonesia, among other places.

➢ The fourth major Sunni school goes back to AHMAD IBN HANBAL, who had studied with AŠ-ŠĀFI'Ī , among others, but called for a return to the literal meaning of the Qur'an. Today, the *Hanbali school* is particularly prevalent in Saudi Arabia.

➢ The regional dominance of individual schools does not undermine the unity of Sunni Islam, and they can also exist side by side: for example, the caliph AL-MUSTANṢIR (1226–42) founded a university in Baghdad (named after him al-Mustanṣir University), where all four Sunni Madhāhib were taught.

➢ The Shiite schools of law are distinctly different from the Sunni schools of law. The most important of these is the *Ja'fari school*, which goes back to the sixth Imam, JA'FAR AL-SADIQ (d. 765) and is the predominant school of law in Iran today.

2304 Fiqh flourished under the Abbasid caliphs, but from the 12th century onwards a certain rigidity set in. The **"gates of Ijtihād"** were closed and only reopened in the 19th century in the face of a completely transformed world.

➢ This development can ultimately be traced back to AŠ-ŠĀFI'Ī, who attributed far more significance to the Qur'an and the Sunnah than to the other two sources, which set limits to the law being further developed by the jurists. The complete rejection of any further development of the Sharī'a through ijtihād was due not least to the decline of the Caliphate and the political crises that accompanied it.

➢ Individual legal scholars, such as the Indian jurist SHAH WALIULLAH DEHLAWI in the 18th century, repeatedly emphasised the necessity of ijtihad. The driving factors were then above all the imposition by the colonial powers of codes of law based on the European model (e.g. the Indian Penal Code of 1860) and the introduction of such codes by Muslim rulers (e.g. the adoption of the French Code Civil in Egypt in 1875, ⇨ par. 3308). This increased the pressure for a modernisation of the Sharī'a to such an extent that in the second half of the 19th century the representatives of an Islamic modernism were able to push through an opening of the "gates of Ijtihād" in order to be able to respond to the innovations in legal life imported by the Europeans.

➢ A first important step in this direction was the Ottoman Civil Code, or *Mecelle*, which was gradually introduced from 1870 onwards. Although it resembled European legal codes in form, it can be seen as a codification of Sharīʿa in content. It remained in force in Turkey until 1926 (⇨ par. 4308).

2. The *leges barbarorum*

2305 During the medieval migration period, the Germanic peoples encountered Roman (legal) culture. Christian ideas and, associated with these, individual elements of Roman law were adopted. At the same time, the Germanic peoples also began to record their own laws based on the model of the Roman legal writings (***leges barbarorum***).

➢ The first to do so were the Visigoths in southern France/Spain (*Edictum Theodorici* 459/461; *Codex Euricianus* 476). The law of the Lombards in Upper Italy was of a high legal quality (*Edictum Rothari* 643, and others). For the area of present-day Austria, the legal records of the Alemanni (*Lex Alamannorum* 725) and Bavarians (*Lex Baiuvariorum*, after 740) were significant.

➢ The *leges barbarorum* were written in Latin but also had insertions in the (Old German) vernacular.

2306 Contrary to a long-held view, the *leges barbarorum* did not contain purely indigenous Germanic law but were a product of the **fusion of Germanic and ancient Roman cultures** as well as Christianity that occurred during the migration period.

➢ This is easily recognisable in the youngest of the *leges barbarorum*, the *Lex Saxonum* of 802; it was not the Saxons themselves who wrote down their law, but rather it was enacted by the victorious Frankish King CHARLEMAGNE after the Saxons had been subjugated and forced to become Christians.

➢ For many other *leges barbarorum*, too, modern research has been able to prove that the occasion of their recording was used to deliberately change the law (i.e. to legislate), for example, in the case of King CLOVIS I's *Lex Salica* of 507/511, which was enacted for the Salian Franks.

➢ Some Germanic kings also enacted separate laws for the Romance population living in their realms, such as the Visigoth King ALARIC II's *Lex Romana Visigothorum* of 506. This law, as well as the *Codex Euricianus*, which applied to the Visigoths themselves, were replaced in 654 by a new *Lex Visigothorum*, which was to apply to all subjects alike, thus creating a bracket for the entire population of the Visigoth Empire (which at that time encompassed most of Spain, ⇨ par. 2103).

2307 The **practical implications** of these *leges* are difficult to assess. In those areas where the (Old) German language developed, the *leges barbarorum* only survived for a short time, if at all; they soon fell into oblivion and were "overgrown" by new customary law. In the Romance territories, on the other hand, they had a lasting effect.

➢ The *Lex Visigothorum*, for example, remained the basis of Spanish law during the Middle Ages and was newly recorded in Spanish (Castilian) by King ALFONSO X of Castile (1252–82) in the *Fuero Real* ("Royal Code") of 1263. Elements of Visigothic law can still be found today in the law codes of Spain and the Latin American countries.

➢ In Pavia, in northern Italy, a law school was founded as early as the 9th century, where Lombard law was taught; it was significant for the subsequent development of legistics in northern Italy (⇨ par. 2319). In the 11th and 12th centuries, Lombard feudal law was recorded in the *Libri Feudorum* and added to the *Corpus Iuris Civilis* by the legists.

➢ A special case was France, where in the north almost only customary law (which was handed down orally) applied (*pays du droit coutumier*), while in the predominantly Romance south written law prevailed (*pays du droit écrit*). In southern France, which had in part belonged to the Visigoth Empire until 507, the *Lex Romana Visigothorum* remained important until the onset of the reception of learned law. This division of France remained in principle until 1804 (⇨ par. 3308).

3. Medieval law in Europe before the reception of learned law

2308 With the Carolingians, early medieval legislative activity reached its climax and conclusion. The subsequent developments in Central Europe primarily followed the path of customary law. Due to a lack of harmonising legislation, there was considerable fragmentation (***iura particularia***).

➢ The "capitular legislation" of CHARLEMAGNE continued to be remembered for a long time, and the knowledge of Roman law also remained present throughout the Middle Ages. However, the latter only had practical significance for clerics (*"ecclesia vivit lege Romana"*), and even then, not unconditionally.

➢ Since the *leges barbarorum* were still the laws of tribal associations (defined by shared ancestry), they became ineffective with the emergence of territorial rule. New laws emerged in the various territorial jurisdictions: imperial law; land law; municipal law; the (rural) *lex familiae* (*Hofrecht*); etc.

➢ The basic rule for the relationship between these "legal circles" was that the narrower took precedence over the wider; the wider legal circle was therefore only of subsidiary rank. Hence, what was agreed for an individual case overruled municipal law, municipal law overruled land law, and land law overruled imperial law.

➢ In addition to these territorial *iura particularia*, there were legal circles with a specific personal and/or material scope of application, in particular ecclesiastical law (*canon law*) and feudal law. Here, too, the rule applied in principle that the narrower circle eliminated the wider one.

2309 Due to this fragmentation, the German law of the Middle Ages cannot be described as a uniform body of law; instead, everyday legal culture was shaped by a **multitude of different bodies of laws**. Still, the actual rules of the various *iura particularia* were often very much in line with each other.

➤ As with Germanic law (⇨ par. 1002), legal historians of the 19th and early 20th centuries were concerned with the reconstruction of a (uniform) German law and therefore emphasised the similarities between the various *iura particularia*. However, these similarities were the result of the far-reaching parallels between their economic and cultural bases, which rarely stopped at national borders; hence, such similarities could just as well be established between them and Old French or Old Slavic law.

➤ However, the concept of a German law (*ius teutonicum*) was certainly present in the minds of medieval people, whereas it would be completely anachronistic to assume the existence of "Austrian laws" in the Middle Ages. The *iura particularia* that existed within the territory of the present-day Republic of Austria did not possess any characteristics that would have distinguished them from other *iura particularia* in Central Europe and would justify considering them as a single entity.

➤ It is therefore more rewarding to look at the factors that caused the similarities and differences between the different *iura particularia*. The great difference between the towns and the countryside is particularly striking; the rural *lex familiae* was the law of a largely static society that lived mainly on its own production and barter trade, with little room for legal innovations. The medieval towns and markets, on the other hand, with their money-based economy and their manifold legal transactions (long-distance trade, arts and crafts, etc.), were the driving force behind the development of medieval law.

2310 The similarities between the *iura particularia* were reinforced through close legal contacts. For municipal law, in particular, the phenomenon of the **municipal law families** is a characteristic feature.

➤ From the 10th century onwards, German settlers increasingly founded new towns, especially in East-Central and Eastern Europe. In these cases, but also elsewhere, the new town usually took over the law of its "mother town" and obtained legal advice from its court (the superior court or *Oberhof*). Thus, for example, the municipal law of Lübeck was widespread in northern Germany and the Baltic States (e.g. Hamburg, Tallinn), and the municipal law of Magdeburg also in Poland and Ukraine (e.g. Cracow, Brody).

➤ The transmission of municipal laws and their variation or replacement were all possible outcomes. In 1291, for example, Pressburg took from Buda (today part of Budapest) a municipal law with southern German (especially Nuremberg) roots, while Buda received a new municipal law around 1421 that was more in line with that of Magdeburg.

➢ The municipal law of Vienna was adopted by some other towns (Krems, Klosterneuburg, Wiener Neustadt, etc.), but in Vienna, in contrast to Magdeburg, for example, no superior court evolved so that no municipal law family in the true sense of the word developed.

2311 Customary law was handed down mainly orally and manifested primarily in chains of (court) cases and verdicts. Occasionally, customary law was recorded in writing, which gave rise to the ***Weistümer***.

➢ The dispensation of justice was still not the task of a specific learned class; rather, the guiding principle was that the judges should come from the same social group as the defendant (principle of equal birth or *Ebenburt*). Thus, for example, a peasant needed to seek justice before the assembled peasant community. The landlord (in later times his deputy) presided over this court meeting (*taiding*) but did not pronounce justice himself. Instead, each individual member of the community was called upon to "find" a verdict, which the entire community was then to follow.

➢ Soon, for practical reasons, the consultation no longer involved the entire community, but individual persons were called upon as "lawmen" (*Schöffen*). Some of these individuals had attended cathedral or monastic schools (⇨ par. 2316) and had acquired a certain knowledge of the law (e.g. EIKE VON REPGOW, ⇨ par. 2313), but they also were not "jurists" in the modern sense.

➢ *Weistümer* were statements by knowledgeable persons about the applicable customary law, which were not made during a trial but with trial-like formality (in a hypothetical trial, as it were). The reasons for this being done and the conditions under which the *Weistümer* were produced remain largely unclear.

➢ *Weistümer* were of great importance especially for the rural *lex familiae*, but similar legal sources also existed in other legal circles (imperial and urban *Weistümer*).

➢ The original function of the *Weistümer* was to ascertain the contested customary law in a binding manner, but in later times landlords often used them to change the law, which meant that the process of ascertaining a *Weistum* could come close to legislation. Sometimes, attempts were made to unify the laws of different manors that were under the same lord, which led to the formation of *Weistum* families.

2312 Thus, the *iura particularia* were neither comprehensive legal systems nor free of contradictions; they did not include abstract legal concepts or figures. Rather, they consisted of **case law** related to specific situations, which was characterized by *functionality* and an *object-centred approach*. Some other characteristics, especially their *formalism* and the *numerus clausus* principle in regard to admissible legal transactions, can be explained by the oral tradition.

➢ In this context, *functionality* means that less attention was paid to legal constructs than to the underlying economic purpose. Thus, for example, two completely different legal institutions from today's point of view, the municipal loan and the municipal land rent, were both given the same name, namely *Burgrecht*, because both had the same economic purpose (a recurring performance by the owner of a municipal property).

➢ The *object-centred approach* manifested itself, for example, in the fact that there was no abstract concept of ownership applicable both to real estate and movable goods (*Fahrnis*). Rather, different *rights in rem* to real estate and movable goods developed based on their actual usage.

➢ Oral tradition always entailed the risk of a variation in the legal rules, which was countered by a certain rigidity regarding legal transactions (*"numerus clausus"*). Contracts could therefore not be freely formulated but had to fit a specific type.

➢ If legal acts were also supposed to affect third parties, they had to be performed *publicly*, in accordance with certain prescribed *formalities* (use of certain words or objects). This was the case, for example, with marriage or the purchase of real estate.

2313 From the 13th century onward, and already in response to the gradual spread of the *ius commune* (⇨ par. 2322), customary law was recorded in **law books**. Most were private works, but some had the same effect as actual laws and to some extent continued to have an impact into the 19th century.

➢ The most important German law book, and the oldest prose work in the (Middle Low) German language, is the *Sachsenspiegel* ("Saxon Mirror"), written around 1225 by EIKE VON REPGOW, a lawman from Quedlinburg in present-day Saxony-Anhalt. The *Sachsenspiegel* was divided into land law and feudal law sections and dealt with private, criminal, procedural, and constitutional law, "reflecting" especially the law of Saxony's peasant (less so the urban) population. It attained extraordinarily wide circulation (over 340 surviving manuscripts, including four magnificently illuminated ones). Its influence extended from the Netherlands to Ukraine. In the Saxon territories it was used for centuries and in some cases even into the 20th century.

➢ In southern Germany and what is now Austria, the "*Kaiserliche Land- und Lehensrechtsbuch*" ("Imperial Land and Feudal Law Book"), written by an unknown author around 1275, became especially important. It was to a great extent based on the *Sachsenspiegel* and was therefore also called the *Schwabenspiegel* ("Swabian Mirror").

➢ Around 1280, an Austrian Land Law, and in the 14th century a Styrian Land Law also emerged; however, unlike the *Sachsenspiegel* and *Schwabenspiegel*, they did not gain supra-regional significance.

➢ All these law books were records created without an official mandate. The mere act of recording the law, therefore, did not change the fact that the law written in these books was customary law.

➢ These law books must be distinguished from collections of laws commissioned by the sovereign, which were also based on customary law but in part modified it, and must therefore be described as *legal codes* (i.e. as normative texts whose validity emanated from the monarch's creative volition). They include the *Constitutiones Regni Siciliae* in particular, which were promulgated in Melfi in 1231 by King FREDERICK II in his capacity as king of Sicily. In 1335/46, Emperor LOUIS IV "the Bavarian" issued the *Upper Bavarian Land Law* for his ancestral land, which was also in force in parts of present-day Tyrol (Kitzbühel, Kirchberg, etc., in part even until 1811).

2314 From the 14th century onward, a trend towards putting legal transactions in writing became noticeable. This trend resulted in extensive *collections of deeds, form books,* and, above all, **registers of legal transactions**, the precursors of modern land registers.

➢ This development had several different origins, one of which was the concept of the *notary*, which originated in Italy and emerged north of the Alps in the Late Middle Ages. Notaries were publicly certified legal professionals who issued certain deeds that could be enforced in court. If only for reasons of efficiency, these deeds followed certain patterns, which were recorded in form books.

➢ Furthermore, many towns maintained public books in which *town clerks* recorded either all or certain legal transactions for the purpose of publicity (e.g. the municipal books of Vienna from 1395 onward).

➢ As early as 1085, WILLIAM I of England ordered that the fees of the entire kingdom be recorded in a land register. Because this register was supposed to describe the final, unalterable state of affairs, it was referred to as "Domesday Book" (Domesday = Judgment Day). Although later changes were no longer recorded, Domesday Book remained an important instrument of the king's central feudal power.

2315 A legal system that was completely separate from the other medieval legal systems – due to the laws on Jews ⇨ par. 2224 – was **Jewish Law** (*halakha*), which governed the legal relations among Jews. It had its sources mainly in the Hebrew Bible and in the Talmud (⇨ par. 1302) and was independently developed by Jewish rabbis.

➢ The most important legal source of the post-Talmudic period was the so-called responsa literature. These were opinions of the rabbis, which came about at the request of the courts (cf. the parallel with the Roman jurists, ⇨ par. 1304). About 250,000 such responsa have come down to us. The rabbis had a great deal of discretion in their interpretation of the Torah and Talmud, which has to do with their legal work also being considered a sacred activity. The rulings of highly respected rabbis were also considered authoritative for other cases, which led to the development of a case law system.

➢ Jewish communities existed in both the Christian and Muslim spheres and were able to maintain contact with each other across great distances. Until well into the 11th century, Babylon was the centre of rabbinic literature also for Jews living in Europe; this period is known as the *Geonim period*, named after the leaders of the Talmud schools there.

➢ In the subsequent *Rishonim period* (11th to 16th century), European rabbis, in particular Ra(bbi) SH(LOMO) YI(TZHAKI), known as RASHI, who taught in France at the beginning of this period, ame to be more influential.

His commentary on the Talmud is still consulted today. MOSES MAIMONIDES, who lived in the 12th century in (then Muslim) Córdoba in Spain and in Cairo in Egypt, is considered the most important Jewish scholar of the Middle Ages. He created a logically structured collection of Jewish laws, the *Mishneh Torah*.

➢ Although the Jews lived in a separate legal system, they still had to observe the laws of the land (and not just the laws on Jews), which sometimes claimed precedence over the Halakha. This principle was also recognised in the Talmud itself (*Dina de-malchuta dina*: the law of the state is [valid] law).

4. Canonistics and legistics

2316 Apart from the Jews, in the Middle Ages, the art of reading and writing was the domain of the church. In *monastic schools* and episcopal *cathedral schools*, mainly clerics, but sometimes also laymen, were instructed in the "seven liberal arts" (*septem artes liberales*), from which other academic disciplines gradually emerged. The ever-increasing influx of students from the 11th and 12th centuries onwards led to the foundation of "communities of teachers and students" (*universitates magistrorum et scholarium*). These **universities** were largely independent of ecclesiastical and secular authorities (*autonomous*).

➢ The "seven liberal arts" were on the one hand the *trivium* – grammar (the study of language), rhetoric (the art of oratory), and dialectic (logic) – and on the other hand the *quadrivium* – arithmetic, geometry, astrology/astronomy, and music. Rhetoric in particular, but also dialectic, offered many opportunities to address legal topics. Prospective notaries, for example, learned how to draw up documents in their proper form (⇨ par. 2314). These activities can be regarded as the first steps towards legal instruction.

➢ The oldest university with law as a key subject of instruction was the University of Bologna in northern Italy, founded at the end of the 11th century. Other early universities developed in Paris, Cambridge, and Montpellier (all before 1220). In addition to these universities, which were established by teachers and students on their own initiative, other universities were later founded for political reasons, especially in Prague in 1348 by King CHARLES IV, in Cracow in 1364 by King CASIMIR III of Poland, and in Vienna in 1365 by Duke RUDOLF IV ("the Founder") of Austria.

➢ Typically, the university was divided into four faculties; graduation from the arts faculty (where the *septem artes liberales* were taught) was usually a prerequisite for attending one of the three "higher" faculties (theology, law, or medicine).

➢ As in the cathedral and monastic schools, most university teachers and students were initially clerics. The decisive difference compared to earlier times was that the universities were not under the authority of an abbot or bishop, but enjoyed *autonomy*, which was mostly guaranteed through papal or imperial privileges. A separate body of university law and a university judiciary for "academic citizens" developed.

➢ The universities were geared towards an international community. Transmigration of both teachers and students was frequent, and academic degrees were usually recognized at other universities. The language of the universities was uniformly Latin. Despite different founding histories and therefore different original conceptions, it is justifiable to speak of "the" European university, which is clearly different from Islamic educational institutions, the *Madāris* (e.g. Azhar in Kairo 975, al-Mustanṣir University in Bagdad 1227).

2317 At the universities, **canonistics**, the study of church law, emerged as an academic discipline independent of theology. Of central importance in this context was the collection of texts published around 1140 in Bologna by the monk GRATIAN, the *Decretum Gratiani*. Together with other sources, it became part of the *Corpus Iuris Canonici* in 1582.

➢ Canon law, the law of the church, was scattered over a multitude of diverse sources from different eras, which often contradicted (or appeared to contradict) each other: the Bible; the decisions of various councils and synods; papal decisions; etc.

➢ The prevailing scholarly method in the Middle Ages was scholasticism, which sought to resolve contradictions between different texts by exposing them as merely apparent. This method allowed scholars to avoid having to question the authority of the sources, but in doing so, the scholastics unknowingly established new doctrines and thus departed from the original messages of the texts that they edited.

➢ In a similar manner, GRATIAN attempted to provide a coherent and comprehensive account of canon law based on the ecclesiastical legal sources, which he systematically arranged into *canones* (rules); hence the original name of his work: *Concordia discordantium canonum*. Because of its completeness, the *Decretum Gratiani* superseded older collections and, although a private work, acquired law-like significance. It was subsequently edited in a scholarly manner by the *decretists*.

➢ The 12th and 13th centuries were an age of prolific papal law-making. The decretals issued by the popes were systematically compiled by GREGORY IX and added to the *Decretum Gratiani* in 1234 as the *Liber Extra*. Subsequent papal legislation made further additions necessary: the *Liber Sextus* in 1298; and the *Clementinae* in 1311. The scholarly treatment of the decretals was undertaken by a school of scholars known as the *decretalists*.

➢ In the wake of the Council of Trent (⇨ par. 2225), Pope GREGORY XIII merged the *Decretum Gratiani* with the above-mentioned collections of decretals and promulgated it in 1582 as the *Corpus Iuris Canonici*. It remained the central source of canon law until the 20th century (⇨ par. 8302).

2318 Canon law was not only relevant for ecclesiastical matters as such but also shaped the development of medieval **private law, criminal law, and procedural law**. For example, one of the most famous legal principles of all, *pacta sunt servanda* (agreements must be honoured), was first recorded in 1234 in the *Liber Extra*.

➢ The phrase *pacta sunt servanda* is considered by some legal philosophers to be the supreme principle of law: whoever makes a promise is obliged to fulfil it. The universality of this principle stands in contrast to many older laws, e.g. classical Roman law, according to which only claims arising from certain types of contract, but not a *nudum pactum*, were enforcable in court.

➢ Building on the Christian doctrine of guilt, canon law helped to establish the principle of culpability in both criminal and tort law: only those who had committed an act intentionally or negligently could be punished or held liable for damages. In contract law, canon law developed the doctrine of the just price (*pretium iustum*), i.e. that a sales contract could be contested on the grounds of an unreasonable purchase price.

➢ Guided by the Bible verse "what therefore God has joined together, don't let man tear apart" (Matthew 19.6), the Church asserted the indissolubility of a marriage that had been validly entered into and consummated. It therefore rejected divorce, which had been permitted in ancient times. The conditions for a marriage to be valid also had to be precisely defined; marriages that had been concluded in an invalid manner could be declared null and void.

➢ Canon law was particularly opposed to the previously existing right of parents to marry off their children against their will and emphasised that only the will of the bride and groom was decisive (*consensus facit nuptias*). However, this meant that marriages concluded without any formalities were also considered valid, provided that there was marriage consensus, which led to many problems. It was not until the Council of Trent of 1563 that formal requirements for marriage were introduced (in particular, a wedding in the church in front of a priest and two witnesses, as well as an entry in the marriage register).

2319 Parallel to canon law, the study of secular law, called **legistics**, developed in northern Italy. However, it studied the *Corpus Iuris Civilis* rather than the (customary) law in force at the time.

➢ As the former centre of the Lombard Kingdom, Upper Italy had always maintained a legal tradition (the Law School of Pavia), and Roman law had never been completely forgotten. The Digest itself, however, had probably been lost since the 7th century. The immediate impetus for the scholarly treatment of the Digest was probably the discovery of a manuscript version (the *Codex Florentinus*) in the southern Italian city of Amalfi, which at that time belonged to Byzantium. A copy of this codex reached Bologna, and it was there that IRNERIUS, a teacher of rhetoric, began teaching legal studies for the first time.

➢ Legal instruction followed the methods developed by scholasticism; the *Corpus Iuris Civilis* was supplemented with explanations written either between the lines (*interlinear glosses*) or in the margins of the legal text (*marginal glosses*). After this activity, the first jurists are called *glossators*.

➢ Introductory texts (*introductiones*) developed into summaries (*summae*). In these, the legal material was systematically presented and, with the help of *distinctiones*, subdivided into ever finer structures. Thereby, the glossators arrived at abstract legal principles under which the concrete facts were to be subsumed. The method of subsumption so typical of continental European legal scholarship today is thus a product of Upper Italian legistics.

➢ The most important glossators were AZO PORTIUS and FRANCISCUS ACCURSIUS, who also taught in Bologna. The *glossa ordinaria*, written by ACCURSIUS, comprised approximately 97,000 glosses and summarised the entire body of glosses to that date. Subsequent jurists, as well as courts, relied exclusively on the *glossa ordinaria*, making it more important in practice than the *Corpus Iuris Civilis* itself: *"quidquid non agnoscit glossa, non agnoscit curia"* ("what is not recognised by the gloss is not recognised in court").

➢ The Greek-language *Novellae* to the *Corpus Iuris Civilis* were not glossed, mainly due to lacking language skills: *"graeca non leguntur"*.

2320 In the 19th century, the jurists of the Late Middle Ages were (pejoratively) called "post-glossators". Today, the term **"commentators"** is more commonly used, as their (now more highly valued) legal work was primarily reflected in commentaries. In addition, they also wrote longer, coherent treatises (*tractates*) and legal opinions (*consilia*, ⇨ par. 2322).

➢ The most important commentators were BARTOLUS DE SASSOFERRATO, who worked mainly in Perugia, and BALDUS DE UBALDIS, who taught in Bologna (among other places). Italy thus remained the centre of legistics throughout the Middle Ages, which is why medieval jurisprudence was later called *mos italicus*. However, important law schools also developed in some cities outside of Italy, such as in Orléans or Montpellier. In Paris, on the other hand, the study of Roman law was banned by the pope in 1219; the reasons for this ban (which remained in place until 1679) are unclear.

➢ Even more so than the glossators, the commentators were concerned with the practical applicability of their scholarship and therefore also incorporated other legal sources into their work, such as the feudal law of the Lombards (⇨ par. 2307) or the municipal laws (*statutes*) of the Upper Italian towns.

➢ This gave rise to the question of how the statutes of different towns related to each other on the one hand and to Roman law on the other. The following principles developed: Roman law was only subsidiarily applicable, but the statutes should be interpreted as narrowly as possible. If several statutes were relevant to the case, the one with the closest connection to the legal matter at hand should be applied (*statute theory*). This was the first step towards the development of *conflict of laws rules*.

➢ From the second half of the 13th century onwards, the *study of criminal law*, which until then had been taught within the framework of legistics, evolved independently of the latter. The earliest complete account of learned criminal law was probably that of ALBERTUS GANDINUS in his *Tractatus de maleficiis (Treatise on misdeeds)* of 1286.

2321 While the law faculties were concerned with canonistics and legistics, the theological faculties (where philosophy was also taught) turned towards the study of **natural law**. Throughout the Middle Ages, the question of the existence of such a supra-human legal order had more philosophical than practical relevance.

➢ Once humans realised that they could change the law, they also began to think about the limits of this changeability and asked themselves whether there were also laws that could not be changed by humans but were instead given by nature. The notion of a natural law is closely related to the question of whether there is such a thing as absolute justice. Thoughts of this kind were expressed as early as in antiquity (by the philosophers of the Stoa, but also by PLATO, ARISTOTLE, etc.).

➢ With the end of antiquity, these teachings were almost forgotten in Christian Europe. In Muslim Spain, however, ARISTOTLE was rediscovered in the 12th century by ABŪ L-WALĪD MUḤAMMAD IBN RUŠD, who wrote commentaries on almost all of the ancient philosopher's works.

➢ In Europe, the writings of IBN RUŠD (known there as AVERROES) caused great excitement and inspired numerous other studies on ARISTOTLE. The most important of these scholars was THOMAS AQUINAS (*Summa Theologiae/Summary of Theology*, 1274), who taught in Paris, Cologne, and Naples. In the spirit of scholasticism (⇨ par. 2317), he tried to reconcile the teachings of the pagan philosopher ARISTOTLE with those of the Bible.

➢ By doing so, THOMAS ended up with three types of law: He argued that God had shaped the world in accordance with an eternal law, the *lex aeterna*. Humans could only imperfectly understand this eternal law; they could only perceive it (via reason) as *lex naturalis*. According to THOMAS, human-made, positive law, the *lex humana*, must conform to the *lex naturalis* to be legally valid.

➢ Of particular influence were THOMAS' teachings on *bellum iustum* (just war), which holds that war is justified only in defence of a just order (which does not altogether preclude a war of aggression). The belligerents must be motivated neither by greed nor hatred nor any other evil intention.

5. The reception of learned law

2322 The term "**reception**" describes the transfer of the results of canonistics and legistics from the universities into legal practice. It was a pan-European process that began in the 13th century, peaked at the transition from the Middle Ages to the modern era (15th and 16th centuries), and finally gave rise to a pan-European law, the ***ius commune***.

➢ Earlier, the glossators had sought to apply their legal knowledge in practice. For example, at the royal court assembly of Roncaglia in 1158, the "quattuor doctores", four students of IRNERIUS, presented a legal opinion on the regalia of Emperor FREDERICK I (who in return granted privileges to the University of Bologna). During the time of the commentators, the writing of legal opinions (*consilia*) had already become such an important part of their work that they were sometimes also referred to as "consiliators".

➢ As the Roman-German emperors saw themselves as the successors of the ancient Roman caesars, the *Corpus Iuris Civilis* was increasingly regarded as imperial law; the *Codex Iustinianus*, in particular, was expanded through statutes of the Roman-German emperors (the *authenticae*) until the 14th century. However, the claim that Emperor LOTHAIR III had (re-)enacted the *Corpus Iuris Civilis* in 1137 by means of a special imperial law (the "Lothairian legend") was proven incorrect by HERMANN CONRING as early as 1643.

➢ The reception did not take place, as was long assumed, as a "direct transfer" of Roman law, but rather needs to be understood as a gradual academisation of legal practice: Graduates of law schools were increasingly employed in the judiciary, in administration, and in politics. They were familiar with Roman and canon law and would apply them whenever the litigants could not prove the existence of a contrary local custom. In this way, the *ius commune* obtained a subsidiary validity, but over time, despite its subsidiary nature, it pushed the various *iura particularia* further and further back.

➢ The process began at the ecclesiastical courts, which first engaged learned jurists, through whom we already see an early reception in the Late Middle Ages. Since these jurists were all clerics, they are also called "clerical jurists".

➢ At the turn of the modern era (in the 15th and 16th centuries), the secular courts, too, began to pay less attention to the principle of equal birth when it came to appointing judges, and more to their academic legal training. The Imperial Chamber Court, established in 1495, was of critical importance in this respect; half of its judges were nobles, the other half jurists, and it had to decide primarily according to the *iura particularia*, but subsidiarily also based on the *ius commune*.

➢ Essential for this development were also certain changes in procedural law; whereas in the Middle Ages the judgement was "found" by the entire (not legally trained) "court community" (⇨ par. 2311), in Roman-canonical civil proceedings as well as in inquisitorial proceedings, the professional, legally trained judge was not only formally in charge of the trial but also the one who passed the sentence.

➢ The need for university-trained lawyers also had repercussions for the universities; while law students initially had to travel to Italy or France for their studies, Roman law gradually became established at an increasing number of universities north of the Alps as well, for example, at the University of Vienna in 1494 (where only canon law had been taught until then). Courses in Roman and canon law were established in Salzburg in 1622/52, in Innsbruck and Linz around 1670, and in Graz in 1778.

➤ The law faculties were also engaged in legal practice insofar as they were asked by the courts to provide scholarly legal advice on specific cases, which also involved sending them the case files (*transmissio actorum*). At the Austrian universities, this phenomenon had only limited significance.

2323 Parallel to and in connection with this academisation of legal practice, an extensive **legislative activity** emerged as the Middle Ages transitioned into the modern era, especially at the municipal and land levels. These *municipal* and *land law "reformations"* were strongly influenced by the *ius commune*, which in turn further stimulated its reception.

➤ The *ius commune* was at the same time the cause, means, and end of legislative activity. Its advance led to considerable legal uncertainty, which was to be overcome by introducing modern statutes. The increasing knowledge of the IUSTINIAN laws then encouraged the princes to actively form the law themselves, and the laws enacted were strongly influenced by the *ius commune*.

➤ One of the main concerns of the early modern period was reform ("reformation"). As in religion, in legal culture, too, the initial aim was merely to remedy grievances and to re-establish the old state of affairs (*"reformare"*). Its outcome was *legislation*: the conscious and deliberate creation of norms by an organ of the state. Although there had already been some attempts in this direction in the Middle Ages (⇨ par. 2313), the number of new laws increased considerably at the beginning of the modern era. Hence, legislation can be described as a newly emerged method of norm-creation.

➤ The towns played an especially pioneering role; they received new, reformed municipal laws (*"municipal law reformations"*) in large numbers, for instance, Nuremberg in 1479, Worms in 1498, Pettau [Ptuj/Slovenia] in 1513, etc. Of particularly high quality was the municipal law for Freiburg im Breisgau (then part of Anterior Austria), written by ULRICH ZÄSI (UDALRICUS ZASIUS) in 1520.

➤ Several territories, such as Bavaria in 1518, also received land law reformations, which helped to spread the *ius commune* farther. For Tyrol, a *"Malefizordnung"* (*maleficium*: an act of wrongdoing) regulating criminal proceedings and substantive criminal law was issued in 1499. A *Land Ordinance* from 1526, which also regulated matters of private law, essentially adopted the customary law tradition in regard to the latter and also did not include a subsidiary applicability of the *ius commune*.

➤ Several drafts of an Austrian Land Law were drawn up from 1526 onwards, but none of them came into effect. The final draft, prepared in 1654 with contributions from JOHANN BAPTIST SUTTINGER, was strongly influenced by the *ius commune*. It later served as the basis for a number of separate laws: criminal law and criminal procedure were regulated in 1656 in a criminal code (*"Ferdinandea"*); the relations between landlords and their subjects (and thereby also some private law matters) were laid down in the *Tractatus de iuribus incorporalibus* (*Treatise on rights in rem*, 1679; and the law of intestate succession was regulated in 1720 in the *Neue Satz und Ordnung vom Erbrecht außer Testament (New ordinance on intestate succession).*

➢ *Policeyordnungen (policey ordinances)* were issued in large numbers; they covered mainly matters of public law (e.g. building law, measures against begging and prostitution) but also some areas of private law, such as certain aspects of labour law (on the concept of *"policey"* in the early modern period, ⇨ par. 3209). *Policeyordnungen* were issued in 1527, 1542, and 1552 for the Lower Austrian group of territories, in 1573 for Tyrol, in 1577 for Styria and Carinthia, etc.

➢ In contrast to the codifications of the 18th century (⇨ par. 3304ff), these early modern laws did not regulate the respective areas in a comprehensive and exhaustive manner but concentrated on individual aspects that were perceived to be important; otherwise, older legal sources or customary law continued to apply as subsidiary provisions. The penalties were also usually not precisely determined; instead, it was left to the judge to find an appropriate penalty (*arbitrary penalties*).

2324 Mirroring the political situation in the 16th century, imperial legislation was not as wide-ranging. However, the *Peinliche Halsgerichtsordnung* of Emperor CHARLES V (**Constitutio Criminalis Carolina, CCC**) of 1532, which covered criminal procedure and substantive criminal law, gained considerable importance.

➢ The CCC was based on the Bamberg *Halsgerichtsordnung* of 1507 and adopted its provisions in part verbatim. With the CCC, the inquisitorial process developed by Italian criminalistics also achieved its breakthrough north of the Alps. For a long time, the Bamberg court master JOHANN VON SCHWARZENBERG was assumed to have been the author of the *"Bambergensis"*, but according to more recent research, it appears that he at least had collaborators.

➢ The CCC was meant to harmonise German criminal procedural law; however, under pressure from the imperial princes, a "salvatory clause" was inserted, which stated that the CCC should have only subsidiary applicability vis-à-vis the territorial laws. Nevertheless, the CCC served as a model for many other criminal law codes and thus shaped the development of criminal law until the 18th century.

➢ Other imperial laws included the *Reichspoliceyordnungen* of 1530, 1548, and 1577, and the *Reichsnotariatsordnung* of 1512.

6. Jurisprudence in the early modern era

2325 In the early modern era, jurisprudence received significant new impulses from the intellectual current of **humanism**. This new approach did not have its origins in Italy but primarily in France (*mos gallicus* instead of the older *mos italicus*).

➢ In southern France in particular, the Roman legal tradition had remained almost unbroken since ancient times. However, a more distanced relationship arose towards the *Corpus Iuris Civilis* as such. While the Roman-German Empire was regarded as the successor to the ancient empire and had therefore adopted the Iustinian law *ratione imperii* (for reasons of imperial continuity), in France, Roman law could only justify its validity *imperio rationis* (on account of its high quality).

➤ Another factor was the rediscovery of antiquity typical of the early modern period (c. 1500), which was reflected not only in art (*Renaissance:* rebirth) but also in intellectual life. While the representatives of the *mos italicus* had ultimately relied only on the *Glossa ordinaria* of ACCURSIUS (⇨ par. 2319), the representatives of the *mos gallicus* sought to regain direct access to classical Roman law.

➤ Therefore, the *Corpus Iuris Civilis* was no longer viewed uncritically as *ratio scripta* but rather as a historically evolved product that had to be cleansed of the interpolations from the times of JUSTINIAN. To achieve this, the jurists began to search for new source material as well as to study the *Corpus Iuris Civilis* using philological/historical methods.

➤ While the legists had written in medieval Latin, the return to the "classical" Latin of antiquity was characteristic of the beginning of the modern era. Because of its superior linguistic quality, the *mos gallicus* was also called "elegant jurisprudence". However, the direct impact of humanist jurisprudence on legal practice remained relatively minor. The *mos gallicus* became important mainly because it enabled better access to the *Corpus Iuris Civilis* (e.g. the first printed edition from 1583 by DIONYSIUS GOTHOFREDUS).

➤ The *mos gallicus* did not attract much attention in Saxony (Leipzig, Wittenberg), where the *mos italicus* was initially retained and customary law prevailed to a larger extent than in the rest of Germany. In 1572, several contentious issues were considered by professors and electoral court councillors and then authoritatively settled by the Elector AUGUSTUS (1553–86) in the *Constitutions of the Electorate of Saxony*.

2326 Initially, traditional customary law received little or no academic treatment. Whereas in the Middle Ages, in the spirit of scholasticism, efforts had been made to describe its rules as only seemingly different from those of the *ius commune* (**concordance literature**), in the early modern period, local customary law was dismissed at first.

➤ The concordance literature of the 14th century sought to identify the similarities and differences between the various regional customs; this helped to preserve them. JOHANN VON BUCH, for example, wrote a gloss on the *Sachsenspiegel* (*"Buchsche Glosse"*, c. 1325) in the style of the glossators.

➤ BERNHARD WALTHER, a native of Leipzig, professor at the University of Vienna from 1540, and *Regimentsrat* to the Lower Austrian government from 1547, is considered the "father of Austrian jurisprudence". In his *Aurei Tractatus iuris Austriaci* (*Golden Tractate on Austrian Law*, 1552–58), he compared the traditional customary law with the learned law.

➤ The *Summa legum brevis levis et utilis* (*Short, Simple, and Useful Summary of the Law*) by RAYMUND VON WIENER NEUSTADT from the 14th century became important in East-Central Europe. The author probably arrived in Hungary from Italy together with the Angevins (⇨ par. 2114) and wrote an easily accessible account of Roman law with references to deviating rules in customary law.

➢ In 1514, Hungarian customary law was recorded by ISTVÁN WERBÖCZY in the *Tripartitum opus iuris* (*Law book in three parts*), with special emphasis on differences to the *ius commune*. It remained the central source of private law in Hungary until 1959 (with a break in 1852–61, when the Austrian Civil Code was in effect).

➢ To make the *ius commune* accessible to a broader, not legally trained audience, several Latin texts were translated into German, and easily comprehensible ("popular") treatises on the *ius commune* were written in German, such as SEBASTIAN BRANT's *Klagspiegel (Mirror of legal actions)* of 1516.

2327 Only in the 17th century did customary law become emancipated; it began to be studied with the same scholarly rigour as the *ius commune*. This scholarly school of the **usus modernus pandectarum** produced a hybrid of *ius commune* and customary law, which was given different names in different parts of Europe (*Ius Romano-Germanicum* in Germany, *Ius Romano-Hispanicum* in Spain, etc.).

➢ The North German polymath HERMANN CONRING's work *De origine iuris Germanici* (*On the Origins of Germanic Law*, 1643), was instrumental in promoting a more open-minded attitude towards the *iura particularia* among jurists. In this work, CONRING described the process of the reception (⇨ par. 2322).

➢ The new legal doctrine was mainly developed by Saxon jurists such as SAMUEL STRYK, who gave it its name with his book *Usus modernus pandectarum*, published in 1690. Another important representative from Saxony was BENEDICT CARPZOV, the author of the *Practica nova Imperialis Saxonica rerum criminalium* (*New Imperial Saxon Practice of Criminal Law*, 1635), who can be regarded as the founder of the modern study of criminal law (historically called "criminalistics", a term that has since taken on another meaning).

➢ Under the *usus modernus*, customary law was subjected to a scholarly process according to the system and method previously reserved for the study of the *ius commune*. Thus, although the terminology of Roman law was predominantly applied, many substantial principles of customary law prevailed (e.g. in the law of possession, or the land charge [*Reallast*]).

➢ The Dutch school of jurisprudence was influenced by both the *mos gallicus* and the *usus modernus*. Its most important representative, HUIGH DE GROOT (HUGO GROTIUS), combined Dutch *iura particularia* with *ius commune* in his *Inleidinge tot de hollandsche rechtsgeleertheid* (*Introduction to Dutch Jurisprudence*, 1619). This Roman-Dutch law also spread to the Dutch colonies; it is still relevant today, for instance, in the Republic of South Africa.

7. The common law

2328 A different development from that in continental Europe took place in England and Wales, where another legal system, the **common law**, developed through the jurisdiction of the High Courts at the king's residence in Westminster. Hardly any *iura particularia* for individual regions emerged beside it.

➤ After the Norman conquest of England in 1066 (⇨ par. 2107), the monarchs introduced a strictly centralised system of government, with the king's court at the very top. Under HENRY II, itinerant justices were sent around the country to dispense justice on behalf of the king, which had a harmonising effect on the law.

➤ In the 12th and 13th centuries, three courts of law emerged from the king's court: The *Court of Common Pleas*, responsible for general civil actions; the *Court of King's Bench*, responsible for royal prerogatives (and thus also for public law); and the *Court of Exchequer*, responsible for financial matters in particular. With their case law, they created a "common law" that applied more or less uniformly throughout England and Wales.

➤ This resulted primarily from the royal courts issuing orders, known as *writs*, to lower-level courts or other authorities. For example, the *writ of certiorari* ordered the court files to be submitted, while the *writ of habeas corpus* ordered a specific person to be summoned. These procedural remedies soon developed into substantive legal principles, such as the *habeas corpus* principle, according to which no one may be arbitrarily arrested, i.e. without a court order. On the other hand, this method led to a very strong emphasis on procedural law and an element of formalism.

➤ For this reason, this (older) common law was rather rigid, which led to inequities. This problem was remedied by the equity jurisdiction of the *Court of Chancery*, which also granted a writ in cases where this was not possible under the older common law but seemed equitable. The equity jurisdiction initially competed with the jurisdiction of the three common law courts but ultimately complemented them and came to be seen as an integral element of the common law itself (*common law in the wider sense).*

➤ In 1873/75, the four above-mentioned courts were merged to form the High Court, where they still partly constitute separate sections (hence today, for example, "High Court, King's Bench division"). The Court of Appeal is the court of second instance. Until 2009, the third and supreme instance was the House of Lords, which was then replaced by a Supreme Court for the entire UK.

2329 Unlike on the continent, a **reception of the learned law did not take place** in England and Wales, and the common law maintained its special position.

➤ As on the continent, a class of clerical lawyers who had studied Roman and canon law at the universities (Oxford, Cambridge) emerged in England during the Middle Ages. However, from the 13th century onwards, they were pushed aside by secular colleagues, who had only partly studied law at the universities and had mainly received their training through associations of their senior colleagues (law societies, etc.). At around the same time, lay juries also gained in importance in England, which also impeded the spread of learned law.

➢ The separation of the English Church from Rome in 1534 (⇨ par. 2118) was critical to this development, since the pope's legal system, canon law, was rejected together with the Catholic Church as such. Indirectly, this led to a certain resurgence of Roman law at the universities; but overall, the influence of learned law on legal practice remained limited.

➢ Unlike in England, in Scotland there was initially a reception of the *ius commune*. After the real union with England in 1707 (⇨ par. 3104), a hybrid of *ius commune* and common law emerged.

➢ With the expansion of the British colonial empire, the common law also became established overseas, although in some cases it was combined with other legal systems, such as French law in Canada (⇨ par. 3113) and Roman-Dutch law in South Africa (⇨ par. 3118).

2330 The common law is largely a product of the courts themselves and is, therefore, **case law**. The statutes passed by the parliament do not supersede the case law but supplement it.

➢ Since a reception of the learned law did not take place, the method of the legists, i.e. the subsumption of facts under abstract norms (⇨ par. 2319), also remained foreign to the common law. Instead, the case law system starts inductively from individual cases and applies these precedents to other cases.

➢ If the cases are sufficiently similar, the decision will follow the precedent (*stare decisis*); if the cases differ to a significant degree, a distinction is made between them. This way, a rich body of case law emerged. The formal removal of a precedent (*overruling*) can usually only be effected by a higher court. It was only in the 19th century that appellate courts began to be bound by their own previous judgements.

➢ A prerequisite for the functioning of a case law system is the collection and publication of court decisions, which has been the case in England since the 14th century. Compare this with Austria, where court decisions have only been published since 1859.

➢ Today, statutes are also becoming increasingly important in England; attempts were made in the 19th century to codify private and criminal law, but these failed (note that the term "codification" was coined by an English lawyer, JEREMY BENTHAM; ⇨ par. 3304).

➢ A similar situation existed in the Scandinavian countries, where, as in England, the reception of learned law was also unable to gain a foothold (or only to a limited extent) and similar developments took place. However, as a result of absolutism, law codes emerged, some of which continue to apply to the present day (e.g. *Danske Lov* 1683).

8. Halakha in Modern Era

2331 The field of *halakha* also underwent a significant transformation at the turn of the Middle Ages to Modern Era, bringing the era of the

Rishonim (⇨ par. 2315) to an end. Legal scholars from the 16th century to the present day are referred to as **Acharonim**.

➤ Rabbi JOSEPH KARO is generally considered to be the turning point between the Rishonim and Acharonim. He was expelled from Spain as a child in 1492 (⇨ par. 2115) and later settled in Palestine. Here, in 1563, he wrote the *Shulchan Aruch*, a comprehensive and easy-to-read summary of the Halakha. This work soon became the subject of numerous commentaries.

➤ The Acharonim had to resolve numerous legal issues that arose for the first time as a result of modern innovations. Therefore, the Acharonim felt more entitled than the Rishonim to overturn decisions made by older rabbis.

Part III

Absolutism, Enlightenment and Natural Law

A Developments

1. The age of classical absolutism (1618–1740)

3101 From 1614, the French Estates General *(états généraux)* were no longer convened, and the king (1643–1715: LOUIS XIV, the "Sun King") had almost unlimited power. Following this example, many other monarchs, such as the "Great Elector" FREDERICK WILLIAM of Brandenburg-Prussia (1640–88), established **absolute monarchies** in their countries.

➢ French absolutism was mainly the work of the two prime ministers ARMAND Cardinal DE RICHELIEU (1624–42) and JULES Cardinal MAZARIN (1642–60). Resistance to their absolutist and centralist politics came mainly from parts of the nobility (*Fronde* uprising of 1648) and the Huguenots. The king and his ministers maintained the upper hand in both instances; in 1685, the Edict of Nantes was revoked again (Edict of Fontainebleau).

➢ The Prussian state was based on the Electorate of Brandenburg (capital: Berlin) and the Duchy of Prussia (capital: Königsberg [Kaliningrad/Russia]), the latter a fief of the Polish crown. Both territories had been united under the Hohenzollern dynasty since 1618. Based on absolutist policies, FREDERICK WILLIAM succeeded in creating a unified state out of his geographically distant territories. In 1660, he cast off the Polish feudal sovereignty over Prussia. This enabled his son FREDERICK (I) to be crowned "King in Prussia" in 1701.

➢ The "Great Elector" responded to LOUIS XIV's Edict of Fontainebleau with the Edict of Potsdam (also issued in 1685), which granted the Huguenots expelled from France refuge in Prussia.

3102 The attempt to establish absolutism in **England** failed. After a republican interlude (1649–60), England became a constitutional monarchy. In the *Bill of Rights* of 1689, the king had to grant parliament far-reaching privileges, in particular the right to pass laws.

➢ In 1629, King CHARLES I (1625–49, House of Stuart) dissolved parliament and ruled in an absolutist manner for eleven years, but he then had to reconvene it in 1640. The conflict between king and parliament developed into a civil war, in which the parliamentarian and army commander OLIVER CROMWELL increasingly gained influence. After the execution of the king in 1649, England was declared a republic ("commonwealth"); CROMWELL received almost dictatorial powers as "Lord-Protector" in 1653.

➤ In 1660, the monarchy was restored under the sons of the executed king. When JAMES II (1685–88), who had converted to Catholicism, ascended the throne and embarked on the re-Catholicisation of England, the House of Stuart was again (and this time permanently) overthrown in the *Glorious Revolution* of 1688/89.

➤ Parliament transferred the crown to JAMES II's daughter, MARY II, and her husband WILLIAM III of the House of Orange, who defeated JAMES II's supporters on the battlefield but was eventually forced to recognise the constitutional system in the *Bill of Rights* of 1689.

3103 The *Thirty Years' War* of 1618–48 devastated the Roman-German Empire and led to a temporary decline of its emperor's power. The **Peace of Westphalia in 1648** consolidated the dualistic system; the imperial princes were granted sovereignty (⇨ par. 3201) over their respective territories.

➤ The Thirty Years' War was ignited by unresolved confessional conflicts; in 1618, the Habsburgs, who wanted to suppress Protestantism in Bohemia, were deposed as kings of Bohemia by the estates, and two governors of the Habsburg king were thrown out of a window of Prague Castle ("Defenestration of Prague", ⇨ par. 3201).

➤ However, the Habsburgs succeeded in defeating their Protestant opponents in the Battle of White Mountain in 1620, whereupon the Protestant kings of Denmark and Sweden, and in 1635 also the Catholic (!) king of France, intervened in the war on the side of the Protestant princes. The Spanish Habsburgs fought on the Catholic side. The war thus mutated into a European power struggle between the Habsburgs and Bourbons, in which religious issues only played a subordinate role.

➤ "Peace of Westphalia" is a summary term for the emperor's peace treaty with France at Münster and the peace treaty with Sweden at Osnabrück. It also included far-reaching constitutional (⇨ par. 2217) and religious provisions for the Roman-German Empire and was expressly adopted as a fundamental law of the Empire by the Reichstag in 1654. France and Sweden thus became guarantors of Germany's internal order.

➤ France was able to overcome Spain's dominance in Europe, which had to accept the independence of Portugal (1640) and the northern Netherlands (1648); the Franco-Spanish War lasted until 1660.

➤ Switzerland, which had already achieved a large degree of independence in the Middle Ages, left the Roman-German Empire *de iure* in 1648, as did the northern Netherlands.

3104 A circle of great powers emerged in Europe, which kept each other in balance through complicated systems of alliances (**"European balance of powers"**). When the Spanish Habsburgs died out in 1700, a war broke out that involved all European powers and was

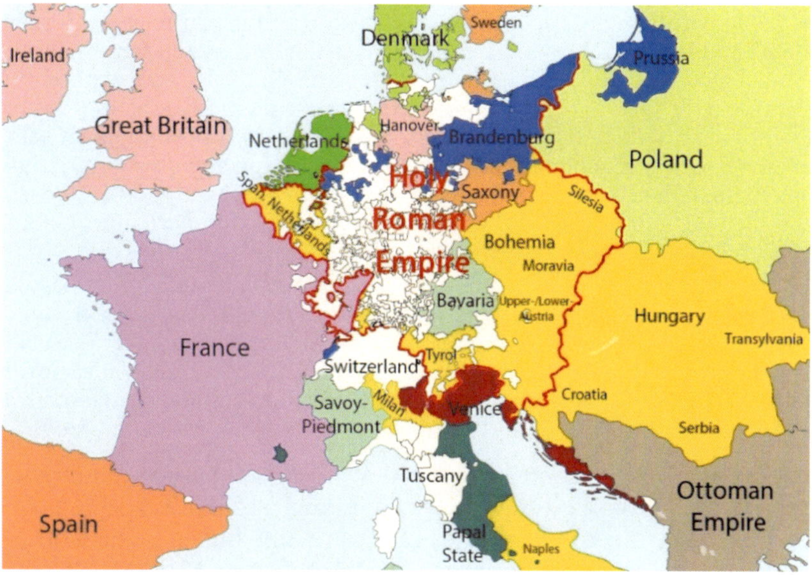

Map 5: Central Europe in 1721

The red line marks the border of the Holy Roman Empire.
Source: https://commons.wikimedia.org/wiki/File:Europa_1721.svg

partly also fought in America (*War of the Spanish Succession*, 1700–14).

➢ The leading great power in the 17th century was France, and the Franco-German border was pushed farther and farther to the east by LOUIS XIV in numerous wars.

➢ The power of the Roman-German emperors had reached a low point by 1648 but was revived to some extent under Emperor LEOPOLD I (1658–1705), especially as a result of the military resistance to the conquests of LOUIS XIV. Upon successfully defending Vienna against the second Turkish siege of the city in 1683, LEOPOLD I was able to (re-)conquer the Kingdom of Hungary in the Great Turkish War of 1683–99 and to transform it into a hereditary monarchy for the Habsburgs (outside the Roman-German Empire!).

➢ Another great power was England, which had been in a personal union with Scotland since 1603 (⇨ par. 2118). In 1707, the two countries entered into a real union through the fusion of the two parliaments, resulting in the *Kingdom of Great Britain*.

➢ In north-eastern Europe, Sweden had developed into a great power in 1648 but was defeated by Russia in the Great Northern War (1700–20). When the Roman-German emperor recognised the imperial rank of the sultan in 1718 (⇨ par. 2119), the Russian Tsar PETER I the Great (1682–1725) adopted the title of *Imperator* to document his equal status vis-à-vis the Roman-German emperor and the Ottoman sultan.

➢ Even before the death of the last Spanish Habsburg in 1700, both LEOPOLD I and LOUIS XIV asserted their claims to the throne, and war broke out immediately after his passing. In order to maintain the balance of power in Europe, both renounced the Spanish throne for themselves as well as for their first-born descendants (*primogeniture*) in favour of subsequent sons or grandsons (*secundogeniture*, ⇨ par. 3107). However, by 1705/11, all members of the House of Habsburg except Emperor CHARLES VI (1711–40) had died. While the emperor now had all the Habsburg hereditary claims to himself, his European allies deserted him.

➢ Spain (= Castile and Aragon including their colonies) therefore passed to a collateral line of the French Bourbons in 1713/14. The Spanish Bourbons have ruled Spain since that time (with occasional interruptions). CHARLES VI was only able to win the Spanish Netherlands (henceforth called the Austrian Netherlands: present-day Belgium and Luxembourg) and some possessions in Italy (permanently only Milan with Lombardy).

3105 The Habsburgs' position as a great power was not based on their imperial title but on their hereditary kingdoms and lands, and thus on a sum of very diverse legal titles that were only linked to each other through the common monarch. The **Habsburg Monarchy** also did not have an official name as a state until 1804 (⇨ par. 3116).

➢ As Roman-German emperors, the Habsburgs held the highest secular rank in Western Christianity but had little actual power. The electoral capitulations (⇨ par. 2117), which all emperors had to sign before their election, increasingly constrained their powers. An attempt to reach a "Permanent Electoral Capitulation" in 1711 failed.

➢ The Habsburgs occupied a dual position in the Roman-German Empire. They were not only emperors but also (by far the most powerful) princes of the empire:

➢ 1. Since the Middle Ages (⇨ par. 2111), they had ruled over the "Austrian hereditary lands" (Austria above and below the Enns River, Styria, Carinthia, Carniola, Tyrol, Vorarlberg, Gorizia, Trieste, etc.), which roughly correspond to the territories of the present-day republics of Austria (without Burgenland and Salzburg) and Slovenia, as well as some parts of Italy (South Tyrol, Trieste).

➢ 2. From 1526, the Habsburgs ruled over the "Lands of the Crown of Saint Wenceslas" (Bohemia, Moravia, Silesia, and, until 1635, also Lusatia, ⇨ par. 2115), and therefore also held the position of the Bohemian elector. These territories roughly correspond to the present-day Czech Republic and south-western Poland.

➢ 3. With the Spanish inheritance, the Austrian Netherlands (present-day Belgium and Luxembourg) and Lombardy in Italy were acquired in 1714.

➢ Outside the Roman-German Empire, the Habsburgs ruled as sovereign kings over the "Lands of the Holy Crown of St. Stephen", i.e. Hungary, Croatia, and Transylvania. This roughly corresponds to the present-day states of Hungary and Slovakia and large parts of present-day Croatia and Romania, as well as smaller parts of present-day Serbia, Ukraine, and Austria (Burgenland).

3106 The diversity of the Habsburgs' legal titles was reflected in the structure of their **central authorities**. Whereas in the 16th century, MAXIMILIAN I and FERDINAND I had at least to some extent established administrative bodies that had jurisdiction over the empire, the kingdoms, and lands as a whole, in the 17th century, separate authorities for the Roman-German Empire on the one hand and the hereditary kingdoms and lands on the other emerged. These authorities were usually based in Vienna, the imperial capital and city of residence.

➢ Their gradual proliferation and differentiation demonstrated the constant expansion of the state's functions. The various chancelleries, in particular, developed from purely clerical offices into authorities with autonomous decision-making powers, since the monarch could no longer personally attend to all affairs himself. But in all cases where the law was unclear, the officials had to seek the monarch's decision (*référé legislatif*).

➢ The *Imperial Chancellery* (from 1559: *Imperial Aulic Chancellery*) had existed since the Middle Ages under the formal leadership of the Elector and Archbishop of Mainz as the Imperial Archchancellor, who was represented by an Imperial Vice Chancellor based in Vienna. A separate *Austrian Aulic Chancellery* for the Austrian hereditary lands was detached from it in 1620, and the Imperial Aulic Chancellery lost its jurisdiction with respect to these territories.

➢ The *Imperial Aulic Council*, which had emerged from various older institutions in the 16th century, was in principle an advisory body to the emperor. Since the emperor continued to lay claim to supreme jurisdiction in the empire even after the establishment of the *Imperial Chamber Court* in 1495 (⇨ par. 2117), the Imperial Aulic Council (also) developed into a supreme court of the empire. In this respect, it competed to some extent with the Imperial Chamber Court, but unlike the latter, it remained dependent on the emperor. The Imperial Aulic Council was also the supreme authority regarding feudal matters and dealt with certain administrative matters (the so-called "privileges") of the Roman-German Empire.

➢ Various other advisory bodies of the monarch emerged as well (*Privy Council*, *Privy Conference*), whose significance and sphere of influence varied depending on the style of government of the respective monarch.

➢ For the lands of the Bohemian Crown, where the Roman-German imperial authorities had almost no jurisdiction due to the Golden Bull of 1356 (⇨ par. 2110), a separate *Bohemian Aulic Chancellery* existed in Prague from 1527 as a central judicial and administrative body. As a result of the Bohemian uprising in 1618, it was moved to Vienna in 1620, and the Bohemian estates' influence on it was reduced to a minimum.

➢ The Austrian Aulic Chancellery had a wider spectrum of competences than its Bohemian counterpart, as it was responsible not only for the political and judicial affairs of the Austrian hereditary lands but also for the affairs of the Imperial House and the greater part of foreign affairs. The *Chancellery Regulations* of 1720 took account of this dual competence by appointing a separate Aulic Chancellor for each of the two portfolios.

➢ From the 16th century onwards, the *Aulic Chamber* was responsible for financial matters (of both the Roman-German Empire and the hereditary lands), and the *Aulic War Council* for war affairs. In 1848, the Ministry of Finance and the Ministry of War emerged from them.

➢ Hungary had a completely independent system of administrative agencies with a Royal Governor (*palatine*), Supreme Court (*curia*), Hungarian Aulic Chancellery, and Chamber. They resided partly in the then Hungarian capital, Pressburg [Bratislava], and partly in Vienna. The administration of the Austrian Netherlands was also decentralised and based in Brussels.

3107 In 1713, Emperor CHARLES VI issued the **Pragmatic Sanction**, which declared the Habsburg hereditary kingdoms and lands indivisible and inseparable, and to this end also decreed harmonised rules for the succession to the throne. Thus, the *de facto* "arbitrary" phenomenon of a common monarch became a legal imperative. The Pragmatic Sanction, which remained in force until the end of the Habsburg Monarchy in 1918, can thus be regarded as the first basic law for the *Monarchia Austriaca*.

➢ During the War of the Spanish Succession, in 1703, several internal agreements, some of them secret, had been concluded within the House of Habsburg to provide a framework for future successions to the throne (⇨ par. 3104). In 1713, these pacts were made public by the last male Habsburg, Emperor CHARLES VI (1711–40) with the Pragmatic Sanction and – with some modifications – reaffirmed.

➢ The Pragmatic Sanction provided succession rules for all constituent parts of the Habsburg Monarchy, following the principle of *primogeniture* (= right of the first-born). Only when all the male descendants had died out should the heir's daughter and her descendants ascend the throne (*subsidiary female succession*).

➢ While the pacts of 1703 only had the character of internal agreements, CHARLES VI also ensured that the Pragmatic Sanction was recognised in each individual territory of the monarchy as a basic (constitutional) law. Hungary was the last of the Habsburg kingdoms and lands to give its consent to the Pragmatic Sanction in 1723 (Statutes I, II, III/1723).

➢ Finally, CHARLES VI also sought recognition of the Pragmatic Sanction under international law in all of Europe, for which he sometimes had to make major concessions, but which he nevertheless did not fully accomplish.

➢ Note that the Pragmatic Sanction only applied to the hereditary kingdoms and lands, not to the Roman-German imperial title. The latter was still not hereditary but was awarded solely by the electors!

3108 The colonisation of **Asia, Africa, and America** continued in the 17th and 18th centuries and in 1770 also reached **Australia**. Increasingly, not only trading posts were established, but also settler colonies, i.e. Europeans took up residence there. Not all of the major powers acquired colonies, although some smaller states (such as the Netherlands and Denmark) also established colonial empires.

➢ Colonies were often not established directly by the state, but by special trading companies, such as the British East India Company, which was founded in 1600. Both the British king and the Mughal emperor (a Muslim ruler who ruled over roughly three quarters of the Indian subcontinent) kept granting this trading company more and more privileges. The British East India Company eventually had a state-like character (with its own military, civil, and criminal jurisdiction) and was more powerful than the Mughal emperor himself.

➢ The Netherlands established a West India Company and an East India Company. These were able to build up a colonial empire in the Caribbean, South Africa, and Indonesia (Dutch East Indies), among other places, although it remained smaller than those of France and Great Britain. The Dutch colony in North America was conquered by Great Britain in 1664, and its capital New Amsterdam was renamed New York.

➢ Note the terminology: due to COLOMBO's mistake in thinking he had landed in India, (Central) America continued to be called the "West Indies" for a long time, while "East India" was the name given to the whole of South Asia, from present-day Pakistan to the present-day Philippines (Spanish East India).

➢ While the European settlers continued to live under the law of the mother country, the indigenous population was subject to a separate jurisdiction. They were disenfranchised and often expelled from their ancestral homelands, which was often justified on racist grounds.

➢ Neither the Holy Roman Empire as such nor the Habsburg Monarchy acquired colonies, but many German princes hired out troops for wars within and outside Europe. The Imperial Ostend Company, founded in 1722, was dissolved as early as 1731 under British and Dutch pressure, so as not to jeopardise the international legal recognition of the Pragmatic Sanction.

2. The age of enlightened absolutism (1740–89)

3109 The philosophy of the Enlightenment brought significant innovations to the concepts of state and law, and several absolutist monarchs developed a new approach to their rule: **enlightened absolutism** (⇨ par. 3207).

➢ The "prototype" of the enlightened absolutist ruler was King FREDERICK II of Prussia (1740–86), whose reign was associated with a series of reforms in the spirit of the Enlightenment (e.g. religious tolerance, abolition of torture).

➢ Under his rule, Prussia developed into a great power, joining the four "old" powers (⇨ par. 3104) and becoming a serious competitor to the Habsburgs in particular (conquest of Silesia 1740–45).

3110 **MARIA THERESA** (1740–80), who became monarch in Austria at the same time as FREDERICK II in Prussia, was still an absolutist ruler of the old type, even though early influences of the Enlightenment were already noticeable under her rule as well. With her centralist reforms, she turned the loose union of the Habsburg territories into a centrally managed, unified state.

➢ In 1740, the male line of the House of Habsburg had died out with the passing of MARIA THERESA's father, Emperor CHARLES VI. Despite the Pragmatic Sanction, MARIA THERESA's succession was disputed, and she had to defend her throne in the *War of the Austrian Succession* (1740–48). Silesia was lost to Prussia in 1745.

➢ A member of the Wittelsbach dynasty (CHARLES VII) was elected Roman-German emperor in 1742, but after his death in 1745, MARIA THERESA succeeded in having her husband FRANCIS STEPHEN OF LORRAINE (1745–65) elected. His coronation made her (like every wife of an emperor) *empress*. The imperial crown now remained in the hands of the *Habsburg-Lorraine dynasty* that they had founded until the end of the Holy Roman Empire in 1806.

➢ MARIA THERESA's experiences in the War of the Austrian Succession motivated her reform efforts, which were intended to also facilitate the reclamation of Silesia (1756–63: Seven Years' War – unsuccessful). However, the Hungarian territories were excluded from most of these reforms, resulting in an emerging dualistic state structure of the Habsburg Monarchy.

➢ In the Bohemian and Austrian provinces, new administrative bodies (known as *gubernias* from 1763 onwards) were introduced, which combined internal and financial administration and were subordinate only to the sovereign, thus bringing absolutism to a temporary climax.

➢ However, the estates continued to exercise their own (rather limited) administrative functions through a "*Landesausschuss*". This resulted in a dual system of central state administration on the one hand and autonomous territorial administration on the other, which persisted until 1925 (⇨ par. 6116).

➢ The absolutist state also did not retain the historical borders of the territories but reorganised the monarchy according to rational aspects, so that the territorial scope of a gubernium (the "governorate district") often comprised not one but several of the existing crown lands (e.g. Styria-Carinthia, Tyrol-Vorarlberg, etc.).

➢ The Bohemian and Austrian Aulic Chancelleries were successively made redundant and then completely abolished in 1749 at the suggestion of FRIEDRICH WILHELM Count HAUGWITZ. New authorities emerged from them, which – in contrast to the previous situation – were no longer distinguished from one another by different territorial spheres of operation but by different substantive responsibilities: the *House, Court and State Chancellery* for handling foreign affairs and the affairs of the House of Habsburg-Lorraine; the *Directorium in publicis et cameralibus* for internal and financial affairs; and the *Supreme Judicial Office* ("*Oberste Justizstelle*") for judicial affairs, including their related administrative matters.

➢ During the Seven Years' War, under the decisive influence of the State Chancellor WENZEL ANTON Prince KAUNITZ, additional reforms were undertaken, which, however, only concerned details of the great reform of 1749:

Table 3: Development of the central authorities, 1740–1848

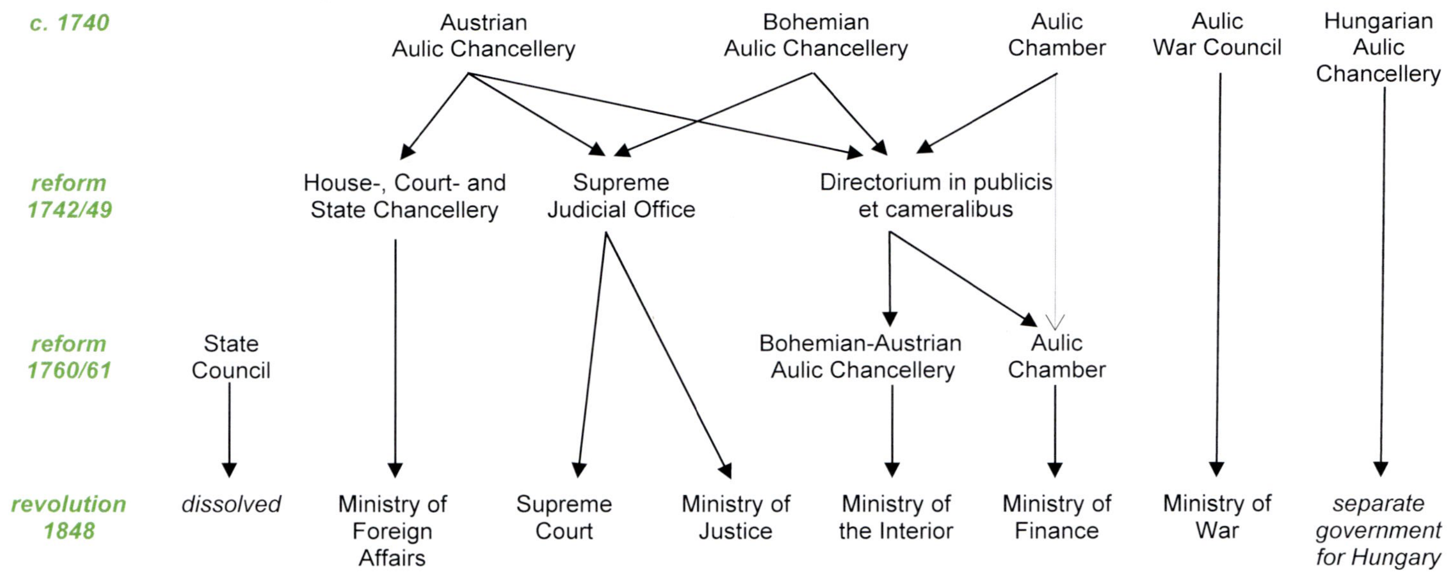

Note: Further restructuring took place from 1782 onwards but was subsequently undone until 1802.

in 1760, a State Council was created as the supreme advisory body of the monarch; in 1761, the *Directorium in publicis et cameralibus* was given up because it turned out to be too large. From then on, internal affairs were handled by the *Bohemian-Austrian Aulic Chancellery* as the supreme authority and financial affairs by the *Aulic Chamber*.

3111 MARIA THERESA's sons, **JOSEPH II** (1765/80–90) and **LEOPOLD II** (1790–92) turned to enlightened absolutism. However, many of their hastily undertaken reforms had to be reversed because of too much resistance, especially from the nobility.

➤ JOSEPH II had already succeeded his father FRANCIS I as the Holy Roman Emperor in 1765 and had been installed by his mother as co-regent in the hereditary lands, but until 1780, he had little say in domestic politics (exception: the abolition of torture in 1776).

➤ JOSEPH's foreign policy was more successful, leading to the acquisition of Galicia in 1772 (⇨ par. 3112) and Bukovina in 1775. His attempts to exchange the Austrian Netherlands for Bavaria, however, failed (apart from the acquisition of the "Innviertel" in 1779), as did the war against the Ottomans that he started in 1788.

➤ After he had become the sole monarch in 1780, JOSEPH II issued numerous patents with which he wanted to radically change almost every sphere of life (*Josephinism*, ⇨ par. 3210). In the process, he often disregarded the reservations of his advisors and also included Hungary in most of his reforms.

➤ Because of their radical nature, the Josephine reforms were often rejected, which escalated towards the end of JOSEPH II's reign into open revolt in Hungary and the Austrian Netherlands. Shortly before his death in 1790, JOSEPH II had to reverse many of his reforms.

➤ LEOPOLD II, who had inherited Tuscany from his father in 1765, made it a model country of enlightened absolutism, but the short duration of his reign in Austria (1790–92) prevented major reforms there. Rather, the unrest that had developed under JOSEPH II could only be calmed by the further reversal of previous reforms.

3112 The Russian Empress CATHERINE II the Great (1762–96) began her reign with enlightened goals but then largely failed to realise them. She expanded the **Russian Empire** in all directions, and, together with Austria and Prussia, annexed the whole of Poland in three "partitions" in 1772/1793/1795, thereby extending Russia into Central Europe.

➤ The Polish state was large in geographical terms, but politically weak, which was exploited by its neighbours to further their imperialist aspirations. The considerable territorial cessions that Poland was forced to make in the First Partition of 1772 led to extensive domestic reforms. On 3 May 1791, Poland became the first European constitutional monarchy. However, precisely this fact led to the three great powers dividing Poland entirely among themselves in two further partitions in 1793/95.

➢ In the First Partition in 1772, Austria acquired territories in the south of Poland (with Lemberg/Ľvív), which were incorporated into the Habsburg Monarchy under the name of *Galicia*. Austria was not involved in the Second Partition in 1793, but in the Third Partition in 1795 it acquired *Western Galicia* with Cracow.

➢ In 1779, Russia assumed the rights previously vested in Sweden under the Peace of Westphalia and thus became (together with France) a guarantor of the internal order of the Roman-German Empire. This role became particularly relevant at the time of the Imperial Recess *("Reichsdeputationshauptschluss")* of 1803 (⇨ par. 3115), which was the result of a Russian-French proposal.

3113 **France** continued to adhere to the classical style of absolutism. Costly wars and a lavish court led to national bankruptcy in 1788, which forced King LOUIS XVI (1774–92) to reconvene the estates, marking the end of the absolute monarchy. The defeat of France by Great Britain was a Pyrrhic victory for the latter, as it indirectly led to the declaration of independence by 13 British colonies in 1789 and the formation of the **United States of America (US)**. France's support of the US in its struggle against Great Britain stimulated a discourse about democracy at home, which would be essential for the outbreak of the French Revolution in 1789.

➢ The expansionist ambitions of France and Great Britain in North America had already led to the French and Indian War of 1754. It merged with the Seven Year's War (⇨ par. 3110) into one war waged in Europe, America, Asia, and Africa, which is why it is sometimes referred to as the "first world war". In it, France fought on the Austrian side and Great Britain on the Prussian side.

➢ In the Treaty of Paris of 1763, France lost its huge possessions in North America (Canada among others). The land east of the Mississippi was awarded to Great Britain, and everything west of it to Spain. When the Native American war chief PONTIAC tried to form an alliance of all Native American tribes against the further expansion of the Whites, the British government imposed a halt to further settlements in 1763, which in turn angered the colonists.

➢ Britain tried to cover the high costs of the war by introducing new taxes without seeking the consent of the colonists. This led the American lawyer JAMES OTIS to describe "taxation without representation" as "tyranny".

➢ In 1764, a "Continental Congress" with representatives of 13 British colonies in North America convened in Philadelphia, which – bypassing the British parliament – addressed its concerns directly to the king, but without success. In 1775, armed conflicts broke out between the British army and the settlers' militia. They escalated and became the American War of Independence (1775–1783), in which France fought on the American side from 1778.

➢ On 4 July 1776, the thirteen British colonies declared their independence and in 1777, with the *Articles of Confederation*, initially joined together as a confederation of states. Their independence from Great Britain was recognised in the Peace of Paris in 1783.

➢ Economic, but above all security policy reasons prompted the founding fathers to transform the Confederation into a federal state. On 17 September 1787, a Constitutional Convention adopted a constitution that was ratified by the individual states and came into force on 4 March 1789. With it, the United States of America was founded as a federal, presidential republic (⇨ par. 6210).

➢ The US Constitution is still in force today and is thus the oldest constitution in the world. Its wording cannot be changed, but amendments can be adopted that expand its content or derogate it in substantive terms. The first ten amendments were adopted as early as 1789 and concerned fundamental rights, which is why they are collectively referred to as the *Bill of Rights*.

➢ US delegates to Paris included BENJAMIN FRANKLIN in 1776–85 and THOMAS JEFFERSON in 1785–89, two of the most important founding fathers of the US (U, who also took the idea of democracy to Europe.

3. The French Revolution and the Napoleonic period (1789–1815)

3114 In the French Assembly of Estates *(états généraux)*, the "Third Estate", the bourgeoisie, seized power on 17 June 1789 and declared itself the National Assembly *(assemblée nationale,* ⇨ par. 4209), which marked the outbreak of the **French Revolution**.

➢ On 4 August 1789, the feudal system was abolished, and on 26 August 1789, human and civil rights were proclaimed. The storming of the Bastille on 14 July 1789, which is still celebrated as the French National Day, had only symbolic significance.

➢ On 3 September 1791, France received a modern constitution in the spirit of constitutionalism. The monarchy was abolished on 21 September 1792, and France became a republic. The deposed king ("Citizen LOUIS CAPET") was executed in 1793; his young son ("LOUIS XVII") probably died in captivity in 1795. The Revolution reached its bloody climax (over 1,000 death sentences within six weeks) in 1794 under MAXIMILIEN ROBESPIERRE's reign of terror. After ROBESPIERRE's fall, the government was led by a five-member Directory (1795–99).

3115 The European monarchies joined forces in several **coalition wars** against revolutionary France but were beaten back after initial successes. The French general NAPOLEON BONAPARTE conquered large parts of Europe and also took sole power in France in a coup d'état (1799).

➢ The threat to the young republic that came from the old monarchies led to a wave of nationalism (with the blue-white-red tricolour and the Marseillaise as national symbols). This, as well as the introduction of universal

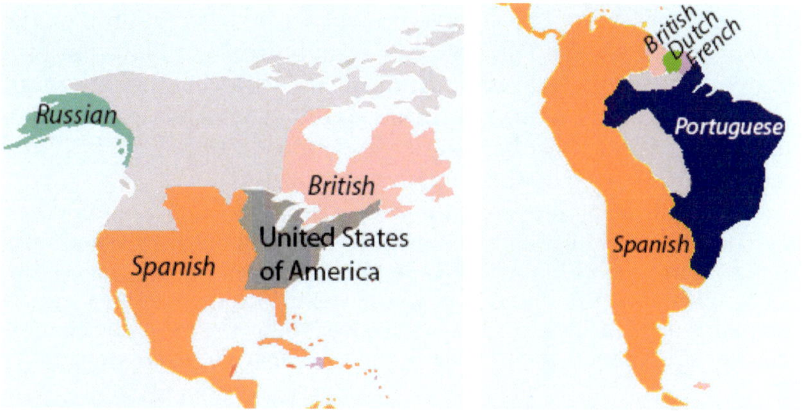

Map 6: The Americas in 1783

Source: https://upload.wikimedia.org/wikipedia/commons/3/3d/Colonial_empires_in_1800.svg (excerpts; colours changed).

conscription in 1793, facilitated a French military hegemony in Europe. BONAPARTE, popular because of his military successes, became "First Consul" with dictatorial powers (including the right to legislate) under the new constitution of 12 December 1799.

➢ In the coalition wars, the Roman-German Empire lost all territories on the left bank of the Rhine River (Peace of Luneville 1801), whereupon a far-reaching restructuring of the empire was undertaken (Imperial Recess 1803). Its ostensible objective – the compensation of the princes from the left bank of the Rhine – was not achieved; rather, the (more than a hundred) smallest and weakest members of the empire lost their imperial immediacy through their incorporation into more powerful imperial estates (*mediatisation*). Almost all ecclesiastical principalities were transformed into secular ones (*secularisation of sovereignty*), and their assets were assigned to secular purposes (*secularisation of property*).

➢ The ecclesiastical territories of Brixen and Trento, for example, were doubly affected by these measures, being both secularised and mediatised into the province of Tyrol. The Prince-Archbishopric of Salzburg, on the other hand, was also secularised but could retain its imperial immediacy as a secular electorate for a little longer. Salzburg was annexed to Austria in 1805/16.

➢ Although the Austrian monarch benefited from the Imperial Recess, his position as the Roman-German emperor was severely compromised because he lost his most important pillars in the empire, namely the small imperial states and the imperial church. For the first time, he was confronted with a Protestant majority in the electoral college.

➢ Of the remaining 34 states, many had reached a size that allowed them to manage entirely without the protection of the emperor. In 1805, NAPOLEON supported the Electors of Bavaria, Saxony, and Württemberg in gaining royal titles.

3116 In 1804, NAPOLEON BONAPARTE crowned himself emperor of the French (NAPOLEON I). The Roman-German Emperor FRANCIS II reacted in the same year by assuming the title of **Emperor of Austria** (as such: FRANCIS I). In 1806, under pressure from NAPOLEON, he laid down the Roman-German imperial crown and declared the **Holy Roman Empire dissolved**.

➢ The creation of an Austrian Empire was a direct reaction to the assumption of the French imperial title in order to maintain equality of rank with NAPOLEON, but also with the Russian emperor, not least because these two held their imperial titles hereditarily, whereas the Roman-German emperorship of Francis II continued to be elective. Following 1803, the chances of the Habsburgs being re-elected as Roman-German emperors were rather remote.

➢ "Austria" in this case did not refer to any specific territory (especially not to the Archduchy of Austria) but was used in a dynastic sense (the dynasty of Habsburg as the "House of Austria"). It was therefore a purely personal elevation in rank that did not in any way modify the constitution of the individual hereditary kingdoms and lands. It was only in later years that the term "Austria" was increasingly used to refer to the monarchy as a whole.

➢ In assuming the title of emperor of Austria, FRANCIS II/I also made it clear that he himself doubted the viability of the Roman-German Empire, which was reinforced by the new kingships of 1805.

➢ In July 1806, 16 German princes joined together to form the *Confederation of the Rhine* and declared their withdrawal from the Roman-German Empire. The Confederation of the Rhine was a mere association (under international law) of sovereign German princes under NAPOLEON's protectorate. Over time, almost all the German states (with the notable exceptions of Austria and Prussia) joined it.

➢ Whether the Roman-German emperor was even entitled to unilaterally declare the end of the empire is doubtful, but given the political situation, it was probably the only reasonable option. Through his declaration, the imperial principalities that had not yet exited the empire also became sovereign.

➢ NAPOLEON's further victories over Prussia in 1806 and Austria in 1809 consolidated his rule over Europe. In numerous states (Spain, Naples, Holland, Westphalia, etc.) he installed relatives as kings; he himself assumed the title of "King of Italy" in 1805.

➢ As early as 1800, NAPOLEON had forced Spain to return the North American territories it had acquired in 1763 to France (⇨ par. 3113). Shortly afterwards, he sold them to the United States, which thus roughly doubled its territory (Louisiana Purchase in 1803).

3117 NAPOLEON's **Russian campaign** of 1812 failed; the European monarchs rallied against him, and he was defeated. NAPOLEON abdicated in 1814 in favour of his two-year-old son ("NAPOLEON II"); however, the allied powers enforced the reinstatement of the Bourbons.

➤ Napoleonic rule over Europe had also led to an awakening of nationalism among the subjugated peoples, which was deliberately fuelled by their monarchs. According to the ideas of the liberal bourgeoisie, the wars of liberation should result in the formation of nation states. After the decisive "Battle of the Nations" at Leipzig in 1813, in which NAPOLEON was defeated by the allies (Austria, Russia, Prussia, Sweden, etc.), the Confederation of the Rhine also disintegrated without being formally dissolved.

➤ NAPOLEON was initially assigned the island of Elba as a sovereign principality but in 1815 attempted to seize power in France again ("NAPOLEON's Hundred Days rule"). After his final defeat at Waterloo in 1815, he was exiled to the island of St. Helena in the South Atlantic, where he died in 1821.

4. The Pre-March period (1815–48)

3118 At the **Congress of Vienna** in 1814/15, Europe was reorganised. Although the far-reaching changes to the European order of states brought about by NAPOLEON were largely reversed, a complete restoration was neither sought nor achieved. Notably, the Holy Roman Empire was not re-established; it was replaced by the *German Confederation*, an association under international law of the sovereign German princes and municipal republics.

➤ The central figure at the Congress was the Austrian Minister of State (from 1821, the State Chancellor) CLEMENS WENZEL Prince METTERNICH, whose policies were geared towards monarchical stability and the restoration of the European balance of power.

➤ The main point of contention at the Congress was the Polish question. The Polish state created by NAPOLEON (the "Grand Duchy of Warsaw") was eventually divided between Russia and Prussia, with Poland's core territory ("Congress Poland") becoming a kingdom tied to Russia in a personal union. (Eastern) Galicia remained with Austria. Cracow became a sovereign city-state.

➤ The principal beneficiaries of the Congress were Russia, which pushed its borders far to the west (Finland, Poland, Moldavia), and Great Britain, which was able to maintain and expand its position as the leading maritime and colonial power. It had entered into a real union with Ireland (⇨ par. 2107) in 1801 by merging their two parliaments, thereby forming the *United Kingdom of Great Britain and Ireland* (UK).

➤ The German Confederation, founded at the Congress of Vienna with the *Act of German Confederation* of 1815 ("*Deutsche Bundesakte*"), essentially encompassed the territory of the former Roman-German Empire; several member states, including Austria, therefore belonged to it only in part (i.e. with the territories that had previously been part of the empire). Its sole organ was the Confederal Assembly in Frankfurt am Main – a gathering of representatives of the individual governments, who were bound by their instructions. It was chaired by the Austrian envoy.

➤ Austria was able to (re-)gain large territories at the Congress (including Tyrol, Vorarlberg, Salzburg, and Lombardo-Venetia as well as parts of

Carinthia and Upper Austria). However, Prussia also made significant territorial gains (Rhineland, Westphalia, northern Saxony, etc.). The Austrian hegemony over Germany was seriously challenged in 1834 by the German Customs Union, which was founded under Prussian leadership, and in which almost all German states except Austria eventually participated.

➤ The Spanish and French Bourbons were restored to their former throne rights. France was able to maintain its position as a great power as well as its territorial status of 1791. Italy was divided into several small states with mostly foreign monarchs (collateral lines of the Habsburgs and Bourbons); the Papal State annexed by NAPOLEON was re-established.

➤ The former Dutch Republic was merged with the former Austrian Netherlands and the Prince-Bishopric of Liège to form the "United Kingdom of the Netherlands", which thus comprised the entire area of today's Benelux countries. At the Congress of Vienna, it had to formally relinquish the Cape Colony (South Africa), which had been conquered by the UK in 1806.

➤ Denmark, with which Norway had been united since 1380 (!), had to cede the latter to Sweden in 1814 (without Iceland and Greenland, which remained with Denmark). This compensated Sweden for Finland, which had been lost to Russia in 1809. Norway became independent in 1905, Iceland in 1944.

➤ The Knights of Malta did not get back the island over which they had ruled from 1530 to 1798 (⇨ par. 2119) and to which they owed their name (and which was part of the British Empire from 1800 to 1964). However, they retained their international legal personality – a unique situation in international law to this day.

➤ The Congress of Vienna contributed significantly to the evolution of public international law, for example by stipulating that diplomats should line up in alphabetical order of the countries they represent, thereby ultimately recognising the principle of the equality of all states. The Central Commission for the Navigation of the Rhine was established as an authority with partly supranational powers that still exists today. And although the Congress participants could not agree on a true ban of the international slave trade, they did agree that it should be condemned.

3119 On 26 September 1815, the (Orthodox) Russian emperor, the (Catholic) Austrian emperor, and the (Protestant) Prussian king proclaimed a **Holy Alliance**, which almost all European monarchs joined, establishing a "brotherhood" founded upon Christianity. This approach also shaped the development of international law.

➤ Throughout the period preceding the March Revolution of 1848 (known as "Pre-March"), there were indeed hardly any armed conflicts between European states. There were, however, several military interventions in individual states by foreign powers aiming to suppress emerging revolutionary movements – the monarchs had united against their own peoples

➤ Parallel to the Holy Alliance, the UK, Russia, Austria, and Prussia formed a "Quadruple Alliance" in 1815, which France also joined in 1818. In the following years, it repeatedly held congresses in various cities to coordinate its members' foreign and security policies. In 1821, Austrian troops

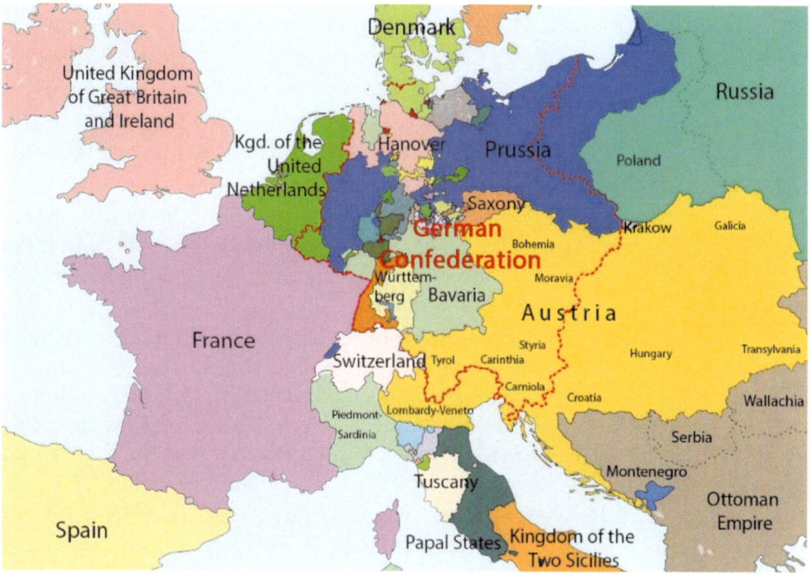

Map 7: Central Europe in 1815

The red line marks the border of the German Confederation.
Source: https://commons.wikimedia.org/wiki/File:Europa_1815.svg

were sent to Naples, and in 1823, French troops were sent to Spain to put down revolutions that had broken out in these states.

➢ Disagreement arose among the European powers in the face of the Greek struggle for independence from the Ottoman Empire, which broke out in 1821, as to whether they should support the (Christian) rebels (the position of Russia, the UK, and France) or the (legitimate) Turkish rulers (the position of Austria and Prussia). The differences eventually became so great that no further congresses were held after 1822. After Russia, France, and the UK had intervened in favour of Greece, the sultan had to recognise Greece's independence in 1829.

➢ Not least because of these events, it became accepted that international law was a matter for Christian states only, to which non-Christian states had no or only limited access. This was linked to the idea that Christian states were "civilised" and thus superior to others. It was used above all to justify the subjugation, colonisation and exploitation of non-Christian states.

➢ The example of Abyssinia (present-day Ethiopia) proves that the recourse to Christianity was only a pretext, concealing racist motives. Although Abyssinia had a Christian culture that dated back right to the beginnings of this religion (see Acts 8:38), it was not considered a "full member" of the international community.

3120 The Holy Alliance could not avert the revolutionary secession of the Spanish and Portuguese colonies in **Latin America** from their mother countries, not least because of the decisive stand taken by the US, whose president JAMES MONROE rejected any interference by European states in American affairs and vice versa in 1823. A large number of new states emerged in Central and South America, mostly republics whose constitutions were inspired by that of the USA. The "Monroe Doctrine" of 1823 characterised the foreign policy of the USA until 1917 (⇨ par. 6102).

➢ At the beginning of the 19th century, more than half of the Americas was still under Spanish colonial rule. The Napoleonic occupation of Spain from 1808–14 weakened the mother country, which greatly intensified the existing tendencies towards independence.

➢ In 1810, uprisings against colonial rule broke out in several Latin American regions, which could only initially be suppressed. In 1816, the United Provinces of the Río de la Plata emerged, followed by Gran Colombia in 1819 (with SIMÓN BOLÍVAR as president 1821–30). Both republics later disintegrated into several successor states (Colombia, Venezuela, Argentina, among others).

➢ Mexico gained its independence in 1821, and the military leader AGUSTÍN DE ITURBIDE was proclaimed emperor. However, as early as 1823, Mexico became a republic. In the Mexican-American War of 1846–48, it lost more than half of its territory to the United States.

➢ In Brazil, the Portuguese crown prince, who was living in the country, took the lead in the independence movement and was crowned Emperor PEDRO I of Brazil in 1822. From then on, two different lines of the Bragança dynasty ruled in the two independent states. Republics were proclaimed in Brazil in 1889 and in Portugal in 1910.

➢ The USA itself continued to expand further to the west, thus increasingly restricting the living space of the Native Americans. Five tribes living in the southeast of the USA (including the Cherokee) who had adopted Christianity and large parts of the Whites' legal culture, came to be known as the "Five Civilised Tribes". But they too were expelled from 1828 onwards and resettled further west in Oklahoma ("Trail of Tears").

3121 In their own countries, the European monarchs ensured that their subjects were watched as closely as possible through a system of informers and strict censorship. With the "**Karlsbad Decrees**" of 1819, METTERNICH succeeded in implementing this surveillance regime throughout the German Confederation.

➢ In 1819, representatives of the most important German states met in Karlsbad (Karlovy Vary/CZ). Their (informal) resolutions were later transformed into formal confederal statutes by the German Confederal Assembly: a *Confederal Press Act* stipulated minimum standards for the exercise of censorship in the German states; a *Universities Act* placed the universities under state supervision; and an *Investigations Act* created a Central Commission of Investigation to take targeted action against revolutionary activities and "demagogues" (i.e. seducers of the people).

➢ The German Confederal Act was supplemented by the Final Act signed in Vienna by a Ministerial Conference ("*Wiener Schlussakte*"). It gave the

Confederal Assembly the right, for instance, to take action against revolutionary unrest in a member state (*confederal intervention*), as well as to intervene militarily against refractory members themselves (*confederal execution*).

➤ In Austria in particular, the stability-oriented policies of the Pre-March period had a paralysing effect on all aspirations for political and economic reform. The situation became even worse when FERDINAND I, who was developmentally disabled, became emperor in 1835, as the State Conference (with four members, among them METTERNICH) that ruled on his behalf was hardly ever able to agree on reforms.

3122 The bourgeoisie was disappointed by the political developments and demanded the formation of nation states (esp. Germany, Italy, Poland) as well as constitutions that would put an end to absolute monarchy and ensure the participation of the bourgeoisie in state power (**constitutionalism**). The French constitutions of 1814, 1830, and 1848 inspired many other European constitutions, making France the "engine of constitutionalisation" in Europe.

➤ The "spearhead" against the restoration policies of the European monarchs were the students, who voiced their concerns at several large-scale events (Wartburg Festival 1817, Hambach Festival 1832). Their focus was on the freedom of the press, since only a free press could effectively enforce all the other aspirations of the bourgeoisie.

➤ Article 13 of the German Confederal Act stipulated that each state should have a *"landständische Verfassung"*. The meaning of this phrase was controversial even among contemporaries. The southern German states of Baden, Württemberg, and Bavaria understood this article to mean that every state should be established as a constitutional monarchy and subsequently issued formal constitutions (⇨ par. 4201).

➤ METTERNICH's advisor FRIEDRICH GENTZ, on the other hand, interpreted Article 13 such that it was sufficient if the constitutions (in the material sense!) of the individual Austrian hereditary lands provided for the existence of diets (i.e. assemblies of the estates), which was the case in almost all of them (even if the diets had no political power). Diets only had to be re-established for Tyrol, Galicia, and Carniola, but for none of these three territories formal constitutional documents in the spirit of constitutionalism were enacted.

➤ The model for the southern German constitutions was the *"Charte constitutionelle"* passed in 1814 under LOUIS XVIII (1814/15–24). Its purpose was to reconcile French Legitimists (= supporters of the "legitimate" Bourbon dynasty), Bonapartists, and Republicans, but this attempt failed (assassination of the heir to the French throne in 1820).

➤ The conservative French King CHARLES X (1824–30) began a confrontation with the parliament established on the basis of the *Charte constitutionelle*. When he dissolved the Chamber of Deputies on 26 July 1830, unilaterally introduced a new electoral law that disadvantaged the industrial bourgeoisie, and abolished the freedom of the press, he was overthrown in the *July Revolution* of 1830. LOUIS PHILIPPE from the collateral line of Bourbon-Orléans was appointed to the French throne and, as

"King of the French" ("Citizen King"), established a monarchy founded entirely on the bourgeoisie; he also issued a revised constitution.

➢ The July Revolution caused commotions in Europe as well; Belgium, which had been united with the Netherlands since 1815, broke away from the latter and received a constitution in 1831 that became a model for other states (Hesse-Kassel, Hanover, Saxony). Thus, by 1848, all the German states except Prussia and Austria had been granted constitutions.

➢ The Polish uprising against Russian rule triggered by the July Revolution failed. Congress Poland was annexed by the Russian Empire in 1832, Cracow by Austria in 1846.

3123 The Swiss cantons, which were re-established in 1815, initially only joined together to form a loose confederation. Only with the Federal Constitution of 12 September 1848 did **Switzerland** become a federal state. At the Congress of Vienna, it proclaimed its "perpetual neutrality", which it maintains to this day.

➢ In 1798, NAPOLEON had conquered the Swiss Confederation and established a "Helvetic Republic" with a centralist constitution. The Federal Treaty concluded on 7 August 1815 then brought about a far-reaching federalisation of Switzerland.

➢ The Federal Constitution of 1848 strengthened the federal central power (Federal Assembly with a bicameral system) but reserved a relatively strong position for the cantons. It also included numerous elements of direct democracy. This constitution was revised in 1874 and applied until a new Federal Constitution came into effect in 2000.

B Structures

1. From the Idea of Sovereignty to the Theory of Absolutism

3201 In the modern era, the relationship between the princes of the Holy Roman Empire and the estates of their territories began to shift in favour of the former. Their previous *dominium territoriale* evolved into a *ius territorii et superioritatis*. This development was also recognised in terms of imperial law by the Peace of Westphalia.

➢ Whereas the *dominium territoriale* (⇨ par. 2216) had been merely the sum of different, historically evolved sovereign rights, the new *ius territorii* was regarded as an originary, comprehensive power from which the concrete sovereign rights were derived. In other words, a reversal of cause and effect had occurred in the perception of the contemporaries.

➢ The modern era brought a considerable expansion of state functions. By virtue of their sovereignty, the princes declared themselves to also be competent to make rules for these newly emerging domains (especially internal administration, known as "*policey*", ⇨ par. 3209). The estates, on the other hand, only retained their historical competences (especially the approval of taxes, participation in civil and criminal legislation) and thus lost importance vis-à-vis the princes.

➤ This often led to conflicts between the princes and the estates. An example of a successful revolt is that of the "States General", i.e. the estates of the northern Netherlands, against the Spanish Habsburg prince in 1579/81 (⇨ par. 2115). The revolt of the Bohemian estates ("Defenestration of Prague") against the German Habsburg king in 1618 (which was also the prelude to the Thirty Years' War, ⇨ par. 3103), on the other hand, failed in the Battle of White Mountain of 1620 and resulted in the complete loss of the political power of the estates (*Renewed Land Ordinance for Bohemia*, 1627).

3202 From the 17th century onwards, some monarchs succeeded in completely overcoming the dualism and made their rule "detached" (*absolutus*) from the estates. The absolutist prince was the sole bearer of **sovereignty** and united all state powers in his person. He was the sole legislator as well as the supreme judge.

➤ The theory of sovereignty as the supreme, original, and comprehensive state power was developed by the French lawyer JEAN BODIN from the Roman legal concept of *imperium* in his *Six Livres de la République* (*Six Books On the Republic*, 1576). BODIN is therefore often described as a theorist of absolutism, which is not quite correct, however, as BODIN also considered the state form of democracy (where sovereignty is vested in the people) a possible option, although he did give preference to absolute monarchy.

➤ Of particular importance was the phrase *princeps legibus solutus est*, from the *Corpus Iuris Civilis* (D 1.3.31), where it had originally referred only to certain marriage laws (the *lex Iulia*, ⇨ par. 1304), whereas now it was interpreted in an extensive manner. BODIN argued that all secular law (*lex*) must be subordinate to the holder of sovereignty. Only divine law (*ius*) was above him. The sovereign was therefore responsible for his actions to God – but only to God.

➤ In his book *Leviathan or the Matter, Form and Power of a Commonwealth Ecclesiasticall and Civil* (1651), the English teacher THOMAS HOBBES compared the state to the monster "Leviathan" or "Bahamut" known from Jewish-Arabic mythology (cf. Job 40:15–32). Like this monster, the state is so powerful that any resistance is futile, which is why one must submit to the state without reservation. HOBBES developed the theory of a (fictitious) social contract, according to which the originally free people had ceded their rights to a sovereign for their own protection. In order for the sovereign to be able to fulfil his tasks, his power had to be unlimited, and the transfer of sovereignty was irrevocable.

➤ A complete elimination of the representation of the estates occurred in France (not convened in 1614–1789, ⇨ par. 3101), where, however, the judiciary of the estates (*parlements*) had a certain substitute function as a public forum. In the Austrian territories, the diets were largely disempowered (especially through the *Dezennalrezesse* of MARIA THERESA: approval of taxes for ten years in advance) but never completely abolished.

3203 The adoption of absolutism meant that the feudal system largely disappeared. Sovereign functions were no longer assigned to vassals for their largely autonomous execution but to civil servants, who were bound by instructions. The development of the **bureaucratic state** is probably the most enduring effect that absolutism had on European legal culture.

➤ Public officials are bound at all times by the instructions of their superiors and thus appear to be their "tools", without any volition of their own. They are not allowed to personally benefit from the goods entrusted to them but receive a fixed salary, and they cannot pass their position on to their heirs. All this results in a close bond with the sovereign and thus in a strengthening of the latter's position.

➤ Attempts to replace the feudal system with a system of officials can be found throughout the Middle Ages, but these attempts regularly failed. However, public officers (*Amtsmänner*) existed, for example, in the towns and manors, and in the modern era, many of them had some legal training, although not in all areas.

➤ In the absolutist period, the bureaucracy was significantly expanded; the civil service developed as a separate profession with its own identity and designated legal provisions governing its work. The criminal laws defined offences related to public office (e.g. abuse of office, accepting of gifts).

➤ Officials were usually appointed for life, but once they reached a certain age, they retired and received a pension. This system provided social security and was intended to make them independent of the influence of third parties; at the same time, however, it was at the root of their frequent lack of motivation to perform.

➤ The creation of the police in the modern sense of the word (⇨ par. 3209), i.e. as special security authorities separate from the other administrative bodies, goes back to JOSEPH II (following first initiatives under MARIA THERESA). From 1782 onwards, police directorates were established in the larger towns of the monarchy.

3204 Remnants of the feudal system persisted mainly in the **justice system** and in the **manors**, where the nobility continued to exert a great deal of influence.

➤ The justice system was one of the elements inherited from the Middle Ages, and hence it continued to be characterised by the dualism typical of the state of estates. In France in particular, the courts (*parlements*) developed into centres of opposition to absolutism, especially during the aristocratic uprising of 1648 (*Fronde*) and in the final years preceding the outbreak of the revolution of 1789.

➤ One of the main aims of MARIA THERESA's state reform of 1749 was to separate the administrative system from the judiciary. However, this had nothing to do with the demands of the Enlightenment (MONTESQUIEU, ⇨ par. 4204); rather, the intention was to free the administrative system from the influence of the estates (which was particularly strong in the judicial system) and to subject it to the sole authority of the monarch.

➢ Above all, however, the manors continued to be the home of the majority of the population. The absolutist state under MARIA THERESA merely set up control bodies (such as the district offices, ⇨ par. 2207); a complete elimination of the autonomous rule of the landlords was not achieved (or even attempted).

➢ However, the judicial system became more homogenous in the higher instances in 1749 with the establishment of the Supreme Judicial Office (the precursor of today's Supreme Court) and in 1782 with the establishment of the Courts of Appeal (the precursors of today's Higher Regional Courts).

3205 The problematic nature of absolutism is evident in the monarchs' **right to intervene** in individual court proceedings by means of a "fiat". Criticism of this practice went to the heart of the monarchs' absolute rule.

➢ The right of jurisdiction had been part of the *dominium territoriale* and thus a historical root of the monarch's sovereignty. For practical reasons, the monarch was represented in most cases by officials/judges, who were bound by his instructions and then decided "in the name of His Majesty". However, the monarch could still refer each individual case to himself and either instruct the judge as to how he should decide or decide himself *ex plenitudine potestate* (out of supreme authority).

➢ It was not until the Enlightenment that a separation of the judicial and political powers was demanded as a means of avoiding arbitrary decisions. The enlightened absolutist King FREDERICK II of Prussia (⇨ par. 3109) therefore promised in his "Political Testament" of 1752 that he would never intervene in court proceedings with a fiat. Nevertheless, in 1779 he broke this promise in the "Miller ARNOLD" case by annulling a civil court ruling that concerned a water mill and had turned out to the disadvantage of the miller, a man called CHRISTIAN ARNOLD. The mill was returned to the miller and the judges were punished, because FREDERICK suspected (but could not prove!) that they had bent the law to the detriment of the miller.

➢ The "Miller ARNOLD" case caused a sensation throughout Europe and brought the practice of fiats into disrepute. In the course of the codification of the Prussian ALR (⇨ par. 3307), the redactors also wanted to include a prohibition on the use of fiats in the new code, which led King FREDERICK WILLIAM II to withhold his sanction of the codification. This significantly delayed the enactment of the ALR. In 1794, it came into effect without a ban on the use of fiats. In Austria, a prohibition of such fiats was included both in the MARTINI Draft and in the West Galician Civil Code 1797 (⇨ par. 3311), but not in the ABGB 1811.

➢ Fiats therefore also continued to be issued during the Pre-March period, although they were less common and less spectacular than that in the case of ARNOLD, the miller. The definitive prohibition of fiats (which were also known as "cabinet justice") in Austria and Prussia occurred when absolutism was overcome and replaced by constitutionalism, i.e. in 1848.

2. Forms of Absolutist Rule

3206 In the course of its historical development, absolutism underwent certain changes. The older form of absolutism (**classical absolutism**) is characterised by the monarch holding court and is therefore referred to in German as *"höfischer Absolutismus"*.

➢ The epitome of classical absolutism was the French King LOUIS XIV, who made his court the glorious centre of the monarchy. All of the state's affairs gravitated around this court, with the king himself as the absolute centre of gravity.

➢ This manner of ruling the state was not only the result of the king's personal thirst for prestige, but also had quite rational reasons; the nobility, who competed with the king for power, should be lured away from their own estates and drawn to the royal court, where they would become dependent on the monarch.

➢ MARIA THERESA's understanding of her rule was somewhat different and can only be explained in terms of her profound religiosity. As a ruler invested by the grace of God, she felt responsible to God alone, but for the same reason also saw herself obliged to provide for the common good of her subjects.

3207 The philosophy of the Enlightenment rejected a religious perspective on the world and took human reason as its starting point. According to a definition by IMMANUEL KANT from 1784, the Enlightenment is the "exit of man from his self-inflicted immaturity. Immaturity is the inability to use one's intellect without the guidance of another". Under the influence of this intellectual current, several absolutist monarchs of the 18th century developed a new understanding of their role: **enlightened absolutism**.

➢ A precursor of the Enlightenment, JOHN LOCKE decisively modified HOBBES' theory of the social contract (⇨ par. 3202) in his *Two Treatises of Government* (1690): the sovereign is appointed for the good of the subjects, so sovereignty comes with obligations and can be withdrawn if these obligations are violated. The people (but not an individual!) therefore have a right of resistance, which, however, can only be exercised in the case of continuous abuse of power by the sovereign.

➢ LOCKE thus not only prepared the intellectual ground for enlightened absolutism, but also laid the foundation for the constitutional theories (⇨ par. 4201) and the fundamental rights theories of the 19th century (⇨ par. 4222).

➢ Enlightened absolutist monarchs, such as King FREDERICK II of Prussia and Emperor JOSEPH II of Austria, deliberately refrained from courtly pomp and regarded themselves as the "first servants of the state". They saw their rule as legitimised by their untiring commitment to the people, and hence there was no need for a divine mission. This understanding of their rule also paved the way for the legislation on religious tolerance that emerged in this period.

➢ Nevertheless, the enlightened absolutist monarchs insisted on their claim to absolute power and rejected any participation of the people in the affairs of state ("everything for the people, nothing by the people"). Their care for their subjects could therefore verge on paternalism.

3. State – Church – Society

3208 The introduction of absolutism took place against the backdrop of the division of faith. The primarily political conflicts between the monarch and the estates gained an additional dimension with the religious question. The Church lost its claim to universality with the schism that followed the Reformation; both the Catholic and Protestant Churches were instrumentalised for political purposes and thus became increasingly dependent on the state (**system of state churches**).

➢ In the Middle Ages, the princes already held certain rights in relation to the Church (*iura circa sacra*, also called the pre-Reformation "church regiment"); they included the right to remedy grievances within the Church, the superiority of princely over ecclesiastical courts (including the right to review decisions of the latter), the approval of the publication of ecclesiastical decrees (*placetum regium*), etc.

➢ In the Protestant territories, this church regiment developed into a *summepiscopate*; the prince acquired supreme power over the Church in his territory, which also considerably strengthened his rule.

➢ In the Catholic territories, a summepiscopate could not develop because of the primacy of the pope. The influence of the Jesuits, in particular, who were bound to unconditional obedience to the pope, was increasingly viewed by the Catholic princes as an obstacle to the further implementation of absolutism. From 1759 onwards, the Jesuit order was outlawed in one territory after the other, and in 1773, especially due to pressure from Spain, it was abolished altogether (but restored in 1814).

3209 The power of the monarchs evolved mainly through a constant proliferation of the functions of the state; facilitated by the takeover of the church regiment, the proactive design of the polity was increasingly seen as a task of the (secular) rulers. This creative volition was expressed mainly in the prince's ***"policey"*** but also in the state's economic policies.

➢ In early modern Germany, "*policey*" was a very general term that encompassed all measures aimed at establishing a well-organised state but also referred to this state itself. Only gradually did it come to be used in a narrower sense to refer to the prevention of dangers (cf., for instance, the German terms *"Baupolizei"* and *"Feuerpolizei"*) and was eventually applied to the modern organisational concept of the police as an agency concerned with law enforcement.

➢ The large number of "policey ordinances" that were issued from the 16th century onwards was a result of the economic and social upheavals of the early modern period (cf. the advance of the money economy!) and the collapse of the medieval regulatory systems. On the other hand, they also contributed significantly to the disintegration of these systems. For example, autonomous law-making by the guilds was replaced by a trade ordinance, church welfare for the poor was replaced by secular welfare, etc.

➢ In the 17th century, the French statesman JEAN-BAPTISTE COLBERT developed the mercantilist economic policy typical of absolutism, which was based on the idea that the wealth of a nation rested primarily on a positive balance of trade. The state should increase exports and avoid imports; therefore, the mercantilist state promoted the establishment of manufactories and, through high customs duties, protected the domestic economy from imported goods.

➢ In the 18th century, mercantilism was replaced by physiocratism, which assumed that economic growth could only come from agriculture, which therefore had to be fostered (cf. the peasant protection legislation in the 18th century, ⇨ par. 2207).

3210 In the Habsburg territories, the reforms of MARIA THERESA and JOSEPH II in particular affected almost all areas of life, often causing them to undergo drastic changes. This brought them increasingly into conflict with the Catholic Church, which became an instrument of the state (**Josephinism**).

➢ In a broader sense, "Josephinism" refers to JOSEPH II's policies in general; however, the term is mostly used in a narrower sense to describe his policies towards the Church. It should be noted that the attitude towards the Catholic Church so typical of JOSEPH II had already begun during the era of MARIA THERESA and continued to have its effect long after the emperor's death.

➢ Thus, under MARIA THERESA, education and censorship were reformed and taken out of the hands of the Church and the Jesuit Order in particular ("nationalisation" of the universities from 1749, ⇨ par. 3316; establishment of a censorship commission in 1751/53; etc.). From 1751 onwards, taxes also had to be paid on the demesne and not just on the tenured land that was cultivated by the peasants; the Church and the nobility therefore now also had to contribute to the state funds.

➢ Radical reforms then took place under JOSEPH II; as early as 1781, he relaxed censorship, and began the process of abolishing serfdom. This was followed by the the almost complete abolition of the death penalty, the tax and urbarial patents of 1785 and 1789 (⇨ par. 2207), and many other reforms.

➢ The instrumentalisation of the Catholic Church was particularly evident in the reform of marriage law: with the Marriage Patent of 1783, the state for the first time assumed the legislative and judicial competence in matrimonial matters. However, marriages were still not to be concluded before a secular authority, but in a church before the priest in charge. After the church service, the parish priests had to read out new state laws to the churchgoers, and they also kept the baptismal, marriage, and death registers for Catholics as well as non-Catholics on behalf of the state. They thus carried out the functional role of state officials. They were educated in state-run seminaries and paid by the state.

➢ The situation was similar in the education system, which was placed under state supervision, but not taken over by the state. Mandatory education was introduced in 1774, but until 1918, more than half of all schools in Austria were still run by the Catholic Church, not the state.

➢ The prerequisite for the instrumentalisation of the Catholic Church was a far-reaching reform of the diocesan structure of the Habsburg Monarchy. In order to prevent bishops who resided abroad (e.g. in Salzburg, Passau) from having direct access to the subjects of his hereditary lands, JOSEPH II established new bishoprics (e.g. Linz in 1782), or relocated them, shifting the diocesan boundaries in the process (e.g. the transfer of the diocese of Wiener Neustadt to Sankt Pölten in 1783). The bishops' communication with Rome was tightly controlled through the *placetum regium*. This meant that no such communication could occur without the consent of the prince.

➢ In 1783, the reform of the dioceses was complemented by a reorganisation of the traditional parish structures, according to rational criteria. Numerous new parishes were established, so that no subject would have more than an hour's walk to his or her parish church.

➢ Religious orders that were neither engaged in education nor in health care nor otherwise "useful" to the state were abolished and their assets confiscated. The money obtained in this way was used to feed religious funds set up in each territory, which were used to finance the state church created in the process (until 1938).

3211 The establishment of the Catholic Church as the state church was not precluded by the fact that JOSEPH II also granted a certain degree of **toleration** to non-Catholic Christians and to the Jews, which did not, however, give them the same rights as Catholics.

➢ The Peace of Westphalia of 1648 (⇨ par. 3103) had essentially reaffirmed the provisions of the Peace of Augsburg of 1555 (⇨ par. 2225), albeit with certain exceptions. However, these exceptions were ignored in the Habsburgs' hereditary lands, where the Catholic Church retained its dominance and the persecution of Protestants continued.

➢ In Hungary and Transylvania, on the other hand, Protestants had been able to practise their religion freely since pre-Habsburg times, so that the legal framework for religion in the Monarchy was very uneven, which led to many problems. Owing to the same reason, there were hardly any forced emigrations from the monarchy in the 18th century, but rather transmigrations within the monarchy, such as from Carinthia to Transylvania in 1734/36. Regarding Salzburg (which only became part of the Habsburg Monarchy in 1805/16), cf. ⇨ par. 2225.

➢ In 1781, Emperor JOSEPH II issued "Patents of Toleration" granting toleration to the Protestant and Greek Orthodox Christians in the various provinces. These patents varied slightly from province to province, but they all granted toleration to these denominations and the right to practice their faith in private. They could only practice their religion in public (processions, ringing of bells, etc.) if they already had this right under previous privileges; otherwise, this right was reserved for Catholics. Accordingly, non-Catholics were allowed to build their own "houses of prayer", but these were not allowed to have bells, towers, or a public entrance from the street. They were also allowed to establish schools.

➢ Tolerance towards the Jews was less far-reaching. Between 1782 and 1785, JOSEPH II issued special edicts on the Jews. These varied considerably from region to region, notably to prevent the emigration of Galician Jews (who made up well over half of all Jews in the monarchy) to the west. The Jews of Vienna were only allowed to practise their religion in private and the synagogue was not allowed to have a street entrance. They were still denied access to most trades and citizenship. Improvements were made, however, particularly in the school system, whereby, under certain circumstances, Jewish children were allowed to attend Christian schools.

➢ The marriage patent of 1783 took account of the new legal situation in religious matters in that both the formalities of concluding a marriage and its legal consequences were largely determined by the respective religious denomination of the spouses. Marriages were therefore officiated by Catholic priests, Protestant pastors, or Jewish rabbis. Divorce was possible under state law if neither of the two spouses was Catholic. These provisions were retained by the Josephinian Code of 1786 and the ABGB of 1811 (until 1938, ⇨ par. 7303).

➢ Backlashes continued to occur in Austria even after 1781. In 1837, more than 400 Protestants from the Zillertal valley were forced to emigrate. This was justified by the fact that the region had only became part of Austria together with Salzburg in 1805/16 and the Josephinian Edict of Toleration had therefore never been promulgated in the area.

3212 The Enlightenment did little to improve the **legal status of women**; rather, their disadvantageous position in society now came to be justified by invoking so-called "natural" differences.

➢ For example, ROUSSEAU argued that women, unlike men, are "constantly reminded of their sex" in all their thoughts and consequently align all their actions with it. KANT believed that women followed their feelings more than reason. Many other men also claimed that women had a reduced ability to make objective decisions, reduced intelligence or reduced artistic talent.

➢ The French Revolution brought only short-term improvements for women, and these were largely reversed with the introduction of the CC. Their position was slightly more favourable under the Prussian ALR and the ABGB. At least CARL ANTON VON MARTINI (⇨ par. 3311) acknowledged that even a supposed superiority in intelligence or skill in one gender did not give that gender the right to oppress the other, while FRANZ VON ZEILLER (⇨ par. 3311) argued that nature itself dictated the distribution of roles between men and women.

➢ Note that the natural law codifications extended the bourgeois model of the family to all classes, thereby eroding the – in relative terms – more favourable position of women in the nobility and the peasantry and reducing it to that of the bourgeois woman.

C Legislation and Jurisprudence

1. The Law of Reason

3301 Natural law had had no practical significance in the Middle Ages and had been studied not by jurists but by philosophers (⇨ par. 2321). This changed radically in the modern era, which is linked to the emergence of a new field of law, **Public International Law**.

➤ The modern term "public international law" was first coined in the 18th century by the English jurist JEREMY BENTHAM (⇨ par. 3304); until then, the term *ius gentium* (law of nations; in German: *Völkerrecht*) had been used. The term had already been used in ancient Rome, but with a completely different meaning. The *ius gentium* of antiquity referred to certain (e.g. private) legal principles that were (allegedly) common to all peoples of the world and that were juxtaposed to the *ius civile* as the particular law of the Romans.

➤ The *ius gentium* of modern times, on the other hand, referred to rules for the legal relationships between peoples and states (hence also: *ius inter gentes*). Although peace treaties had existed since ancient times (see the Treaty of Ebla and Abarsal, ⇨ par. 1101), it was only with BODIN's concept of sovereignty (⇨ par. 3202) that the distinctive nature of public international law came to the attention of contemporaries. In his book *Zum ewigen Frieden* (*Perpetual Peace,* 1795), IMMANUEL KANT wrote: "The idea of international law presupposes the separate existence of many independent but neighboring states."

➤ As there was initially very little positive law relating to public international law, jurists resorted to natural law. This occurred in the context of "Spanish late scholasticism" in Spain, which was at that time establishing its colonial empire. FRANCISCO DE VITORIA (*De Indiis/On the Indians,* 1532), for example, argued on the basis of natural law that the rule of the pagan Indians over their territories was legitimate, but also that Christians had a right to proselytise, which they could enforce if necessary.

3302 The Dutchman HUGO GROTIUS (⇨ par. 2327) is considered the "father of modern public international law" on account of his work De *jure belli ac pacis libri tres in quibus ius naturae et Gentium: item iuris publici praecipua explicantur (Three Books on the Law of War and Peace: wherein are explained the Law of Nature and Nations and the principal points relating to government*, 1625). In this book, he argued that there must be certain legal principles (not only, but especially in public international law) that were evident from reason and hence had to be valid whether God existed or not. In doing so, he became a pioneer also of the modern, secularised natural law—the **law of reason**.

➤ In the Eighty Years' War (1568–1648), Protestant Holland fought for its independence from Catholic Spain (⇨ par. 2115). At the same time, it sought to build its own colonial empire, largely also in the context of its struggle against the Spanish. In this context, GROTIUS, as early as 1604/05, wrote an expert opinion for the Dutch East India Company (⇨ par. 3108) according to which there are no exclusive rights to the sea, which is instead open to all who want to sail it (*mare liberum*). This principle has gained general acceptance and, with the exception of coastal waters, still applies today.

➢ In *De jure belli ac pacis* GROTIUS established a set of fundamental rules for interstate engagement, which should also apply in war. In view of the religious schism of his time, however, he did not invoke God as the source of all law. Like the Enlightenment in philosophy (⇨ par. 3207), modern natural law in jurisprudence sought to make human reason the starting point of all cognition. This is also the origin of the term "law of reason".

➢ This new natural law acquired great significance not only for public international law, but for all areas of law. GROTIUS, for example, argued that it was obvious from reason alone that one must replace what one has taken from others and fulfil one's promises. He also considered the principle whereby wrongdoers are punished for their offences to be immediately apparent from reason.

➢ But whereas in the areas of private and criminal law, natural law entered into a kind of competitive relationship with positive law (⇨ par. 3303) and ultimately merged with it (⇨ par. 3305), it maintained a dominant position in public international law well into the 19th century. At the universities, international law was taught (only) in the context of natural law; cf. for Austria the textbook *Lehrbegriff des Natur-, Staats- und Völkerrechts* (*On Law of Nature, State and Nations*) by CARL ANTON VON MARTINI from 1783, which was required reading for law students until 1848 (⇨ par. 3311).

3303 The older theories of the law of reason assumed that natural law, like human reason, was unchangeable and must therefore remain the same regardless of time and space (**absolute law of reason**). Only later, the idea that natural law could take on different shapes depending on time and space gained ground (**relative law of reason**).

➢ In his work *De iure naturae et gentium libri octo* (*Eight Books on the Law of Nature and of Nations*, 1672), the German jurist SAMUEL PUFENDORF developed the idea that one could derive from reason not only certain fundamental principles but also, by using a logical and deductive method *(more geometrico)*, a complete legal order that was independent of time and space. PUFENDORF was thus a typical representative of philosophical rationalism (cf. BARUCH DE SPINOZA's *Ethica, ordine geometrico demonstrata/Ethics, Demonstrated in Geometrical Order,* 1677) and exerted great influence on philosophers such as JOHN LOCKE or JEAN-JACQUES ROUSSEAU. However, the relevance of his insights for legal practice was limited.

➢ It was not until the end of the 17th century that the Saxon jurists CHRISTIAN THOMASIUS and CHRISTIAN WOLFF succeeded in bringing together their relative natural law with the *ius romano-germanicum*, which continued to dominate positive law. Natural law was taken as a guideline for positive law, but not every deviation was rejected as invalid. Rather, they acknowledged that there could be different manifestations of natural law depending on time and space.

➢ This more flexible approach to natural law was a great success, and consequently, the full body of positive law was subjected to a comprehensive critique from a natural-law perspective, most notably criminal law by the Italian jurist CESARE BECCARIA in his book *Dei delitti e delle pene* (*On Crimes and Punishments*, 1764). He criticised both torture and the death penalty as being unreasonable, which actually led to their abolition in many countries.

2. Codifications based on the law of reason

a) General remarks

3304 The word **"codification"** (*codicem facere* – to make a book) was coined by BENTHAM. In general terms, "codification" refers to any larger collection of laws, but in a narrower sense, it includes only such codes that exhibit the following characteristics:

➢ It contains either the entire legal order (*universal codification*) or at least a specific area of the law in its entirety (*partial codification*, e.g. civil law, criminal law). The collection

➢ must be *systematic* (e.g. based on the institutional or the pandectic system) and *free of inconsistencies*;

➢ must consist of *abstract legal propositions* (i.e. it is not a collection of concrete cases);

➢ must be endowed with *exclusive applicability* (= *exclusivity,* i.e. there can be no subsidiary validity of older statutes or customary law): "Whatever is not in the code of Laws, ought not to be Law" (BENTHAM);

➢ and must be enacted *by the body competent to pass new laws* (depending on the constitutional situation, the absolute monarch, parliament, etc.).

3305 Under the influence of natural law, large-scale **codification efforts** took place in numerous European states from the second half of the 18th century onwards. The fragmentation of the *ius romano-germanicum* resulting from the plurality of legal sources was to give way to a consistent legal order. Positive law should be examined in the light of natural law and reformed when necessary.

➢ The codifications should establish legal certainty. This was especially true for the only universal codification ever completed, the ALR (⇨ par. 3307), which was particularly committed to using plain language so that lay people could also understand it.

➢ The second major aim of the codifications was to harmonise the law in the territories where the respective code was intended to apply. For the Habsburg Monarchy, this was an important step towards the creation of a unified Austrian state; as a "general law", the codification was to be enacted in all territories concerned *by one single legislative act*. The downside of this trend was that the pan-European *ius commune* was abandoned in favour of national legal systems.

➢ Thirdly, the natural law codifications were also used to implement many reforms in the spirit of enlightened absolutism. However, their general validity (which means that the code should be equally binding for all estates) was only partially effective in levelling out the differences between the different social groups. The Prussian ALR had separate chapters for each estate; the Austrian General Civil Code (ABGB) allowed for a different treatment of the estates through references to "political laws".

3306 Precursors of the natural law codifications were the collections of laws created under the Bavarian Elector MAXIMILIAN III JOSEPH (1745–77), the most important of which is the **Codex Maximilianeus Bavaricus Civilis** (**CMBC**; also *Kurbayrisches Landrecht/State Law for the Electorate of Bavaria*) of 1756.

➢ The CMBC contained civil law, feudal law, and some smaller areas of public law; it was drafted mainly by the Bavarian State Chancellor WIGULÄUS XAVERIUS ALOYSIUS Baron VON KREITTMAYR. The impetus for the CMBC had come from the natural law school; nevertheless, it had only limited natural law influences and was strongly influenced by the *ius commune*. The *ius commune* was also to continue to apply as a subsidiary source of law. Therefore, the criterion of exclusivity did not apply to the CMBC.

➢ The CMBC thus soon came to be regarded as outdated. Still, it remained valid in (parts of) Bavaria until the German Civil Code (BGB) came into effect in 1900, and in the *Innviertel* (then Bavaria, part of Upper Austria since 1779/1815) until the ABGB was introduced in 1817.

3307 In Prussia, King FREDERICK II the Great initiated the creation of a universal codification in 1746. The project was not completed until after his death; the **Allgemeines Landrecht für die preußischen Staaten** (ALR, *Prussian General State Laws*) was therefore enacted by his successor FREDERICK WILLIAM II in 1794.

➢ After a failed initial attempt in 1746–55, a committee led by JOHANN HEINRICH CASIMIR VON CARMER prepared a draft for a "General Code for the Prussian States" in 1780–91.

➢ Criticism of the draft, especially regarding the inclusion of "royal fiats" (⇨ par. 3205), resulted in further delays. The code (without the abolition of the said prerogative) was only published on 5 February 1794 and entered into effect on 1 June 1794 under the more conservative title *Allgemeines Landrecht* ("General State Laws").

➢ The ALR covered civil, commercial, criminal, ecclesiastical, and administrative law. It thus qualifies as a universal codification, even though it was meant to be only of subsidiary applicability to provincial laws, which contradicts one of the main principles of the concept of codification.

➢ Its vast number of sections (over 19,000) was the result not only of the great number of matters it covered but also the language of the law, which, although vivid, was also very casuistic. Although this casuistic approach helped to make the ALR popular, it was also one of the reasons – along with its adherence to the traditional system of estates – for the ALR soon being regarded as outdated. It was therefore not adopted for the territories that were incorporated into Prussia after 1815.

➢ The criminal provisions of the ALR ceased to apply in 1851 (⇨ par. 4302) and the civil provisions in 1899 (⇨ par. 4307). Some administrative provisions survived until the 20th century; a few sections are still in place today in formerly Prussian states.

3308 In France, five codifications (*cinq codes*) consolidated the legal achievements of the French Revolution of 1789. As the most modern codes of their time, the five codifications became models for other codes around the world, especially the **Code Civil** (**CC**, Code NAPOLEON) of 1804.

➢ To overcome the division of the country into the *pays du droit coutumier* and the *pays du droit écrit* (⇨ par. 2307), LOUIS XIV had established uniform provisions for criminal and criminal procedural law as well as civil procedural law and commercial and maritime law through several *ordonnances*. However, these were not yet codifications as defined above.

➢ The French Revolution gave rise to numerous individual statutes (*droit intermédiaire*); as early as 1791, the *assemblée nationale* declared it one of its tasks to create a civil code for the whole of France. However, it was only under NAPOLEON's consulate that a commission was set up for this purpose. The most prominent jurist on this commission was JEAN-ETIENNE MARIE PORTALIS, but NAPOLEON also took an active part in the discussions.

➢ The *cinq codes* were: the CC (civil law, 1804); the *Code de procédure civile* (civil procedure, 1806); the *Code de commerce* (commercial law, 1807); the *Code d'instruction criminelle* (criminal procedure, 1808); and the *Code pénal* (criminal law, 1810).

➢ Based on the French borders at the time, the CC also applied in the German regions on the west bank of the Rhine (Cologne, Mainz and others) and remained in force there even after 1815 (until 1900; ⇨ par. 4307). In Belgium, which was part of France from 1797 to 1814, the CC was only replaced by a new codification in 2019.

➢ In 1812, the CC was also implemented in the then French territories in present-day Slovenia, East Tyrol, Upper Carinthia, etc. (the "Illyrian provinces") but replaced by the ABGB in 1815 after the territory had been won back by Austria.

➢ The CC was also adopted in several German states during the Napoleonic period (e.g. as *Badisches Landrecht* in the Grand Duchy of Baden in 1809), in most Italian states, in the Netherlands, and in Poland (sometimes in a modified form); it also influenced legislation in several Swiss cantons (Geneva, Fribourg, etc.).

➢ In the post-Napoleonic period, the CC also served as a model for codifications in Romania (1863), Italy (1865), Portugal (1867), and Spain (1888/89), as well as in several American and African states (e.g. Louisiana 1825, Quebec 1866, Peru 1852, Argentina 1871, Egypt 1875). It is still used today in France, making it the world's oldest surviving civil code.

b) Austria

3309 In the Habsburg Monarchy, codification efforts began under MARIA THERESA but initially did not lead to satisfactory results. The ***Constitutio Criminalis Theresiana*** (**CCTh**), which covered criminal procedure and substantive criminal law, was already considered outdated at the time of its adoption; the draft for a codification of civil law and civil procedure (***Codex Theresianus***, **CTher**) never came into effect.

➢ The CCTh brought almost no innovations; it primarily served to standardise criminal law and criminal procedure in the Bohemian-Austrian lands. It was based on FERDINAND III's criminal code for Austria below the Enns from 1656 (*Ferdinandea*) and JOSEPH I's criminal code for the Bohemian lands from 1707 (*Josephina*). Hence, it still contained, for example, provisions on witchcraft as well as on torture. Nevertheless, it was approved by MARIA THERESA on 31 December 1768 and came into effect on 1 January 1770.

➢ Similarly, the draft of the CTher was primarily a compilation of the laws applicable in the individual hereditary lands and otherwise followed the *ius commune* with little evidence of influences from the law of reason. Because of its length and textbook-like character, MARIA THERESA, on the advice of her State Council, denied this draft her sanction. As preparatory work for later codification efforts, however, the CTher was of great significance.

3310 Under JOSEPH II, codification efforts were resumed and resulted in new legislation in civil, criminal, and procedural law. They were heavily influenced by the spirit of the **Josephinian reforms** (*Josephinism*, ⇨ par. 3210).

➢ In 1781, the General Code of Civil Procedure (*"Allgemeine Gerichtsordnung"*), which had already been commissioned under MARIA THERESA, received its official sanction.

➢ Criminal law and criminal procedure were regulated in two separate codes (Josephinian Criminal Code 1787; Code of Criminal Procedure 1788). By almost entirely abolishing the death penalty, the new criminal code realised one of the aims of the Enlightenment; however, capital punishment was replaced by harsh labour sentences.

➢ In 1774, the State Council member JOHANN BERNHARD HORTEN drafted a civil law codification based on the CTher that was only about half as long ("HORTEN Draft"). Based on this draft, the *"Allgemeines bürgerliches Gesetzbuch, I. Theil"* (*General Civil Code, Part I*) was sanctioned in 1786 (to distinguish it from the ABGB 1811, it is now called the "Josephinian Code"). It contained the law of persons and family law; a patent on the law of succession was also passed in the same year.

➢ The Josephinian codifications not only led to a standardisation of the law in the Habsburg Monarchy but also to sometimes radical reforms in the spirit of Josephinism (⇨ par. 3210), such as the secularisation of marriage law or the abolition of many of the nobility's privileges. A typical example of natural law is the rule introduced in 1786 (and still in force today) whereby the relatives with a right of inheritance – regardless of gender – are divided into certain lines (*parentelae*) and, in the absence of a will, the position within the parentelae determines who is entitled to the inheritance.

➤ The sanctioning of Part II, which would have included the law of property and the law of obligations, did not occur because of JOSEPH II's early death in 1790. Due to the radical nature of the Josephinian reforms and the widespread disturbances that they had sometimes caused, his successor LEOPOLD II decided not to continue the codification efforts any further at the time; the commission that had been working on it was dissolved.

3311 The Austrian codification efforts were resumed under FRANCIS II. The resulting early drafts, which were prepared with substantial contributions from CARL ANTON VON MARTINI, were implemented in **Western Galicia** and (Eastern) Galicia in 1796/97; the insights gained there were incorporated into the final draft.

➤ MARTINI, who originally came from South Tyrol, became the first professor of "natural law" at the University of Vienna in 1753. His draft of a civil code from 1796 ("MARTINI Draft") was characterised in particular by a detailed introduction containing provisions similar to fundamental rights (see the proximity in time to the human rights declarations in the USA and France, ⇨ par. 4222). For example, the MARTINI Draft states that the purpose of the state is to "ensure the protection of persons, property and all other rights of its members".

➤ Another significant innovation in the MARTINI Draft was the abolition of the previously customary *référé législatif* (⇨ par. 3106): In unclear cases, the judges no longer had to seek the monarch's decision, but the law itself contained a set of rules on how it was to be interpreted and how any gaps could be closed by means of analogy. Consistent with this, the MARTINI Draft also contained a prohibition of fiats (⇨ par. 3205).

➤ (Eastern) Galicia fell to the Habsburg Monarchy in 1772 as part of the First Partition of Poland and Western Galicia in 1795 with the Third Partition of Poland (⇨ par. 3112). The latter was lost again in 1809 during the Napoleonic Wars, whereas Galicia remained part of the Habsburg Monarchy until 1918. Whether the codifications were introduced in these provinces "on a trial basis" or whether the need for modern codifications was particularly urgent there remains a matter of dispute.

➤ In 1797, the MARTINI Draft was enacted as the *Civil Code for Western Galicia* (*Westgalizisches Gesetzbuch*, WGGB); in 1798, it was also implemented in Eastern Galicia and Bukovina (it is therefore also known as the "Galician civil code"). A *West Galician Criminal Code*, which contained both substantive criminal law and criminal procedure law, was also enacted in 1797.

➤ The *West Galician Code of Civil Procedure*, which was sanctioned in 1796, was implemented not only in Galicia and Bukovina but also in the territories that were reunited with Austria after 1815 (Tyrol, Vorarlberg, Salzburg, etc.), while the General Code of Civil Procedure 1781 remained in force in the other crown lands; both remained valid until the new Code of Civil Procedure came into effect in 1898 (⇨ par. 4311).

3312 In the last phase of the codification process (as of 1797), FRANZ VON ZEILLER, a disciple of MARTINI and his successor at the University of Vienna, had a great influence on the legislative process. The **Criminal Code** (*Strafgesetzbuch*, **StGB** 1803) was sanctioned in 1803, and the **General Civil Code** (*Allgemeines bürgerliches Gesetzbuch*, **ABGB** 1811) was sanctioned in 1811. The provisions of the Criminal Code 1803 on criminal procedure were applied until 1850 and those on substantive criminal law until 1974. The ABGB 1811 remains the central source of Austrian private law to this day.

➢ In 1797, work resumed on the StGB and also on the ABGB in 1801, and new commissions were established. While ZEILLER was the "expert advisor" for the ABGB and for the first part of the StGB dealing with crimes (i.e. he prepared the text and presented it to the commission), JOSEPH VON SONNENFELS assumed this role for the second part of the StGB, dealing with misdemeanours and "serious police offences" (i.e. administrative criminal law). The latter also attempted to draft a "political code" that was to encompass the entire body of administrative law, but without success.

➢ The StGB received its imperial sanction on 3 September 1803 and the ABGB on 1 June 1811; both came into effect on 1 January of the following year. Their territorial scope was initially reduced by the Napoleonic conquests (⇨ par. 3308); it was not until 1815/17 that the Austrian codifications were also extended to Salzburg, Tyrol, and Vorarlberg, which were (re-)acquired at the Congress of Vienna, as well as to Lombardo-Venetia and the Illyrian provinces (= parts of Carinthia, Slovenia, and Croatia).

➢ During the period of neo-absolutism (⇨ par. 4106), in 1852/53, the ABGB and the StGB were extended to Hungary (then including Croatia and Transylvania). Since the procedural part of the StGB had meanwhile been abrogated (⇨ par. 4310), and the court had issued several decrees that dealt with substantive criminal law, the StGB of 1803 was repromulgated as the Criminal Law (*Strafgesetz*) of 1852, incorporating the earlier court decrees.

➢ After the end of neo-absolutism, Hungary returned to its traditional civil and criminal law, which was based primarily on customary law, whereas the Austrian codifications remained in force in Croatia (until 1946) and Transylvania (until 1943/45).

➢ As early as 1812, the ABGB was also introduced in Liechtenstein, where it is still in force today; the Serbian Civil Code of 1844 also follows the ABGB to a considerable extent. The ABGB also had significant influence on the civil codes of several Swiss cantons (including the Bernese Civil Code 1826), Parma, and Romania, as well as on some German drafts (Bavaria, Saxony).

➢ After the disintegration of the Habsburg Monarchy, the ABGB was adopted in the successor states, and its territorial scope was occasionally even extended within these states, in particular to the new Austrian province of Burgenland, where it was introduced on 1 January 1924.

➢ Thus, for decades after the fall of the Habsburg Monarchy, the "Austrian civil law realm" still encompassed a major part of Central Europe. Its disintegration essentially only occurred after 1945, when the Socialist civil codes came into effect (Czechoslovak Civil Code 1950 etc., ⇨ par. 5301). To

Table 4: Codifications in Austria

<table>
<tr><th>CIVIL LAW</th><th>CIVIL PROCEDURE</th><th>CRIMINAL LAW</th><th>CRIMINAL PROCEDURE</th></tr>
<tr><td colspan="2">*Codex Theresianus*
(draft, 1766)</td><td colspan="2">Constitutio Criminalis Theresiana
1768</td></tr>
<tr><td>Josephinian Code
1786</td><td>General Code of
Civil Procedure 1781</td><td>Josephinian Criminal Code
1787</td><td>Code of Criminal Procedure
1788</td></tr>
<tr><td>Western Galician
Code 1797</td><td>Western Galician Code of
Civil Procedure 1796</td><td colspan="2">Western Galician Criminal Code
1796</td></tr>
<tr><td>**General Civil Code**
(ABGB) 1811
(in force since 1812)</td><td></td><td colspan="2">Criminal Code
1803</td></tr>
<tr><td></td><td></td><td>Criminal Code 1852</td><td>Code of Criminal Procedure
1850
Code of Criminal Procedure
1853</td></tr>
<tr><td></td><td>**Code of Civil Procedure**
(ZPO) 1895
(in force since 1898)</td><td></td><td></td></tr>
<tr><td></td><td></td><td>**Criminal Code (StGB) 1974**
(in force since 1975)</td><td>**Code of Criminal Procedure**
(StPO) 1873
(in force since 1873,
repromulgated 1975)</td></tr>
</table>

this day, the ABGB remains a subsidiary source of law in Croatia and Slovenia, but its practical significance is limited.

3313 The ABGB is a typical **natural law codification**, which is reflected in many of its provisions as well as in its systematic approach and overall structure. Its avoidance of casuistry, but especially the exclusion of all "political" provisions, were important reasons for the first major amendment not taking place until more than 100 years after its enactment. More than half of the original text of the code (818 of the initially 1,502 sections) is still in force today.

➢ The structure of the ABGB, like that of the CC of 1804, was influenced by GAIUS' *Institutiones* (⇨ par. 1303; called the "institutional system"): a short introduction is followed by a First Part, which covers the "law of persons" (including marriage law and parent and child relations); a Second Part comprises the "law of things" (which, in present-day terminology, covers property law as well as the law of succession, matrimonial property law, and the law of obligations); and a Third Part contains general rules (e.g. provisions on limitation periods).

➢ The influence of natural law on the ABGB is most evident in its § 7, which instructs the judge to decide "according to the principles of natural law" if neither interpretation of the law nor legal analogy led to a clear result. Still, the ABGB is largely based on the *ius commune*, which is most evident in its provisions on the law of obligations. To a lesser extent, the ABGB also reflects influences of local customary law (especially in property law) and canon law (especially in matrimonial law).

➢ The ABGB is of a more abstract nature than the ALR. Therefore, many of its provisions could take on a new meaning under different political and social conditions, not least because the wording of the law as such promised freedoms, which, in the reality of 1812, were restricted by "political" laws (to which the ABGB, however, only made general references). When these "political" laws disappeared (notably in the wake of the revolution of 1848), the same provisions of the ABGB could also provide the private-law framework for a (more) liberal society; they were, therefore, according to a dictum of the later Minister of Justice FRANZ KLEIN, a "bill of exchange payable at a future date".

➢ Thus, the ABGB covered institutions that, at the time when it came into effect in 1812, existed either only among the nobility (e.g. the familial *fideicommissum*) or only within the rural manorial system (e.g. *emphyteusis*), but did not restrict their applicability to these estates; instead, it opened them up (at least seemingly) to all strata of the population. The opinion occasionally expressed that the ABGB was a "(neo-)corporative codification" might therefore be misleading.

➢ Great significance has been attributed to § 16 ABGB, which has remained unchanged to this day and recognises that "every man has inborn rights, which are already apparent from reason", imposing a general ban on slavery and serfdom. Formulated by ZEILLER himself, it was intended to compensate for the approach – previously adopted in the WGGB but rejected in the final drafting of the ABGB – of placing some provisions resembling fundamental rights before the main text of the codification. Today, it serves as the reference point for the personality rights.

➢ The StGB 1803 was also a natural law codification and was widely recognised and used as a model, for example, in Latin America. However, it was less progressive than, for example, the Josephinian codifications.

3. Exegetical jurisprudence

3314 In the wake of the codifications, natural law scholars were primarily concerned with the scholarly examination of the new codes. This was achieved mainly through a detailed interpretation of the individual provisions (**exegetical jurisprudence**).

➢ The Exegetical School emerged as soon as the first codifications had been issued (JOSEPH VON BANNIZA, *Gründliche Anleitung zum ABGB/ Thorough Instructions On the ABGB*, 1787).

➢ A four-volume Commentary on the ABGB (1811–13), written by ZEILLER, gained considerable significance due to the author's role in the creation of the ABGB. The commentary is still sometimes used in studies on the current law.

➢ ZEILLER's disciple CARL JOSEPH PRATOBEVERA VON WIESBORN published the first legal journal in Austria, Materialien für Gesetzkunde und Rechtspflege in den Oesterreichischen Erbstaaten (Materials for the study of law and justice in the Austrian hereditary states), from 1815.

➢ Scholarly work on the ABGB in Italian was particularly prolific in Lombardo-Venetia, especially in comparing the ABGB with the CC (applied in Upper Italy until 1815). However, it had little influence on developments in the German-speaking world.

➢ While in Austria the Exegetical School dominated jurisprudence until around 1850, in France the *école de l'exégèse*, which operated in a similar manner, continued to exist for almost the entire 19th century; detailed studies on the CC were also undertaken in the parts of Germany on the left bank of the Rhine, where the CC continued to be used until 1900 ("Rhenish law"). A different development unfolded in Prussia (on the right bank of the Rhine), where the emergence of the Historical School of Law (⇨ par. 4301) precluded an exegetical treatment of the ALR.

3315 The exegetes did not intend to change anything about the law in the codifications. Nevertheless, their work sometimes had the effect of a covert extension of the law. In a parallel development, a **conscious evolution** of the law occurred through "authentic interpretations".

➢ The work of the 19th-century exegetes was similar to that of the medieval legists; their goal was to complete a comprehensive analysis of individual legal provisions but without questioning their authority. However, their interpretations repeatedly deviated from the historical volition of the legislator and thus resulted in a further evolution of the law in certain areas.

➢ The ABGB had adopted the rules of interpretation of the MARTINI draft largely unchanged; the judge was also no longer obliged to seek a decision from the monarch in unclear cases (⇨ par. 3311). However, § 8 of the ABGB authorised the legislator to "explain a law in a generally binding manner". Such an explanation was referred to as an "authentic interpretation"; however, it is not an interpretation in the jurisprudential sense, but an amendment to the original statutory text (with *effect ex tunc*, i.e. from the entry into force of the ABGB).

➢ A formal amendment of the codifications was initially deemed incompatible with the fact that these codes were based on natural law; hence, they were considered unalterable. From the 1820s onwards, however, plans were made to amend both the StGB and ABGB, and commissions were set up for that purpose.

3316 In **legal education**, the new codifications became the focus of legal instruction.

➢ Until the middle of the 18th century, the Austrian law faculties had taught almost exclusively Roman and canon law. It was not until MARIA THERESA's university reform (⇨ par. 3210), which had been proposed by GERARD VAN SWIETEN, that designated chairs were established in 1753 for Natural Law as well as for Public and Feudal Law and Imperial History.

➢ As the codifications placed the legal system on a new footing, the academic curriculum was also reformed and at the same time brought under government control. The law curriculum of 1810, developed mainly by ZEILLER, focused on the study of Austrian private law based on the ABGB. Roman and canon law, on the other hand, were increasingly marginalised.

➢ Imperial History, established in 1753, was given up in 1810. This early precursor of today's Legal History had lost its practical significance with the end of the Holy Roman Empire, where historical knowledge had often been required to understand its operation.

➢ Practical relevance was a central theme of the curricular reforms of 1753 and 1810; the law faculties' primary purpose was to train civil servants, and only little emphasis was placed on legal scholarship. The course of study was tightly organised and taught like at secondary school. Textbooks were prescribed by law, and annual or semester examinations were held at the end of each year or semester. In such a system, there was no room for freedom of teaching and learning.

➢ These academic reforms went hand in hand with a thorough subjugation of the once autonomous universities to the absolutist state; academic jurisdiction was abolished in 1783. The professors were state officials appointed by the emperor, received a government salary, and were subject to the government's disciplinary authority.

Part IV

The Age of Constitutionalism and Imperialism

A Developments

1. The Revolution of 1848 and its aftermath (1848–51)

4101 The European Revolution of 1848 began in France, where LOUIS PHILIPPE was overthrown in February 1848, and the (Second) Republic was proclaimed (**"February Revolution"**).

➢ The "Citizen King" LOUIS PHILIPPE had not succeeded in balancing the different movements in his country; rather, under his rule, his supporters (the Orléanists) struggled for power with Republicans, Bonapartists, and Legitimists alike.

➢ The February Revolution of 1848 was, like its predecessors, mainly driven by the bourgeoisie, but it also showed some early radical democratic and Socialist tendencies. At the same time that the revolution was raging in France, KARL MARX and FRIEDRICH ENGELS published the "Communist Manifesto" in London (⇨ par. 4313).

➢ LOUIS NAPOLEON BONAPARTE, a nephew of NAPOLEON I, was elected president of the French Republic and quickly gained great popularity. He carried out a coup d'état on 2 December 1851, extending his power further. A referendum turned out in favour of the restoration of the monarchy; in 1852, BONAPARTE ascended the throne as Emperor NAPOLEON III ("Second Empire", until 1870).

4102 News of the overthrow of the Citizen King spread across Europe like wildfire, lighting the torch of revolution everywhere. In March 1848, it also broke out in the German Confederation, including Austria (**"March Revolution"**). METTERNICH was forced to resign (13 March 1848). A Constituent National Assembly meeting at St. Paul's Church in Frankfurt (*"Paulskirchenversammlung"*) sought to create a German Reich in lieu of the German Confederation.

➢ Only a few days after the revolution had broken out in France, uprisings also occurred in southern and western Germany. The protesters demanded, among other things, the abolition of censorship and the convening of a German National Assembly. On 31 March, a revolutionary "pre-parliament" met in Frankfurt.

➢ The German Confederal Assembly gave in to this pressure and asked the German states to hold elections for a National Assembly, which they did. The National Assembly met on 18 May 1848 at St. Paul's Church and elected the popular Archduke JOHN as *"Reichsverweser"*, i.e. provisional head of state. The Confederal Assembly then vested its competences in him.

➢ The most urgent concern for the assembly at St. Paul's was the creation of a catalogue of "fundamental rights of the German people". This catalogue was sanctioned by the *Reichsverweser* on 28 December 1848. Discussions on the organisation and borders of the German Reich – which had yet to be established – were postponed, which meant that a significant amount of time was lost and the counter-revolutionary forces were able to gain strength.

➢ Hence, the problem of the extent to which Austria should belong to the German Reich was not resolved at this stage. While the representatives of the *"Greater German Solution"* propagated the inclusion of those parts of Austria that had so far been part of the German Confederation (not all of Austria!) into the German Reich, the supporters of the *"Smaller German Solution"* were in favour of excluding Austria completely.

➢ This debate was also linked to the question of who should be the future head of the Reich; while under the "Greater German Solution", the Austrian emperor was realistically the only potential monarch, the representatives of the "Smaller German Solution" regarded the Prussian king in particular as a candidate for the German throne. Republican ideas were only held by a minority.

➢ Proposals that aimed to unite the entire Austrian monarchy with the German states in an (economic) alliance that would encompass the whole of Central Europe remained entirely unrealistic (*Greater Austrian Solution, Plan of the Seventy Million*).

4103 Under the pressure of events, the monarchs of Austria and Prussia, who at that stage were the only princes of the German Confederation that continued to hold on to absolutism, now also promised to introduce constitutions in their states. On 25 April 1848, Austria received its first constitution in the formal sense – the **Pillersdorf Constitution**, named after its main redactor, the Minister of the Interior FRANZ VON PILLERSDORF – and was thus transformed into a constitutional monarchy.

➢ As early as 14 March, the Austrian emperor agreed to the most urgent demands of the revolutionaries: the abolition of censorship, and the establishment of a "national guard", i.e. a citizen army that would serve as a counterweight to that of the emperor. In the "constitutional promise" of 15 March, this was again reaffirmed and, in addition, the promise was made that "deputies of all provincial estates" would take part in the drafting of a constitution, and that the bourgeoisie in particular would be more strongly represented than originally envisaged. A central assembly of the estates was indeed established, but its influence on the constitution was rather limited, and the latter, especially its chapter on fundamental rights, was primarily PILLERSDORF's work.

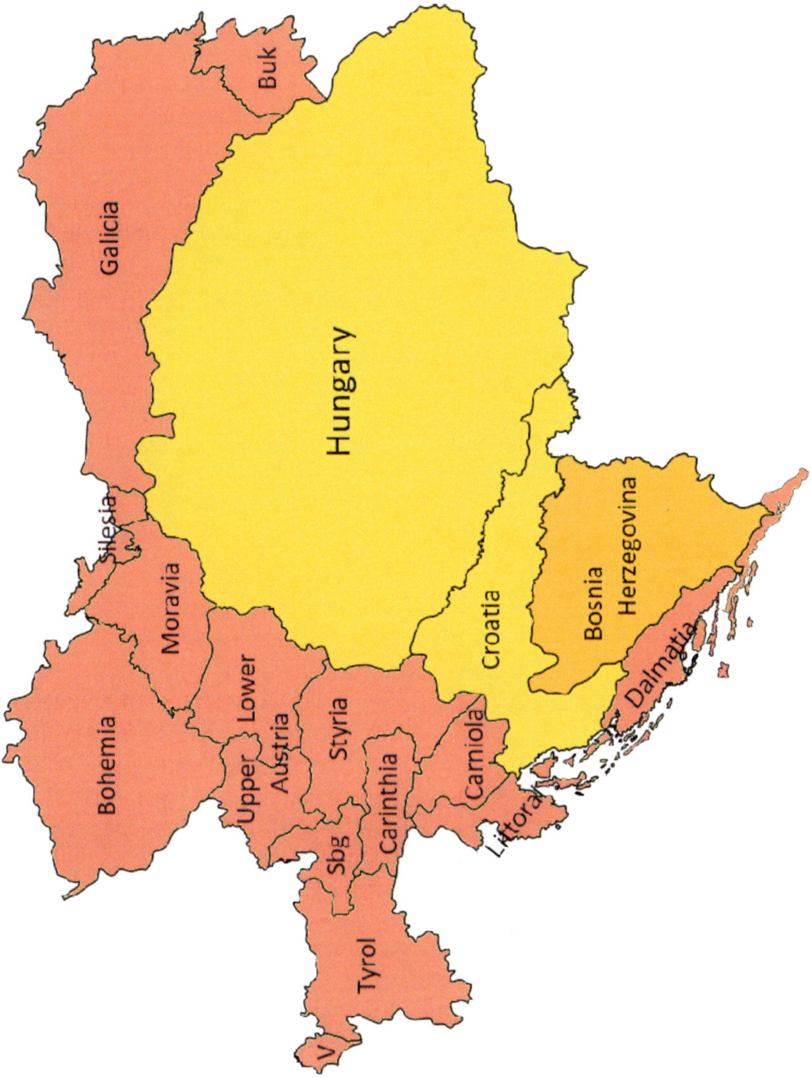

Map 8: The Kingdoms and Countries of the Habsburg Monarchy

Buk = Bukovina, Sbg = Salzburg, V = Vorarlberg
Source: https://commons.wikimedia.org/wiki/File:Austria-Hungary_map_de.svg (slightly revised)
Copyright: public domain

➢ Lombardo-Venetia was excluded from the constitution's scope of application, as this crown land had – as a consequence of the revolution – openly seceded from Austria, expelled the Austrian army, and sought incorporation into an Italian kingdom (yet to be created).

➢ Also excluded was Hungary, since the emperor (in his capacity as king of Hungary) had already two weeks earlier, on 11 April, sanctioned 31 statutes that can be considered a constitution (in the material sense) for Hungary and its other territories (= "Transleithania", i.e. the countries on the other side of the border river Leitha). With these statutes, Hungary became a constitutional monarchy, linked to the rest of Austria only through the person of the shared monarch.

➢ The Bohemian territories, on the other hand, were included in the scope of the Pillersdorf constitution, even though the emperor had also promised to enact a separate constitution for Bohemia.

➢ Thus, the Pillersdorf constitution applied in Bohemia, Moravia, and Silesia as well as in Austria above and below the Enns, Salzburg, Styria, Tyrol and Vorarlberg, Galicia, Bukovina, Illyria (= Carinthia, Carniola, and the Austrian Littoral), and Dalmatia. These territories for the most part continued to form a constitutional entity; they were called "Cisleithanian" and distinguished from the "Transleithanian" territories.

4104 The Pillersdorf constitution was typical of the early-constitutionalist era. Above all, its bicameral system and restrictive electoral law caused outrage among the bourgeoisie and led to a second wave of revolution in May 1848, which resulted in a significant amendment. The *Reichstag* convened for the first time in July 1848 but was relocated from Vienna to the small Moravian town of Kremsier due to a **third revolutionary wave in October 1848**. While most of the revolutionaries' achievements were short-lived, the transformation of the previously collegial court offices into monocratically run ministries has been of lasting significance to this day.

➢ The Pillersdorf constitution provided for a Reichstag that was to be divided into two chambers, the Senate and the Chamber of Deputies, following the British model. Against legislative resolutions of the Reichstag the emperor had an absolute right of veto (⇨ par. 4205). In addition, provincial assemblies should continue to "represent the interests of the provinces" but should have no legislative power of their own.

➢ The House, Court, and State Chancellery was transformed into the *Ministry of Foreign Affairs*, the Bohemian-Austrian Aulic Chancellery into the *Ministry of the Interior*, the Aulic Chamber into the *Ministry of Finance*, and the Aulic War Council into the *Ministry of War*. The administrative matters concerning the judiciary were moved from the Supreme Judicial Office to a new *Ministry of Justice*. The Supreme Judicial Office was thus left with the role of a court of final instance and was therefore renamed the Supreme Court of Justice (*Oberster Gerichtshof*, OGH).

➢ The new ministries – unlike the previous, collegially organised aulic authorities (⇨ par. 3110) – were *monocratically* organised, i.e. led by a single person, which was a prerequisite for assigning the legal responsibility for all actions taken by a ministry to the respective minister. The supreme government body was the *Council of Ministers*, whose meetings were chaired by a *minister-president*. The State Council and the State Conference were dissolved.

➢ The publication of the electoral rules for the Chamber of Deputies on 9 May, which excluded groups such as day labourers, weekly wage earners, and servants from the franchise, led to renewed unrest in Vienna (*May Revolution*). This was also because the elections to the German National Assembly (which also took place in those provinces of Austria that belonged to the German Confederation) had been conducted according to much more progressive electoral rules. Following the "Storm Petition" of 15 May, the Senate was abolished (even before its first meeting) by an imperial proclamation of 16 May. The Austrian Reichstag – now consisting of a single chamber – was declared a constituent assembly (i.e. was tasked with drafting the definitive constitution) and new electoral rules were issued on 30 May.

➢ On this basis, the Reichstag was eventually elected and convened in Vienna on 22 July. Its first and most important task was to pass a resolution on the liberation of the peasants (⇨ par. 2208).

➢ Meanwhile, a fierce dispute broke out with Hungary over the question of whether it should be allowed to pursue its own foreign policy and have its own army. On 3 October, Emperor FERDINAND I (as King of Hungary: FERDINÁND V) dissolved the Hungarian parliament – which the latter ignored.

➢ When the Austrian Minister of War, THEODOR Count BAILLET-LATOUR, planned to send troops to Hungary, another uprising erupted in Vienna ("October Revolution"), during which LATOUR was lynched on 6 October. The emperor and his government fled to Olmütz [Olomouc/CZ], and the Austrian Reichstag was moved to neighbouring Kremsier [Kroměříž/CZ], where the deliberations on a constitution continued.

➢ In Olmütz, FELIX Prince of SCHWARZENBERG was appointed as the new minister-president; unlike his predecessors, who had only been able to remain in office for a few weeks, he succeeded in establishing a lasting government (until 1852). On 2 December, Emperor FERDINAND I abdicated in favour of his 18-year-old nephew FRANCIS JOSEPH I (1848–1916).

4105 The nationalism that openly erupted everywhere in 1848 almost led to the collapse of the Habsburg Monarchy, but its army was able to suppress the revolution throughout the empire and thus preserve its unity for the time being. Both the German *"Paulskirchenversammlung"* and the Austrian Reichstag failed, and the constitutions that they had drafted did not become valid. On 4 March 1849, Emperor FRANCIS JOSEPH decreed ("octroyed") the **March Constitution** (*"Oktroyierte Märzverfassung"*), which introduced a central government for the entire monarchy.

➢ Lombardo-Venetia, which had already seceded from Austria, was won back, preventing the formation of an Italian nation state. Vienna, where the revolution was still ongoing, was besieged and fell; the Hungarian revolutionary army rushing to its aid was forced back. Uprisings in Bohemia and Galicia were also suppressed.

➤ The draft constitution prepared by the Austrian Reichstag ("Kremsier Draft") was a progressive, "high constitutionalist" document that subscribed to the principle of the sovereignty of the people. For this reason, in particular, it was met with disapproval by the SCHWARZENBERG government, and the Reichstag was dissolved on 4 March 1849, even before a formal resolution on the draft had been passed. The fact that the Reichstag of Kremsier, unlike the emperor and his government, did not represent the entire monarchy (especially not Hungary) was used to justify this measure.

➤ Together with the dissolution of the Reichstag, the emperor promulgated the "March Constitution". A constitution for the entire monarchy, it was based on the Kremsier Draft but introduced a number of elements that favoured the monarch; it can therefore be described as "early constitutionalist". This constitution was supplemented by a fundamental rights patent, which only applied in the Cisleithanian territories.

➤ Hungary responded to the constitutional octroi by deposing the House of Habsburg and declaring its sovereignty; LAJOS KOSSUTH took over the government as *"Reichsverweser"*. The Hungarians could only be defeated with Russian armed assistance (capitulation at Világos, 13 August 1849). A bloody punishment of the revolutionaries ensued.

➤ Meanwhile, the proponents of the "Smaller German Solution" had gained the upper hand at St. Paul's. The *Constitution of the German Empire* adopted by the assembly on 28 March 1849 only permitted Austria to join the German Empire if it reduced its relationship with Hungary to a mere personal union, which went against the centralist Austrian March Constitution that had been enacted only a few days earlier.

➤ Apparently in anticipation of Austria's rejection of the constitution, the delegates elected not FRANCIS JOSEPH but the Prussian King FREDERICK WILLIAM IV as the new "Emperor of the Germans". However, the latter had by then also defeated the revolution in his country (constitutional octroi of 5 December 1848) and now refused to accept the "revolutionary crown". The National Assembly had thus failed and was for the most part disbanded; a radical rump parliament in Stuttgart was dissolved by Württemberg troops in June 1849.

➤ After a lengthy and ultimately inconclusive tug of war between Prussia and Austria, the German Confederation was re-established in its old form in 1850.

2. The post-revolutionary era (1852–67)

4106 The March Constitution of 1849 became only partially effective; there were no Reichstag elections and the emperor *de facto* exercised the right to legislate on his own ("pseudo-constitutionalism"). On 20 August 1851, essential parts of the constitution were suspended in the *"August Decrees"*; on 31 December 1851, it was fully repealed in the *"Sylvester Patents"* (named after the day of the feast of St. Sylvester, which coincides with New Year's Eve). The era of **neo-absolutism** began.

➢ As a result of the revolution, a "state of siege" (i.e. a state of emergency) prevailed over large parts of the monarchy (Vienna, Prague, all of Hungary, Galicia, Lombardo-Venetia); the administration of these areas was in the hands of the military, and fundamental rights did not apply or applied only to a limited extent.

➢ Since a new parliament was not convened after the dissolution of the Kremsier Reichstag, new legislation was enacted either by means of transitional provisions or by using the emergency decrees provided for in the March Constitution. On paper, however, the validity of the March Constitution was upheld for the time being. Hence, the period 1849–51 can be described as "pseudo-constitutional".

➢ From about 1850 onwards, the young emperor attempted to emancipate himself from his dominant minister-president SCHWARZENBERG and initiated the realisation of the Reichsrat, which had been envisaged in the constitution as a supreme advisory body alongside and in competition with the Council of Ministers. The Reichsrat took up its work in April 1851.

➢ The March Constitution was abolished in 1849 in a two-stage coup d'état; with the "August Decrees" of 20 August 1851, the Reichsrat was released from its ties to the Council of Ministers and transformed into a crown council, and ministerial responsibility was abolished. The Reichsrat and the Council of Ministers were instructed to debate whether the March Constitution of 1849 should be retained.

➢ On 31 December 1851, the March Constitution and the supplementary fundamental rights patent were each repealed by one of the "Sylvester Patents". A simple letter from the emperor to the minister-president of the same day provided the basic outlines of a future organisation of the state, which were, however, only partially implemented.

➢ After SCHWARZENBERG's death in 1852, the Council of Ministers as such was dissolved, and the ministers only met for "conferences". The emperor concentrated all powers in his hands; the constitutional practice of the years 1852–59 is therefore described as "neo-absolutism".

➢ Hungary, subjugated by military intervention, unsuccessfully demanded a return to its "31 statutes" of 1848. Instead, it was deemed to have lost all its privileges, and Austrian laws were introduced there as well. A new Press Code reintroduced censorship throughout the monarchy in 1852. By 1854, it became possible to lift the state of emergency throughout the empire.

➢ FRANCIS JOSEPH's strictly centralist policy was his reaction to the separatist efforts of the individual nationalities during the revolution. He relied on the army, the civil service, and the Catholic Church. A concordat was concluded with the latter in 1855, which restored its great influence on education and suspended the secular marriage law in relation to Catholics (⇨ par. 4221).

4107 Together with NAPOLEON III, the King of Piedmont-Sardinia succeeded in unifying Italy (**"*Risorgimento*"**); Austria's domination of the Apennine Peninsula was brought to an end. On 14 March 1861, VICTOR EMMANUEL II of Piedmont-Sardinia assumed the title of "King of Italy".

➢ In 1848, CHARLES ALBERT of Piedmont-Sardinia (1831–49) had already made himself the head of the Italian unification movement as the only "national" king (in contrast to the other rulers on Italian soil – the Habsburg and Bourbon monarchs and the pope), but he had been defeated by the Austrian army (⇨ par. 4105).

➢ In the Russian-Turkish Crimean War (1853–56), in which the UK and France fought on the Turkish side against the hegemonic claims of the Russian Empire, Piedmont-Sardinia distinguished itself as an ally of France. The two nations formed a defensive alliance that was directed against Austria. Austria, on the other hand, was isolated internationally precisely because it had remained neutral in the Crimean War.

➢ In 1859, Austria went to war with a pre-emptive strike against Piedmont-Sardinia, which then received help from France. They succeeded in defeating Austria at the Battle of Solferino. In the Peace of Zurich, FRANCIS JOSEPH had to cede Lombardy; only Veneto remained with the Habsburg Monarchy (until 1866).

➢ Subsequently, the small states of central Italy and the Kingdom of Sicily joined Piedmont-Sardinia (following referenda on this matter). The territorial scope of the constitution imposed on Piedmont-Sardinia by CHARLES ALBERT on 4 March 1848 (*"Statuto Albertino"*) was thus successively extended to the entire peninsula. The deposed princes went into exile.

➢ The Papal State was able to assert itself (in a reduced form) until 1870, on account of NAPOLEON III's pro-church policy; hence, Florence was initially chosen as the capital of Italy instead of Rome.

➢ FLORENCE NIGHTINGALE had already laid the first foundations for modern war nursing during the Crimean War when the Battle of Solferino prompted the Swiss HENRY DUNANT to establish the Red Cross in 1863. On 22 August 1864, twelve states signed the "Geneva Convention for the Amelioration of the Condition of the Wounded in Armies in the Field" that had been drafted by the Red Cross. It stipulated, among other things, that wounded and sick soldiers be treated humanely and not be killed or injured. The role of the Red Cross was to effectively protect such individuals. Many other states joined the agreement later, Austria in 1866.

4108 The military defeat in Italy and the resulting financial crisis forced FRANCIS JOSEPH to abandon his neo-absolutist policy; nevertheless, he refused to return to constitutionalism. However, with the **October Diploma of 1860**, he promised to establish representative bodies of the estates and once again granted Hungary a special position within the monarchy.

➢ To close the huge budget gap that resulted from the war, Finance Minister KARL VON BRUCK in 1859 recommended issuing state bonds and also convening "men of trust" from among the population who were to supervise the financial affairs of the state.

Table 5: Constitutional developments 1848–1867

Austria	Hungary
25 April 1848: Pillersdorf Constitution early constitutionalist; Reichstag is convened and sits from July 1848 to March 1849	11 April 1848: 31 statutes const. monarchy
1848/49: Kremsier constitutional draft high-constitutionalist, federalist; never came into existence	*Revolution*: „forfeiture of the constitution“
4 March 1849: Octroyed March Constitution early constitutionalist; Reichstag is not convened, constitutional reality: pseudo-constitutionalism	⇨ in force also in Hungary
31 Dec. 1851: **Sylvester Patents** Constitutionalism is abandoned; neo-corporative system is only envisaged; constitutional reality: neo-absolutism	⇨ in force also in Hungary
20 Oct. 1860: October Diploma attempted reform: neo-corporative system amended before the Reichsrat convenes	⇨ in force also in Hungary, but special status
26 Feb. 1861: February Patent Reichsrat and diets based on a neo-corporative system. Largely effective, but "wider Reichsrat" is boycotted by Hungary	⇨ in force also in Hungary, but special status
20 Sept. 1865: **"Sistierungspatent"** temporarily suspends the Basic Law of 1861	⇦ compromise negotiations
21 Dec. 1867: December Constitution (five Basic Laws) constitutionalist; limited federalism; becomes effective; Czech boycott until 1879	**Compromise** (statute XII/1867) Return to the constitution of 1848

➢ Accordingly, on 5 March 1860, Emperor FRANCIS JOSEPH convened a "reinforced" Reichsrat, to which – in addition to the existing members of the Reichsrat– a number of politicians who enjoyed the confidence of the nobility and bourgeoisie were appointed. The draft budget for 1861 was submitted to the new body for consultation. Not long afterwards, on 17 July, the emperor declared that he would from now on only undertake certain actions in relation to the state finances (in particular the introduction of new taxes and the taking out of loans) if they had been approved by this reinforced Reichsrat.

➢ The reinforced Reichsrat met between May and September 1860 and used the debates on the budget for an extensive criticism of the emperor's centralist and neo-absolutist policies.

➢ FRANCIS JOSEPH responded to this criticism on 20 October 1860 with an "Imperial Diploma Governing the Internal Constitutional Affairs of the Monarchy" (the "October Diploma"). Henceforth, legislation was to involve the "participation" of the diets or the Reichsrat, and the diets were to send deputies from their midst to the latter. Their right of approval was limited to certain financial matters; otherwise, their "participation" was of an advisory nature only.

➢ Note the – at first glance confusing – German terminology; the word *Reichstag* was avoided for being "too constitutionalist", and the central body was instead referred to as the *Reichsrat*, although it was actually no longer a crown council but a parliament. The "old" Reichsrat (i.e. the crown council created in 1851) was initially retained, renamed the "State Council" in 1861, and finally abolished in 1868.

➢ In addition to the October Diploma, Provincial Statutes were passed for four of the Cisleithanian crown lands (Styria, Carinthia, Salzburg, Tyrol), which determined the composition of their parliaments. They were not parliaments in the constitutionalist sense, but rather (neo-)corporative assemblies of the estates with only an advisory function (⇨ par. 2220). The clergy and the nobility were given same weight as the bourgeoisie and the peasants. The new Provincial Statutes met with strong criticism, and it was decided that further Provincial Statutes for the other Cisleithanian crown lands should not be enacted.

➢ The Transleithanian diets (of Hungary, Croatia, and Transylvania) were also structured along the divisions between the estates in accordance with the model that had already existed before 1848. However, in contrast to the Cisleithanian diets, they had a genuine right to pass laws; furthermore, their competences were much wider, as they were also responsible for civil, criminal, and trade law, among other things. In Cisleithania, these matters fell under the competence of a "narrower" Reichsrat, which was the Reichsrat without its Transleithanian members.

➢ The parliament for the monarchy as a whole, on the other hand, was called the "wider" Reichsrat; it had only limited competences pertaining to conscription to the military, imperial finances, etc. Certain matters (the *"prerogatives of the crown"*) remained excluded from parliamentary participation at all and continued to be decided by the emperor alone.

➢ The centralised administration was also partly abandoned; the (until then centralised) ministries of the interior, culture, and justice were dissolved, and their competences passed to a *minister of state* in Cisleithania, a *court chancellor* in Hungary, and another *court chancellor* in Croatia. The foreign, war, and finance ministers, on the other hand, remained competent for the entire monarchy. All ministers and court chancellors met in the Austrian *Council of Ministers*, which was now once again headed by a *minister-president*.

4109 The corporative system of the Provincial Statutes of 1860 in particular met with strong criticism from the bourgeoisie; thus, FRANCIS JOSEPH decided to make substantial changes to the rules passed only four months earlier (**"February Patent" 1861**). This allowed for the reconvening of the diets and a central parliament, the Reichsrat, in the spring of 1861 – after a hiatus of more than twelve years. However, the February Patent was still not a constitution in the constitutionalist sense, and in Hungary, the entire system created in 1860/61 was rejected.

➢ The February Patent of 1861 was intended as a means to implement the October Diploma of 1860, but it also modified it in a number of important respects. The Reichsrat and the diets were given genuine legislative rights; although their internal structure remained neo-corporative, it was still substantially modified in favour of the bourgeoisie.

➢ The Reichsrat was now divided into two chambers: a House of Lords (⇨ par. 4209), and a House of Deputies (⇨ par. 4211). The distinction between a "wider" and a "narrower" Reichsrat, i.e. with or without Hungarian deputies, was retained.

➢ In formal terms, the February Patent consisted of a promulgation patent and 46 annexes, including a *Basic Law on Imperial Representation*, which determined the composition and competences of the Reichsrat. Each of the 15 Cisleithanian crown lands had a *land ordinance*, *electoral rules* for the respective diet, and a *formula for the number of deputies* that each diet was to send to the House of Deputies of the Reichsrat.

➢ Under the promulgation patent, these annexes, together with the Pragmatic Sanction of 1713, the October Diploma of 1860, and the remaining legal acts of October 1860, formed the "Constitution of Our Empire" (misleadingly referred to in modern literature as the *Imperial Constitution 1861*). However, this was not a constitution in the constitutionalist sense either. Of the three powers (in the sense of MONTESQUIEU, ⇨ par. 4204), only legislation was covered; there were no provisions on fundamental rights, the separation of powers, ministerial responsibility, etc.

➢ The theory previously taught by legal historians that the October Diploma was "federalist", whereas the February Patent was "centralist", has been superseded by more recent research. The distribution of competences between the state and the crown lands hardly changed between 1860 and 1861; the Transleithanian lands were not affected by the February Patent of 1861 at all, since their diets convened according to the regulations of 1860.

➢ In Hungary, all of the above-mentioned norms met with opposition, and the country demanded a return to its 31 statutes from 1848. The Hungarian diet did convene but was soon dissolved again, and Hungary boycotted the wider Reichsrat. The Cisleithanian diets and the narrower Reichsrat, on the other hand, convened in the spring of 1861 and established a parliamentary continuity that remained (almost) unbroken until 1918.

4110 In the German Confederation, the antagonism between Prussia and Austria became increasingly acute and finally led to the *Austro-Prussian War* of 1866. Prussia's victory led to Austria's exclusion from the German Confederation. A unification of Germany according to the "Smaller German solution" (⇨ par. 4102) was prevented by France, thus only a **North German Confederation** (*"Norddeutscher Bund"*) was initially established.

➢ The Prussian Minister-President OTTO VON BISMARCK (1862–90), in particular, pushed for a decision on the "German question" not through negotiations but through "iron and blood". A convention of the German princes in Frankfurt in 1863, which had been summoned by Austria for the purpose of reforming the German Confederation, was boycotted by Prussia and thus doomed to fail.

➢ In the German-Danish War of 1864, Austria and Prussia jointly conquered Schleswig-Holstein, which was linked to Denmark in a personal union; the dispute over the political future of this territory was the trigger for the Austro-Prussian War of 1866. In this war, most of the German states were on Austria's side, while Prussia formed an alliance with Italy, thus forcing Austria into a war on two fronts. The decisive battle of Königgrätz ended with an overwhelming Prussian victory.

➢ Prussia annexed several states allied with Austria (Hanover, Hesse-Kassel, Nassau, Frankfurt) as well as Schleswig-Holstein, but spared the Habsburg Monarchy, which only had to cede Veneto to Italy and agree to the dissolution of the German Confederation.

➢ The early termination of the war by Prussia was not least due to the threat of France's entry into the war. On 14 July 1866, two weeks after Königgrätz, BISMARCK notified NAPOLEON III that he would abandon the plan to create a German Empire; instead, Prussia was only to unite with the states north of the Main River to form the North German Confederation.

➢ Despite its English designation as a "confederation", the North German Confederation was not an alliance under international law but a federal state. Sovereignty lay with the Federal Council, in which the constituent states were represented by members of their governments; it was chaired by Prussia. The Reichstag was directly elected by the entire male population and had legislative power, together with the Federal Council (⇨ par. 4209). The executive branch was headed by the federal chancellor, a position BISMARCK held alongside that of Prussian minister-president.

4111 In the United States, tensions between the industrialised northern states and the agrarian, slave-owning southern states grew and led to the secession of eleven southern states in 1860/61, which loosely joined together to form the "Confederate States of America". In the

American Civil War (1861–1865), the Confederate States were defeated and forced to rejoin the Union. In 1865, slavery was abolished in the United States.

➢ The rift between the northern and southern states was not directly caused by the slavery issue; some northern states also allowed slavery. In the south, however, a large part of the economy (including extensive cotton plantations) was based on slavery. The demand for its abolition (*abolitionism*) seemed unacceptable to those with economic power.

➢ When the abolitionist ABRAHAM LINCOLN (1861–65) was elected president of the USA in 1860 with the votes of the Northern states alone, the split manifested itself openly. One month after the election, South Carolina seceded from the Union, followed by other states (Georgia, Texas, etc.). The Union, on the other hand, disputed the right of the federal states to secede.

➢ After their military defeat in 1865, the southern states were initially occupied by the Union; self-government was restored from 1869. The US Constitution was amended in 1865/70 to include three amendments that abolished slavery, established the equality of all citizens before the law and prohibited electoral discrimination on the basis of race. However, the southern states passed laws that enforced racial segregation, which the US Supreme Court found to be constitutional in 1896. It was not until a century after the end of the civil war that the civil rights movement, led by MARTIN LUTHER KING Jr., succeeded in eliminating this racial discrimination with the Civil Rights Act of 1964.

➢ In 1862, France, Spain, and the UK used the temporary weakness of the USA for a military intervention in Mexico aimed at forcibly collecting irrecoverable debts. Subsequently, in 1864, NAPOLEON III appointed a puppet government under the Habsburg archduke MAXIMILIAN as "Emperor of Mexico". It was only after the end of the Civil War that the USA was able to enforce the withdrawal of French troops, causing the puppet regime to collapse; MAXIMILIAN was shot dead by Republican troops in 1867.

3. The Austro-Hungarian Monarchy (1867–1918)

4112 FRANCIS JOSEPH was politically compromised by the military defeats in Germany and Italy and forced to radically restructure his empire. The negotiations for a solution to the Hungarian question, which had already been resumed in 1865, culminated in the **"Austro-Hungarian Compromise"** of 1867.

➢ The attempt at reconciliation between the imperial government and the Hungarian estates, which had begun with the October Diploma and the February Patent, had ultimately failed in the summer of 1861. The negotiations, which had reached a "dead end", were only resumed in the spring of 1865, when the Hungarian politician FERENC DEÁK acknowledged the Pragmatic Sanction of 1713/23 (⇨ par. 3104) as the basis for relations between Hungary and the other territories of the Habsburg Monarchy and concluded from this that certain matters (the "pragmatic affairs", ⇨ par. 4115) would necessarily have to be regulated by both sides together.

➢ In order to be able to negotiate with DEÁK and the other representatives of the Hungarian estates on his own, the emperor once again decided to infringe on the constitution. With the *"Sistierungspatent"* of 20 September 1865, he temporarily suspended the Basic Law on Imperial Representation of 1861 and dissolved the Reichsrat. For two years (1865–67), Cisleithania was again ruled as an absolute monarchy.

➢ On 8 June 1867, FRANCIS JOSEPH was crowned King of Hungary. The 31 statutes of 1848 were reinstated but also supplemented by the statute XII/1867 (the Hungarian Compromise Act), which reorganised relations with Cisleithania. When the latter issued its own Compromise Act within the framework of the December Constitution (⇨ par. 4113), this led to a series of conflicts, as the two statutes differed in some respects.

➢ FRANCIS JOSEPH now referred to himself as "Emperor of Austria, King of Bohemia, etc. and Apostolic King of Hungary" (note the word "and" - expressing a certain distance!). Joint authorities for both parts of the empire were referred to as "k.u.k." (*"kaiserlich und königlich" – imperial and royal*), with authorities responsible only for Cisleithania as "k.k." (*"kaiserlich-königlich" – imperial-royal*), and authorities responsible only for Hungary as "m.k." (*"magyar királyi"* – royal Hungarian).

➢ The monarchy itself was renamed the "Austro-Hungarian Monarchy"; its legal nature was a matter of dispute. Hungarian constitutional lawyers, in particular, held the view that Hungary and Austria were merely linked to each other in personal and real unions, but that there was no (federal) state (?) uniting the two.

4113 With the **December Constitution** of 21 December 1867, the non-Hungarian ("Cisleithanian") crown lands were given a constitution that would essentially last until 1918.

➢ The monarch's far-reaching concessions towards Hungary met with massive protest in Cisleithania. The (narrower) Reichsrat was not reconvened until the deal had been sealed; it met again in 1867 after a two-year break. When the government demanded that it accept the Compromise with Hungary, the Reichsrat in turn demanded constitutional reforms in Cisleithania.

➢ As a compromise, the Constitutional Committee of the House of Deputies in July 1867 offered not to adopt a new constitution but to modify the February Constitution and the Basic Law of 1861, as well as to supplement them with additional statutes. These were subsequently drafted by the Reichsrat and received their imperial sanction on 21 December 1867 (*December Constitution*).

➢ Unlike in Hungary, in Cisleithania, the theory of the continued existence of an Austrian state in which Hungary only had a special position initially prevailed. Thus, the term "Austria" as a synonym for Cisleithania was avoided, and the cumbersome designation "the kingdoms and lands represented in the Reichsrat" was used in official texts instead ("Cisleithania" itself was never an official state name!). Only from 1915 onwards was Cisleithania officially referred to as "Austria", which might be interpreted as a success of the Hungarian point of view.

4114 The December Constitution was not a uniform constitutional document but consisted of several basic laws (**"Staatsgrundgesetze"**). These were:

➢ The *Basic Law on Imperial Representation of 1861*, which governed the composition and competences of the Reichsrat (with some amendments made in 1867);

➢ the *Basic Law on the General Rights of Nationals for the Kingdoms and Lands Represented in the Reichsrat*, with a catalogue of fundamental rights that was essentially modelled on the catalogue from 1849;

➢ the *Basic Law Establishing an Imperial Court,* whose main task was to protect the fundamental rights;

➢ the *Basic Law on the Judiciary*, which, among other things, guaranteed the independence of the judiciary and the separation of powers, and introduced administrative jurisdiction;

➢ the *Basic Law on the Executive*; which, among other things, governed the requirement of countersignature and ministerial responsibility (referring to an already existing law, the Ministerial Responsibility Act 1867, ⇨ par. 4218); and

➢ the *Delegation Act*, a basic law that governed the affairs common to all lands of the Austrian-Hungarian Monarchy and how they should be managed (the Austrian Compromise Act), albeit with some deviations from the Hungarian Compromise Act.

4115 Following the Compromise, Austria (Cisleithania) and Hungary (Transleithania) were bound together by the person of the monarch and the **pragmatic affairs**. In addition, some other **("dualistic") affairs** were treated separately in formal terms but managed according to the same principles. Austria-Hungary also constituted a *customs and economic union*. Nevertheless, both parts of the "Dual Monarchy" were independent of each other in most areas.

➢ Accordingly, two governments with equal status existed in Vienna and Budapest, each under a minister-president (k.k. and m.k. respectively), as well as two parliaments: the k.k. *Reichsrat* for Cisleithania; and the m.k. *Országgyűlés* for Transleithania.

➢ Foreign affairs, warfare, and the financial affairs pertaining to them were defined as common (*pragmatic*) affairs. A joint Austro-Hungarian (k.u.k.) minister was appointed for each of the three portfolios.

➢ *Dualistic affairs* were, in particular, customs, certain indirect taxes, the coinage and monetary systems, and the "determination of the military system" (universal conscription was adopted in 1868).

➢ In dualistic affairs, the Austrian and Hungarian parliaments and ministries should formally enact independent laws and ordinances, but their content should be the same (*harmonised legislation*).

➢ For legislation in pragmatic affairs, on the other hand, the two parliaments were to form delegations from among themselves, which would usually deliberate separately and only communicate with each other in writing, thus avoiding the impression of a joint parliament. A joint session was only permissible in exceptional cases and occurred only rarely.

➢ While the Austrian Compromise Act stipulated that legislation in pragmatic matters should be passed by concordant resolutions of the Austrian and Hungarian delegations, under the Hungarian Compromise Act, only the two parliaments themselves were competent to pass new laws, and the latter approach prevailed. Thus, in practice, laws on pragmatic matters (after preliminary deliberation in the delegations) were passed by concordant resolutions of the Austrian and the Hungarian parliaments, i.e. almost in the same way as laws on dualistic matters.

➢ Although warfare was a pragmatic affair, and a k.u.k. army and fleet existed accordingly, Hungary demanded and was granted its own body of military troops, the m.k. *Honvéd*. For reasons of parity, a k.k. *Landwehr* was established in Ciseithania in 1869, which meant that three armed forces existed alongside each other. However, care was taken to ensure that the Honvéd, in particular, could not turn against the k.u.k. army; for example, it had no artillery.

4116 The **ethnic question**, which had remained unresolved in 1867, became Austria-Hungary's main constitutional problem in the following years. The conflicts between the different nationalities obstructed parliamentary life, in particular, and thus led to a partial return to authoritarian power structures.

➢ Of those surveyed in the 1910 census, around 24 percent gave German, 20 percent Magyar, 17 percent Czech or Slovak, 10 percent Polish, 8 percent Serbo-Croat, 8 percent Ukrainian, 7 percent Romanian, 3 percent Slovenian, and 2 percent Italian as their mother tongue or everyday language. Thus, the Slavs, with a total of around 46 percent, constituted the largest segment of the population; nevertheless, the Germans and Magyars were the politically dominant ethnicities in the monarchy.

➢ The Czechs, in particular, protested against the special status granted to the Magyars in the Compromise of 1867 and boycotted the Reichsrat from 1867–79. In 1871, the Bohemian diet demanded a revision of the Compromise and a reorganisation of the monarchy based on an Austro-Bohemian-Hungarian trialism ("Bohemian Fundamental Articles"), but due to the resistance of the German Liberals and the Hungarians, this was never realised.

➢ The crown lands of Voivodina and Transylvania, which had been separated from Hungary in 1849/50, were reunited with Hungary in 1860 and 1868 respectively, and the Magyar language was made the state language throughout the kingdom. A ruthless policy of Magyarisation ensued. Only Croatia was granted a certain degree of autonomy in the "Hungarian-Croatian Compromise" of 1868 (independent legislation in civil and criminal law matters, etc.).

➢ In Cisleithania, on the other hand, the equality of the ethnic groups was constitutionally guaranteed (Article 19 of the Basic Law on Fundamental Rights). Hence, at least theoretically, every language spoken in these crown lands should have had equal status in the communication between the authorities and individuals ("external official language") and their internal

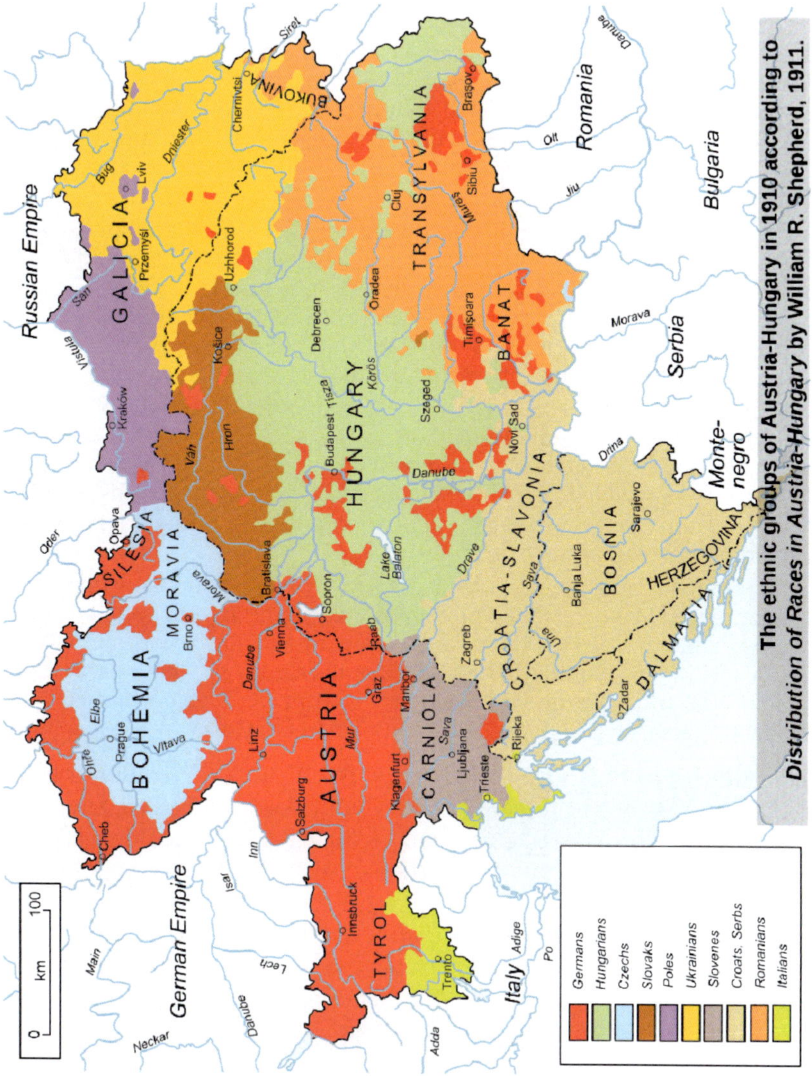

Map 9: The Ethnic Groups of the Habsburg Monarchy
Source: https://upload.wikimedia.org/wikipedia/commons/4/47/Austria_Hungary_ethnic.svg
Copyright: public domain

operations ("internal official language"), as well as at state schools. However, this constitutional imperative was often ignored in practice, even by supreme authorities, and the German language was clearly favoured.

➢ The courts of public law (Imperial Court and Administrative Court) regarded Article 19 as a directly applicable norm and developed a rich body of judicature on it. The House of Deputies took hardly any initiatives to solve the ethnic problem; on the contrary, non-German deputies were discriminated against there as well (e.g. by not recording speeches in languages other than German).

➢ A decree for Bohemia initiated in 1897 by Minister-President KASIMIR Count BADENI (1895–97) stipulated that the Czech language should have equal status with German as both an external and internal official language (*"Badenische Sprachverordnung"*). However, as this would have meant that German-speaking civil servants would have had to learn Czech, this led to major riots. BADENI had to resign and his decree was repealed.

➢ Around the turn of the century, the ethnic conflict became increasingly acute; disruptive incidents rendered the Reichsrat incapable of doing its work for months at a time, and the governments – which since 1893 had hardly ever been able to stay in office for more than a few months – had to rely more and more on emergency decrees under § 14 of the Basic Law on Imperial Representation (⇨ par. 4207).

➢ A promising approach to solving the ethnic problem, at least with regard to the electoral rules, was adopted in Moravia, where from 1905 onwards those eligible to vote cast their votes in separate ballots according to their ethnic affiliation; the number of German and Czech-speaking parliamentarians was predetermined as well (the "Moravian Compromise"). This model was also adopted in Bosnia and Bukovina in 1910.

4117 The **electoral reforms** initiated by the Minister-Presidents EDUARD Count TAAFFE in 1882, KASIMIR Count BADENI in 1896, and MAX VLADIMIR Baron VON BECK in 1907 (⇨ par. 4212) considerably extended the franchise and thus led to an upheaval of the distribution of votes in the Cisleithanian Reichsrat. While the parliament had until then been dominated by the conflict between the German liberals on the one hand and the conservative and national parties on the other, the new mass parties – the Social Democrats and the Christian Socials – now entered the Reichsrat.

➢ The Czech boycott of the Reichsrat from 1867–79 increased the parliamentary power of the German Liberal Party, which dominated political life in this era. It had already played a decisive role in the drafting of the December Constitution (and was thus also called the Constitutional Party). Under the governments led by the brothers KARL (1867/68) and ADOLPH Prince AUERSPERG (1871–79), many of the principles laid down in the Constitution were translated into simple laws (e.g.: the Confessional "May Laws" of 1868 and 1874, ⇨ par. 4221; the direct election of the House of Deputies in 1873, ⇨ par. 4209; the Code of Criminal Procedure 1873 with the general introduction of jury trials, ⇨ par. 4310; the creation of the Imperial Court in 1869 and the Administrative Court in 1876; etc.).

➢ The 1879 election radically changed the political situation; the Liberals went into opposition, and Minister-President TAAFFE (1879–93) was able to establish a government based on a coalition of German Clericals, Slavs, and Romanians (the "Iron Ring"). During this period, the first social security laws were passed (accident insurance in 1887, health insurance in 1888).

➢ In 1888/89, at the Hainfeld Party Congress, VIKTOR ADLER succeeded in uniting the social democratic movements into the Social Democratic Workers' Party. Representing primarily the interests of the working class, it fought for universal suffrage and against restrictions on the freedom of the press; in terms of its ideology, it relied mainly on Marxism, of which it developed an Austrian variant ("Austro-Marxism").

➢ Pope LEO XIII established a tradition of Catholic social teaching in 1891 with the encyclical *"Rerum Novarum"* (⇨ par. 7213). It was the ideological basis for the new Christian Social Party formed under KARL LUEGER (Mayor of Vienna 1897–1910). As the party of mainly the petty bourgeoisie and peasants, it too advocated an extension of the franchise but also emphasised its loyalty to the Imperial House. Its religious and social orientations coincided with resentment against the Jewish upper middle classes, which eventually manifested itself in anti-Semitic policies (⇨ par. 7202).

➢ Liberal and conservative parties disintegrated or were absorbed into the new mass parties as the latter became more established. A radical residue of the former Constitutional Party, the German National Party, regrouped under GEORG Ritter VON SCHÖNERER. This party also propagated social reforms but was especially characterised by its anti-Semitism and anticlericalism. Adhering to the "Greater German Solution", it sought to solve the ethnic question by detaching the German parts of Austria from the monarchy and annexing them to Germany.

4. The European Empires and the World

4118 **Spain**, which lost almost all its colonial possessions during the 19th century, was shaken internally by conflicts over the throne as well as civil wars. The end of Spanish colonial rule in America (1898) also marked the beginning of the **USA's** colonialist ambitions.

➢ When Queen ISABELLA II was to succeed her father to the Spanish throne in 1834, this met with opposition from her uncle, who claimed the throne himself as "CHARLES V". This led to the "Carlist Wars"; ISABELLA was able to stand her ground against the Carlists but was overthrown in 1868, following a military coup. The crown was now offered to others, among them a distant relative of the Prussian king (the "Hohenzollern Candidature for the Spanish Throne"), who was then forced to renounce it due to pressure from France, which in turn triggered the Franco-German War of 1870/71 (⇨ par. 4119).

➢ In 1873, Spain became a republic; in 1874, a coup d'état led to the restoration of the monarchy under the Bourbons. The last American colonies (Cuba and Puerto Rico) as well as the Philippines were lost in a war against the USA in 1898.

➢ In 1902, Cuba became a formally sovereign state, but remained dependent on the USA; Puerto Rico and the Philippines became US colonies. While the Philippines gained independence in 1945, Puerto Rico is still an "unincorporated territory" of the USA and thus remains in a quasi-colonial situation.

➢ In the United States' interior, the Native Americans were cruelly persecuted and their living space was progressively diminished. Often, they were forcibly relocated. In 1890, the last pockets of armed resistance were crushed.

4119 The long-standing rivalry between Prussia and France led to the Franco-Prussian War in 1870. The victory of the allied German troops led to the formation of the **German Reich** in 1871.

➢ In formal terms, this was achieved by the southern German states joining the North German Confederation, whose constitution was adopted with minor changes. The German Reich was thus also a federal state. Although the Prussian King WILLIAM I assumed the title of "German emperor" on 18 January 1871, the other princes were not deposed (unlike in Italy). Sovereignty remained with the Federal Council, the representative body of the German states. It exercised the legislative power together with the Reichstag, which was elected by the people. The "federal chancellor" became an "Reich chancellor". Until 1918, this office was almost always held by the man who was also the Prussian minister-president (1867/71–90: OTTO VON BISMARCK).

➢ NAPOLEON III was captured by German troops, and the *Third French Republic* was proclaimed in Paris on 4 September 1870. Attempts to establish a Socialist government (Paris Commune 1871), as well as efforts to restore the Bourbon monarchy, failed.

➢ France withdrew its troops from Rome in 1870, which was subsequently conquered by Italy and declared its capital (end of the Papal State). It was not until 1929 ("Lateran Treaties") that the pope was again granted (symbolic) sovereignty over the "Vatican State" (0.44 sq km).

4120 Reich Chancellor BISMARCK sought to secure the newly won German unity through an **alliance system of European powers**. After his resignation in 1890, however, the German Emperor WILLIAM II (1888–1918) increasingly headed for a confrontation with the other great powers.

➢ France had been forced to cede Alsace-Lorraine to Germany in the war of 1870/71, resulting in deep discord. BISMARCK initially succeeded in isolating France internationally and formed alliances with Austria-Hungary and Russia (the "Three Emperors' Alliance").

➢ WILLIAM II, on the other hand, vigorously pursued the construction of a German fleet and a German colonial empire, which posed a threat to the British Empire. This allowed France to enter into alliances with its former archenemies, the UK and Russia; this *"Entente"* encircled Germany and its ally Austria-Hungary (the "Dual Alliance").

4121 The imperialist aspirations of the great European powers led to the **colonisation of almost all of Africa and large parts of Asia** by 1914, which gave rise to numerous conflicts between the great powers. The colonies were ruthlessly exploited as sources of raw materials and sales markets. European (legal) culture was also exported to the colonies, albeit often at the price of destroying the autochthonous cultures.

➢ In India, the 1857 uprising against the British East India Company was violently suppressed by the UK. The Mughal Emperor (⇨ par. 3108), who had formally led the uprising, was deposed, but the British East India Company was also dissolved and India (comprising the present-day states of India, Pakistan, Bangladesh, and Myanmar) was declared a British crown colony. In 1876, Queen VICTORIA (1837–1901) assumed the title of Empress of India, thereby establishing herself as successor to the Mughal Emperors, but also claiming equality of rank with the European emperors.

➢ In Africa, the European colonial powers had long been content with trading posts on the coast. Only in South Africa had there been a settler colony (initially Dutch, then British) since the 17th century (⇨ par. 3118). In 1830, France began conquering Algeria, which until then had been part of the Ottoman Empire. Egypt (which formally belonged to the Ottoman Empire until 1920) was effectively ruled by the UK from 1882.

➢ Around the same time, other European countries also became increasingly interested in a complete subjugation of Africa. The Berlin Conference of 1884/85, at which 12 European countries, the United States and the "International Congo Society", agreed on free trade throughout the Congo River Basin, among other things, is commonly regarded as the starting point of the subsequent "Scramble for Africa". During this period, the UK and France in particular subjugated huge parts of the continent; smaller parts went to Germany, Portugal, Spain, and Italy. Only Ethiopia and Liberia were able to maintain their independence.

➢ The "International Congo Society" was run by the Belgian King LEOPOLD II himself, who, as a result of the Berlin Conference, became the de-facto ruler of the Congo Basin (today's Democratic Republic of Congo) . Its indigenous population was subjected to brutal oppression, and millions of people were killed or maimed. It was only in 1908 that LEOPOLD II was forced to cede the Congo to the Belgian state, which continued to exercise colonial rule until 1960.

➢ With the Madrid Convention of 1880, the European powers agreed not to subject the Kingdom of Morocco to a single colonial regime, but to mutually recognise their separate spheres of influence. When France nonetheless occupied two Moroccan cities in 1911, Germany also deployed military forces to Morocco, which almost triggered a world war (Morocco crisis). Ultimately, France was able to make Morocco a French colony in 1912, while Germany was compensated with areas in Cameroon.

➢ Austria-Hungary did not participate in the Scramble for Africa; it did not establish a colonial empire at all, mainly due to its weakened international position after the defeats suffered in 1859/66, as well as its Balkan

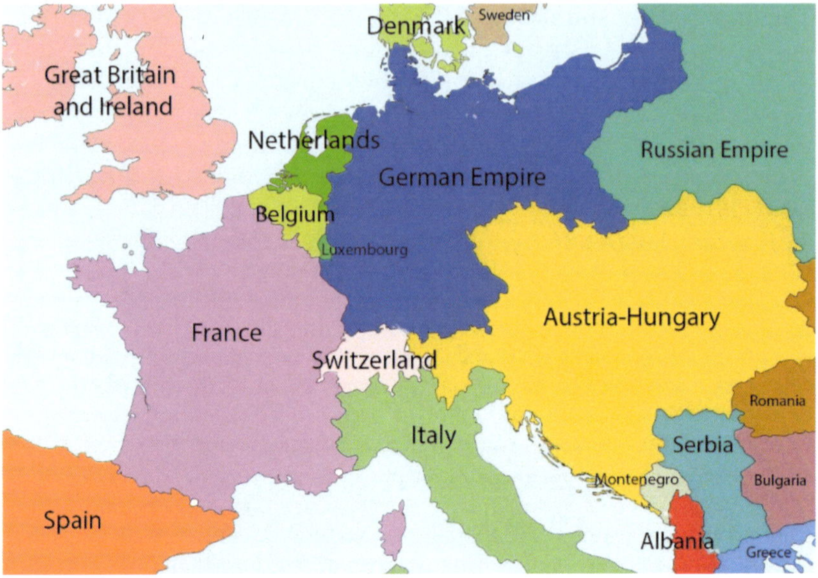

Map 10: Central Europe in 1914

Source: https://commons.wikimedia.org/wiki/File:Europa_1914.svg

Map 11: The Europeanisation of the world in 1914

Only major powers and other colonial powers are shown in colour. Source: https://upload.wikimedia.org/wikipedia/commons/4/45/World_1914_empires_colonies_territory.PNG (colours and labels modified).

policy, which absorbed all its remaining foreign policy capacities (⇨ par. 4124). However, it was involved in many international treaties, such as the Madrid Convention of 1880 or the Congo Act of 1885, and also participated in the economic exploitation of Africa. In Egypt alone, around 7,000 Austrians lived at the beginning of the 20th century.

4122 The **Chinese Empire** did not become a colony, yet it did find itself in a state of dependency on several European powers, from which it tried in vain to free itself during the Boxer Rebellion. The **Japanese Empire**, on the other hand, developed its own imperialist ambitions.

➤ This dependency was mainly the result of agreements known as the "unequal treaties" in which the European powers secured trade privileges and their own jurisdiction (so-called *consular jurisdiction*) over European merchants operating in China and Japan, without having to provide anything in return. Furthermore, individual Chinese cities came under the direct control of a colonial power; Hong Kong, notably, was a British crown colony from 1843 to 1997.

➤ There was growing resistance in China to the increasing European influence, which found its most prominent expression in the secret society of the "Boxers". The revolt which they instigated was suppressed in 1900/01

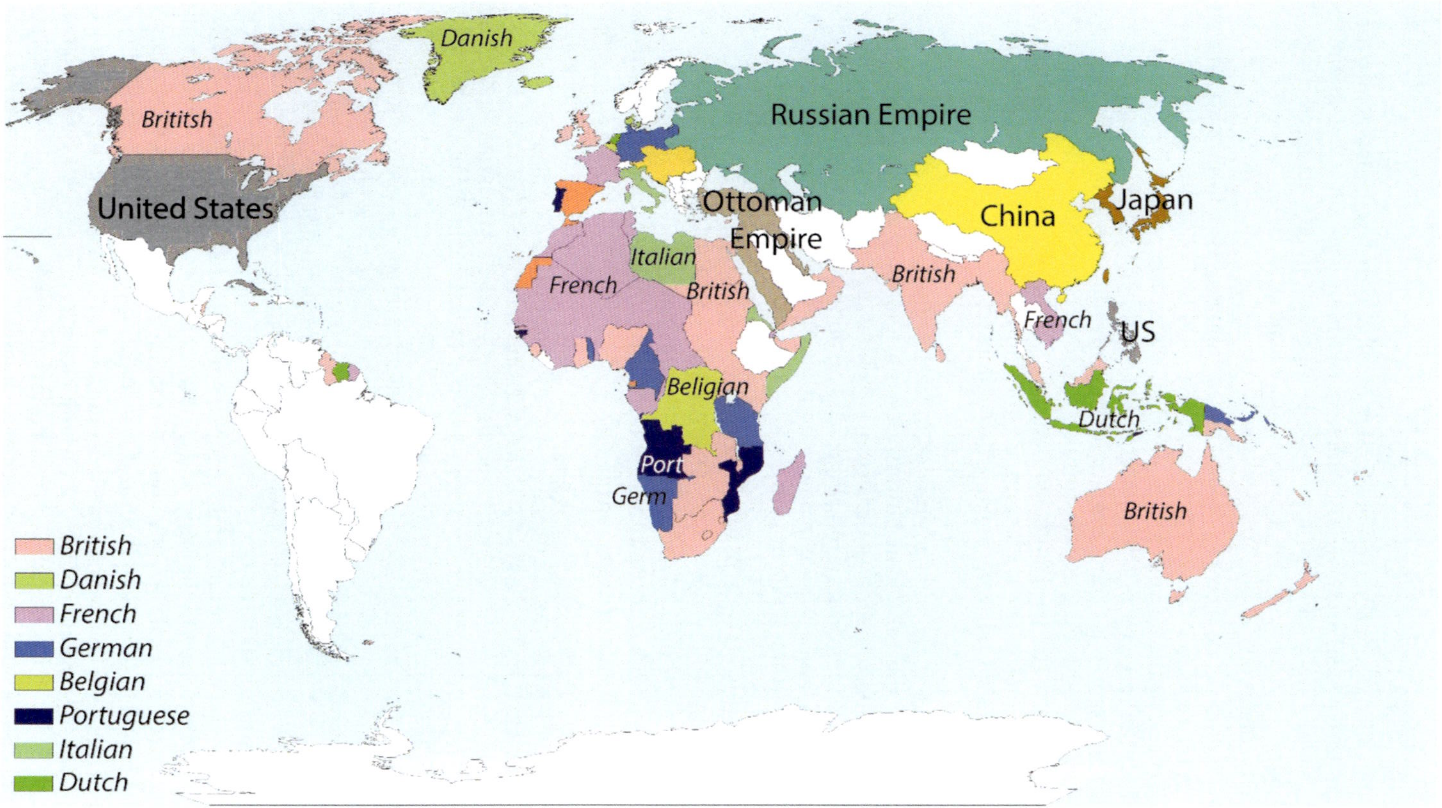
Danish
Britith
United States
Russian Empire
Ottoman
Empire
China
Japan
Italian
French
British
British
French
US
Beligian
Dutch
Port
Germ
British
British
Danish
French
German
Belgian
Portuguese
Italian
Dutch

by an alliance of eight colonial powers (in which Austria-Hungary also took part with a small contingent), which made China even more dependent. As a result, among other things, the allied powers jointly acquired Tianjin; Austria-Hungary did not, however, fully exploit its rights associated with this acquisition.

➢ Japan had deliberately isolated itself from the West from the 17th century onwards, but from 1853 it was also forced to accept "unequal treaties". Japan's constitution resembled the European feudal system (⇨ par. 2202). Since the 12th century, its supreme ruler had been the Shōgun, while the head of state, the Tennō, essentially had only religious and ceremonial significance. With the Meiji Restoration of 1867/68, the Shōgun was deprived of his power and the Tennō, who was now regarded as equal to a European emperor, took over the government himself. The state and the legal system were modernised, with Japan often following European models (⇨ par. 4307).

➢ In 1894/1911, Japan succeeded in freeing itself from the "unequal treaties" with the European powers. It even took part in the international intervention to suppress the Boxer Rebellion in China in 1900/01. In the Russo-Japanese War of 1904/05, an Asian power was for the first time able to defeat a major European power. In 1895, Taiwan became a Japanese colony, followed by Korea in 1910.

4123 Overshadowed by growing fears of an impending world war (⇨ par. 4126) and following a Russian initiative, two international conferences were held in The Hague in 1899 and 1907; their resolutions (*Hague Conventions*) remain of decisive importance for the **international law of war** to this day.

➢ The traditional right to war (*ius ad bellum*) remained uncontested in principle. However, factors like the influence of philanthropists such as Henri Dunant (⇨ par. 4107), the Austrian pacifist Bertha von Suttner (Nobel Peace laureate 1905), and the US president Theodore Roosevelt (1901–09, Nobel Peace laureate 1906) had given rise to the desire to codify just actions in war (*ius in bello*) in order to prevent the worst atrocities.

➢ The Russian tsar had already initiated an international conference in Brussels in 1874, but the resolutions adopted there were ultimately not accepted by the participating states. The resolutions of 1899 and 1907, on the other hand, were ratified by a number of states, including Austria-Hungary, and also became part of customary international law, so that they can now claim worldwide validity.

➢ The most important of the documents signed in 1899 was the Convention with respect to the Laws and Customs of War on Land. It significantly expanded the Geneva Convention of 1864, prohibiting among other things the killing of prisoners. In 1907, this convention was further expanded.

➢ Other documents prohibited certain weapons, such as, in particular, asphyxiating poisonous gases, or the forcible collection of debts due from one state to another (as had occurred in Mexico in 1862, ⇨ par. 4111). The territory of neutral states was declared inviolable; belligerents should not move troops or munitions of war across the territory of a neutral power.

➢ The conference of 1899 also adopted a convention for the Pacific Settlement of International Disputes. This established the Permanent Court of Arbitration, which is still operating in The Hague today.

4124 The **Balkans** developed into a "powder keg", where Austria-Hungary and Russia, in particular, competed with each other.

➢ From the beginning of the 19th century, the peoples of the Balkans (inspired by the Greek example) had sought independence from the Ottoman Empire (⇨ par. 3119). In 1817, Serbia gained internal autonomy as a principality but remained liable to pay tributes to Turkey.

➢ In the Russo-Turkish War of 1877, Russia conquered a large part of the Balkan Peninsula and pursued the establishment of a Greater Bulgarian principality dependent on it (Peace of San Stefano 1878). Austria-Hungary thus saw its own position in the Balkans jeopardised. BISMARCK was able to ward off the threat of war by convening an international conference. At the Congress of Berlin in 1878, Serbia, Montenegro, and Romania each gained their sovereignty; the much smaller Bulgaria became a principality but had to pay tributes to Turkey.

➢ Austria-Hungary occupied Bosnia-Herzegovina in 1878, based on the terms of the Congress of Berlin. Since there was no agreement on whether the country should be administered by Cisleithania or Transleithania, it was – as another "pragmatic matter" – placed under the administration of the k.u.k. Minister of Finance.

➢ In 1908, the Young Turk revolution successfully demanded the reconvening of the Turkish parliament, which had been dissolved in 1878, and the question of the constitutional position of Bosnia and Bulgaria within the framework of the Ottoman Empire became relevant again. Bulgaria declared its independence, and Austria-Hungary formally annexed Bosnia. This put a severe strain on Austria-Hungary's traditionally good relations with Serbia, which had been hoping to acquire Bosnia itself.

➢ The annexation of Bosnia in 1908 significantly strengthened the South Slavic element in the Habsburg Monarchy. The heir to the Austrian-Hungarian throne, FRANZ FERDINAND, in particular, supported the demands to unite the South Slavic peoples distributed across Cisleithania (Dalmatia, the Austrian Littoral, Carniola, Southern Carinthia, Lower Styria), Transleithania (Croatia), and Bosnia and to make them a separate entity of the monarchy ("Austro-Hungarian-South Slavic trialism").

➢ Further Balkan wars in 1912 (independence of Albania) and 1913 aggravated the situation; the European part of Turkey was reduced to approximately its present size.

4125 The Russian Revolution of 1905 forced Tsar NICHOLAS II (1894–1917) to enact a constitution. However, this did not mean that **Russia** had become a genuinely constitutional monarchy.

➢ Under Emperor ALEXANDER II (1855–81), there had already been comprehensive reforms (abolition of serfdom in 1861; independence of the judiciary in 1864). His plans to constitutionalise Russia did not materialise, as he fell victim to an anarchist assassination plot in 1881. In the period that followed, Russian domestic politics continued to be marked by anarchist terror.

➢ The extreme differences between the rich and the poor resulted in bloody riots in 1905, which finally led to the unilateral enactment of the constitution of 1906. Russia was thus formally a constitutional monarchy, but the parliament (*Duma*) had little power.

➢ Of great significance for Russia was the split of the Social Democratic Party in 1903 into a moderate minority (*Mensheviks*) and a radical majority (*Bolsheviks*). The Bolsheviks (from 1918: Communists) under VLADIMIR LENIN did not aim for a democratisation of Russia but a "dictatorship of the proletariat".

4126 When Austria-Hungary declared war on Serbia on 28 July 1914, the **First World War** (1914–18) broke out. It was a conflict between the "Central Powers" (Austria-Hungary, Germany, Turkey, Bulgaria) and the "Entente" (Russia, France, UK) with their Allies Serbia, Belgium, Japan, Italy, Romania, USA, Brasilia, etc.).

➢ The war was triggered by the assassination of FRANZ FERDINAND by Serbian nationalists in 1914. Austria-Hungary's smouldering ethnic conflicts erupted openly during the war; Minister-President KARL Count VON STÜRGKH (1911–16) suspended several fundamental rights and, resorting to emergency decrees, ruled in an almost dictatorial manner. He was thus assassinated by the radical Socialist FRIEDRICH ADLER in 1916.

➢ After the death of the Austro-Hungarian Emperor and King FRANCIS JOSEPH in 1916, his successor CHARLES I/IV (1916–18) failed to prevent the disintegration of the monarchy. Its independence-seeking nations placed great hopes in US President WOODROW WILSON's declaration of 8 January 1918 ("14 Points"), in which he presented the outlines of a post-war order and promised the peoples of Austria-Hungary "the freest opportunity to autonomous development".

➢ When the military situation became desperate in autumn 1918, Austria-Hungary proposed an armistice. In response to WILSONS' "14 Points", CHARLES I/IV issued a manifesto on 16 October 1918, in which he called on all members of the Reichsrat to come together in "National Councils" based on their respective ethnicities and to work towards a transformation of Austria (not Hungary!) into a federal state in which each ethnic group should have its own polity.

➢ However, WILSON declared on 18 October that mere "autonomy", as promised in Emperor CHARLES' *People's Manifesto*, was not a sufficient basis for future peace negotiations. The Czechoslovak Republic was proclaimed as a sovereign state on 28 October, followed by the establishment of a "State of Slovenes, Croats, and Serbs" on 29 October and the foundation of the German-Austrian state on 30 October (⇨ par. 6107). Hungary terminated the real union with Cisleithania on 31 October. On 1 November, the West Ukrainian People's Republic (later annexed by Poland) was proclaimed. Thus, within a week, all the peoples of the Habsburg Empire (with the exception of the Poles, Romanians, and Italians, who wanted to join the respective nation-states) had established their own states.

➢ The political end of the Austro-Hungarian Monarchy was inevitable when CHARLES I/IV relinquished every participation in the affairs of the state in respect to German-Austria (on 11 November 1918) and to Hungary (on 13 November 1918) (⇨ par. 6109). However, the k.u.k. army was not legally dissolved until 19 December 1918 and the k.u.k. diplomatic service not until 8 November 1920.

B Structures

1. General remarks

4201 The overcoming of absolutist regimes, as it occurred in the revolutions of 1688, 1789, 1830, and 1848, did not (or at least not permanently) lead to a complete elimination of the monarchies but to a division of sovereignty between the monarch and the people ("monarchical legitimacy" versus "popular sovereignty"). The legal relations between the two sovereigns were codified in a **constitutional document**.

➢ Constitutionalism was the logical progression from enlightened absolutism; the state should not only act in the interest of its subjects, but the subjects themselves should also be involved in state affairs. The transformation from an "association of subjects" to the "people of a state" played a major role in the emergence of nationalism and, conversely, nationalism became a driving force of constitutionalism. Hence, there had already been attempts to codify the constitution in some enlightened-absolutist states (especially in Tuscany by the Grand Duke – and later Emperor – LEOPOLD II).

➢ The oldest constitutional monarchy was England (from the 17th century). Its constitutional system was described several times by continental European jurists, such as CHARLES DE MONTESQUIEU in his book *De l'Esprit des lois* (*The Spirit of the Laws*, 1748) or RUDOLF VON GNEIST in his *Englisches Verfassungs- und Verwaltungsrecht* (*English Constitutional and Administrative Law*, 1857/60). It became the model for constitutional movements on the continent. English law was, however, often inaccurately reproduced, and mere buzzwords were used in calling for its achievements to be adopted in other countries as well.

➢ Of greater practical significance for the rest of Europe than the English constitution were the various French ones, some of which were adopted without modifications. Most of the English institutions only reached Germany and Austria through this indirect route.

➢ The act of codifying the constitution in a special document was of great importance beyond its normative content and contributed to the formation of a national identity, which is why the constitutions usually included solemn preambles, provisions on state symbols (such as coats of arms, flags, anthems, etc.) and programmatic provisions. They appeared in large numbers in the constitutional monarchies after 1791 (Poland, France).

➢ This distinguished the continent from England, where a codified constitution does not exist to this day. Rather, English constitutional law is based on a bundle of laws from different eras, and partly also on customary law. Similarly, Hungary did not have a codified constitution until 1945.

➢ The codification of constitutions also led to a new understanding of the term "constitution". Whereas previously a constitution was understood to mean only the basic order of a state, without regard to its content, it was now subject to very specific substantive requirements. Thus, Article 16 of the French Declaration of the Rights of Man and of the Citizen 1789 states: "Any society in which no provision is made for guaranteeing rights or for the separation of powers, has no constitution." This new understanding also provides the background for the dispute over Article 13 of the German Confederal Act 1815 (⇨ par. 3122).

4202 In early constitutionalist states, the constitutional document was issued unilaterally by the monarch (**constitutional octroi**). A high constitutionalist understanding of the constitution, by contrast, would have required joint enactment by the monarch and the people's representatives would have required joint enactment by the monarch and the people's representatives (**constitutional compact**).

➢ The labels "early constitutionalist" and "high constitutionalist" should be understood not only in a temporal sense but also in a conceptual one; in early constitutional monarchies, the monarch still had a predominant position, and many constitutionalist demands were not fully realised.

➢ The creation of a constitution in the form of a constitutional compact corresponded to the Enlightenment idea of the social contract (⇨ par. 3207). In practice, constitutional compacts were rare (e.g. Württemberg 1819; to some extent also the Austrian December Constitution 1867).

➢ The question of how the constitution was enacted was not least important for the question of who was competent to subsequently amend or repeal it. In 1837, when King Ernest Augustus I of Hanover repealed the constitution octroyed by his predecessor in 1833, seven professors of the University of Göttingen protested publicly against this ("Göttingen Seven", among them Jacob and Wilhelm Grimm); however, they were unable to do anything against what they considered to be an inadmissible course of action by the king and were removed from their posts (*Hanoverian constitutional conflict*).

4203 The constitutional documents were usually divided into two parts, one of which covered the **organisation of the state**, and the other the **fundamental rights**.

➢ Sometimes, already existing fundamental rights catalogues were incorporated into the constitution, for example the French *Déclaration des droits de l'homme et du citoyen* 1789 into the constitution of 1791, or the *Fundamental rights of the German people* 1848 into the constitution of the German Empire 1849.

➢ In other cases, the organisation of the state and the fundamental rights were debated together but laid down in separate documents. Cf. for Austria, for example, the two-part draft of the Kremsier Reichstag 1848/49, or the octroyed March Constitution 1849 with the complementary Fundamental Rights Patent 1849.

➢ In Austria, the fragmentation of the constitution into different statutes (⇨ par. 4114, par. 6113) resulted in a rather unusual way of dealing with it; the constitution was repeatedly extended in a casuistic manner by adding more and more specific constitutional laws, which soon led to considerable legal uncertainty.

2. The Separation of Powers

4204 The organisation of the state during the period of constitutionalism was based on the principle of **separation of powers**. The distribution of state power among different organs prevented the concentration of power at a single point and thus ensured mutual control (*checks and balances*). Since the time of the Enlightenment, three powers have been distinguished from each other, namely the *legislative, executive, and judicial powers*. In respect to each of the three powers, constitutionalism aimed to limit the originally universal power of the monarch and give the people or their representatives an opportunity to participate in them.

➢ JOHN LOCKE is regarded as the founder of the doctrine of separation of powers. In his *Two Treatises of Government* (1690), he sought to separate legislative from executive power (⇨ par. 3207). MONTESQUIEU had already distinguished three powers in 1748: *puissance législative*; *puissance exécutrice*; and *puissance de juger*. Although they had to be separate from each other, each of them still had to be able to exert some influence on the other powers in order to prevent their abuse. Even if only two of these powers were concentrated in one hand, there could be no such thing as freedom.

➢ According to MONTESQUIEU, there would be no freedom even if only one of these powers were entrusted to just one of the three social forces (the crown, nobility, and bourgeoisie); instead, each of the three powers had to be divided fairly among these three forces.

➢ The constitutions of the constitutionalist period in the 19th century adopted MONTESQUIEU's ideas with certain important modifications; in particular, the role of the administration was extended at the expense of the judiciary. The nobility was able to maintain its special legal position almost only in the context of the bicameral system (⇨ par. 4209) but remained the *de-facto* leading political caste until 1918.

➢ MONTESQUIEU's doctrine of the separation of powers conflicts with the democratic principle, which stipulates that all state power must emanate from the people; it was therefore rejected, for example, by JEAN JACQUES ROUSSEAU (⇨ par. 6202). HANS KELSEN also said that the proponents of the monarchy used this doctrine as an argument against unrestricted parliamentary rule.

4205 **Legislation** was usually carried out jointly by the parliament and the monarch. In early constitutionalist monarchies in particular, the monarch was clearly more powerful than the parliament.

➢ In most constitutions, this supremacy of the monarch was ensured by the monarch's right to dissolve and convene parliament and to issue emergency decrees (⇨ par. 4208), among other things. Many early constitutionalist systems also gave the monarch the sole right to introduce legislative proposals, whereas typically, in high constitutionalist systems, the parliament could also proceed on its own (through members' bills).

➢ Early constitutionalist systems, but also, for example, the December Constitution of 1867 (§ 13 of the Basic Law on Imperial Representation) provided that no parliamentary resolution could become law against the will of the monarch (*absolute veto*). High constitutionalist systems, such as the French Constitution of 1791 or the Kremsier Draft, on the other hand, stipulated that the monarch could not prevent the entry into effect of a statute but only delay it (*suspensive veto*).

4206 The monarch had his strongest position in the area of **administration**, which he carried out with the help of responsible ministers. Besides this *state administration*, however, the *autonomous self-administration* of the regional bodies (crown lands, municipalities) and professional interest groups (chambers) existed as well. This was justified in terms of state theory by the fact that these self-governing bodies had a certain "natural sphere of activity", which should remain "free of state interference".

➢ The monarch could appoint and dismiss ministers according to his will. They reported to parliament on their activities and could be held accountable for violations of the law. However, in contrast to ministers in democratic systems, they were not dependent on the majority in parliament and were therefore *legally* but not *politically accountable* (⇨ par. 6209).

➢ The monarch himself remained unaccountable for his actions, but each of his acts needed to be countersigned by a minister, who thereby assumed the legal responsibility (*requirement of countersignature*).

➢ The administrative organisation at the lower and intermediate levels was completely reorganised in 1849/68; the governorate districts were abolished in 1849, the counties (*"Kreise"*) in 1868, and the administration of the state as a whole was now tied to the (crown) lands, which were subdivided into districts from 1849 onwards. Each administrative district was now also supposed to be an autonomous territorial authority with the right to self-administration, which gave rise to a "dual structure".

➢ Accordingly, the *communal association of the highest order* was the crown land, where a representative of the emperor, the *"Statthalter"* (appointed by the emperor and subordinate to the k.k. ministries) was responsible for state administration. A provincial committee elected by the diet and headed by a governor was responsible for the autonomous administration of the crown land (although with only limited competences). Similar structures for the county (until 1868) and district levels were planned (*communal associations of intermediate order*) but only realised in a few crown lands.

➢ The *lowest order of communal association* was the local municipality, which encompassed the towns, markets, and villages (concept of the *"standard municipality"*). In the municipalities, the mayor and the municipal council had their own autonomous sphere of action as well as a delegated sphere of action in which they exercised certain state functions.

➢ Note that according to the contemporary view, only the state as a whole was considered "the state".

4207 The most extensive limitation of monarchical power was in the **judiciary**, which was conducted by *independent* judges whom the administration could *neither remove nor relocate*. The people were involved in the administration of justice through *jury trials*.

➢ The constitutional requirement that judges should be independent was mainly directed against the fiats ("cabinet justice", ⇨ par. 3205) that had been common in the absolutist era and were now forbidden. However, the monarch could still grant pardons and amnesties and also stop criminal proceedings.

➢ To protect the judges, they could be relocated to another position or completely removed from office against their will only on the basis of specific legal provisions and upon a judicial decision (Article 6 of the Basic Law on the Judiciary 1867). However, the appointment of the judges as such and also their promotion to a higher position were left to the discretion of the monarch, meaning that they also continued to depend on his goodwill.

➢ For political and press trials in particular, there were therefore demands for a participation of the people in the administration of justice. *Jury trials* should realise a maximum of judicial independence. They were introduced in Austria in 1848 for press trials and in 1850 for certain other proceedings but were abolished immediately after the onset of neo-absolutism in 1852. They were reintroduced after the return to constitutionalism for press trials in 1869 and for certain other proceedings in 1873.

➢ A special constitutional law passed in 1873 allowed the government to suspend jury trials in certain areas for up to one year if this was in the interest of the independence of the judiciary. In practice, this right was often abused, and, for example, jury trials were suspended throughout Austria in 1914–18.

➢ The constitutional requirement to separate the judiciary from the administration on the one hand and the abolition of patrimonial jurisdiction on the other made it necessary to completely reorganise the judicial system. This was done in 1849/50, resulting in the creation of the judicial system that is essentially still in place today. The supreme judicial body in civil and criminal matters was the Supreme Court, below which were the Higher Regional Courts (successors to the Courts of Appeal and usually serving more than one crown land), the Regional Courts, and the District Courts. Special courts were retained only for a few specific matters (e.g. commercial law), and military jurisdiction was restricted.

➢ The multitude of new authorities that emerged from 1848/49 onwards led to numerous problems in the details. During the period of neo-absolutism, in 1852, it was therefore decided that, outside of the large towns and where it was feasible, the district administration and the district court should be merged into a single authority (*mixed district office*). Although this allowed for small-scale organisational structures, which benefited the rural population in particular, the mixed district offices were dissolved again in 1868, as they undermined the principle of separation of powers.

4208 The monarch's right to issue **emergency decrees** was inconsistent with the principle of separation of powers. It was seen as a relic of absolutism but was largely accepted as a necessity.

➢ The basic idea was that situations could arise (such as war or an uprising) in which legal measures had to be taken quickly but parliament was unable to pass a timely resolution, e.g. because it was not in session or was physically prevented from convening.

➢ For such emergency situations, the monarch was given the right to issue decrees that had the legal quality of statutes ("emergency decrees"). However, abuse was always possible; for example, the right to issue emergency decrees in § 87 of the Austrian March Constitution 1849 was one of the foundations of FRANCIS JOSEPH's sham constitutional rule without a parliament in 1849–51.

➢ The December Constitution of 1867 sought to bind the right to issue emergency decrees to tight constraints; thus, each emergency decree had to be countersigned by all ministers and immediately submitted to the Reichsrat for approval – first to the House of Deputies, then to the House of Lords (§ 14 of the Basic Law on Imperial Representation). The right to issue emergency decrees under § 14 was of great practical importance, especially when the Reichsrat became incapacitated around 1900 due to ethnic conflicts, as well as during the First World War (cf., for instance, the three partial amendments to the ABGB, ⇨ par. 4309).

➢ In 1914, the government was given the right (by means of a § 14 emergency decree!) to issue emergency decrees itself. There were hardly any procedural barriers to this right; however, it was only to be used to implement economic measures that became necessary due to the war. This right was confirmed by the Reichsrat in 1917 in the War Economy Enabling Act (*Kriegswirtschaftliches Ermächtigungsgesetz*, KwEG). The KwEG was also incorporated into the body of law of the First Republic, where it would become particularly significant in 1933/34 (⇨ par. 7103).

3. Parliamentarism and suffrage

4209 Some of the constitutionalist parliaments were able to build on already existing representations of the estates (especially in England and Hungary, ⇨ par. 2218), while others were newly founded in the course of revolutions. Following the example of the English parliament, they were mostly organised according to the **bicameral**

system, with the first chamber representing certain privileged estates (high nobility, clergy) and the second representing the people.

➢ The underlying problem already emerged at the onset of the French Revolution; the three curiae of the Estates-General (*états généraux*) that reconvened in 1789 had traditionally been of equal weight, but the first two (the ecclesiastical and secular nobility) represented only about 2 percent of the share of the population that had a say in political affairs, while the Third Estate (the bourgeoisie) represented about 98 percent. The deputy EMMANUEL SIEYÈS, in particular, therefore saw the Third Estate as the true representative of the people; upon his initiative, the Third Estate unilaterally declared itself the National Assembly and took power in a revolutionary act.

➢ In England, the bicameral system dating from the Middle Ages remained in place. Following electoral reforms (especially the Reform Bill of 1832), the House of Commons represented an increasing proportion of the population (but ⇨ par. 4211) and was therefore regarded as the representation of the people (in contrast to the House of Lords). Nevertheless, both houses continued to have equal weight until the 20th century. Only since the Parliament Act 1911 has the House of Lords (insofar as it is involved in the legislative process at all) merely been able to delay, rather than prevent, decisions of the House of Commons (*suspensive veto*).

➢ In the course of the 20th century, the composition of the House of Lords underwent significant changes. By far the largest group of members (including women since 1958) are appointed for life (*life peers*), while the number of *hereditary peers* and *lord spirituals* has been steadily reduced.

➢ Following the British example, the Pillersdorf Constitution of 1848 provided for a division of the Reichstag into a Senate and a Chamber of Deputies. After the "Storm Petition" of 15 May 1848, the Senate was abolished, so that the finally convening (constituent) Reichstag of Vienna/Kremsier had only one chamber, thereby avoiding any preferential treatment of certain estates.

➢ Another type of bicameral system is found in the US Constitution, with its division of the Congress into the Senate and the House of Representatives; there, the purpose of the first chamber is not to take into account the interests of certain estates but to represent the states in federal legislation. In Austria, such a structure was envisaged for the Reichstag in the Kremsier Draft of 1848/49 and also in the octroyed March Constitution of 1849; it was, however, not realised.

➢ The North German Confederation (1867–70) and the German Empire (1871–1918) established the – not further subdivided – Reichstag (as the representation of the people) together with the Federal Council (as the representation of the states) as their legislator. This model was also followed by the Weimar Constitution 1919 (Reichstag/Reichsrat), the German GG 1949 (Bundestag/Federal Council), and especially also the Austrian B-VG 1920 (National Council/Federal Council).

4210 Under the Austrian **February Constitution** 1861, the Reichsrat consisted of the House of Lords (*Herrenhaus*) and the House of Deputies (*Abgeordnetenhaus*). The former was modelled on the first chamber of the British parliament; the latter consisted of delegates of the diets (and thus corresponded to the first chamber of the US parliament). Austria therefore had "two first chambers" (BRAUNEDER) but no representation of the people (the respective second chambers of the British and US parliaments). It was not until 1873 that direct popular elections to the House of Deputies were introduced.

➢ All adult princes of the imperial dynasty as well as the heads of certain noble families belonged to the House of Lords *by birth*, as did certain archbishops and bishops *by virtue of their office*. The emperor was entitled, according to § 5 of the Basic Law on Imperial Representation, to *appoint* men who had rendered outstanding services to "the state or the Church, science or the arts" as members of the House of Lords for life.

➢ Since the number of peers was not fixed (§ 5 of the Basic Law on Imperial Representation), the emperor could manipulate the balance of power at any time by appointing new peers. Not least because of this, the House of Lords had little political weight; however, the large number of high-profile jurists in its ranks gave it a certain authority. It was not until 1907 that the number of members that could be appointed under § 5 was limited to 150–170, in order to reduce the emperor's influence.

➢ As for the legislative process, the House of Lords and the House of Deputies remained of equal weight until 1918; laws could only be passed with the consent of both houses (and the sanction of the emperor), and thus each of the three institutions could prevent a bill from being passed.

➢ The Basic Law on Imperial Representation (§ 6) and the formula for the allocation of seats from 1861 (⇨ par. 4109) determined how many deputies per crown land and curia would be delegated to the House of Deputies; in the event that no delegation took place, the emperor could order a direct election as an exceptional measure (§ 7 of the Basic Law on Imperial Representation).

➢ Since the Bohemian diet refused to send its representatives to the House of Deputies after 1867, direct elections under § 7 of the Basic Law on Imperial Representation were initially held in Bohemia in 1868; in 1873, direct elections to the House of Deputies were generally introduced with the electoral law reform under the Minister of the Interior JOSEF LASSER. This did not change anything in the balance of power between the individual crown lands and curiae.

4211 Despite the self-perception of the parliaments (or their second chambers) as the representation of the people, **suffrage** was subject to numerous restrictions; in particular, it was usually made dependent on a certain tax contribution, the census, which favoured primarily the economically prosperous bourgeoisie. On the other hand, suffrage based on membership in a certain curia led to a (partly *de facto*, partly *de iure*) preferential treatment of the nobility and the clergy (⇨ par. 2220).

➢ The basic idea behind the census suffrage was that only those who contributed financially to the state should also be allowed to vote. However, exceptions to the census requirement were made for certain members of the clergy, civil servants, military officers, and university graduates (known as the "intelligence").

➢ The census was initially set so high that, for example, in France in 1814 only about 0.3 percent of the population were entitled to vote; in England, even after the major electoral reform of 1832, only 4 percent of the rural and 7 percent of the urban populations could vote. Only gradually was the census lowered and thus the right to vote extended.

➢ Universal suffrage for all men of age, independent of a census, was introduced in France in 1848 and in England in 1918. For elections to the (northern) German Reichstag, universal male suffrage existed from the beginning (1867), but in some of the German states it was not established until 1918. In Hungary, too, the right to vote was reserved for about 7 percent of the population until 1918.

➢ The three-class electoral law that was in place for the elections to the Prussian diet from 1849 to 1918 was extremely timocratic (= based on tax revenue). There, all male citizens over 24 years of age were ranked according to their tax contributions and then divided into three classes, such that the sum of the tax contributions was the same in each class. Each class elected an equal number of electors, which meant that the votes of the individual voters were as unequal as their tax contributions; for example, in the Prussian elections of 1903, 3.36 percent of all men of age voted in the first class, 12.07 percent in the second class and 84.57 percent in the third class. On the other hand, this system at least also granted suffrage rights in the last class to men who had no income at all.

➢ The Austrian municipal electoral law, on the other hand, tied the three-class system to a census. In Vienna in 1886 (i.e. before the incorporation of the working-class suburbs) only 5.9 percent of the resident population were entitled to vote based on their census, and these were again divided into three electoral bodies such that approximately 0.5 percent were entitled to vote in the first, 1.4 percent in the second and 4 percent in the third electoral body.

➢ In the elections to the Austrian diets (from 1861) and to the House of Deputies (from 1873), the census also reduced the number of voters to about 6 percent of the population. The electorate was organised according to the curial electoral system (large landowners, towns, chambers of commerce and trade, rural communities, ⇨ par. 2220), which led to considerable imbalances; whereas (in 1873) 59 voters elected one deputy in the Reichsrat curia of the large landowners, one deputy from the curia of the towns represented approximately 1,580 voters and one deputy from the curia of the rural communities approximately 8,400 voters.

4212 The **struggle for universal suffrage** for the House of Deputies was the dominant theme of Austrian domestic politics at the turn of the 19th and 20th centuries (⇨ par. 4117). Limited success was achieved in 1896/1907 with the introduction of universal male suffrage. Women were on the losing end; already existing modest foundations of a **women's suffrage** were even repealed again.

➢ Since the laws concerning suffrage were initially formulated in a gender-neutral way, women also had the right to vote in the (rare) cases in which they met the census. While the Municipalities Act 1849 still stipulated that female voters needed to be represented by a man, the electoral rules for the diets from 1861 said that the vote had to be cast in person (except in the curia of the large landowners). In this respect, women's suffrage existed in some (but not all) Austrian diets until 1918, albeit in a very limited form. In some diets, such as the Lower Austrian one in 1888, it was expressly abolished.

➢ When the direct election of the House of Deputies was introduced in 1873 with Minister of the Interior LASSER's electoral law reform, the substantive electoral law of the diets was taken over almost without modification, but women's suffrage was only retained for the curia of the large landowners (in which they needed to be represented by a man). With the elimination of the large landowners' curia in 1907, this "women's suffrage" ended as well.

➢ Even the mass parties, which campaigned for universal suffrage, treated the issue of women's suffrage as secondary at best and regarded the attainment of universal male suffrage as their primary goal. This also had to do with the prohibition of women's membership in political parties (until 1918, ⇨ par. 6215).

➢ A first extension of men's suffrage for the House of Deputies took place in 1882 through a reduction of the census to five Gulden of direct taxes per year, which increased the number of eligible voters in the towns by about a third and in the rural communities by about a quarter (electoral law reform under Minister-President TAAFFE). With the electoral law reform of 1896 under Minister-President BADENI, the census was reduced again, this time to four Gulden, and in addition to the already existing curiae, a general curia was created, in which all men over the age of 24 (including the voters of the four "old" curiae!) were entitled to vote.

➢ Although BADENI's electoral law reform of 1896 introduced universal male suffrage for the first time, the electoral rules were extremely unequal, since in the general curia there were approximately 70,000 voters for every deputy (cf. the above-mentioned 59 voters in the large landowners' curia, 1,580 voters in the curia of towns, and 8,400 voters in the curia of rural municipalities). Moreover, those who had already been eligible to vote before 1896 now had two votes. See also ⇨ par. 2220.

➢ It was not until the electoral reform under Minister-President BECK in 1907 that the curiae were abolished and all men over the age of 24 were given general and, in principle, equal voting rights. However, distortions still existed due to the varying organisation of the constituencies, which favoured the German-speaking electorate. Also, many persons (including those who had been residing at the place where they were to cast their vote for less than a year) were excluded from suffrage.

➢ Initially, the right to vote was exercised in public and largely carried out via electoral colleges; the principles of secrecy of the ballot and direct suffrage were only gradually introduced (ultimately in 1896 and 1907 respectively).

Table 6: Three-Class vs. Curial Electoral System

a) The 1903 elections to the Prussian House of Deputies (an example of a three-class electoral system)

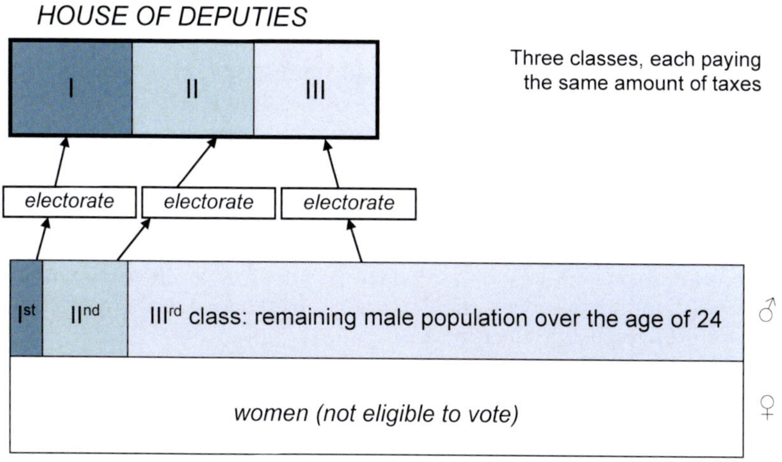

b) The 1897 elections to the Austrian House of Deputies (an example of a curial and census-based electoral system)

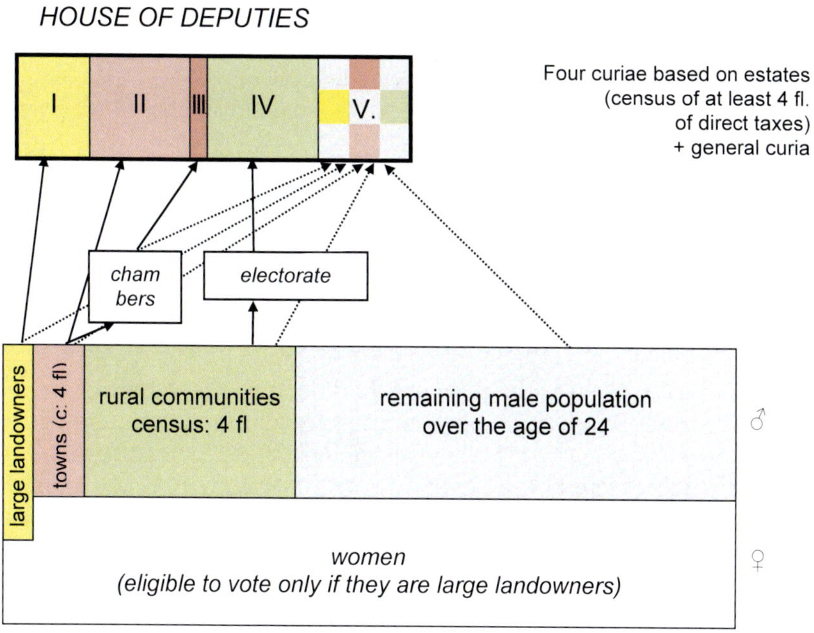

➢ Unlike the House of Deputies, the diets retained the curial system until 1918; however, a general curia was also established for most of the diets (modelled on the 1896 reform for the House of Deputies).

4213 In exercising their mandate, the members of parliament were not bound by any instructions from the electorate (**free mandate**). The constitutions granted them immunity to protect them from arbitrary acts by the authorities.

➢ Through the free mandate, the idea of representation of the people by the deputies became a fiction, as it allowed the deputies to consciously go against the will of their voters.

➢ The French Constitution of 1795 already justified the free mandate by stating that the deputies should not each represent their own constituency, but that they should all together represent the nation as a whole (Article 52). The deputies should therefore (after thorough discussion) jointly arrive at a solution that would result in satisfactory outcomes for the entire nation. This would not be possible if the deputies were strictly bound by the mandates of their respective electorates.

➢ In order to strengthen the reliance of the parliamentarians on their electorate, the first French constitutions (1791, 1793) provided that deputies could either not be re-elected at all or could only be re-elected once. This was later recognised as inefficient and eliminated in order to be able to ensure a certain degree of continuity in the governance of the state.

➢ The principle of immunity dates back to the French Revolution of 1789, when members of the National Assembly had to fear arrest by the police, who were following the king's orders. It was later adopted in virtually all constitutions.

➢ An arrest or detention of a member of parliament by the police required the prior consent of the parliament; if he was arrested red-handed, the parliament had to be informed immediately and, at its request, the parliamentarian had to be released (*extra-professional immunity*; *immunity in a narrow sense*). Under no circumstances could he be held responsible for his voting behaviour or statements made in parliament (*professional immunity*).

4. Courts of Public Law

a) Administrative Jurisdiction

4214 The independence of the judiciary had been won at a high price. For at around the same time as the monarchs relinquished their right to intervene (⇨ par. 3205), they restricted the scope of the courts to private and criminal law. **Public law proceedings**, i.e. legal disputes concerning, for example, trade, construction or tax matters, were decided exclusively by the administrative authorities (which continued to be controlled by the monarch).

➢ As late as the 18th century, public law proceedings (*contentiosa publica*) had been treated in the same way as those under private law. With the state reform of MARIA THERESA in 1749 (⇨ par. 3204), the distinct nature of public law proceedings was made explicit for the first time, and special senates were formed to decide on them. However, as the 18th century progressed, legal recourse to these senates was increasingly denied – precisely because the monarch could no longer impose his fiats on them.

➢ Instead, from around 1800 onwards, the only recourse against the decisions of the administrative authorities was to lodge a complaint, without any formal requirements and with little legal regulation, with a higher authority, ultimately with the monarch.

➢ A similar development took place in the other German states and especially also in France. It was not halted by the French Revolution, but rather gained momentum. In 1790, the French courts were expressly forbidden to "interfere" in administrative matters, since the administrative authorities – unlike the courts – were seen as the executive organ of the people's will.

➢ France subsequently began to establish a distinctive form of administrative justice, an organisation separate from the civil courts that was to provide legal protection for individuals. Since 1799, the Council of State (Conseil d'Etat) has been the highest instance, although neither it nor its subordinate authorities possessed the constitutional guarantees of a court.

➢ Many German states, including Austria, set up a system based on the French model, which, however, complied even less with the principle of the rule of law than the latter. Key procedural principles, such as the right to be heard, were either not regulated at all or only in a very sketchy manner. This left the state with a great deal of leeway.

➢ In England, on the other hand, the principle that legal disputes of any kind may be brought before the high courts (or, since 1873, the High Court, ⇨ par. 2328) is upheld to this day. During the Pre-March period, many liberal German jurists considered the English system to be exemplary and called for the abolition of administrative justice based on the French model. This demand was also incorporated into the German constitution drawn up by the *"Paulskirchenversammlung"* (⇨ par. 4105), but due to the failure of the 1848 revolution, it was not realised.

4215 This dispute over legal policy was linked to an important discussion in legal theory: while the idea that individuals could also have subjective rights in public law had initially been rejected, the existence of **subjective public rights** was now increasingly being recognised.

➢ Initially, the existence of such rights was only recognised in relation to the rights guaranteed under constitutional law, known as fundamental rights. According to the draft constitutions developed at the *Paulskirche* and the *Reichstag* at Kremsier respectively, these rights were to be protected by a special Imperial Court (*Reichsgericht*).

➢ From the second half of the 19th century, the idea that not only constitutional law but also administrative law established subjective public rights, which were essentially different from private rights, was gradually gaining ground.

➢ During the deliberations on the December Constitution of 1867, the protection of fundamental rights was still given priority over more general legal protection. The former was comprehensively regulated in a separate law, the Basic Law Establishing an Imperial Court (⇨ par. 4114), and assigned to an Imperial Court, while an Administrative Court was only promised in very general terms in an article of the Basic Law on the Judiciary; it was not initially clear how the competences of the two courts would differ. Only over time did the principle take hold that the Administrative Court could be called upon to protect subjective rights that were not guaranteed in the constitution (but, for example, in a simple law).

4216 The Imperial Court commenced its activities in 1869, the Administrative Court in 1876. While the former was only able to determine the violation of fundamental rights (i.e. it had only *declaratory jurisdiction*), the Administrative Court was given the power to rescind unlawful administrative acts (i.e. it had the **power of cassation**). It was only in 1919 that the Constitutional Court, as the successor to the Imperial Court, was also given the power to rescind unconstitutional administrative acts.

➢ In a parallel development to Austria, Prussia had also established an administrative court system in 1876. The Prussian system was particularly progressive and provided for a multi-level organism that would hand down (*reformatory*) decisions in certain, exhaustively listed administrative matters in place of the administrative authorities.

➢ In Austria, on the other hand, a single administrative court was set up that did not replace the existing administrative justice but was simply "superimposed" on it. It was therefore still necessary to lodge a complaint against an administrative act with the higher-level administrative authority. Only after all administrative channels had been exhausted could an appeal be lodged with the Imperial Court (on grounds of unconstitutionality) or with the Administrative Court (on grounds of other violations of the law).

➢ The Imperial and Administrative Courts did not review the entire administrative dispute but only determined whether the administrative act issued by the administrative authority that had ultimately decided on the matter was lawful. Questions of fact and discretionary decisions could not be reviewed by the supreme courts, which is why they could not issue a new decision (reformatory jurisdiction) but only pronounce the cassation of the previous one. The administrative authority then had to issue a new administrative act based on the court's legal opinion.

➢ However, in contrast to what was the case in Prussia, the jurisdiction of the Austrian Administrative Court was formulated in broad terms, so that, with a few exceptions, all administrative law was covered from the very beginning (*general clause system*). It was not until 1960 that the general clause system was also universally introduced in Germany.

b) Impeachment

4217 Impeachment, i.e. the **legal accountability of ministers** to parliament, is a typical element of a constitutional monarchy, and once again, England and France were models in this respect. While in England it always remained tied to the general criminal jurisdiction, the French system developed a specific form of ministerial accountability under constitutional law.

➤ The concept of ministerial responsibility corresponds to the basic constitutionalist demands for the separation of powers and *"checks and balances"*. While the monarch himself was "sacred, inviolable, and unaccountable" (as stated in Article 1 of the Basic Law on the Executive of 1867), the ministers could be held personally accountable, which gave the parliament control over the executive power.

➤ By contrast, ministerial responsibility as just described was alien to the absolutist state. When Emperor FRANCIS JOSEPH I abolished the ministerial responsibility introduced in 1848 on 20 August 1851, this was – justifiably – seen as a logical preliminary step towards the establishment of (neo-)absolutism (⇨ par. 4106).

➤ In England, proceedings against ministers and high-ranking officials had been taking place since the 14th century. The *House of Commons* brought the charges, while the *House of Lords* passed the sentence. Since the *House of Lords* was not only a legislative body but also, until 2006, England's highest court (⇨ par. 2328), the political judiciary was embedded in the ordinary one. One significant example was the proceedings against THOMAS WENTWORTH, 1st Earl OF STRAFFORD in 1640/41, which resulted in his execution (and marked the beginning of the English Civil War, ⇨ par. 3102). The impeachment proceedings introduced in the United States (1778) and Hungary (1848), for example, were modelled on the English system, with the lower house acting as the prosecuting authority and the upper house as the sentencing authority.

➤ France, on the other hand, developed an impeachment procedure that was separate from the ordinary judiciary in 1791. This was to be carried out by a special impeachment court, and the parliament was authorised to bring charges. Most of the other European constitutions were based on this model.

4218 The great importance attributed to impeachment in theory was in stark contrast to its practical significance. In reality, ministerial impeachments were rare and convictions almost unheard of. This was also the case in Austria, where a special **Impeachment Court** (*Staatsgerichtshof*) was established in 1867 to enforce ministerial responsibility, but it never heard a case.

➤ The dismissal of a minister against the will of the monarch was in effect equivalent to a revolution. Impeachment of a minister did therefore not occur for every minor offence, but only in extraordinary cases. The first such trial in France was that of JULES POLIGNAC, which took place in the wake of the July Revolution of 1830, but only after King CHARLES X, who had protected Polignac, had himself abdicated (⇨ par. 3122).

➢ In Austria, a "responsible ministry" had already been formed in March 1848, but initially there were no provisions for its impeachment. The March Constitution of 1849 provided for an "Imperial Supreme Court" as the competent forum, but this was not established before ministerial responsibility was abolished by the August Decrees of 1851.

➢ In the period leading up to the December Constitution, the Ministerial Responsibility Act of 25 July 1867 re-established the legal responsibility of the imperial and royal ministers to parliament; both the House of Deputies and the House of Lords had the right to bring charges before a special Impeachment Court. It consisted of 24 members, half of whom were elected by each of the two houses of the Reichsrat, and who were not allowed to sit in either of the two houses themselves.

➢ A conviction by the Impeachment Court would have resulted in the loss of office and, depending on the circumstances, potentially also in criminal prosecution and the imposition of damages. However, not a single minister was impeached before 1918, let alone convicted.

➢ The Austro-Hungarian ministers also had their own impeachment court provided for in the Compromise Acts (⇨ par. 4115), but there was no implementing law, with the result that this court never became active either.

5. State – Church – Society

a) General remarks

4219 The triumph of constitutionalism was an indirect consequence of the greatest social upheaval since humans had become sedentary: the **Industrial Revolution**. With the emergence of new economic structures, the bourgeoisie in particular gained significant power at the expense of the nobility. At the same time, there was an exodus from the countryside, and the working class emerged as a fourth estate alongside the nobility, the bourgeoisie, and the peasants.

➢ The roots of the Industrial Revolution are to be found in Great Britain (invention of the steam engine in 1763, the mechanical loom in 1785, the steam locomotive in 1802/04, etc.). The movement of *"Manchester Liberalism"*, which had its origins in the town of this name (a centre of the textile industry), called for the abolition of protective tariffs and other trade barriers because they were regarded as detrimental to the advancement of prosperity. The demand for liberalism in economic terms, as advocated DAVID HUME or ADAM SMITH, among others, was combined with political liberalism in many ways.

➢ However, economic liberalism could also exist independently of political liberalism; thus, liberal approaches can be discerned in Austrian economic policy both in the Pre-March period and in the neo-absolutist era (e.g. in the Industrial Code 1859). At times, attempts were even made to counterbalance the disappointment of the liberal bourgeoisie with the political situation by granting them economic concessions.

4220 **Liberalism** as a political movement broke through in Austria with the revolution of 1848 and again from 1861/67. In socio-political terms, it resulted in the introduction of liberal fundamental rights; in governance and economic terms, it led to a reduction of state functions and the emergence of business legislation that was (almost) purely based on private law, while the influence of the authorities was pushed back. The market was supposed to regulate itself. Initially, this liberal concept seemed to work (*"Gründerzeit"*); however, it came to an abrupt end with the stock market crash of 1873. State intervention in the economy and the development of modern social law were the results of this development.

➢ The Social Democrat FERDINAND LASSALLE described a completely liberalised state that was limited to its core functions of monitoring internal and external security (derogatorily!) as a "night-watchman state".

➢ The positive development of the Austrian economy from 1867 onwards led to increasingly daring speculations, which resulted in a crash of share prices on the Vienna Stock Exchange during the Vienna World Exhibition (9 May 1873: "Black Friday"). The stock boom of the *"Gründerzeit"* ended; the middle classes sought refuge in fixed-interest bonds.

➢ The state again had to take the place of private investors (including the successive nationalisation of the railways); efforts to establish protective tariffs also re-emerged.

➢ The first attempts of the workers to organise themselves (formation of trade unions, strikes) were regarded by the constitutionalist governments as dangerous to the state and therefore suppressed (German Socialists Act 1878); to some extent, the social legislation that began to emerge at the same time can be seen as a means of reconciling the state with the working class.

4221 The main opponent of liberalism was the Catholic Church, which became a stronghold of conservatism and anti-modernism but at the same time also took the first steps towards its own social teaching (⇨ par. 7213). In several European countries, a **cultural struggle** unfolded between Catholic-conservative forces on the one hand and national-liberal forces on the other.

➢ The cultural struggle not only unfolded around the issue of freedom of faith and conscience (although this was the cause of many conflicts), but in many cases also gave both sides the opportunity to make their mark by addressing a range of socio-political issues.

➢ In Austria, the Concordat of 1855 was a step backwards compared to the Josephinian reforms. The Church was granted far-reaching influence on schooling and education in general. The ABGB provisions on marriage were suspended for Catholics and court cases concerning Catholic marriages had to be heard by ecclesiastical judges. The Church was recognised as the owner of the religious funds.

➢ When the Liberals returned to power, their "May Laws" of 1868 restored the ABGB-based marriage law for Catholics, brought education under the control of state authorities, and made it possible for people to freely change their denomination or leave the Church. In special cases, in particular if the bride and groom did not belong to any legallwas meant to be allowed from 1868/70 (*"Notzivilehe"*).

➢ In 1870, the Concordat was formally terminated, and in 1874, the legal status of the Catholic Church and the fate of the religious funds were regulated by state laws, such that the state could now again exert greater influence over these matters.

➢ The culmination of the cultural struggle in Austria was the sentencing of the Bishop of Linz, FRANZ JOSEPH RUDIGIER (1853–84), to 14 days in prison for his criticism of the May Laws (he was, however, immediately pardoned by the emperor). In Prussia, which was predominantly Protestant, the conflict between BISMARCK and the Catholic Church was much more severe; in 1874/75, of the eleven Catholic bishops of Prussia, five – almost half of them – were temporarily imprisoned

b) Fundamental Rights

4222 The idea of **fundamental rights** is intricately linked with the idea of natural law. The various theories of natural law regularly postulated the existence of pre-positive, inalienable human rights. In the course of constitutional codification, attempts were made to positivise these human rights and incorporate them into the constitutions. This led to a change in the concept of fundamental rights, which now came to denote constitutionally guaranteed rights.

➢ In the course of the English constitutional conflicts (⇨ par. 3102), which ended with the establishment of constitutionalism in England, the English Parliament had enacted several laws granting English citizens certain basic rights. The great importance of these rights at the time can only be understood against the political background of their origins: In 1679, it was decreed that a writ of habeas corpus (⇨ par. 2328) must not be ignored (*Habeas Corpus Act*), and in 1689 that anyone could petition the king without fear of reprisals and that subjects who are Protestants may have arms for their defence (*Bill of Rights*).

➢ In 1689, influenced by the English constitutional conflicts, JOHN LOCKE wrote his *Two Treatises of Government* (⇨ par. 3207), in which he explained that the people had not given up all their rights with the social contract. Some rights, specifically life, liberty, and estate, are inextricably linked to humanity and thus inalienable.

➢ During the 18th century, the concept of fundamental rights gained increasing prominence. When the 13 British colonies in North America declared their independence on 4 July 1776, they began their declaration with the words: "We hold these truths to be self-evident, that all men are created equal, that they are endowed by their Creator with certain unalienable Rights, that among these are Life, Liberty and the pursuit of Happiness." This wording goes back to THOMAS JEFFERSON (US President 1797–1801).

➢ Only a few weeks earlier, in June 1776, a convention in the future US state of Virginia had adopted a *Declaration of Rights* alongside a constitution. Among other things, it proclaimed the equality of all citizens, freedom of press and of religion, and it forbade cruel and unusual punishments, baseless search and seizure, to name just a few. The Virginia Declaration of Rights became the model for all subsequent human rights catalogues, in particular the French Declaration of the Rights of Man in 1789 and the US Bill of Rights in 1791. With the Napoleonic conquests, the idea that human rights should be codified spread throughout Europe.

➢ The codification of fundamental rights led to their substantive transformation. The notion of general "human rights" lost importance; the primary subjects of fundamental rights were male, white citizens. Women and foreigners enjoyed these fundamental rights only to a very limited extent, if at all.

➢ In 1791, the Frenchwoman Olympe de Gouges published her *Declaration of the Rights of Woman and of the Female Citizen* in which she called for equality between men and women. However, she did not live to see its success; in 1793 she was executed on the pretext of being a royalist.

➢ Even slavery was able to persist for a long time in countries with constitutionally guaranteed rights. Since in the modern era the trade in Muslim slaves dried up, people from sub-Saharan Africa were increasingly enslaved, and remained enslaved even if they converted to Christianity. Therefore, religious justifications of slavery came to be replaced by racist ones.

4223 In Austria, the **development of modern fundamental rights** began with the revolution of 1848 and the first constitution in the formal sense, the Pillersdorf Constitution of 25 April 1848.

➢ In absolutist Austria, the idea of codifying human rights was rejected (on the Martini Draft see ⇨ par. 3311). However, § 16 ABGB included the provision that "every man has inborn rights" and that slavery and serfdom were prohibited (⇨ par. 3313). Considering that serfdom in Russia was only abolished in 1864, slavery in the USA in 1865 and in Brazil in 1888, it is evident how progressive this provision was at the time.

➢ The fundamental rights of the Pillersdorf Constitution had been largely formulated by Pillersdorf himself. Based on the English model, they included the right of petition and habeas corpus, as well as freedom of religion and freedom of the press (but not the right to bear arms).

➢ The most comprehensive discussion of fundamental rights in an Austrian parliament to date took place in 1848/49 in the Reichstag at Kremsier, where a separate draft of a fundamental rights catalogue was drawn up alongside the draft of the constitution. It substantially exceeded the fundamental rights of the Pillersdorf Constitution. Among other things, it proclaimed the equality of all citizens before the law (⇨ par. 4226).

➢ The March Constitution of 1849 itself contained only a few fundamental rights provisions (including the abolition of serfdom, equality of citizens before the law, protection of property). It was supplemented by a fundamental rights patent issued at the same time, which provided for a few additional fundamental rights (freedom of belief, freedom of the press, freedom of science, among others), but – unlike the actual constitutional document – only applied in the Cisleithanian lands.

➤ Of the two Sylvester Patents of 31 December 1851, the first repealed the March Constitution, but confirmed equality before the law and the abolition of manorialism. The second Sylvester Patent repealed the Fundamental Rights Patent of 1849, but confirmed the rights already granted to the legally recognised churches and religious communities, especially with regard to public religious practice.

➤ The Fundamental Rights of the German People of 1848, which were adopted by the assembly at St. Paul's in Frankfurt, were also quite comprehensive. They were, however, repealed by the German Confederal Assembly in 1851.

4224 It was only after the end of neo-absolutism and the return to constitutionalism in 1861/67 that fundamental rights could be re-established in Austria. The **Basic Law of 21 December 1867 on the General Rights of Nationals** is still one of the most important Austrian fundamental rights catalogues today.

➤ The *Law on the Protection of Personal Liberty* and the *Law on the Protection of the Home* had already been enacted in 1862. They stipulated that an arrest or a search of a house by the police could generally only be carried out on the basis of a corresponding judicial order. In 1867, both laws were declared part of the Basic Law on the General Rights of Nationals, and thus given constitutional rank. While the Law on the Protection of Personal Liberty was replaced by a new law in 1988, the Law on the Protection of the Home is still in force today and is thus the oldest valid Austrian constitutional law.

➤ In 1867, the right of equality of all citizens before the law, the inviolability of property, the preservation of the secrecy of correspondence, freedom of assembly and association, freedom of the press, freedom of belief and conscience, freedom of research and academic teaching, the equality of all nationalities and numerous other rights were added.

➤ Article 20 of the Basic Law on the General Rights of Nationals provided for the temporary or local suspension of individual fundamental rights (freedom of the press, freedom of association and assembly, etc.), an option repeatedly used in times of crisis and war (especially during the First World War from 1914 to 1918).

4225 The constitutions from the era of constitutionalism in the 19th century and their catalogues of fundamental rights regularly granted the right of **freedom of belief and conscience**, including Article 14 of the Basic Law on the General Rights of Nationals, which is still in force today. This law also guaranteed the legally recognised churches and (non-Christian) religious communities the right to public worship (Article 15), while other religious beliefs were granted the right to "domestic" (private) religious practice (Article 16).

➢ The Pillersdorf Constitution of 1848 already guaranteed "full freedom of belief and conscience" for all citizens. § 2 of the Fundamental Rights Patent of 1849 added the right to public worship for legally recognised churches and religious communities. The Fundamental Rights Patent of 1849 was repealed in 1851 (⇨ par. 4106), but the right to public religious practice was expressly confirmed on this occasion.

➢ The Pillersdorf Constitution also contained a promise that the unequal treatment of people on religious grounds would be gradually abolished. This applied above all to the Jews, hence the discriminatory laws relating to them were successively repealed. Their legal status was comprehensively regulated in the Israelite Law of 1890, which is still in force today, albeit with numerous amendments.

➢ The concordat concluded in 1855 between Austria and the Holy See favoured the Catholic Church in terms of its relationship with the state (⇨ par. 4219), but had no effect on the freedom of religion and conscience. The Protestants Patent of 1861 granted full equality of rights to the Protestants of the Augsburg and Helvetic confessions. It was replaced by a new law in 1961.

➢ As of 1849/67, the Catholic, Protestant, and Greek Orthodox Christians as well as the Jews were considered "legally recognised" within the meaning of § 2 of the Fundamental Rights Patent of 1849 and Article 15 of the Basic Law on the General Rights of Nationals 1867. In 1874, the Minister of Religious Affairs was authorised by the *Recognition Act* to recognise further denominations by decree, but during the time of the monarchy this was only used twice: in 1877 for the benefit of the Old Catholic Church (which had split from the Catholic Church in the wake of the First Vatican Council of 1870/71) and in 1880 for the benefit of the Moravian Church.

➢ The official recognition of Islam, which had become necessary as a result of the annexation of Bosnia in 1908 (⇨ par. 4124), was formalised by the *Islam Act* of 1912. Initially, its scope was limited to the Hanafi rite. The intention behind this law was to avoid recognition under the Recognition Act of 1874. Among other things, it was stipulated that Muslim marriages should continue to be officiated by a state authority (⇨ par. 4221).

➢ Freedom of religion and conscience also guarantees the right not to belong to any religion at all! However, the legal status of those without a religious affiliation – as well as that of followers of religious communities not legally recognised by the state – remained unclear and uncertain until the end of the monarchy.

4226 The introduction of the general principle of equality into Austrian constitutional law in 1848 did **not** immediately result in the **equality of women**. In some areas, such as voting rights (⇨ par. 4212), their situation actually deteriorated.

➢ Under the fundamental rights catalogues adopted between 1848 and 1867, the principle of equality (Article 2 of the Basic Law on the General Rights of Nationals) always applied only to "citizens" among themselves, which, given the language use of the time, could have included female nationals or excluded them. However, the genesis of the law clearly shows that it was intended to apply exclusively to men. In the entire period up to 1918, there was not a single complaint by a woman based on Article 2 of the Basic Law on the General Rights of Nationals because of discrimination on the grounds of her sex.

➢ Even where the law seemingly postulated the equality of men and women, such as in the Industrial Code of 1859, the subordination of the wife to her husband under family law meant that women could rarely exercise these rights to the same extent as men.

➢ A particularly controversial issue was the right to equal education for women. From 1878, women were allowed to take their school-leaving exams (*Matura*), but it was not until 1897 that they were also allowed to study at university. In 1919, they were eventually also allowed to study law.

4227 The fundamental rights catalogues were initially only conceived as state objectives; it was only with the establishment of the Imperial Court that they became legally enforceable **subjective public rights**.

➢ As "state objectives", they primarily set out principles that the administrative authorities ought to follow, meaning that non-compliance would not have entailed any legal consequences. An example of this is the Pillersdorf Constitution.

➢ The draft constitution of Kremsier envisaged that anyone whose constitutional rights had been violated could have brought a civil action for full redress of the injury by the state before the Imperial Court. According to contemporary views, this would probably have meant not only monetary compensation but also the restoration of the lawful state of affairs.

➢ The March Constitution of 1849 also provided for a constitutional court that would have had jurisdiction over "violations of political rights", but without specifying the effects of such a decision. A constitutional court was not established.

➢ Only in 1869 was an Imperial Court actually established under the Basic Law Establishing an Imperial Court of 1867. It was responsible for "complaints by nationals regarding violations [by administrative authorities] of the political rights guaranteed to them by the constitution" (⇨ par. 4216).

C Legislation and Jurisprudence

1. From Historical School of Law to Conceptual Jurisprudence

4301 The **Historical School of Law** emerged at the beginning of the 19th century as a countermovement to codification and natural law. Leaving aside a few earlier contributions, FRIEDRICH CARL VON SAVIGNY and KARL FRIEDRICH EICHHORN, both professors at Berlin University, are considered the true founders of this school.

➢ The 19th century was the century of historism; the continuing effect of the past was felt in all areas of life, including the law. The rejection of the law of reason by the Historical School of Law (which might be better described as "historicist") went hand in hand with the rejection of the Enlightenment and, as its result, the French Revolution.

➤ SAVIGNY first set out his academic agenda in 1814 in his treatise *Vom Beruf unserer Zeit für Gesetzgebung und Rechtswissenschaft* (*Of the Vocation of Our Age for Legislation and Jurisprudence*). It had been provoked by the demand of the Heidelberg professor ANTON THIBAUT for a civil code for Germany, which SAVIGNY vehemently opposed.

4302 Its underlying concept was that the law could not be logically construed; rather, since it was derived from the "spirit of the people" (***Volksgeist***), it had evolved organically and could therefore only be understood by studying its history.

➤ In regard to older cultures, this spirit was assumed to express itself in the shape of customary law, whereas in more advanced civilisations it was thought to manifest in judicature and jurisprudence, which both refine the law over time. Statutes only serve to complement this "organically" emerging law but cannot replace it (cf. the common law, ⇨ par. 2329).

➤ In his programmatic treatise from 1814, SAVIGNY argued that the times he lived in were not yet mature enough for a codification of German civil law. This could only be addressed, if at all, after a full historical reappraisal of the law. SAVIGNY therefore opposed the idea of codification. As the Prussian Minister of Justice (1842–48), he rejected a comprehensive revision of the ALR; therefore, only a new criminal code was enacted to replace the criminal law provisions of the ALR in 1851, whereas the civil law provisions continued to apply until 1900.

➤ The followers of the Historical School of Law worked with historical legal material and sought to make it directly usable for contemporary law by forcing it into a modern system. This was called the "historical-systematic" method.

➤ From a present-day perspective, the historical-systematic method was ultimately an unhistorical approach to the historical legal sources that did not do justice to their specific nature. The Historical School of Law is therefore not the same as present-day legal history!

4303 SAVIGNY and his disciples turned to the study of Roman law as the most important foundation of positive law (*Romanism*, **pandectistics**). The branch founded by EICHHORN, on the other hand, aimed to reveal the Germanic foundations of the law (**Germanism**).

➤ Of lesser practical importance, on the other hand, was another branch of the Historical School of Law that worked neither in a Germanistic nor a Romanistic style, but instead pursued a "global history of law" (e.g. the later Pandectist JOSEPH UNGER, who in 1850 published *Die Ehe in ihrer welthistorischen Entwicklung*, about the evolution of marriage in world history).

➤ In the academic dispute between Pandectists and Germanists, contemporary legal-political concerns were often "projected back", i.e. historical sources were searched for arguments that would support one's own position (for example, in the dispute over the nature of the legal person).

➢ While the Romanists were able to build on the *Corpus Iuris Civilis* (and were called Pandectists after its main part, the pandects), the Germanists first had to painstakingly piece together their sources (e.g. *Deutsche Rechtsalterthümer* [*Legal antiquities*, 1828] by JACOB GRIMM). However, by today's standards, their work was inaccurate and often joined together sources that came from widely different places and times (⇨ par. 1002). Their efforts to find their "own" (i.e. Germanic or German) legal past must be placed in the context of 19th/20th-century nationalism (⇨ par. 4201). Roman law was demonised as "alien law" and blamed for numerous social ills that had emerged since its reception.

➢ The different situations regarding their sources soon led to the Pandectists/Romanists working more systematically and dogmatically. They focused mainly on civil law, while their Germanistic colleagues were more interested in historical questions (e.g. in the study of the sources) and, in their research, paid greater attention to the history of public law. This split is still noticeable today at the University of Vienna, for example, where the subject "Romanistic Foundations of European Private Law" is of a more dogmatic nature, while the discipline "Legal and Constitutional History", which emerged from legal Germanism, is mainly historically oriented.

4304 Later developments brought a complete separation of the systematic and historical methods; **conceptual jurisprudence** and **legal history** developed into different fields.

➢ The systematic method of the Historical School of Law gave rise to (what later became known as) conceptual jurisprudence, with the Pandectist GEORG FRIEDRICH PUCHTA, a disciple of SAVIGNY, considered its founder. Conceptual jurisprudence attempted to derive, in an inductive way, abstract concepts from the "legal material" (i.e. positive law) – for instance, the concept of "contract" from a sales contract, a work contract, or a rental contract, etc. – and to develop further, even more abstract, "generic concepts" from these (the concept of "legal transaction" from a contract, a will, a promise, etc.).

➢ These concepts would then be arranged into a fully consistent system, from which – in a deductive manner – solutions for all kinds of legal problems could be derived (e.g. from the nature of a legal transaction, different principles would result, which would then also apply to all types of legal transactions, such as a purchase). The judge was therefore regarded as a "subsumption automaton" that, following formal logic, derived the decision for each individual case from these abstract terms.

➢ The legacy of conceptual jurisprudence lies in the creation of a precise legal terminology, on which modern jurisprudence is still based today. The difficulty with conceptual jurisprudence lies primarily in the fact that, while it pretended to reach its conclusions solely based on formal logic and the posited law, it actually created new norms and also failed to recognise the judge's function as a creator of new law (in the case above, for example, rules that positive law has for the work contract are understood as general rules for any legal transaction and then applied to other situations, such as a purchase; however, this is actually a case of analogy).

➢ With conceptual jurisprudence, the original concern of the Historical School of Law (i.e. the rejection of a system derived from logic) was abandoned. The Pandectists after PUCHTA were therefore quite open to the idea of codification.

➢ Pandectist codifications include the Civil Code for the Kingdom of Saxony from 1863 and the Code for the Russian Baltic provinces (= today's Estonia, Latvia, and Lithuania) from 1864, which was also written in German.

➢ In a parallel development, legal history was established as an independent discipline, which, although in terms of methodology increasingly oriented towards the historical disciplines, also attempted to preserve its propaedeutic (introductory) function for legal education (⇨ par. 0001).

4305 The departure from natural law led to a focus on positive law. Combined with the rapid increase in legislative activity in the 19th century, this resulted in **legal positivism**.

➢ This legal positivism was thus stronger in places where positive law was already expressed in statutory form, such as in the countries of the Rhenish law (⇨ par. 3314). In countries that had remained without codification, on the other hand, positive law was mainly derived from the textbooks of law professors; this gave rise to a type of positivism based on academic knowledge.

➢ *Positivism* regarded positive law as the sole source of law. Initially, its validity was uncritically attributed to the fact that this was the actual, effective legal order (⇨ par. 6304). Positivism became particularly influential in public law and contributed significantly to the development of the principle of legality.

4306 In Austria, the Historical School of Law was unable to establish itself at first on account of the strong position of the ABGB. It was not until **THUN's curricular and university reform** in 1852/55 that the Historical School, and in particular its pandectist branch, gained momentum.

➢ Under the Austrian Minister of Education LEO Count THUN-HOHENSTEIN (1849–60), a fundamental educational reform took place, which sought to implement the principle of the unity of research and teaching in Austria. This reform was based on the model of the University of Berlin, where WILHELM VON HUMBOLDT had been involved in founding the institution in 1810, and later came to be known as the Humboldtian ideal of education. Until then, secondary school (*"Gymnasium"*) had lasted for six years, followed by a two-year philosophical course at the arts faculty, which was a prerequisite for admission to the law faculty (⇨ par. 2316). With the reform, grammar school was extended by two years and the two-year *"Philosophicum"* was given up. The school-leaving exam (*"Matura"*) was henceforth sufficient for admission to one of the four faculties, which all had equal status (theology, law and political science, medicine, and philosophy).

➢ The school-like character of university studies, which had persisted in the Pre-March period, was abandoned in favour of the freedom of teaching and learning; instead of annual intermediate examinations, final examinations (state examinations, *rigorosa*) on the entire course material were introduced, thus realising a central demand of the revolution of 1848.

➢ THUN, however, rejected the revolution itself and the movements that had led to it. The doctrine of natural law, which was given a share of the "blame" for the outbreak of the revolution, was pushed back both in the legal curriculum and through a rigorous personnel policy; it was replaced by the Historical School of Law "imported" from Germany, which meant that almost half of the law curriculum consisted of legal history subjects.

➢ From around 1840, individual Austrian jurists, such as EMIL FRANZ RÖSSLER, had already conducted legal historical research in the spirit of Germanism, but they did not diminish the dominant position of exegetical jurisprudence. Only the triumph of pandectistics in the wake of THUN's curricular reform marked the end of the Exegetical School in Austria as well. Pandectistics' most prominent representative was JOSEPH UNGER, who had THUN as his patron. In his (unfinished) *System des österreichischen allgemeinen Privatrechts* (*System of Austrian General Private Law*, 1856ff), he described Austrian private law for the first time not according to the structure of the ABGB itself, but according to the pandect system – an approach that most textbooks on Austrian civil law still follow today.

➢ With the strong emphasis on legal history in the curriculum, THUN had hoped to instil patriotism and conservatism in the students, which did not materialise. The extent to which the legal history subjects were taught was therefore reduced further and further from one curricular reform to the next, so that since 2006 (in Vienna) it has become limited to about a sixth of what it was in 1855; still, the legal history subjects have been able to maintain their position as compulsory subjects in the first stage of the established degree programme to the present day.

2. The pandectistic codifications

4307 After the German Reich was established in 1871, the harmonisation of the law was addressed. The **German Civil Code** (*Bürgerliches Gesetzbuch*, **BGB**), which was adopted in 1896 and came into effect on 1 January 1900, was a product of pandectistics and remains the private law code of Germany to this day.

➢ Until 1899, the individual German states applied either state codifications (CMBC, ALR, CC, Saxon civil code), *ius commune*, or even the *Sachsenspiegel*.

➢ In individual areas, the law had already been harmonised before 1871, such as the Bills of Exchange Act (*Wechselordnung*) 1848 and the General German Commercial Code 1861, which had been introduced in all German territories, including Austria (there under the name *Allgemeines Handelsgesetzbuch*, General Commercial Code, 1862). The draft of a uniform law of obligations from 1866 (the "Dresden Draft") never came into effect because of the German Confederation's dissolution soon after its completion.

➢ At the same time that the German Empire was established in 1871, a new criminal code came into effect that was primarily based on the Prussian Criminal Code of 1851. In 1879, the *Reichsjustizgesetze*, which included the German Code of Civil Procedure and the German Code of Criminal Procedure, came into effect, which – although they have been amended many times – are still applied in Germany today.

➢ In 1873, the Reichstag was given the competence to harmonise private law, and a commission was appointed for this purpose in 1874. Its most prominent members were the two Pandectists BERNHARD WINDSCHEID and GOTTLIEB PLANCK. The first draft that it submitted in 1888 was a thoroughly pandectistic codification. It was widely criticised (not only, but also for this reason), especially by the Germanist OTTO VON GIERKE, and was therefore revised again; the determining influence of pandectistics, however, remained.

➢ In a parallel development, a Commercial Code (*Handelsgesetzbuch*) was also debated and adopted in 1897. It came into effect together with the BGB on 1 January 1900.

➢ The BGB is characterized by a high level of abstraction, which means that it is difficult for non-jurists to understand. It reflected an individualistic, capitalist social and economic order; GIERKE's and also ANTON MENGER's criticism (⇨ par. 4311) was therefore also aimed at the code's lack of social quality. Nevertheless, it served as a model for several other codifications, such as the Japanese Civil Code 1898, the Swiss Civil Code 1907, the Greek Civil Code 1946, and even – not because of its content, but because of its "perfect" legal technique – the Soviet Russian Civil Code 1922.

4308 The **Swiss Civil Code** 1907, largely the work of EUGEN HUBER, came into effect in 1912.

➢ In the 19th century, several cantons had adopted civil codes, some of them based on the CC (e.g. Geneva), others on the ABGB (e.g. Bern). A largely independent creation was the Zurich Civil Code 1856, in which JOHANN CASPAR BLUNTSCHLI had been involved. A harmonisation of the law for all Swiss cantons was first achieved in the Code of Obligations (*Obligationenrecht*); it was passed in 1881 and came into effect throughout Switzerland in 1883.

➢ In 1886–93, EUGEN HUBER, a jurist from the canton of Zurich, wrote a four-volume account of Swiss private law and its history; even before he had completed this work, he was commissioned by the Federal Council in 1892 to prepare a draft for a civil code, which he presented in 1904. After about three years of deliberations, the new civil code was unanimously adopted by the Swiss Parliament on 10 December 1907. The code of obligations from 1881 was revised but not integrated into the civil code; instead, it was repromulgated as a separate statute in 1911 and came into effect together with the civil code in 1912.

➢ Unlike the German BGB, its Swiss counterpart is written in a language accessible to the general public (no abstract "general provisions"); it is derived from the Historical School of Law, but not only from its Romanist branch. It also incorporates local particularities.

➢ The provision on how to fill gaps in the law in article 1 of the Swiss Civil Code is particularly well-known; it instructs the judge to decide in accordance with customary law and, in the absence of customary law, in accordance with the rule that he or she would make as a legislator. The Swiss Civil Code thus encourages judges to engage in law-making.

➢ The Swiss Civil Code was taken up by Turkey in 1926, which since the 19th century – but especially under ATATÜRK (⇨ par. 6101) – had been seeking to bring its legal culture closer to the European model.

4309 In Austria, the civil law scholar JOSEPH UNGER (⇨ par. 4306) initially advocated an overall reform of the ABGB based on the principles of the Historical School of Law. Later, he abandoned this approach and demand merely "mosaic-like amendments". This demand was accommodated with the three **partial amendments to the ABGB** in 1914, 1915, and 1916.

➢ UNGER initially assumed that the redactors of the ABGB had tried to codify Roman law and accused them of having misunderstood many of its aspects in the process. Only when in 1888/89 JULIUS OFNER published the previously unknown consultation minutes on the ABGB commission did it become apparent that the redactors had quite deliberately deviated from Roman law on numerous occasions, which also prompted UNGER to view their work more favourably.

➢ In 1911, a bill for the comprehensive amendment of the ABGB was submitted to the Reichsrat and adopted (with modifications) by the House of Lords in 1912. Before the bill could be adopted in the House of Deputies, the First World War broke out, and parliament was not reconvened until 1917; the civil law reform was therefore implemented through three emergency decrees issued by the emperor. The "partial amendments" were passed in 1914, 1915, and 1916, respectively, and had a profound impact on the text of the ABGB; about one-third of the sections were modified, and in numerous areas, the provisions were aligned with those of the German BGB.

➢ In many cases, the partial amendments reflected the socio-economic changes brought about by the Industrial Revolution, such as the provision that a contractual partner who makes use of a vicarious agent is liable for this agent's harmful conduct as if it were his own (§ 1313a ABGB). Long-obsolete provisions, such as a rule that prohibited physicians and lawyers from charging for their services, were eliminated, and a prohibition on usurious contracts was added (§ 879 ABGB). The introduction of a statutory right of inheritance for spouses was probably a consequence of the drastic decline in marriage contracts in the 19th century.

4310 A recodification of Austrian **criminal procedure law** was undertaken by the criminal law professor and Minister of Justice JULIUS GLASER, resulting in the Code of Criminal Procedure 1873. Attempts to codify substantive criminal law, on the other hand, failed (⇨ par. 8303).

➢ Austrian criminal procedure law after 1848 was subject to numerous changes that reflected the prevailing constitutional situation ("Criminal procedure law is applied constitutional law").

➢ Hence, in 1850, the procedural part of the StGB from 1803 was replaced by a modern Code of Criminal Procedure, which went back to a draft by JOSEPH VON WÜRTH. It accommodated the demands of the 1848 revolution for the abolition of the inquisitorial system and the introduction of accusatory trials, based on the French model.

➢ In 1853, during the period of neo-absolutism, the Code of Criminal Procedure was enacted, which in many aspects reverted to the legal regime of 1803. Its main redactor was ANTON HYE VON GLUNEK, who later became Minister of Justice.

➢ The December Constitution of 1867 eventually provided the constitutional framework for a return to the modern accusatory system. After several unsuccessful attempts, the reform was eventually implemented during the term of office of the Minister of Justice GLASER (1871–79). The Code of Criminal Procedure adopted in 1873 is still in force today (with significant amendments, ⇨ par. 8303).

3. Alternative Approches

4311 The conceptual jurisprudence imported from Germany was met with criticism (especially in Austria), which led to the development of various **alternative approaches**. In particular, the limited value attributed by conceptual jurisprudence to the work of the judges was criticised.

➢ EUGEN EHRLICH, a native of the Austrian Bukovina, founded the Free Law movement, which advocated the elaboration and complementation of statutory law by the courts. According to EHRLICH, the law is developed less by legislation than by the society in which it operates, making him a pioneer of modern legal sociologyO.

➢ The counter-currents to conceptual jurisprudence also included the various social legal theories, which in Austria were represented primarily by the civil proceduralist ANTON MENGER and the later state chancellor KARL RENNER ("Socialists of the chair"). MENGER also achieved fame beyond the borders of the monarchy, not least through his criticism of the "First Draft" of the German BGB from 1888, which only formally guaranteed equality before the law and did not consider the actual inequalities in society, which is why he referred to it as the class law of a minority.

➢ MENGER's disciple FRANZ KLEIN published a series of essays in the journal *Juristische Blätter* in 1890/91 entitled *Pro futuro (For the future)*, in which he emphasised the important role of the judge and called for the strengthening of the latter's position in civil proceedings. KLEIN was thereupon commissioned to draft a new Code of Civil Procedure, which the Reichsrat adopted in 1895 without any significant changes.

➢ It came into effect in 1898 and attracted worldwide attention. Plans in the interwar period to also introduce it in Germany (whereas Austria was to adopt the German BGB) were not realised, but the German Code of Civil

Procedure was amended in 1933 along the lines of the Austrian model. In Austria, it is still in force today but has been amended several times.

4312 The most consequential alternative to conceptual jurisprudence, however, was developed by one of its former main representatives, the Viennese Romanist RUDOLPH VON JHERING. It was called the **jurisprudence of purpose** and was influenced by social Darwinist ideas.

➤ JHERING had been a follower of PUCHTA's teachings for a long time but then spectacularly broke with his previous ideas. He first presented his new agenda in a lecture called *Der Kampf ums Recht* (*The Struggle for Law*), given to the Vienna Law Society on 11 March 1872, and then described it in greater detail in his book *Der Zweck im Recht* (*Law as a Means to an End*, 1877/83).

➤ In his book *The Origin of Species by Means of Natural Selection, or the Preservation of Favoured Races in the Struggle for Life* (1859), CHARLES DARWIN, in keeping with the philosophy of his time, had developed the idea of the natural selection of biological species through the *"survival of the fittest"*. JHERING applied these thoughts to human coexistence; the title of his lecture was a conscious reference to DARWIN's *Struggle for Life*.

➤ For JHERING, "purpose" was the actual "creator of all law". Every legal claim was subject to competition by those who were using it to pursue certain objectives. He argued that there were not only egoistic objectives (self-preservation, pleasure, etc.) but also those of "ethical self-assertion", for instance, "the ethical". With this approach, he confronted both positivism and the traditional theory of natural law by considering law neither detached from the reason of its emergence nor as a direct product of reason.

4. Marxist Legal Theory

4313 **Marxism** was founded in the 19th century by KARL MARX and FRIEDRICH ENGELS and further elaborated in the 20th century, especially in the Socialist states of East-Central and Eastern Europe (⇨ par. 5201).

➤ MARX studied in Bonn and Berlin during the Pre-March period and counted various disciples of the philosopher G. W. F. HEGEL among his teachers. He then worked mainly as a journalist. ENGELS, the son of a textile manufacturer, who had encountered and described in detail the miserable living conditions of factory workers in England in 1842, became his lifelong friend; together, they published the *Communist Manifesto* in 1848.

➤ MARX's main work is *Das Kapital* (*Capital*, 1867). Marxism, which he and ENGELS established, is a comprehensive worldview that encompasses its own philosophy of history and economic and social theory, as well as a theory of law. MARX had already outlined the fundamental concepts of the latter in his *Zur Kritik der Politischen Oekonomie* (*A Contribution to the Critique of Political Economy*, 1859).

4314 Marxism's theoretical foundation is a **materialist philosophy of history**, which describes the course of history as determined by the economic structure of a society. This structure constitutes the material "base", from which a legal and political "superstructure" arises; this base is also associated with certain social "forms of consciousness" (religion, philosophy).

➢ In this, MARX to some extent followed HEGEL's approach but, in his own words, turned HEGEL's ideas "upside down", since the latter had taught an idealist philosophy of history according to which the course of history was determined by ideas.

➢ History, according to MARX, is a process that unfolds as a matter of necessity and which is to a certain extent also predictable; while humanity initially lived in a state of *primitive Communism*, its history since the advent of private property has been characterised by class struggles. In ancient *slave society*, the society of medieval *feudalism*, and in modern *capitalism*, the propertied classes have always exploited the classes without property, the proletariat.

➢ But, according to MARX, capitalism already carries the seeds of its own decay, as more and more wealth is concentrated in the hands of an increasingly small number of people. The ever-growing proletariat would therefore one day seize power and establish a "dictatorship of the proletariat". The *Socialism* thus realised, however, was only a transitional stage which, after the abolition of all private property and thus of all class antagonisms, would lead to *Communism*, a classless society.

4315 In Marxism, the **law of bourgeois society** is conceived as a means for the ruling class to consolidate its rule.

➢ The extent to which law, as part of the "superstructure", merely reflects the transformations of the "base" (the underlying economic structures) or is consciously used by the ruling classes as an element of its agency, is debated within Marxism.

➢ Class struggle, according to the Marxist view, is primarily economic in nature and driven into the juridical-political sphere by the law of bourgeois society.

4316 In Communism, the law appears to be dispensable because the class struggle has been overcome; it will therefore "**die off**" together with the state. According to an alternative Socialist theory, however, the law could also be employed to develop a Socialist social order.

➢ The (mostly non-Marxist) "Socialists of the chair" (⇨ par. 4311) in particular propagated a "social jurisprudence" that would use the law to bring about changes in society.

➢ ENGELS, on the other hand, thought that the Marxist theory of law was useful only for a (negative) critique, and that it could not be used for a (positive) reform of the law.

Part V

The Age of Far-Left Dictatorships

A Developments

5101 In Russia, the disastrous course of the First World War led to the fall of the tsar in February 1917. In the "**October Revolution**" of 1917, the Communists (Bolshevists) under LENIN succeeded in gaining power in Russia.

➢ After Tsar NICHOLAS II's abdication in the "February Revolution" of 1917, a bourgeois government had proclaimed a republic. However, because it remained in the war, it was overthrown in the Bolshevik "October Revolution" (which had more the character of a coup than a popular uprising). LENIN became the new head of government and immediately concluded first an armistice, then also peace with the Central Powers (⇨ par. 6101).

➢ The elections to a constituent assembly held in November 1917 returned only 23.5 percent of the vote for the Bolsheviks. In a parallel move, however, the workers and soldiers had formed councils (*soviets*, ⇨ par. 5205), in which the Bolsheviks prevailed. When the constituent assembly refused to recognise "soviet power", it was forcibly dissolved by LENIN in January 1918.

➢ An "All-Russian Soviet Congress" adopted a constitution on 10 July 1918, transforming Russia into a soviet republic. LENIN was only able to fully establish himself after a bloody civil war that lasted until 1921. The former tsar and his family were shot dead by the Bolsheviks on 17 July 1918.

5102 In 1922, the **Union of Soviet Socialist Republics** (USSR, Soviet Union) was founded. For a long time, it was the only socialist state in the world, with the exception of Mongolia. It was only after World War II that dictatorships modelled on the USSR emerged in numerous other states in Europe (⇨ par. 8106) and outside Europe (⇨ par. 8104), with the support of the Soviet Union.

➢ The USSR was the result of a merger of Soviet Russia with Ukraine, Belarus, and Transcaucasia (= Armenia, Georgia, and Azerbaijan), where the Communists had also gained power and formed soviet republics. In 1936, more soviet republics were created through secessions. Despite the federal structure, Russia remained the dominant power within the union.

➢ The history of Soviet Russia resp. the Soviet Union can be divided into five phases: war communism, New Economic Policy, Stalinism, Post-Stalinism, and Perestrojka. During the first period (1917–21), attempts were made to implement communist ideology with great severity and without regard for the actual feasibility of the measures. Mass expropriations took place, but workers' right to strike, for example, was also banned. This phase culminated in a catastrophic famine in 1921/22.

➢ In 1922, LENIN decided to loosen the grip of the dictatorship, allowing a limited degree of private ownership of the means of production again. This phase, which lasted until 1928, was known as the "New Economic Policy".

➢ Even before LENIN's death in 1924, JOSEPH STALIN (1922–53) took power as General Secretary of the Communist Party of the Soviet Union (CPSU). He ordered political "cleansings" and forced collectivisations of especially the peasantry, which resulted in millions of deaths. In Ukraine, a famine was deliberately caused in 1931/32 (*Holodomor*). The last democratic elements of the Soviet constitution gave way to a totalitarian dictatorship (*Stalinism*), which some – paradoxically, but tellingly – call "left-wing fascism" (⇨ par. 7201).

➢ After 1918, attempted communist coups took place in numerous European countries, including Austria. Communist regimes emerged briefly in Bavaria, Hungary, and Slovakia, but had not been able to survive in the long term. Only Mongolia, which had broken away from China with Russian military assistance in 1921, managed to permanently establish a Soviet-style people's republic (until 1990). The "world revolution" that MARX had regarded as inevitable had thus failed to materialise, but STALIN now advocated the thesis that "Socialism in one country" alone was also viable. The international isolation in which the USSR initially found itself was eased, and in 1934 it joined the League of Nations (⇨ par. 6102).

➢ Stalin remained in power until his death in 1953. In 1956, a "de-Stalinisation" process was set in motion, marking the beginning of the fourth phase in the history of the Soviet Union, which lasted until 1985. The dictatorship was relaxed to some extent, but the political structures became ossified and ultimately proved resistant to reform. This proved fatal in the fifth phase, in which a restructuring (*"perestroika"*) was attempted in earnest from 1985 (⇨ par. 8133).

B Structures

5201 Like the "bourgeois democracies" of the West, the **Socialist dictatorships** (or "people's democracies") of Eastern and East-Central Europe also adopted constitutional documents that regulated the state powers and the legal status of the individual (*constitution in the material sense*) and, at least in theory, were of a higher rank than simple laws (*constitution in the formal sense*).

➢ Soviet Russia was the first Socialist country to adopt a constitution on 10 July 1918, which was followed by the USSR's first constitution on 26 July 1923. Both were replaced by new constitutions under STALIN in 1936 and 1937 respectively, whereby much "ideological ballast" was discarded in favour of increased pragmatism; however, the dictatorial element also gained in strength.

➢ After the Second World War, the states of East-Central Europe in the Soviet sphere of power also adopted constitutions that were strongly influenced by the Soviet model (ČSR 1948, Poland 1952, etc.). The constitution of the GDR from 1949 had a special position, as it was partly based on the Weimar Constitution of 1919, in order not to jeopardise the reunification of Germany – a project to which the GDR was still committed at the time.

➢ From 1968 onwards, most Socialist constitutions were amended or replaced by new ones (ČSSR 1968; Hungary 1972; Soviet Union 1977; etc.). They sought to cover not only the state but also the entire socio-political order. The different national traditions were also taken into account more than before, so that they differed more markedly from each other. The GDR, on the other hand, abandoned its old ties to Weimar and its commitment to German reunification with its constitution of 1968.

5202 The political system of the Socialist people's democracies was primarily determined by the **claim to leadership of the Communist party** ("dictatorship of the proletariat").

➢ The ideological basis of the Communist parties was the doctrine developed by MARX and ENGELS (⇨ par. 4313), which was further developed by LENIN and others in the 20th century (*Marxism-Leninism*).

➢ The states led by Communist parties described the contemporary (transitional) order of the state as Socialism ("to each according to his merit"); it was to be developed further towards Communism ("to each according to his needs"). Several states included the word "Socialist" in their official names (Union of Soviet Socialist Republics – USSR, Czechoslovak Socialist Republic – ČSSR, Socialist Federal Republic of Yugoslavia, etc.).

➢ The "dictatorship of the proletariat" as a transitional phase *en route* toward a classless society was most acutely expressed in the Soviet Russian constitution of 1918, which, for instance, excluded from the right to vote people who "used wage labour for profit" or "lived on unearned income". On the other hand, foreigners working in Russia enjoyed the same political rights as nationals (Articles 20, 65). Later constitutions departed from this radical conception.

➢ The Communist party was usually the only legally permitted party. Some states (GDR, ČSSR) formally had – and the People's Republic of China still has – a multi-party system, but even in these cases, the Communist party (which in the GDR was called the Socialist Unity Party of Germany) makes a claim to leadership that is accepted by the other parties.

➢ The legislative bodies were elected in such a way that only a single list was available, from which the voters could delete individual candidates; in practice, this had little influence on the election results. The composition of parliament – as well as, as in the case of the GDR, the ČSSR, and China, the distribution of mandates among the individual parties – was thus essentially already decided before the election.

➢ Although secrecy of the ballot was constitutionally guaranteed in some states, making use of this right was considered a hostile act and *de facto* rarely granted.

5203 The constitutional reality in the Socialist states can only be fully understood against the background of the **Marxist conception of law** (⇨ par. 4315–4316).

➢ According to this view, the law was only a tool of politics and subordinate to the latter. Considerations of political expediency took precedence over juridical subsumptions. In the latter, the "class character" of the norms always had to be taken into account.

➢ Since the Communist party claimed to be the guarantor of the right policies, its actions could not be restricted by legal norms. Rather, it argued that the law should be applied according to considerations of expediency.

➢ The "bourgeois" principle of legality was replaced by the principle of "Socialist legality"; while the law should be strictly observed, it should always be interpreted in accordance with the requirements of social progress. The hidden contradiction in this postulate was consciously accepted and resulted in the diminished importance of the law and the constitution.

➢ The actual significance of the formal constitution rested in its propagandistic function; it codified the ideology of the state. This was also reflected in extraordinarily long preambles, which often referred to certain historical events. All this resulted in a disconnect between the written constitution and the *"Realverfassung"*.

5204 The organisation of the state followed the idea of the **unity of state power**. The separation of powers was rejected, and federalism could barely evolve either.

➢ The idea that the parliamentary representatives of the people held a superior position vis-à-vis the administration and the courts was an illusion; in reality, they were utterly powerless. The actual political decision-making occurred within the Communist party, especially in its "Politburo", and the General Secretariat.

➢ The political penetration of all state organs by the Communist party and the cumulation of responsibilities ensured the unity of state power. The general secretary of the Communist party was often also the head of state. A combined identity of party leader and head of government was untypical but still sometimes the case (e.g. STALIN in 1941–53).

➢ The USSR as well as (since 1968) the ČSSR were established as federal states, but their federalism was poorly developed; in the GDR, the Länder were eliminated in 1952 in favour of a centralised state structure. The only Socialist state where the individual provinces had a significant degree of autonomy was Yugoslavia.

➢ Although most socialist constitutions contained fundamental rights catalogues, these had little practical significance. Despite the promise of freedom of religion and conscience, religious communities were often subject to repression. On the other hand, as early as 1846, Pope PIUS IX condemned communism, which was confirmed in even stronger terms by Pope PIUS XI in 1937 as a reaction against the 'sorry effects' of this doctrine in Russia.

➢ Constitutional courts were only introduced in Yugoslavia in 1964 and in Poland in 1986; in the ČSSR such a court was promised in 1968 but never realised. Administrative courts, such as those that existed in the successor states of the Habsburg Monarchy, were dissolved; instead, only informal complaints to the administrative authorities were possible. The public prosecutors were also to ensure compliance with the laws not only in criminal law but in administrative law as well; the individual had no legal right to the authorities taking action.

5205 The parliamentary assemblies were composed according to the **soviet system** (from the Russian word for "council"); the deputies were not allowed to vote based on their own convictions but were bound by the mandate of their voters (*bound mandate*).

➤ The basic idea behind the soviet system was grassroots democracy; the population would elect delegates in every town, factory, army unit, etc., who in turn would elect delegates, etc., all the way up to the Supreme Soviet (= the central parliament of the USSR). Through the bound mandate, the will of the people should propagate upwards.

➤ The principle of the bound (or "imperative") mandate seemed to realise the democratic idea more successfully than that of the free mandate (⇨ par. 4213). However, this also meant that parliament lost its role as a place for the political elite to exchange ideas, since discussions could not effect a change in their voting habits. The actual political decisions needed to be taken outside parliament.

➤ Hence, the system proved impracticable, and soon after the October Revolution, it was gradually modified until the parliamentary assemblies finally lost all power. With the Soviet constitution of 1936, the principle of delegation was replaced by the direct election of the Supreme Soviet, so that the grassroots element disappeared.

➤ Nevertheless, the Socialist constitutions retained the possibility to recall a deputy who "violated his or her duties" prior to the next election (e.g. Article 57 of the GDR Constitution 1968). However, such provisions had hardly any practical significance.

5206 The **property regime** was characterised by its division into consumer goods and means of production. With few exceptions, the latter could only be owned by the state or cooperatives.

➤ The phrase "means of production" was coined by MARX. He used it to refer to work equipment and work objects, e.g. tools, raw materials, and finished goods.

➤ The most important means of production was real estate. Peasants were expropriated on a large scale, often by violent means, and agricultural production was carried out by state (*sovkhozes*) and cooperative farms (*kolkhozes*).

➤ The system of a centrally planned economy that was introduced in lieu of a market economy caused private initiative to wither away; luxury goods were virtually unheard of. At best, it could cover the basic needs of the population, but often not even those.

5207 In many of the **dictatorships of East Asia**, doctrines were developed that referred to themselves as advanced versions of Marxism, but had little to do with the original ideas. The writings of MARX and ENGELS are barely taught anymore in these countries.

➢ For example, the Khmer Rouge regime in Cambodia (1975–1979) placed peasants at the centre of its ideology, instead of workers, in line with the actual situation in the country. This was seen by some as the purest form of Marxism, while others saw it as a complete departure from it. The radical, inhumane measures of this regime, which were aimed at returning the country to a state of complete barbarism (e.g. by murdering people because of their ability to read and write), were (disparagingly) referred to as *"stone age communism"* in German political science.

➢ In North Korea, Marxism-Leninism was replaced by the *Juche idea* from the 1970s onwards, which focuses on the autarky of the country and the cult of personality surrounding the ruling KIM family.

➢ The teachings of the first communist president of China, MAO ZEDONG (1949–59; de facto China's leading figure until his death in 1976), which were collected in the "Little Red Book" from 1964 (*Maoism*), became of particular importance. He also sought to combine nationalism with communism and to replace the working class with the peasantry. In line with the Russian revolutionary LEON TROTSKY, MAO proclaimed that the revolution must be "perpetual" in order to maintain its strength. This led to the so-called Cultural Revolution from 1966 to 1976, which claimed millions of lives.

➢ Under DENG XIAOPING (as "paramount leader" China's dominant political figure 1978–89), China's centrally planned economy was phased out (including the abolition of the *rénmín gōngshè*, which were comparable to the Soviet *kolkhozes*) and the country increasingly transitioned to a capitalist market economy. These changes, however, did not go hand in hand with a democratisation of China; attempts towards a more democratic system were violently suppressed (as in particular in 1989 in Beijing).

C Legislation and Jurisprudence

5301 A specific type of jurisprudence and a **Marxist approach to legislation** emerged in the Socialist states.

➢ Soon after the "October Revolution" in 1917 (⇨ par. 5101), it became clear that even the Soviet republics, at least temporarily, could not exist without a legal system. Thus, Russia passed statutes on family law and labour law aimed at creating a Communist society. In 1922, the Russian Civil Code followed, which was influenced by the German BGB (despite the latter's "bourgeois character").

➢ During the same period, the Soviet People's Commissar for Justice PËTR STUČKA, who had played a decisive role in the creation of the above-mentioned laws, but also LENIN himself, developed a Soviet legal theory. The theory of the "death of the state", which had already become questionable with the establishment of the Soviet Union, was permanently abandoned under STALIN.

➢ The Soviet Russian codifications served as a model for the legislative efforts in the other Soviet republics and – after 1945 – also in the Socialist states of East-Central Europe. New Socialist civil codes came into effect in the ČSR in 1950 and in Hungary in 1960.

➢ The GDR held on to the German BGB from 1896 until 1975 in order not to jeopardise German reunification. However, it was reinterpreted in the context of the "class struggle". The theoretical foundations for this reinterpretation were established in particular at the Babelsberg Conference in 1958. Like in Russia, family law in the GDR was excluded from the general civil code and given its own statutory regime in 1965. The codification efforts regarding the general private law, which began in 1952, were not completed until 1975. On 1 January 1976, the civil code of the GDR came into effect and remained valid until Germany reunification in 1990 (⇨ par. 8131).

Part VI

The Age of Democracy

A Developments

1. Europe 1918–1933

6101 Despite Russia's early withdrawal in the spring of 1918, the First World War was decided in favour of the Entente in the autumn of the same year, which was mainly the result of the USA entering the war on its side in 1917. On 3 November 1918, an armistice was signed with Austria-Hungary, and another on 11 November with Germany. The Russian, German, and Austrian emperors, the Turkish sultan, and the German princes fell. The **Peace Treaties of 1918/19/20** created a plethora of new states in Central and Eastern Europe.

➢ In 1918, Russia and Ukraine signed the peace treaties of Brest-Litovsk. The peace treaties with the "Central Powers" were concluded in the Paris suburbs of Versailles (Germany 1919), St. Germain-en-Laye (Austria 1919, ⇨ par. 6110), Neuilly (Bulgaria 1919), Trianon (Hungary 1920), and Sèvres (Turkey 1920).

➢ The autumn of 1918 by no means marked the end of hostilities in Europe; on the contrary, local conflicts (Poland/Russia, Hungary/Romania, Greece/Turkey, etc.) dragged on for years. In other respects, too, the "interwar period", as the era 1918–39 is often called, was frequently marked by military conflicts, civil wars, revolutions, coups d'état, and other acts of violence.

➢ New states were: Finland, Estonia, Latvia, Lithuania, and for a short time also Belarus and Ukraine (all of them previously Russian); Poland (made up of previously Russian, German, and Austrian territories); Czechoslovakia (ČSR, previously Austrian and Hungarian territories). The until then German city of Danzig [Gdańsk], and Fiume [Rijeka], which had previously belonged to Hungary, became sovereign city-states. Serbia merged with Montenegro and the "State of Slovenes, Croats, and Serbs" (created shortly before from Austro-Hungarian territories) to form the "Kingdom of Serbs, Croats, and Slovenes" (SHS State; from 1929: Kingdom of Yugoslavia).

➢ The Republic of (German-)Austria also considered itself a new state, but this was disputed by the victorious powers (⇨ par. 6110).

➢ Hungary lost more than 63 percent of its national territory, but unlike Austria, it maintained its continuity as a successor of pre-war Hungary. From November 1918 to February 1920, Hungary was a republic (March-

August 1919: Communist soviet republic), after which it was declared a kingdom again. The throne remained vacant and the royal administrator MIKLÓS HORTHY (1920–44) acted as head of state. When ex-King CHARLES IV (the Austrian ex-Emperor CHARLES I) tried to regain the Hungarian crown by military means in 1921. He was captured and exiled to Madeira, where he died in 1922.

➤ Significant territorial gains were achieved by Romania (Transylvania, Moldavia), Italy (South Tyrol, Trieste, Istria), and France (Alsace-Lorraine) in particular. Germany had to give up not only its colonies but also about 13 percent of its European territory and was obliged to make extensive reparations. Bulgaria lost its access to the Mediterranean.

6102 To safeguard the new order of peace, an international organisation of states, the **League of Nations**, was founded; it can be regarded as a precursor of the UN. Although it was initiated by US President WOODROW WILSON (as point 14 of the "14 Points"), the USA (as well as the USSR until 1934) remained outside the League of Nations, which was one of the main reasons for its limited political significance. The seat of the League of Nations was in Geneva.

➤ Its covenant was not an independent treaty but was incorporated into all the Paris Peace Treaties (using an identical text). Nevertheless, only states that had emerged from the First World War as victorious powers were among the founding members of the League of Nations. While Austria was admitted as early as 1920, Germany did not join until 1926.

➤ After 1919, the USA returned to the MONROE Doctrine (⇨ par. 3119), meaning that it did not want to interfere in European affairs any more than was absolutely necessary, and therefore refused to join the League of Nations. The Soviet Union still clung to the idea of a "world revolution" for a long time (⇨ par. 5102), which made interactions with the "bourgeois states" in the context of official international relations almost impossible.

➤ The League of Nations had three main organs: the Assembly, the Council, and the Secretariat. While in the Assembly, each member had one vote, the Council originally consisted of four permanent members (UK, France, Italy, and Japan) and four members elected for a fixed term. After Germany was admitted to the League of Nations, it was also given a permanent seat on the Council, which met with fierce resistance in some quarters.

➤ The Permanent Court of International Justice, founded in 1920, was not formally an organ of the League of Nations, but the two were closely linked both politically and legally. It complemented the International Court of Arbitration, which had been established in 1899 (⇨ par. 4123) and also had its seat in The Hague.

➤ In order to secure not only peace between the states but also peace within the states, the Paris Treaties also incorporated the statute of an International Labour Organisation (ILO), which still exists today. It is primarily dedicated to improving working conditions and fighting unemployment.

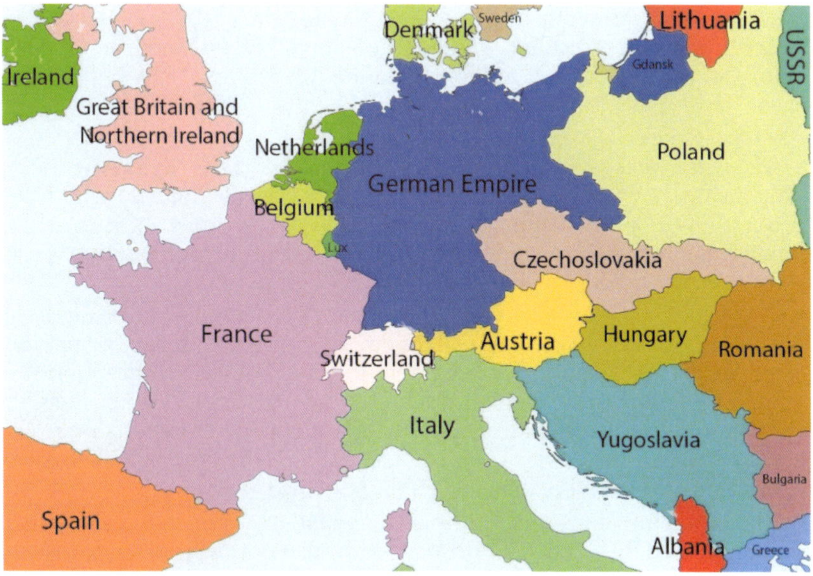

Map 12: Central Europe in 1929
Source: https://commons.wikimedia.org/wiki/File:Europa_1929.svg

➢ In the treaties, religious and ethnic minorities were granted basic guarantees (e.g. schooling in their own language; public religious practice). Inthe event of a violation of these guarantees, they could appeal directly to the League of Nations. In 1921, the Norwegian FRIDTJOF NANSEN was appointed High Commissioner of the League of Nations for Refugees and developed, among other things, a passport for stateless persons ("Nansen passport").

➢ In 1928/29, following an initiative of the US Secretary of State FRANK B. KELLOGG and his French counterpart ARISTIDE BRIAND, 43 states, including Germany and Austria, signed an agreement in which they renounced the right to wage wars (⇨ par. 4123) and promised to resolve conflicts peacefully (KELLOGG-BRIAND Pact). The only exceptions were self-defence and sanctions imposed by the League of Nations.

6103 With the Treaty of Sèvres, the Allies intended to completely **destroy the Ottoman Empire** and significantly enlarge Greece. The Middle East was to be divided into spheres of influence for the UK, France, and Italy. However, the Turkish general MUSTAFA KEMAL ATATÜRK was able to defeat the Greek army in the Greek-Turkisch War (1919–22) and subsequently regained some other former Ottoman possessions. The *Treaty of Lausanne* in 1923 gave Turkey the borders that it has essentially retained to this day. The agreements reached in 1920, however, had long-term significance for Palestine and the Arab world.

➢ Greece was ultimately unable to gain territory at Turkey's expense. The Treaty of Lausanne resulted in the largest forced resettlement in modern history so far. Around 1.2 million Orthodox Christians ("Greeks") had to leave Turkey, while around 400,000 Muslims ("Turks") had to leave Greece.

➢ The sultan was overthrown in 1922 and replaced as a religious figure by a (politically powerless) caliph, who, however, was also forced to abdicate in 1924. As State President of the Turkish Republic (1923–38), ATATÜRK pursued a policy of Europeanisation and secularisation for his country, e.g. by introducing the Swiss Civil Code in 1926 (⇨ par. 4308).

➢ During the war, the Turkish army had murdered hundreds of thousands of Armenians on suspicion of collaboration with the Entente (*Armenian genocide*, to this day not recognised by official Turkish historiography). The efforts to establish an Armenian state in 1919 consisting of former Russian and Ottoman territories failed; only an Armenian Soviet Republic was established within the Soviet Union (⇨ par. 5102), the border with Turkey being approximately the same as before the World War.

➢ The plans for the formation of an independent Arab state, which had been developed during the World War, were also not realised. HUSSEIN BIN ALI, a direct descendant of the Prophet, from the Hashemite dynasty that had ruled over Mecca for centuries, assumed the title of "King of the Arabs" in 1916. He had to relinquish this title under pressure from the Entente. When the Ottoman Caliphate was abolished in 1924, HUSSEIN declared himself the new caliph. Following this, he was overthrown by the Wahhabi sheikh ABDULAZIZ IBN SAUD, who created the Kingdom of Saudi Arabia in 1932.

➢ As "League of Nations mandates", Syria and Lebanon came under French rule, Palestine, Jordan, and Iraq under British rule. The agreement concluded by HUSSEIN's son FAISAL in 1919 with CHAIM WEIZMANN (first president of Israel from 1949 to 1952) on the formation of a Jewish state in Palestine (*Faisal-Weizmann agreement*) therefore did not come into force. FAISAL himself became King of Iraq in 1921, where the Hashemites ruled until 1958. In Jordan, another line of this dynasty has continued to reign as kings from 1921 to the present day.

6104 The **British Empire** had reached its greatest expansion (around one quarter of the world's population) through the Paris Peace Treaties, but lost prominence in world politics to the USA. The extreme expansion of the colonial empire stretched British resources, and the *British Empire* was transformed into the *British Commonwealth of Nations*.

➢ Especially Ireland and the "settler colonies", i.e. the colonies with large populations of British descent (Canada, Australia, New Zealand, South Africa, Newfoundland) became increasingly autonomous from the 19th century onwards and developed into *"dominions"*. In 1926, the equal status of the dominions in relation to the British mother country within the British Commonwealth was proclaimed (BALFOUR Declaration). The *Statute of Westminster* in 1931 gave them almost full internal and external autonomy, but they remained monarchies under the British Crown.

➢ Ireland, which had been in a real union with Great Britain since 1801, politically seceded from Great Britain in 1922 as the Irish Free State and formally left the Commonwealth in 1948 as a republic. Only the predominantly Protestant province of Ulster remained part of the United Kingdom of Great Britain and Northern Ireland.

➢ In 1922, Egypt and in 1932, Iraq were formally granted independence (although the UK still retained some influence). In many other colonies, there was a growing desire for independence, particularly in British India, where MAHATMA GANDHI sought to realise India's independence through non-violent means from 1914/20. The end of the caliphate in 1924 led to major protests among Indian Muslims.

➢ As a new war would only have weakened the power of the British even further, their external policies in the interwar period were to a large extent characterised by *appeasement* (cf. for instance the Munich Agreement with National Socialist Germany of 1938, ⇨ par. 7110).

6105 Although **Italy** emerged from the war as a victorious power, it was disappointed by the results of the peace negotiations, which fuelled the nationalism that had existed since the Risorgimento (⇨ par. 4107). The Fascist Party (*Partito Nazionale Fascista*, PNF) under BENITO MUSSOLINI (called the "Duce") emerged victorious from the clashes between far-left and far-right forces. He seized power by force in 1922 and established the world's first fascist state, which became a model for many other right-wing movements and systems (⇨ par. 7102; par. 7201).

➢ In the Treaty of St. Germain, Italy was able to acquire South Tyrol, Trieste and Istria. However, hopes of further territorial gains in the eastern Adriatic (where a large proportion of the population had been Italian since Venetian times) and in Anatolia and the Caucasus at the expense of Turkey were not realised. The Italian poet GABRIELE D'ANNUNZIO spoke of a "mutilated victory".

➢ Immediately after the signing of the Treaty of St. Germain, in October 1919, D'ANNUNZIO, at the head of a group of irregular combatants, seized the city of Fiume (Rijeka), which was disputed between Italy and Yugoslavia. The peculiar constitution he drafted for Fiume combined socialist and anti-democratic demands with utopian ideas of a new society that would not be torn apart by political parties, often borrowing from Roman antiquity. These ideas later became a model for fascism.

➢ At around the same time, the Italian Socialists grew more radical. There were calls for the expropriation of large landowners; strikes occurred and workers violently occupied factories, which in turn provoked equally violent counter-reactions by initially only loosely organised combat groups (*Fasci di combattimento*). These were mainly recruited from former soldiers and were largely financially supported by the large landowners and factory owners. In the summer of 1922, they succeeded in violently breaking a general strike called by the socialists.

➢ BENITO MUSSOLINI (who had been expelled from the Italian Socialist Party in 1914) placed himself at the helm of these fighting groups, the anti-

Marxists, and the nationalists, and in 1921 founded a new party, the *Partito Nazionale Fascista*, from these heterogeneous movements. In October 1922, he organised a mass movement centred on the "March on Rome" (which started from various cities). This enabled MUSSOLINI to force the king to appoint him as prime minister (until 1943, ⇨ par. 7111).

6106 Germany became a republic in 1918; it was called the **Weimar Republic** after its constitution of 11 August 1919, which had been adopted in Weimar. The economic consequences of the lost war and the harsh peace conditions of Versailles resulted in the rejection of parliamentarism among broad sections of the German population. Right from the start, there was the threat of a Communist takeover, soon followed by violent attempts by right-wing radicals to overthrow the government.

➤ After the fall of the monarchy, the Social Democrat PHILIPP SCHEIDEMANN proclaimed a republic on 9 November 1918; on the same day, the Communist KARL LIEBKNECHT proclaimed a "Socialist republic". Workers' and soldiers' councils were formed based on the Russian model; however, a general congress of soviets rejected the establishment of a soviet republic on 19 December 1918 and called for elections to a constituent national assembly. An uprising of the disappointed Left in January 1919 ("SPARTACUS uprising") was crushed, and LIEBKNECHT was murdered.

➤ For the first time, women were also entitled to vote for the National Assembly; it convened on 6 February 1919 (for security reasons not in Berlin but in Weimar) and elected the Social Democrat FRIEDRICH EBERT, who had headed a provisional government since the collapse of the monarchy, as the *"Reichspräsident"* (until 1925).

➤ The Weimar Constitution strengthened the central state power; the Reichstag took centre stage, whereas the Reichsrat (successor to the previous Federal Council) was essentially left with only a suspensive veto. Great weight was attached to the role of the president (after the 1925 direct popular election: PAUL VON HINDENBURG) through his right to issue emergency decrees and call referenda. The chancellor and ministers were appointed by the president but were politically accountable to the Reichstag.

➤ In contrast to the Constitution of 1871, the Weimar Constitution also had a catalogue of fundamental rights (and fundamental duties!), which did not take precedence over ordinary legislation, however.

➤ Of the numerous radical right-wing groups, the National Socialist German Workers' Party (*Nationalsozialistische Deutsche Arbeiterpartei* – NSDAP, named thus from 1920 onwards) under ADOLF HITLER, which had been founded in 1919, soon became the most prominent. In 1923, it instigated a coup in Munich (the "Beer Hall Putsch"), which failed; HITLER was sentenced to five years in prison (but released early in 1924). During his imprisonment, he began to write the book *Mein Kampf* (*My Struggle*) and decided not to seize power in Germany by force, but through democratic means.

➤ In the Reichstag, both the German Communist Party (*Kommunistische Partei Deutschlands*, KPD) and the NSDAP gained an increasing number of seats, and the remaining democratic parties were no longer able to govern on their own. The governments increasingly had to make use of the president's right to issue emergency decrees ("presidential cabinets").

2. Austria 1918–1933

a) The birth of the republic

6107 In light of the disintegrating Austro-Hungarian Monarchy, the German-speaking members of the Austrian Reichsrat formed a **Provisional National Assembly** in October 1918 and decided on 30 October 1918 **to establish the state of German-Austria** (*Staatsgründungsbeschluss).*

➢ In accordance with Emperor CHARLES I's People's Manifesto of 16 October (⇨ par. 4126), the German-speaking parliamentarians had already convened on 21 October in the building oft he Lower Austrian diet (as opposed to the Reichsrat building). It soon became apparent, however, that the Provisional National Assembly would not discuss a reorganisation of the monarchy, as envisaged in the Manifesto, but rather the creation of a new state.

➢ After the Czechoslovaks and the South Slavs had proclaimed their own states on 28 October and 29 October respectively, the Provisional National Assembly decided on 30 October 1918 to assume the "supreme power in the state of German-Austria" and thereby created the new state (*Staatsgründungsbeschluss,* § 1).

➢ From the perspective of the monarchical constitution, the members of the Reichsrat were not authorised to take this step, which would even have qualified as high treason! The foundation of German-Austria thus took place in breach of legal continuity, i.e. through a revolution in the legal sense. The new republic refused to be seen as a legal successor to the monarchy and adopted a status of *formal discontinuity* relative to it.

➢ However, a *material continuity* between the monarchy and the republic resulted from the wholesale adoption of the previous legal system into the body of law of the republic (*Staatsgründungsbeschluss*, § 16).

➢ §§ 2–15 of the *Staatsgründungsbeschluss* contained a provisional constitution for the new state, which defined the competences of its supreme organs (even if only rudimentarily for the time being). While legislation was to be the responsibility of the Provisional National Assembly itself, governmental power was entrusted to a State Council consisting of the three presidents of the Provisional National Assembly as well as twenty other parliamentarians; one of them was to act as "state notary" and certify official documents, while another was to run the chancellery, which gave rise to the office of state chancellor.

➢ The three presidents of the Provisional National Assembly (and until 19 December also the state chancellor and state notary) as the *State Council Directorate* constituted the (collective) head of state of German-Austria.

➢ The administrative functions at the state level were not conducted directly by the State Council but by a state government appointed by it, which consisted of state secretaries. From 19 December 1918, this govern-ment was headed by the state chancellor (the Social Democrat KARL RENNER), who thus functioned as the head of government.

➢ Members of the three traditional parties (the German National [from 1920: Greater German], Christian Social, and Social Democratic parties) were represented in all these newly established organs; they thus became (in a political, not a legal sense) the bearers of continuity.

6108 The state of German-Austria was to include **all German-speaking territories** of the former Austrian half of the monarchy as well as the ethnically German part of western Hungary (*Burgenland*). These areas, which did not constitute a contiguous territory, had a combined population of about 10 million.

➢ The new state laid claim (1) to the seven German-speaking Alpine countries, i.e. Vorarlberg, Tyrol (without its Italian-speaking territory), Salzburg, Carinthia, and Styria (in both cases excluding the Slavic areas), and Upper and Lower Austria (including the adjacent German-speaking areas in the north).

➢ It also claimed (2) the German-speaking Sudetes and the German-speaking north-west of Bohemia; these areas formed two new Länder, namely Sudetenland and German-Bohemia, as well as (3) the cities of Brünn [Brno], Iglau [Jihlava], and Olmütz [Olomouc] with their adjacent regions, which each constituted German linguistic exclaves ("language islands") within Czech territory.

➢ Finally, German-Austria also laid claim to (4) the German-populated areas in the west of Hungary that directly bordered on its other territories. This was not a single political unity but comprised parts of the four Hungarian counties of Pressburg [Pozsony/Bratislava], Wieselburg [Moson], Ödenburg [Sopron], and Eisenburg [Vas], which later gave rise to the name "Burgenland".

➢ In the seven "historical" and two "new" Länder, Provisional Provincial Assemblies were also formed in a revolutionary manner (but in consultation with the Provisional National Assembly). Thus, all nine Länder were legally new creations, just like German-Austria itself. The composition of the Provincial Assemblies was not based on the results of the most recent elections in the crown lands, as these had still followed an electoral system based on curiae and census, but according to the respective outcomes of the Reichsrat election of 1911.

➢ With the *Law on the Assumption of State Power in the Länder* of 14 November 1918, the Provisional National Assembly formally acknowledged the Provincial Assemblies and granted them the right previously vested in the diets to legislate in the Länder. Thus, although German-Austria was not a federal state, it was, like Cisleithania before it, a decentralised unitary state.

6109 On 30 October, the House of Lords and on 12 November, the House of Deputies held their last sessions; on 11 November, Emperor

CHARLES I renounced his "share in the affairs of the state". Under the influence of these events, the Provisional National Assembly decided on 12 November to **proclaim the Republic of German-Austria** as a constituent part of the German Republic.

➢ The formula chosen by Emperor CHARLES I was deliberately not a formal renunciation of the throne, since such an act was out of the question for the monarch. It only applied to German-Austria; with regard to Hungary, he issued a similar declaration on 13 November (⇨ par. 4126).

➢ In the Provisional National Assembly's resolution of 30 October 1918, the question of the form of government had been intentionally left open; however, since the provisional constitution did not provide for a monarch as an organ of the state, it had implicitly already decided in favour of the republican form of government. A "renunciation of the throne" (and also a "deposition" of the monarch) had no legal significance for the new state because of the formal discontinuity of the republic vis-à-vis the monarchy; these acts must therefore be understood as merely political moves.

➢ The former emperor remained in Austria until March 1919, continuing to exercise imperial prerogatives such as the conferring of noble titles, and then went into exile, on which occasion he revoked his declaration of 11 November 1918. Only afterwards, on 3 April 1919, was he formally deposed by the Habsburgs Act and expelled from the country. The remaining Habsburgs were allowed to remain in the country, provided they renounced their membership in the archducal house and pledged allegiance to the republic. The assets of the Habsburgs, insofar as they were not of a purely private nature, were confiscated.

➢ When the republic was proclaimed by one of the three presidents of the Provisional National Assembly, FRANZ DINGHOFER (of the German National Party), on the ramp of the parliament building on 12 November, a riot provoked by the newly founded Austrian Communist Party claimed two lives.

➢ In the public consciousness, 12 November soon replaced 30 October as the day of the "founding of the republic" and was declared a state holiday in 1919. The section of Vienna's Ringstrasse where the parliament and the university are located was named the "Ring of 12 November".

6110 The name "German-Austria" was intended to demonstrate not only a certain distance from the Habsburg Monarchy but also above all a commitment to the German nation; since the new state was not considered viable on its own, its ***"Anschluss"* (annexation) to the German Reich** was envisaged from the very beginning.

➢ The desire for an *"Anschluss"* to the German Reich corresponded to the national sentiment of the majority of the population but also appeared to be necessary for economic reasons, especially since the disintegration of the monarchy had also torn apart an economic area that had existed for centuries. The German-Austrian territories hardly seemed capable of surviving on their own. This became even more pronounced later in 1918, when the ČSR annexed German-Bohemia and Sudentenland as well as the German language islands, a measure against which German-Austria could only voice its protest but not mount any military resistance.

➢ The fact that German-Austria declared itself a "constituent part" of the German Republic on 12 November had no legal consequences, as there was never a corresponding official declaration by Germany. However, negotiations on an *"Anschluss"* were initiated between the two governments. According to the Weimar Constitution, Austrian delegates should also be included in the representative body of the German Länder, the Reichsrat, but should not have the right to vote until the *"Anschluss"* was realised.

6111 The victorious powers of the First World War referred to German-Austria as "Austria" and regarded it, alongside Hungary, as one of the legal successors of Austria-Hungary, which, together with its former allies, was responsible for the war. The **Treaty of Saint Germain-en-Laye** of 10 September 1919 determined, among other things, the borders of the new state, but contrary to the post-war order propagated by WILSON in 1918 ("14 Points", ⇨ par. 4126), these rarely followed the linguistic boundaries. An annexation to Germany was implicitly forbidden.

➢ According to the German-Austrian view, German-Austria, like the ČSR and the SHS state, had come into being in a revolutionary manner, and the Austrian Empire had thus ceased to exist without a legal successor. However, this could not be in the interest of the Entente, who intended to conclude peace treaties with the states responsible for the war and impose heavy reparation payments on them.

➢ Accordingly, the Treaty of Saint Germain also contained reparation obligations for Austria (which RENNER described as "downright absurd" because of their extent). Due to the disastrous economic situation, they proved to be irrecoverable and were first deferred, then completely waived in 1929 (whereas Germany paid reparations until 1932).

➢ The Treaty of Saint Germain essentially established the Austrian-Czechoslovak border along the historical borders of Bohemia and Moravia with Upper and Lower Austria (with minor deviations in favour of the ČSR), which meant that Austria also had to officially relinquish German-Bohemia and Sudetenland (which had *de facto* already been lost in 1918) as well as the three language islands with a combined population of over 3 million.

➢ In defining the border with Italy, neither linguistic nor historical, but rather (military) geographical criteria were used to determine the border. Therefore, the Brenner Pass was chosen, which meant that South Tyrol, with about a quarter of a million German-speaking South Tyroleans, became part of Italy.

➢ Armed conflicts (the so-called *"Abwehrkampf"*) broke out on the border with the SHS state (Yugoslavia). In southern Carinthia, the Allies ordered a referendum, which on 10 October 1920 resulted in the area concerned ("Area A") remaining with Austria. A second referendum regarding another contested area ("Area B"), which also included Klagenfurt, was then not held. The Austrian-Yugoslavian border in Styria, on the other hand, was determined without a referendum (also to Austria's disadvantage).

➢ The only territorial gain for Austria (at the expense of Hungary) was Burgenland, which was also due to Hungary being one of the defeated powers. Moreover, the latter was under Communist rule at the time, so the Allies did not take its interests into consideration. After a corresponding provision had also been included in the Treaty of Trianon (⇨ par. 6101), the area was officially vacated by the Hungarian army, but for some time, irregulars (i.e. armed individuals who did not officially belong to the Hungarian army) prevented the takeover of Burgenland by the Austrian military.

➢ The Hungarian resistance could only be pacified through Italian mediation (Venice Protocol of 13 October 1921). A referendum in the area of Ödenburg (Sopron), agreed upon by Austria and Hungary, returned a vote in favour of Hungary, and Austria had to give up Ödenburg (which had been the intended capital of Burgenland) and its surroundings.

➢ The *"Anschluss"* to the German Reich was not explicitly forbidden in Article 88 of the Treaty of Saint Germain, but it was made dependent on the consent of the League of Nations, which realistically could not be obtained. A corresponding provision was also included in the Treaty of Versailles (⇨ par. 6101). The Austrian members of the German Reichsrat had to withdraw from it.

➢ The Treaty of Saint Germain also contained fundamental rights for religious and ethnic minorities; furthermore, Austria had to accept certain military restrictions (including the abolition of compulsory military service and a ban on maintaining an air force).

➢ Austria accepted the peace conditions only "under solemn protest". Non-binding referenda in Vorarlberg in 1919 and in Tyrol and Salzburg in 1921 brought overwhelming majorities in favour of an annexation of the respective Länder to Switzerland and Germany respectively. Due to international pressure, the federal government was forced to ignore their results and prohibit further referenda.

➢ The change of name from "German-Austria" to "Austria", which was effected in terms of international law in the Treaty of Saint Germain, was domestically implemented with a law of 21 October 1919. However, the republic on this occasion again refused to be seen as the universal legal successor to the monarchy and to assume any obligations other than those expressly named in the treaty.

b) The Federal Constitutional Law 1920

6112 Even though the Provisional National Assembly consisted of elected delegates, they had in fact been elected into a different role (namely as members of the House of Deputies), hence the democratic legitimacy of the Provisional National Assembly as the creator of a new constitution seemed questionable. For this reason, it did not itself adopt a definitive constitution but left this task to a newly elected **Constituent National Assembly**. For the first time, women could also vote and be elected under the same conditions as men; another important innovation was proportional representation instead of the previous majority voting system (⇨ par. 6214). The

Social Democrats emerged from the election as the strongest party, and, under State Chancellor RENNER, formed a grand coalition with the Christian Socials.

➢ At the time of the election (16 February 1919), the borders of the republic had not yet been defined. Of the 255 deputies provided for in the law, only 159 could be elected. Eleven deputies for South Tyrol and Lower Styria were appointed to the Constituent National Assembly according to a system of proportional representation, but they had to resign their mandates after the conclusion of the Treaty of Saint Germain. No such appointments took place for the German-Bohemian and Sudeten German constituencies, which were already regarded as lost at that point.

➢ On 14 March 1919, the Constituent National Assembly decided on amendments to the provisional constitution; while the Provisional National Assembly had had three presidents of equal status, the Constituent National Assembly elected a first president (the Social Democrat KARL SEITZ) and two deputies (as second and third presidents). The first president now also served as head of state.

➢ The State Council was abolished, as it was seen as too cumbersome, and a "Main Committee" of the Constituent National Assembly was created in its place, which was to be responsible for "liaising between legislation and executive", but which had considerably less political weight than the State Council.

➢ The state government, on the other hand, was given a more significant role and was now directly elected by the Constituent National Assembly. Its members (the state chancellor and state secretaries) were subject to both political and legal ministerial responsibility.

➢ On the basis of the provisional constitution, a great deal of legislative activity ensued (in particular concerning social reforms), whereas the question of the definitive constitution was initially not addressed. The left, radical wing of the Social Democrats became increasingly dominant, which, although it averted the danger of the Communists entering parliament (an attempted Communist coup on 15 June 1919 failed), made cooperation with the Christian Socials increasingly difficult.

➢ When the grand coalition collapsed in the summer of 1920, plans were made for new elections to the Constituent National Assembly, although by its very nature the latter was not supposed to be a permanent legislative body. Just before the dissolution of the Constituent National Assembly, which was scheduled for 31 October, the Federal Constitutional Law was finally adopted.

6113 On 1 October 1920, the Constituent National Assembly adopted the **Federal Constitutional Law** *("Gesetz womit die Republik Österreich als Bundesstaat eingerichtet wird"* or *Bundes-Verfassungsgesetz*, **B-VG**) as the definitive constitution for the Republic of Austria. It was a makeshift consensus between the two major parties, which had only been made possible by the fact that many ideologically sensitive matters had been sidelined by retaining the legal status of the monarchy "for the time being". Accordingly, the B-VG was not a definitive codification of the constitution but merely a "constitutional torso".

➢ In May 1919, the Social Democratic State Chancellor RENNER commissioned HANS KELSEN, a professor at the University of Vienna (⇨ par. 6204, par. 6303), to draft a federal constitution. Once the Treaty of Saint Germain was concluded, MICHAEL MAYR, a Christian Social professor from Innsbruck University, was appointed state secretary and entrusted with the constitutional reform.

➢ Independently of the state government's endeavours, representatives of the Länder discussed the constitutional question at conferences in Salzburg in February and Linz in April 1920. MAYR presented a draft to the Salzburg conference that was based on KELSEN's work and additional contributions (known as the "private draft MAYR", as it was not formally approved by the government). This became the basis for the subsequent consultations.

➢ When the grand coalition collapsed in the summer of 1920, however, a decision on the constitution seemed to be a distant prospect. MAYR introduced a Christian Social constitutional bill in the Constituent National Assembly, whereupon RENNER published a divergent draft in a newspaper, the *Wiener Zeitung*, which made the differences of opinion between the parties evident.

➢ Contentious points were, among others, the establishment of a chamber of the Länder (the Federal Council) and its possible role in federal legislation, the introduction of the office of a federal president, the distribution of competences between the federal government and the Länder, and fundamental rights.

➢ The constitutional committee of the Constituent National Assembly established a sub-committee under the leadership of the Social Democrat OTTO BAUER and the Christian Social IGNAZ SEIPEL; KELSEN was called in as a non-partisan expert. This sub-committee decided to submit those parts of the constitution on which a consensus could be reached to the Constituent National Assembly for its decision and to exclude the remaining parts for the time being.

➢ Therefore, the B-VG contained neither a catalogue of fundamental rights nor provisions on the distribution of competences in the areas of education and public finances; rather, the respective legal frameworks of the monarchy (i.e. the *Basic Law on the General Rights of Nationals* in particular) were provisionally retained. A general division of competences between the federal and Länder levels was also formally adopted, but a Constitutional Transition Act stated that this division would only come into effect at a later point in time; until then, the respective laws of the monarchy would continue to apply (⇨ par. 6116).

6114 The B-VG came into effect on 10 November 1920. It was (and still is) based on the **democratic**, **republican**, **federal**, and **legality** principles. However, the federal element was initially rather weak and political power was concentrated at the federal level, specifically in the National Council, which also elected the federal government.

This also entailed a dilution of the principle of separation of powers (parliamentary democracy, ⇨ par. 6208).

➢ The National Council was elected every four years on the basis of the equal, direct, secret, and personal suffrage of men and women over the age of 20, and according to the principle of proportional representation (⇨ par. 6214).

➢ The members of the Federal Council were elected by the diets, with each of them having a number of votes corresponding to its number of citizens (but at least 3 and not more than 12). This, as well as the fact that its members usually did not vote by Länder but by parties, meant that the balance of power in the Federal Council was usually similar to that in the National Council. Moreover, since the Federal Council only had a suspensive veto against National Council resolutions that the National Council could override with a second vote, the Federal Council had very little political weight.

➢ The members of the National and Federal Councils together formed the Federal Assembly, which elected the federal president. The federal president had mostly representative functions.

➢ The federal government, consisting of the federal chancellor and federal ministers, was elected by the National Council and was also politically and legally accountable to the latter (⇨ par. 6208).

➢ The B-VG also contained very detailed provisions on the Länder constitutions, which were not allowed to contradict the federal constitution. The distribution of powers between the federal government and the Länder continued to be governed by the provisions from 1861 and 1867. These, however, had given the diets only very limited powers, so that Cisleithania had not been referred to as a federal state at the time. Hence, the Republic's designation as a federal state (Article 2 B-VG) was highly controversial in legal circles.

➢ Unlike the democratic, republican, and federal principles, the principle of the rule of law was not explicitly proclaimed at the outset. However, it was enshrined in a number of provisions, in particular in Article 18 B-VG, in the same way as the other aforementioned principles. According to this article, not only was unlawful administrative action prohibited, but the entire administration was only allowed to act on the basis of explicit legal authorisation.

➢ The organisation of the ordinary courts and the administrative court was carried over largely unchanged from the monarchy and therefore remained an exclusive federal competence. The B-VG brought major innovations with regard to constitutional jurisdiction.

➢ As Lower Austria comprised more than half of Austria's inhabitants, the B-VG provided for an internal autonomy for regional Lower Austria on the one hand and Vienna on the other. It also allowed for a complete separation of the two by means of concerted laws of the Viennese and Lower Austrian diets, and this was eventually the option chosen in 1921 with the *Separation Act*, which entered into effect on 1 January 1922. On the same date, Burgenland (⇨ par. 6111) also became a constituent state with equal rights to the other eight. Since then, the federation has been made up of nine Länder.

c) Constitutional developments 1920–33

6115 The main problem in Austrian domestic affairs after 1918 was the social hardship Austrians endured because of the lost war, the collapse of the monarchy, and the harsh peace conditions of the Treaty of Saint Germain. Inflation "took on ever more unearthly qualities" (ZÖLLNER) and could ultimately only be stopped by a League of Nations loan, which Austria received based on the **Geneva Protocols** of 4 October 1922 (the "Geneva loan"). In return, Austria had to commit to far-reaching constitutional and administrative reforms as well as to maintaining its economic and political autonomy.

➢ The Alpine regions were economically underdeveloped. More than 2 million people lived in the "waterhead of Vienna" (i.e. almost one third of the Austrian population). The cost of living rose over 2,600 times within three years. Attempts by the Christian Social Chancellor SEIPEL (1922–24, 1926–29) to obtain loans domestically were obstructed by the UK and France, which sought to make Austria dependent on them.

➢ The protocols signed in Geneva with the UK, France, Italy, and the ČSR guaranteed Austria a loan of 650 million Goldkronen. In return, Austria had to commit to economic, constitutional, and administrative reforms to reduce public spending. A Commissioner-General of the League of Nations supervised the economic reform programme, but due to his far-reaching powers, Austria was effectively deprived of its financial sovereignty. Austria was obliged to maintain its political and economic independence; this time, there even was not an option to revoke the commitment via a procedure pursuant to Article 88 of the Treaty of Saint Germain.

➢ The Geneva Protocols also stipulated that the Austrian federal government should be given special legislative powers to ensure efficient reforms. Due to pressure from the opposition Social Democrats, the federal government could only exercise this right together with members of the National Council in an "extraordinary cabinet council". In practice, only twenty legal acts were passed in this way.

➢ The loan allowed Austria to introduce a new currency, the Schilling, on 1 March 1925 (10,000 Kronen = 1 Schilling), and its stability became the most important principle of Austrian economic policy after 1925.

➢ The downside of this economic policy was a steady increase in the number of unemployed, from around 120,000 in 1923 to 193,000 in 1929 (counting only those who received unemployment benefits). When those who depended on welfare payments are included, the number of unemployed probably reached 280,000 already in 1929 (i.e. before the Great Depression). Corporate insolvencies also rose significantly from 1924 onwards.

6116 As a result of the Geneva Protocols, Austria undertook far-reaching constitutional and administrative reforms, with the **constitutional amendment of 1925** as its core. Essentially, the amendment revised the existing constitution in line with previous developments.

In particular, the provisions on the distribution of competences between the federal government and the Länder (Articles 10–15 B-VG) came into effect, and the "dual structure" of federal and Länder administration was eliminated. Administrative procedural law was codified; however, a comprehensive reform of administrative jurisdiction, which had also been planned, remained unrealised.

➢ Although the distribution of competences between the federal level and the Länder included a general clause in favour of the latter (Article 15 B-VG), the most important competences, including the "competence-competence", were at the federal level (Article 10 B-VG). Although this structure had been adopted already in 1920, it only came into effect, after minor modifications, on 1 October 1925.

➢ The distribution of competences in finance could be resolved as early as 1922 with a separate constitutional law on public finances. The distribution of competences in education and municipal law was not resolved until 1962.

➢ The main problem with the reform was the administrative organisation's dual structure (⇨ par. 3110), which in essence dated to the reign of MARIA THERESA: in the monarchy, the central state had its own authorities in the crown lands, while the crown lands themselves autonomously exercised certain administrative functions through their own committees (*"Landesausschüsse"*). In 1918, the central state administration at the Länder level was placed under the control of a governor (*"Landeshauptmann"*) and two deputies, which meant that Länder authorities were now acting on behalf of the federal government ("indirect federal administration").

➢ In the new republic, two separate administrative apparatuses existed side by side: the Länder administration on one side and the indirect federal administration on the other. Not until the constitutional reform of 1925 was a full organisational integration of these apparatuses achieved by establishing an "Office of the Provincial Government" in each of the Länder. This new institution was created to conduct both the affairs of the provincial administration (under the authority of the Länder governments) and the indirect federal administration (under the authority of the governor).

➢ Meanwhile, the district administrative offices (*Bezirkshauptmannschaften*) were converted into authorities of the Länder. They too were to act in matters of Länder as well as indirect federal administration. Indirect federal administration became the standard type of all federal administration, and the exercise of administrative functions by separate federal authorities was limited to certain specified areas of public administration.

➢ The main element of the reform of administrative procedure was the General Administrative Procedure Act 1925, which was to be applied by both federal and Länder authorities, thereby achieving standardisation and a simplification of administrative procedure throughout the country.

➢ The Court of Audit's review functions were extended to the Länder, and the Constitutional Court was given the right to determine competences in abstract terms.

6117 Paramilitary units formed outside the parliamentary system and armed conflicts erupted. Following the **fire in the Palace of Justice in 1927**, the atmosphere between the Christian Socials and the Social Democrats, who had been in opposition since 1920, was characterised by open hostility.

➢ Immediately after the end of the First World War, armed self-defence groups ("*Frontkämpfer*") arose, and from them, the *"Heimwehr"* paramilitary groups were created. In terms of party affiliation, they were associated with the Christian Socials, but increasingly also sympathised with Italian fascism ("Korneuburg Oath" of 1930). From 1930 onwards, they became the *"Heimatblock"*, a separate political faction in the National Council.

➢ Since the army (based on provisions of the Treaty of Saint Germain set up as a professional army) was also dominated by Christian Socials, the Social Democrats formed their own paramilitary organisation in 1923/24, the *"Republikanischer Schutzbund"*. The Austrian National Socialists, largely subordinated to their German sister party since 1924, founded a *"Sturmabteilung"* (SA) and a *"Schutzstaffel"* (SS) based on the German models.

➢ Violent clashes occurred repeatedly between these groups, especially in 1927 in Schattendorf, when an invalid and a child were killed by *Frontkämpfer* during an armed encounter with the *Schutzbund*. When the defendants in the subsequent "Schattendorf trial" were acquitted, violent demonstrations on 15 July 1927 ensued, culminating in the burning of the Palace of Justice in Vienna. The police were ordered to shoot into the crowd, and 89 protesters and four police officers were killed.

➢ Austria was thus on the brink of civil war. Yet the Social Democrats were indecisive about mounting active resistance against the federal government, and also failed to persuade Chancellor SEIPEL to resign. From the bourgeois point of view, this was a sign of weakness. With the danger of a Socialist coup (which had been smouldering since 1917) averted, the Social Democrats were pushed into an utterly defensive position. Thus, the *Heimwehren* demanded a complete revision of the constitution along the lines of Italian fascism, if necessary, by force.

6118 Unlike the constitutional reform of 1925, the **amendment in 1929** was not a continuation of previous constitutional developments but transformed the hitherto parliamentary system into a parliamentary-presidential system. The second major reform project, namely the establishment of a parliamentary representation of the "estates" (i.e. corporative groups), was not realised.

➢ The fear of a coup d'état by the *Heimwehren* motivated the federal government to initiate a constitutional amendment itself, thereby reducing the threat posed by extra-parliamentary forces. For the same reason, the Social Democrats agreed to the reform and only slightly mitigated some particularly drastic amendments included in the government bill. Thus, the two-thirds majority necessary for a constitutional amendment was obtained.

➢ The focus of the constitutional reform of 1929 was on the federal president, whose powers were significantly increased to satisfy the demand for a "strong man". To give him more political weight, it was decided that he should henceforth be directly elected by the people (⇨ par. 6210). He was given the right to issue emergency decrees (subject to such complicated rules that it remained practically meaningless, cf. Article 18 [3–5] B-VG), as well as the supreme command over the army.

➢ The National Council's position was weakened, however; it was henceforth convened and dissolved by the federal president. The federal government, appointed by the president and therefore no longer elected by the National Council, also remained politically accountable to the latter, which led to a twofold dependency (⇨ par. 6211).

➢ Plans were also made to transform the Federal Council into a council of the Länder and corporative groups, although the exact composition (a bicameral system within the Federal Council?) and competences (an absolute veto against National Council decisions?) of this reformed Federal Council remained unclear. Only a declaration of intent was inserted into the B-VG to the effect that a respective constitutional law would follow (which never happened).

➢ Under the banner of "depoliticization", parliamentary rights of participation in the appointment of judges of the Constitutional Court were reduced to the benefit of the federal government, which was granted nomination rights. However, this change resulted only in a "re-politicization" (in favour of the ruling Christian Socials): through a constitutional provision, the existing judges were dismissed and only two of them carried over into the new Constitutional Court. One of those affected was KELSEN, who subsequently left Austria. In regard to the Administrative Court, on the other hand, appointment by parliament was replaced by a right of self-renewal (i.e. new judges were appointed based on proposals made by the court's plenary assembly), which in the long term indeed resulted in substantial depoliticization.

➢ Despite the far-reaching reforms, the constitutional amendment of 1929 was not considered a "total revision" of the constitution, which would have required a referendum under Article 44 (2) B-VG. In this respect, the amendment of 1929 continues to be a benchmark for how far a merely partial amendment of the constitution may extend.

6119 The culmination of the *Great Depression* in 1929 led to a closer alignment of Austria with the German Reich; however, a bilateral **customs union plan in 1931** had to be abandoned due to an advisory opinion of the Permanent Court of International Justice. As compensation, Austria received another League of Nations loan in 1932 ("Lausanne Protocol").

➢ Despite the prohibition of a union between the two countries in the treaties of Saint Germain (Article 88) and Versailles, Austria and Germany continued to aim for the closest possible relationship also after 1919. For example, the two governments discussed whether Austria might adopt the German Civil Code and Germany the Austrian Code of Civil Procedure. Efforts were also made to achieve a joint codification of criminal law. However, none of these projects came to fruition.

➢ The New York Stock Exchange crash on 24 October 1929 plunged the entire world economy into its worst crisis to that date. In Austria, the unemployment rate rose to over 26 percent by 1933.

➢ The customs union plan (SCHOBER-CURTIUS Plan) presented by the Austrian Federal Chancellor JOHANN SCHOBER and the German Foreign Minister JULIUS CURTIUS on 19 March 1931 provided for the elimination of the Austrian-German customs border and the creation of a unified customs area through coordinated legislation. The planned customs union was therefore not a supranational community (⇨ par. 8117) but a loose association that was also open to the accession of other states and subject to termination after three years.

➢ France reacted to Austria's customs union plans by withdrawing funds (which resulted in the collapse of the *Creditanstalt*, one of Austria's largest banks, in 1931) and demanding in the League of Nations that the customs union plan be examined by the Permanent Court of International Justice. On 5 September 1931, the Court ruled that while the customs union plan did not violate Article 88 of the Treaty of Saint Germain, it was incompatible with the "economic independence" to which Austria had committed itself in the Geneva Protocols of 1922.

➢ To alleviate economic hardship, Austria was granted another League of Nations loan of 300 million Schillings by the UK, France, Italy, and Belgium in the Lausanne Protocol of 15 July 1932. As in 1922, Austria once again had to commit to maintaining its independence.

B Structures

1. The Essence and Value of Democracy

6201 The idea of **democracy** had been discussed since the 5th century BC, especially by philosophers (⇨ par. 1203). The term underwent considerable changes in its meaning over the course of time. The origins the modern theory of democracy lie in the 18th century, when, in reality, democracy in the modern sense of the word did not exist.

➢ The vast majority of medieval and early modern theorists of the state rejected democracy because they believed that the people were fickle and incapable of forming a common interest, as everyone was jealous of the others (e.g. THOMAS HOBBES, 1651). Monarchy was almost universally accepted as the best of all systems of governance (e.g. THOMAS AQUINAS, c. 1273).

➢ It was not until the Enlightenment period, with its emphasis on natural law, that the freedom and equality of all human beings were recognised – principles that are indispensable for a modern understanding of democracy. Thus, in the 17th and 18th centuries, the idea of democracy gradually acquired a positive meaning and replaced the concept of the *politie* (e.g. SAMUEL PUFENDORF, 1673).

6202 JEAN JACQUES ROUSSEAU (*Du contrat social/The Social Contract,* 1762) became an important thinker for the modern theory on democracy with his doctrine of **popular sovereignty**. However, ROUSSEAU was quite sceptical about the idea of democracy and its feasibility; he rejected a parliamentary system such as it already existed in Great Britain at that time.

➢ In contrast to LOCKE (⇨ par. 3207), ROUSSEAU thought that the submission to the social contract was both absolute and unconditional (*aliénation totale*). However, contrary to Hobbes' theory, ROUSSEAU's social contract does not establish the rule of an individual, because before the people can grant the rulership to an individual, they must first establish themselves as an entity.

➢ According to ROUSSEAU, the function of the social contract could therefore only be to transform the people into a political body entrusted with sovereignty. A separate contract could then transfer individual sovereign rights – but never sovereignty itself – to a government. The government was only the executive organ of the common will of the people (*volonté générale*) and could be dismissed if necessary.

➢ ROUSSEAU also argued that the common will could not be exercised by representatives, thereby contradicting the idea of parliament as the "representation of the people". Thus, it was acceptable – because of the deputies' free mandate – for the British parliament, for example, to override the will of the people. The British people were only free during the elections; at all other times, they were "slaves" to the parliamentary rule.

6203 The constitution of the United States of 17 September 1787 (⇨ par. 3113) was a ground-breaking document, as it created the first democratic state (in the modern sense of the word). It was discussed and defended against its critics by ALEXANDER HAMILTON, JAMES MADISON, and JOHN JAY in several newspaper articles published in 1787/88, which came to be known as the **Federalist Papers**.

➢ The Federalist Papers did not regard the fact that the USA was (and is) not a direct but an indirect (representative) democracy as a necessary evil that comes with a certain size of a state; rather, they preferred a parliament to a people's assembly because it contributed to political stability and was better suited to keeping particular interests in check in relation to the general good.

➢ Unlike ROUSSEAU, the authors of the Federalist Papers endorsed the principle of separation of powers as a means of preventing the abuse of authority. The legislative power, in particular, should not be in the hands of one person alone; with this argument, the Federalist Papers justified the bicameral system (⇨ par. 4209) as well as the federal structure of the USA ("vertical separation of powers" between the Union and the states). The power of the state should be further limited by fundamental rights – which originally were not included in the US constitution. They were only created in 1791 with the *Bill of Rights*.

6204 In the 19th century, theorists of democracy such as JOHN STUART MILL (*On Liberty*, 1859) saw democracy as the system of governance that best guaranteed the **freedom of the individual**. For HANS KELSEN (*Vom Wesen und Wert der Demokratie/The Essence and Value of Democracy*, 1920/29), this notion was a fiction; for him, the value of democracy lay in securing domestic peace, as it enabled a "balance of class forces".

➢ Even democracy is a form of domination and necessarily restricts the freedom of the individual. Democracy therefore does not realise the "return to nature" postulated by ROUSSEAU; this would be anarchy.

➢ MILL presented the democratic movement mainly as a struggle for freedom from tyranny. But he too already recognised the risk that in a democracy, the majority party might tyrannise the minority. Here, MILL drew heavily on the account of US democracy given by the French author ALEXIS DE TOCQUEVILLE in his *De la Démocratie en Amérique* (*Democracy in America*, 1835/40), who had argued that even in a democracy, the majority party should not have unlimited power.

➢ KELSEN recognised the idea of freedom as the "ideology" of democracy and argued that it justified the majority principle in voting; namely, only if existing norms can be changed as easily as possible will those who are in favour of the change be "free". In the real world, however, absolute freedom cannot be achieved. According to KELSEN, it is typical of a democracy that majorities can change at any time (through elections), reversing the roles of government and opposition. Therefore, no party is condemned to permanent impotence, and, at least theoretically, everyone is given the chance to participate in government. This leads to political conflicts not being fought out violently in the streets but peacefully within democratic institutions, such as parliament.

2. Forms of democracy

6205 **Direct democracy** comes closest to the "pure" concept of democracy but is difficult to realise in practice. The large states of the modern era, however, regularly chose the system of indirect (representative) democracy, which is sometimes supplemented by elements of direct democracy.

➢ Direct democracies existed especially in antiquity, when they were only possible because of the small size of the *poleïs*. In IUSTINIAN's Institutions (1.2.5), this is explained using Rome as an example; at the time of the city-state, laws were still passed by a popular assembly at the Campus Martius. As the empire grew and the convening of popular assemblies became more difficult, popular votes were increasingly replaced by senate decisions.

➢ Today, representative democracy is generally recognised as a requirement of the modern state once the latter reaches a certain size. In some states, especially in Switzerland, there are also opportunities for citizens to influence policies through direct democratic means (initiatives, referenda).

Popular assemblies with legislative rights exist today only in the Swiss cantons of Glarus and Appenzell-Innerrhoden.

➢ Modern technology (the internet in particular) has given rise to the idea of reviving direct democracy, which, however, is rejected by some for practical reasons (such as the complex needs of modern legislation). This problem became evident in Switzerland in 1978, for example, when a referendum was to be held on a question of economic policy and two thirds of the respondents in a poll were unable to even roughly explain the issue on which they were voting.

➢ Direct participation of the people is widely accepted when it comes to certain fundamental decisions. In France, for example, all constitutions since 1791 (except for the *Charte constitutionelle* of 1814) have been confirmed by a plebiscite; cf. also the Austrian vote on joining the EU in 1994, or the British one on leaving it in 2016. Whether the voters in these cases were fully aware of the consequences of their decision is debatable.

➢ Experience has shown that referenda are often abused in a manipulative manner by demagogues seeking validation of their policies (⇨ par. 7205). Therefore, the German GG does not provide for them (with one exception: a new delimitation of the federal territory, Article 29).

➢ The varying traditions of the individual states regarding referenda became apparent, for instance, in the (failed) ratification of the European constitution in 2005, when referenda were held in some states (such as France) but not in Germany or Austria (⇨ par. 8140).

6206 The Austrian federal constitution provides for three types of direct involvement of the electorate in the legislative process: **referenda**; **popular initiatives;** and **consultations**. In 2009, the **citizens' initiative** was introduced at the EU level.

➢ According to Article 44 (3) – previously (2) – B-VG, any total revision of the constitution must be submitted to a referendum; so far, this has happened only once (in 1994, concerning Austria's accession to the EU). A referendum can also take place if this is demanded by one third of the members of either the National Council or the Federal Council (this happened in 1978, leading to the rejection of a proposed nuclear power plant in the Lower Austrian municipality of Zwentendorf).

➢ In Austria, popular initiatives aimed at introducing legislative proposals in the National Council are becoming increasingly relevant. If an initiative reaches 100,000 votes (until 1981: 200,000 votes), the National Council must consider it. During the First Republic and in the early years of the Second Republic, these direct democratic means were rare. It was not until the (successful) initiative on the independence of the Austrian Broadcasting Corporation in 1964 that its importance gradually increased. Following a significant simplification of the procedure in 2018, countless initiatives have been launched every year. The most successful were those against the construction of a conference centre in Vienna (1982) and against genetically modified foods (1997), each with more than one million votes.

➢ However, as popular initiatives became more frequent, the legislators' willingness to take the *vox populi* into account diminished. While it was initially taken for granted that a successful initiative would also lead to a corresponding change in the law, later initiatives remained ineffective even if they had reached a very high number of votes, such as the two petitions of 1982 and 1997 mentioned above. Proposals to introduce mandatory consultations of the electorate once an initiative has surpassed a certain number of votes have not yet been realised, not least because this would bypass parliament as a regulative institution and make legislation dependent on the mood of the electorate.

➢ In 1989, and not least as a consequence of this situation, the National Council was given the option to conduct consultations – which are not legally binding – on "fundamental" issues. So far, only one such consultation has taken place (on the retention of compulsory military service, 2013).

➢ According to Article 11 (4) TEU, one million citizens from "a significant number of Member States" can call on the Commission to take action on a specific matter (*European citizens' initiative*). So far, ten such citizens' initiatives have reached the required threshold.

6207 In **representative democracies**, only a few state organs are usually directly elected by the people; the remaining ones are appointed by those organs and are therefore only indirectly democratically legitimised, which at least in theory results in a certain hierarchy. The two main types of representative democracy are *parliamentary democracy* and *presidential democracy*.

➢ The direct election of a state organ strengthens its political significance. It would therefore be problematic if not only the highest but also the lower organs were elected, because then the highest organs would find it difficult to enforce their will against the lower ones.

➢ For this reason, during the transition to democracy, only the highest levels of the state were usually democratised, whereas the administrative and judicial apparatus, whose structures to some extent still go back to absolutism, were kept largely unchanged. The bureaucracy is linked to the democratically legitimised government through the latter's right to issue instructions, as well as through the principle of legality, which thus acquires a specifically democratic function.

➢ In Austria, the administration was to some extent made more democratic as early as 1862, through the establishment of "district municipalities" (⇨ par. 4206), i.e. self-governing bodies at the district level. They were only introduced in Bohemia, Galicia, and Styria. The B-VG also provided for the possible introduction of "territorial municipalities" (cf. today's Article 120 B-VG), but this was not developed further. After 1924, the district representations in Styria (which had survived from the monarchy) were no longer elected but appointed by the provincial government.

6208 In a **parliamentary democracy**, parliament is in theory the most important institution; it is the only organ that is directly elected by the people, while all other organs, especially the government, derive their democratic legitimacy directly or indirectly from parliament. This type of democracy was chosen by Austria in the years 1918–29 and has been in place in the Federal Republic of Germany since 1949.

➢ Austria chose a particularly radical form of parliamentary democracy in 1918–19, when the organ entrusted with government, the State Council, was elected by the Provisional National Assembly from among its members in such a way that all parliamentary parties were also represented in the State Council. The State Council was thus an "executive committee" of the Provisional National Assembly.

➢ In 1919–29, the state/federal government was elected by the Constituent National Assembly and the National Council respectively (Article 70 B-VG); this also ensured that at least half of parliament agreed with the political line of the government. The political supremacy of parliament was also expressed, among other things, in the fact that in 1918–20, the three presidents of the Provisional National Assembly and later the first president of the Constituent National Assembly were also the heads of state. In 1920, a new organ was introduced, namely the federal president, who was elected by the Federal Assembly and essentially had only representative functions until 1929. Even the supreme command of the federal army was initially formally vested in parliament.

➢ Similarly, according to Article 63 GG, the German Bundestag elects the federal chancellor of the FRG.

6209 Parliamentary democracy is a state form in which the separation of powers developed in the context of constitutionalism (⇨ par. 4204) is not applicable, or is only applicable to a very limited extent, not least because of the **political responsibility of the ministers**. In practice, the government has more political power than parliament.

➢ This conjunction of state powers usually only concerns the executive and legislative powers of a democratic state, whereas in Austria at least, the judiciary is as independent of or dependent on the other powers as during the time of the constitutional monarchy.

➢ *De iure*, the executive and legislative branches are linked in that a government (or an individual minister) that has lost a vote of no confidence in parliament will be removed from office (*political ministerial responsibility*, Article 74 B-VG). Such a vote of no confidence (in contrast to the impeachment of a minister in the case of *legal ministerial responsibility*) does not require an alleged violation of the law but may be called whenever the government or minister no longer follows the same political line as the parliamentary majority.

➢ *De facto*, the executive and legislative branches are linked through the political parties whose functionaries are represented in both the government and parliament. In political practice, ministers enjoy the confidence of parliament for as long as their party (alone or together with coalition parties) holds the majority of votes.

➢ Votes of no confidence are therefore rare in times of political stability; they can lead to considerable destabilisation. This happened in the Weimar Republic, where three governments were overthrown between 1923 and 1926, making it rather difficult to form a stable new government. Article 67 of the GG therefore stipulates that the German Bundestag can only remove a chancellor from his or her office if it elects a new chancellor at the same time (*constructive vote of no confidence*). This was the case when HELMUT SCHMIDT (SPD) was overthrown with the election of HELMUT KOHL (CDU) in 1982.

➢ The only vote of no confidence in Austria to date took place on 27 May 2019; five days earlier, Federal President ALEXANDER VAN DER BELLEN had appointed an ÖVP-led minority government based on a proposal by Federal Chancellor SEBASTIAN KURZ. The vote was directed against the entire government, which was removed from office by the federal president the following day. Unlike in Germany, a vote of no confidence in Austria does not automatically result in the election of a new chancellor. Therefore, the Federal President dismissed only the Federal Chancellor within one day and entrusted the previous ministers with the continuation of government business until, six days later, he succeeded in appointing a "technocratic government" (which was considered "apolitical" and therefore tolerated by all parties) for the period until the next National Council election (⇨ par. 8146).

➢ As long as a government has the confidence of parliament, the *clash of interests between the legislative and executive branches* (typical of constitutional monarchies) is eliminated. In fact, the system of parliamentary democracy often results in key political decisions being taken by the government, with parliament only used as a "voting machine".

➢ According to the British author WALTER BAGEHOT (*The English Constitution*, 1867), the traditional dichotomy of government versus parliament is replaced by the division of state powers between the government/parliamentary majority on the one hand and the opposition on the other. The parliamentary minority rights, i.e. the rights of the opposition parties, are therefore essential for the functioning of democratic structures.

➢ These minority rights include, in particular, the right to participate in committees and plenary debates, to introduce draft legislation, and to demand a referendum.

➢ Under Article 34 of the Weimar Constitution, one fifth of the members of the German Reichstag could set up a committee of inquiry; under Article 44 GG, the threshold is one quarter of the members of the Bundestag. In Austria, committees of inquiry could originally only be set up by majority vote (and were thus quite rare); since 2015, only a quarter of the members of the National Council has been required (*right of inquiry*).

➢ Only a specific and concluded event or process pertaining to an area of public administration that falls under the competence of the federal level can be the object of such an inquiry (Article 53 B-VG). Its findings do not have any direct legal consequences but may be politically significant.

➢ With the elimination of the conflict of interests between the legislative and executive branches, the extra-professional immunity of parliamentarians (⇨ par. 4213) has lost its purpose. Its retention (cf. Article 57 B-VG) can be regarded as a privilege for which there is no democratic justification.

6210 In a **presidential democracy**, the head of state is directly elected by the people and, given his or her constitutional powers, competes to a certain extent with parliament, which means that the "classical" separation of powers becomes more important.

➢ The oldest presidential system of government is that of the USA, where the president is elected by the people; he or she is both head of state and head of government. Most Latin American constitutions are modeled on this example. In Europe, the system of presidential democracy is not currently implemented in its pure form in any constitution.

➢ In these systems, if the president belongs to a different party from the majority of the members of parliament, conflicts of interest may arise – for example, if a bill introduced by the government is rejected or, conversely, if the president vetoes parliamentary resolutions (e.g. Article 1 Section 7 of the US Constitution). In a parliamentary democracy, such a scenario would be very unlikely.

➢ The sociologist MAX WEBER argued (in 1919, when he was unaware of what was to follow!) for a "plebiscitary leader democracy" also in Germany, in which a president directly elected by the people should counterbalance parliamentary rule and at the same time provide an "outlet for the people's need for leadership".

➢ In 1930, the German constitutional lawyer CARL SCHMITT (who would join the NSDAP in 1933), argued that the president of the German Reich was a politically neutral authority whose role was that of a "guardian of the constitution". KELSEN, on the other hand, believed that an elected president, as someone who holds a political position, could never be neutral; for him, the idea that an individual could represent an entire nation was a fiction. According to KELSEN, only a constitutional court could act as the "guardian of the constitution".

➢ The strong position of the German Reich's president (who was directly elected by the people from 1925) in the period 1919–34 was mainly based on his right to issue emergency decrees (Article 48 of the Weimar Constitution), of which he made extensive use (⇨ par. 6106). The GG learned its lesson from the negative example of the Weimar Constitution and granted the federal president only very limited powers.

6211 Many democratic states have implemented **hybrid forms** of parliamentary and presidential democracy. This was the case in Austria from 1929–34 and has been again since 1945. Similar constitutional systems have been in place in Italy since 1948 and in France since 1958. In political practice, however, the French president has far more power than his Austrian and Italian counterparts.

➢ With the constitutional amendment of 1929, it was decided that the federal president should henceforth be directly elected by the people. However, special laws repeatedly suspended this popular election, so that it did not actually take place until 1951, when THEODOR KÖRNER was elected. Since then, the federal president has enjoyed the same direct democratic legitimacy as the National Council.

➢ Furthermore, the amendment stipulated that the federal president should appoint the federal government; at the same time, the federal government's political accountability to the National Council was maintained. The federal government is thus caught in a twofold dependency.

➢ This creates a certain tension, which became particularly evident during the formation of the government in 2000, when the FPÖ/ÖVP parliamentary majority was able to install a coalition government against the declared will of the federal president (⇨ par. 8144). This political "showdown" demonstrated that the Austrian federal president, although his or her constitutional powers are hardly inferior to those of his or her French counterpart, *de facto* has hardly any more political power than before 1929.

➢ In particular, the federal president can exercise almost all of his or her powers only upon the initiative of the federal government or a minister (Article 67 B-VG). The right to issue emergency decrees, which the federal president has held since 1929, is so complex (approval by a standing parliamentary committee; inadmissibility of constitutional amendments or interventions in certain sensitive matters such as the protection of tenants) that it has never been applied, not even during the constitutional crises of 1933/34.

3. Excursus: Republic

6212 A monarchy can only also be a democracy if the role of the monarch is largely limited to representative functions, whereas political power is largely vested in parliament (*parliamentary monarchy*). This is the case in almost all monarchies that still exist in Europe today, such as the one in the UK. Most European democracies, however, including Austria, chose the **republic** as their form of government.

➢ On the history of the term "republic" see ⇨ par. 1104 above. The dichotomy of the republic vs. the monarchy relates only to the position of the head of state and, in particular, whether he or she can be held accountable for his or her actions. Another typical, though not essential, distinguishing feature is whether he or she is elected to his or her office for a limited period, or whether he or she ascends the throne for life by virtue of a hereditary right.

➢ In the 18th and 19th centuries, the British monarch steadily lost political influence, so that the transformation from a constitutional to a parliamentary monarchy occurred gradually; since 1707, no parliamentary decision has been challenged, and since 1834, every government (which is still formally appointed by the monarch) has been dependent on the trust of parliament.

➢ Austria made a radical departure from the monarchical form of government in 1918, first entrusting a collegial body (the State Council Directorate, 1918–19), then the president of the Constituent National Assembly (1919–20) with the responsibilities of a head of state. Since 1920, another monocratic organ, the federal president, has been the head of state.

➢ The Austrian federal president is legally responsible for his or her actions and can be brought before the Constitutional Court by the Federal Assembly for violating the federal constitution (Article 142 B-VG). He or she is also politically responsible for his or her actions and, at the initiative of the Federal Assembly, can be removed from office in a referendum (Article 68 B-VG). Neither of these cases has so far occurred.

4. Electoral law and political parties

6213 According to ROUSSEAU, the ideal of democracy (though unattainable in practice) is that "rulers" and "ruled" should be the same. Therefore, a democratic electoral system aims to realise the principles of **universality, equality,** and **freedom**.

➢ Even in democratic states, women (and in states where slavery was still legal, also slaves) were for a long time excluded from all political participation, yet this did not compromise the self-perception of these states as democracies. Universal suffrage for men and women was first introduced in the British colony of New Zealand and in the US state of Colorado in 1893, while the US did not introduce women's suffrage at the federal level until 1920. In Europe, it was first introduced in Finland (then part of the Russian Empire) in 1906, followed by Norway, Denmark, and Iceland in 1913/15.

➢ It was only the political and social upheaval caused by the First World War that led to the introduction of women's suffrage in many other European states in 1917–19; Estonia; Latvia; Russia; Austria (here for the first time in the election to the Constituent National Assembly in 1919, ⇨ par. 6112); Germany; Czechoslovakia; Poland; etc. Remarkably, women's suffrage was introduced very late in some countries with a long democratic tradition, in England fully only in 1928, in France in 1944, and in Switzerland in 1971 (at the federal level) resp. in 1990 (in all cantons).

➢ The exclusion of children from the right to vote continues to be taken for granted, even though they also are subjects of state rule. There has at least been a tendency to include younger persons in the electorate. In Austria, for example, the minimum age for the right to vote, which was 20 in 1918, was lowered to 19 in 1968, to 18 in 1992, and to 16 in 2007. Foreign citizens are not entitled to vote, even if they have been living in the country for years. However, the Maastricht Treaty granted all Union citizens the right to vote in municipal elections in the municipality in which they reside (Article 22 TFEU).

➢ Until 2012, people who served extended prison sentences were invariably excluded from the participation in elections; following a decision of the ECtHR in 2010, this general limitation on the right to vote was removed, but the sentencing court can still ban a person from voting on an individual basis.

➢ The obligation to keep individual voting behaviours secret serves to protect the free franchise, as especially the negative example of the referendum in 1938 demonstrated, when conducting a secret ballot was allowed but not obligatory. For this reason, the method of postal voting that was introduced in 2007 is also highly questionable, as there is no guarantee that the voter can cast his or her ballot in a free and secret manner.

➢ The principle of immediacy is *not* an essential element of a democratic electoral law. An indirect election (e.g. the election of the US president and, until 1913, the election of the senators) is also regarded as a democratic election. However, elections that are not decided by the people directly but indirectly via an electoral college can lead to significant distortions of the will of the electorate. In 1876, 1888, 2000, and 2016, a candidate was able to win the majority of electoral votes and thus the presidential election even though fewer primary voters had cast their ballots for him than for his opponent.

6214 Although all votes may have the same *counting value*, they may have different *success values*, depending on the electoral system. The main types are the **majority** and the **proportional electoral systems**. Modern electoral systems seek to compensate for the shortcomings of either system through hybrid forms, such as preferential or second votes.

➢ In the context of electoral law, "equality" means that every vote counts the same ("one person, one vote"); curiae, classes of voters, and the like are therefore not allowed. However, this does not preclude an unequal success value of the votes cast.

➢ The majority voting system is the older of the two; it divides the territory into constituencies, each of which elects only one member of parliament. Such systems favour large parties and ensure stable majorities in parliament; however, they hinder the establishment of new parties and distort the voters' will, as the votes cast for the defeated candidates are not considered at all.

➢ A proportional electoral system was first introduced in Belgium in 1899 and gradually became established in other states as well (in Austria and Germany in 1918). In this case, the division of the territory into constituencies is either dispensed with altogether, or they are organised in such a way that each constituency elects several deputies proportionally to the votes cast. The advantage of this system is that it better reflects the will of the electorate; the disadvantage is that the election is not "personalised" (the voters merely "tick off a list" instead of choosing an individual candidate), and that parliament becomes more fragmented.

➢ An extreme majority voting system was introduced in Italy in 1923, where a party that won 25 percent of the votes could win 66 percent of the seats in a constituency; this favoured the fascists. In 1945–93, Italy went to the other extreme of a purely proportional electoral system, resulting in an unusual diversity of parties and no government being able to stay in office for more than a few months. The electoral law that has been in place in Italy since 2016 is a hybrid system of majority and proportional representation.

➢ The system of proportional representation introduced in Austria in 1918 was at first substantially mitigated by the creation of relatively small constituencies, where many "residual votes" were not considered. With the electoral law reforms of 1971 and 1992, special "investigative procedures" were introduced to also consider these residual votes. This significantly strengthened the principle of proportional representation and also improved the diversity of the Austrian party spectrum (⇨ par. 8128).

➢ The counting of residual votes, however, only benefits those parties that have already won a "basic mandate" in at least one constituency, or – since 1992 – at least 4 percent of all valid votes nationwide, which is meant to prevent an excessive fragmentation of parliament.

➢ In 1949, Austria created an opportunity for voters to prioritise or delete individual candidates; since 1971, only *preferential votes* in favour of individual candidates, but neither deletions nor down-rankings, have been allowed. In practice, such preferential rankings are rarely successful: in 1983, an SPÖ candidate managed to enter the National Council through preferential votes, and in 2004, an FPÖ candidate entered the European Parliament in the same way.

➢ In Germany, on the other hand, the concept of a *second vote* has been in place since 1953: each voter gives his or her first vote to an individual, and his or her second vote to a party. Under the original concept, the member of parliament who received the most votes in a constituency received a mandate, which could lead to a party receiving more mandates (via the first votes) than it was entitled to (according to the number of second votes). Therefore, reforms were introduced in 2013 and 2023 to restore full proportionality.

6215 Democracy, by definition, requires a clash of opinions and thus also a diversity of opinions. The Political Parties Act 1975 and the new Political Parties Act 2012, which replaced it, therefore declare the "**existence and diversity of political parties**" to be "essential elements of the democratic order".

➢ Until 1975, political parties were usually established under the Associations Act 1867 (for instance the FPÖ, founded in 1955). This act subjected "political associations" to rigorous checks (including the submission of lists of their members to the state authority); women were not allowed to join political parties until 1918 (⇨ par. 4212).

➢ The parties established in 1945 (⇨ par. 8110) were not created under the Associations Act. Rather, until 1975, the SPÖ, ÖVP, and KPÖ derived their existence directly from the Austrian Declaration of Independence, which they have signed.

➢ The Political Parties Acts of 1975 and 2012 both include certain sections that have the rank of constitutional laws and guarantee the freedom to found political parties. Their statutes must be published on the internet (until 2011: in a newspaper) and deposited with the Ministry of the Interior; unless the new party is classified as a National Socialist organisation (⇨ par. 8201), the Ministry of the Interior cannot object to its statutes. Parties that were founded under the Political Parties Act are the Greens (1986), the Liberal Forum (1993; merged with NEOS, founded in 2012), and the BZÖ (Alliance for the Future of Austria, 2005), among others.

6216 The **obligation to vote according to the party line** – which has never been laid down in law – can be seen as a necessary consequence of an electoral system that is based on party lists. There is a certain tension between this situation and the principle of the **free mandate**, which has survived from the time of an electoral system in which voters could choose from individual candidates.

➢ In the era of the majority electoral system, in which the voters chose from a list of candidates, the latter still mainly campaigned for their election

Table 7: Majority vs. Proportional Electoral System

A) Majority electoral system: 6 constituencies, each electing 1 MP

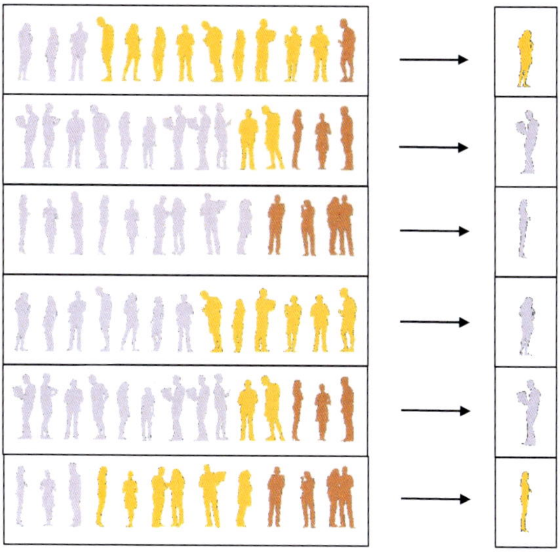

B) Proportional electoral system: 6 members are elected proportionally

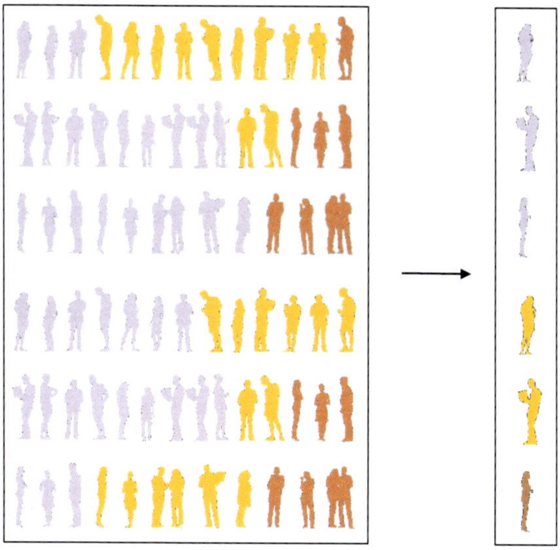

on an individual basis; only when they entered parliament did they join together to form interest groups. The proportional representation system, on the other hand, presupposes the existence of parties, since in this case not individuals but groups of persons ("party lists"), which have come together at least for the purpose of their joint candidacy ("electoral party"), are elected.

➢ The *political parties* that are governed by the Political Parties Act need to be distinguished from the *electoral parties* that compete in the elections. However, behind every electoral party there is almost always a political party (usually of the same name) or sometimes also an alliance of several political parties.

➢ From a legal point of view, the fact that parties rather than individuals are elected does not infringe on the direct quality of the election, since the parties are required to publish lists of the persons whom they intend to send to parliament before the election takes place.

➢ In terms of the principles of democracy, however, the fact that the parties do not have any constitutional means of forcing the deputies who have entered parliament via their party lists to vote in a certain way does pose a problem. The obligation to vote according to party policy, which usually results in the deputies of a party voting as a group, is based on an (in theory) voluntary agreement between them. If a deputy departs from the party line, he or she (merely) risks being expelled from the parliamentary group or party or might not be allowed to stand as a candidate for that party again in the future. However, he will remain a member of parliament until the end of the legislative period.

➢ This problem is exacerbated when parliamentarians not only break away from the party that nominated them but also found a new party or join an existing one. The first case happened in 1993 and 2005 with the emergence of the Liberal Forum and the BZÖ respectively, both founded by former FPÖ parliamentarians. The second case occurred in 2015 when several parliamentarians of the party "Team Stronach" joined the parliamentary group of the ÖVP.

5. Constitutional Justice

6217 Constitutional jurisdiction in the broader sense refers to all judicial competences for the protection of the constitution. Constitutional jurisdiction in the narrower sense refers to **judicial review** of general norms (laws and ordinances). Even in democracies, its existence is not immune to controversy.

➢ In the Habsburg Monarchy, constitutional jurisdiction in the broader sense was exercised by the Imperial Court with its right to control administrative acts for their constitutionality (⇨ par. 4216, par. 4227) and the Impeachment Court (⇨ par. 4218). In 1919, both competences were vested in a *Constitutional Court*, but it was only with the B-VG 1920 that this court was also granted the right to review the constitutionality of legal norms.

➢ Insofar as the court that is tasked with judicial review also has the authority to repeal laws, it acts as a "negative legislator" and, in this regard, has the same political power as the "positive legislator" (parliament). In particular, states with a strong democratic tradition have been reluctant to accept such judicial review because it appears to limit the omnipotence of parliament, which represents the will of the people.

➢ The prerequisite for the development of a judicial review of legal norms is the existence of "constitutional law in the formal sense". This is created in a special procedure (e.g. a two-thirds majority in parliament) and limits the powers of the "ordinary legislator". The doctrine of the hierarchical structure of the legal system (⇨ par. 6304) proved particularly influential for the development of constitutional jurisdiction; HANS KELSEN referred to the Constitutional Court (in a reply to the anti-democratic CARL SCHMITT, who had rejected the notion of constitutional jurisdiction) as the "guardian of the constitution" (⇨ par. 6210).

6218 In **Great Britain**, a constitutional court in the sense described above has not evolved, because Great Britain does not have constitutional law in the formal sense. The legislative power of parliament is, in theory, unlimited.

➢ According to the British view, the constitution describes the organisation of the state, i.e. what is usually meant by "constitution in the substantive sense". The idea that a particular statute has a special legal quality ("constitution in the formal sense") and therefore takes precedence over other statutes is alien to English law. Note that the UK, to this day, does not have a constitutional charter (⇨ par. 4201)!

➢ The British Parliament can therefore enact laws of any content without having to follow special procedural rules. The omnipotence of the British Parliament became particularly clear in 1716, when it extended its own legislative period from three to seven years. The British constitutional lawyer ALBERT VENN DICEY (*Introduction to the study of the law of the constitution*, 1885) saw this as proof that sovereignty lies not with the British people, but with parliament. Accordingly, a simple majority in parliament was sufficient for the Brexit Act 2020, for example, whereas the Brexit referendum in 2016 did not have any binding effect.

➢ The *Human Rights Act 1998* authorises the English courts to review laws for their conformity with the ECHR. However, in the event of a violation of the Convention, they can only make a declaratory finding of the violation but cannot repeal the offending law (*declaratory effect*). The situation is therefore comparable to that of the Imperial Court in the Habsburg Monarchy with regard to violations of the Basic Law on the General Rights of Nationals (⇨ par. 4216).

6219 The earliest example of constitutional jurisdiction was established in North America at the end of the 18th century against the backdrop of the 13 colonies' fight for independence from the British mother country (⇨ par. 3113). The **American model of constitutional jurisdiction** is characterised by *decentralisation* and *incidental judicial review*, as well as the merely *declaratory character* of the judgment.

➢ When the British Parliament introduced new duties for the colonies with the *Stamp Act* of 1765, without the involvement of the colonies' inhabitants, a Virginia court declared in 1766 that this law was incompatible with the Virginia Constitution and therefore not applicable. The principle that unconstitutional laws are null and void was first recognised by the US Supreme Court in 1803 in the case of MARBURY VS. MADISON.

➢ The American model does not provide for special constitutional courts or constitutional complaints. Rather, each court is required to (*incidentally*) review the laws that are to be applied in the proceedings pending before it for their constitutionality. If the court comes to the conclusion that the law is *unconstitutional*, this means that the law was null and void from the outset, i.e. non-existent (*absolute nullity*), which merely requires a formal pronouncement by the court (*declaratory competence*).

➢ Note the Anglo-American legal system of case law (⇨ par. 2330), whereby such decisions are also considered as precedents for other courts.

6220 In Europe, the concept of a **judicial review** based on the American model was the subject of extensive discussion but initially rejected. The December Constitution of 1867 allowed the courts to review ordinances, but not "duly promulgated laws" (Article 7 of the Basic Law on the Judiciary).

➢ Although Austrian constitutional law recognised the concept of a constitution in the formal sense (amendments to the December Constitution could only be adopted with a two-thirds majority in the House of Deputies and the House of Lords), a violation of this provision had no legal consequences, since even an unconstitutional simple law was considered valid if it had been ("duly") promulgated in accordance with the constitution.

➢ Ordinances could be reviewed by all courts and, for the specific case, declared invalid, a procedure similar to the American system of judicial review. However, due to the lack of a case-law system, this could lead to situations in which one court deemed an ordinance valid, while another court considered it invalid.

➢ In Germany, the idea of a judicial review only gradually gained acceptance and was in principle recognised by the German *Reichsgericht* (the supreme court of the German Reich in civil and criminal matters) in 1925; however, it did not acquire any practical significance.

6221 Besides the American model, a second model has received worldwide attention and imitation. It was developed for the B-VG with significant input from HANS KELSEN (⇨ par. 6113) and can therefore be described as the **Austrian model**. In contrast to the United States, it was not introduced primarily to provide better legal protection for individuals, but rather to serve as a system of *checks and balances* within the federal state. For this reason, it also followed completely different principles, namely the *centralisation* of constitutional jurisdiction in a single court and the *constitutive effect* of its decisions.

➢ As early as 1919, KELSEN had put forward the idea that a special court should be able to control provincial laws that contradict federal laws. (At that time, it was still envisaged that after Austria's transformation into a federal state, federal laws would take precedence over provincial laws, as is still the case in Germany today under Article 31 of the German Basic Law.)

➢ As the constitution evolved, it was decided that federal and provincial laws should have equal status. Accordingly, Article 140 B-VG stipulates that both the federal government and the Länder governments can challenge federal laws before the Constitutional Court. Such requests for review do not necessitate any specific occasion (*abstract judicial review*).

➢ It is only through the constitutional court's decision that the laws are repealed (constitutive effect: announcement in the Federal Law Gazette); until then, they are – provisionally – valid. MERKL coined the term *"Fehlerkalkül"* ("error calculus") to describe the phenomenon of the merely relative nullity of unconstitutional laws.

➢ The Constitutional Court is the only court competent to review legal norms; the other courts are barred from doing so, which ensures the consistency of jurisprudence (principle of centralisation). The review of ordinances was also entrusted to the Constitutional Court; with regard to this, certain courts, in addition to the governments, were given the right to submit requests for review to the Constitutional Court.

6222 The Austrian model of constitutional jurisdiction subsequently underwent a process of continuous expansion. **Incidental judicial review** gained in importance compared to abstract judicial review, and it is by far the more prevalent of the two in practice today. However, the principles of centralisation and of the constitutive effect of the decisions also apply in this context.

➢ Upon KELSEN's initiative, in 1920 the Constitutional Court was granted the right to examine *ex officio* the constitutionality of a law in a pending case if there are doubts about its constitutionality (Article 140 B-VG).

➢ This provision has gained particular importance for the review of unconstitutional administrative decisions within the scope of the Constitutional Court's special administrative jurisdiction (⇨ par. 4216): When the Constitutional Court reviews an administrative decision in terms of its constitutionality and doubts arise as to whether the law on whose basis the decision was issued is in conformity with the constitution, the review procedure of the administrative decision is suspended and the law itself is reviewed (and potentially repealed). Only then will the review of the administrative decision be continued and, if the underlying law is no longer in force, the decision will likewise be repealed.

➢ In 1929, the Supreme Court and the Administrative Court were also granted the right to apply to the Constitutional Court for a judicial review if they had doubts about the constitutionality of the laws they had to apply. This right was gradually extended to all other courts (both ordinary courts and administrative courts) by 2014.

6. State – Church – Society

6223 A state-church system is difficult to reconcile with the pluralistic nature of democracy; it occurs almost exclusively in parliamentary monarchies. The transition to a republic typically associated with democracy (⇨ par. 6212) also implies a complete rejection of state power legitimised by religion and is the basis for a (more or less profound) **separation of church and state**.

➢ In England, Norway, and Denmark, for example, the Crown is also the secular head of the respective state church; however, this position results not so much in privileges for the state church but in paternalism (approval of ecclesiastical legal acts by the Crown or parliament, etc.).

➢ A far-reaching separation of church and state was achieved in the USA, with the First Amendment of 1791,and in France, with the Law on the Separation of the Churches and the State in 1905.

➢ The Republic of Austria also maintains a separation of church and state; if it abandoned its denominational neutrality, this would be qualified by some legal scholars as affecting the principle of republicanism and thus as a total revision of the federal constitution pursuant to Article 44 (3) B-VG. However, the legally recognised churches and religious societies in Austria (like those in Germany) are considered public corporations and still enjoy a privileged position compared to secular private associations; to some extent, they are also eligible for state funding.

➢ The State of Israel was also founded in 1948 as a secular democracy, even though, for example, its name and flag refer to the Jewish religion. Its marriage law is not regulated by the state but is a matter for the 14 recognized religious communities. To this extent, but only to this extent, Halakha is therefore authoritative for the majority of the Israeli people.

➢ The secularisation of ecclesiastical property, which took place in Germany particularly as a result of the Imperial Recess of 1803, made it necessary to find new sources of funding for the churches. At the end of the 19th century, several German states introduced church taxes; this concept was generally recognised in Article 137 of the Weimar Constitution (which is still applicable today!). Church tax is levied by the state together with income tax; its administration is the responsibility of the churches.

➢ In Austria, on the other hand, the Catholic Church was financed mainly from the religious funds (⇨ par. 3210), until the latter's dissolution by the National Socialist regime. Since then, members of the Catholic Church have been required to pay church contributions (per a law of 28 April 1939), which – in contrast to the German church tax – is considered a membership fee governed by civil law and must therefore be claimed in civil court proceedings if necessary.

➢ The end of the Austrian monarchy also meant the end of the prince's right to nominate bishops (⇨ par. 2223). Since the Concordat of 1933, the selection of bishops has been the sole prerogative of the pope (except for in Salzburg, where the cathedral chapter was able to retain a remnant of its old voting rights). The Austrian federal government may raise objections of a general political nature against a candidate but has so far never exercised this right.

6224 Freedom of religion and of conscience, guaranteed in Austria since 1867, has led to a **plurality of religions and world views** across a broad spectrum, and the state has the task of ensuring a fair balance between the interests of these groups.

➢ As of 1918, only four other Christian confessions besides the Catholic Church, plus Judaism, and Islam, were legally recognised in Austria. The recognition of the Moravian Church (granted in 1880) was withdrawn in 2012, as it does not maintain a single parish in the territory of the present-day Republic.

➢ With the Treaty of St. Germain, all religions present in Austria, regardless of whether they were officially recognised or not, were granted the right of public worship (⇨ par. 6111). However, official recognition has not lost its significance. It continues to be relevant, among other things, for state subsidies and for the right to religious education within the public school system.

➢ Official recognition under the Recognition Act of 1874 was thus granted to the Methodists in 1951, to the Mormons in 1955, to the New Apostolic Church in 1975, and to the Buddhists in 1983. In 2003, a separate law was passed for the Oriental Orthodox Churches (Armenians, Syrians and Copts [Egyptians]), which were gradually recognised from 1973.

➢ Under the Islam Act of 1912, only Muslims of the Hanafi rite were covered by the official recognition (⇨ par. 4225). This restriction was repealed by the Constitutional Court in 1987 because it violated the principle of equality. A new Islam Act was passed in 2015.

➢ Given the large number of religions, the requirements for recognition under the Recognition Act of 1874 were significantly tightened in 1998 (including a minimum population share of 2% and a fundamentally positive attitude towards society and the state). To compensate for this, the possibility of registering as a "religious denomination" was created. This meant that many communities that are not very widespread in Austria (e.g. Hindus) also acquired legal personality, but not the status of a corporation under public law.

➢ After this reform, only Jehovah's Witnesses in 2009 and the Alevis in 2013, as well as the Free Churches, which joined together specifically for this purpose, achieved recognition under the Recognition Act of 1874.

6225 In a democracy, it can be challenging to define the tasks of the state in general terms; its nature is that of an "**open society**" (KARL R. POPPER) that is, in principle, compatible with a wide variety of social and/or economic models. However, the issue of the "core functions of the state", which has emerged in recent times in the context of the ever-increasing "outsourcing" of former state functions, poses a problem for democratic theory that needs to be taken seriously. If persons endowed with state authority are not democratically legitimised themselves and their actions cannot be predetermined by instructions from democratically legitimised organs, then this conflicts with Article 1 B-VG.

➤ After 1918, in Germany as well as in Austria, the state's tasks grew significantly as a result of the expanding social laws (pension insurance, unemployment insurance, etc.). However, this was not so much a consequence of the introduction of the democratic principle as a necessary reaction to the economic consequences of the First World War.

➤ The welfare state is enshrined in the constitution of the Federal Republic of Germany by the programmatic provision of Article 20 GG ("The Federal Republic of Germany is a democratic and social federal state"). In Austria, there is no such provision; there, the discussion of whether the welfare state should be incorporated in the constitution occurs more in the context of the debate about the creation of basic social rights.

➤ Due to the outsourcing of state functions, which has become increasingly common in recent times, the enforcement of entire areas of the law is no longer undertaken by state organs but by autonomous legal entities that are only under relatively loose state supervision. This may seem reasonable in some areas (railways? postal services? universities?) but is (still?) rejected for good reasons in regard to the police, the judiciary, and the army.

6226 The democratic principle of the **equality of all people with regard to their rights and dignity** has also contributed to the breakthrough of the principle of equality in the area of fundamental rights and made it the most important constitutional principle of all. The equality of men and women, in particular, has become almost a reality within the democratic system.

➤ The constitutions of the 19th century had already made regular provision for the equality of all citizens (⇨ par. 4226), but in practice this was given little importance. In 1920, the principle of equality was the only fundamental right incorporated into the B-VG (Article 7) and, following the example of the Weimar Constitution, supplemented by a demonstrative enumeration, according to which "privileges based on birth, gender, status, class, and confession are prohibited". This enumeration must be understood in its historical context (abolition of the nobility in Autria in 1919; establishment of the dictatorship of the proletariat in Russia in 1917, ⇨ par. 5202); notably, racial discrimination is not included in this list.

➤ In constitutional theory, it has been recognised from around 1926 that the principle of equality not only binds the executive, but also the legislator; laws may not include any non-objective differentiations, i.e. differentiations that based solely on the subject. The Constitutional Court has recognised this principle since 1931.

➤ Even with Article 7 of the B-VG, full equality between men and women had still not been achieved; differentiations based on gender were often legitimised by the Constitutional Court on the grounds that they were "objective" because they were rooted in the "nature of women". This only began to change in 1990, when the Constitutional Court ruled that different retirement ages for men and women were unconstitutional. It was only from around this time that formal equality of men and women was gradually established in practically all areas of life. Nonetheless, women still faced a range of disadvantages in practice. This led to the demand for "positive discrimination", i.e. specific measures to legally favour women, with the ultimate aim of achieving true equality between men and women. Article 7 was amended to include such a provision in the constitutional amendment of 1998.

C Legislation and Jurisprudence

1. General Remarks

6301 In the period 1918–1933, there were relatively few legal reforms in Central Europe, especially as modern codifications were already in place: the German Civil Code (BGB, ⇨ par. 4307) and the Swiss Civil Code (ZGB, ⇨ par. 4308). The Austrian General Civil Code (ABGB), in the version of three partial amendments, now also largely met the requirements of the early 20th century (⇨ par. 4309). However, due to the political upheaval, numerous laws were created in the field of **labour and social law**; highly controversial politically was the **reform of the marriage law**. As for criminal law, see ⇨ par. 8303.

➢ The end of the Habsburg Monarchy in 1918 did not mean the end of the Central European legal realm that it had created, especially since all successor states pursued a policy of substantive continuity (⇨ par. 6107) and only gradually replaced the old laws with new ones. Therefore, the ABGB, for example, remained in force in southern Poland until 1945 and in Czechia until 1950 (⇨ par. 3312).

➢ In the wake of the Russian October Revolution, workers' councils were set up in many countries, including Austria, although they did not achieve any substantial political influence. In Austria, the workers' councils developed into works councils in 1919, which still have significant co-determination rights in the management of businesses (but also not more than that). The eight-hour working day was introduced in Austria in 1918 and child labour was drastically reduced.

➢ While divorce (irrespective of the religious denomination of the spouses) was introduced in Czechoslovakia in 1919, in Austria it was opposed by the Christian Social Party in particular. Instead, it became common practice for the provincial governors to grant a dispensation to people who had been separated from their first spouse in terms of both "table and bed" (but were still formally married). This enabled them to remarry while their first spouse was still alive (known as "dispensation marriages" or, after the governor of Lower Austria, ALBERT SEVER, also as "Sever marriages").

➢ This practice was based on the (very vaguely formulated) § 83 ABGB, but was never recognised by the Austrian civil courts, which resulted in judicial chaos. When the Constitutional Court denied the civil courts the authority to rule on the validity of dispensations, this led to the dismissal of almost all its judges by a constitutional law of 1929 (⇨ par. 6118). The newly constituted Constitutional Court did in indeed revise its opinion; the underlying problem, however, remained unresolved until 1938.

6302 The doctrine of civil and criminal law was not significantly reformed either. Building on JHERING's theories, the Tübingen civil law scholar PHILIPP HECK developed the **jurisprudence of interests**, which argues that every new norm emerges through the weighing of conflicting interests. These would need to be identified and evaluated by the judge.

➢ HECK's thoughts were of particular significance for the theory of legal gap-filling; the identification of a gap in the law is in itself already an evaluative process, since the judge determines that a norm, although desirable, is missing. The law serves to resolve social conflicts and is, as it were, a "diagonal of powers of contending factors".

➢ The "teleological method" advocated by the Graz civil law professor ARMIN EHRENZWEIG was similar. EHRENZWEIG's *System des österreichischen allgemeinen Privatrechts* (*System of Austrian General Private Law*, 1923/25) would influence Austrian civil law scholarship for decades.

➢ The study of international law, whose existence had been contested in the 19th century (especially by the German philosopher G. W. F. HEGEL) experienced a major upturn after 1918. In 1922, two chairs for international law were created for the first time at the University of Vienna.

2. The pure theory of law

6303 The pure theory of law is a positivist legal theory developed by HANS KELSEN (⇨ par. 6113, par. 6204) in Vienna at the beginning of the 20th century; it is therefore also known as the "**Vienna school of legal theory**". A summary of his theory was published by KELSEN himself in 1934 in his book *Reine Rechtslehre* (*The Pure Theory of Law*).

➢ KELSEN was a professor of constitutional law at the University of Vienna from 1918 to 1930 and a judge at the Austrian Constitutional Court from 1919 to 1930. He had originally conceived his theory for constitutional law; his disciples ADOLF J. MERKL and ALFRED VERDROSS later transferred it to the fields of administrative law and international law. Its influence remained limited in the areas of civil and criminal law.

➢ After KELSEN's departure from Vienna in 1930 (⇨ par. 6118), the "Vienna School" gradually fell into decline; in the 1960s, however, the pure theory of law experienced a renaissance in Austria. Today, it is recognised all over the world, especially in Southern Europe and Latin America, and in recent times also increasingly in Germany.

6304 In contrast to older positivist theories, the pure theory of law rejects the idea that the validity of norms can be derived from factual power

Table 8: The Hierarchical Structure of the Legal System
and Public Law Jurisdiction in Austria 1869–2013

The Administrative Court reviewed
the legality of administrative decisions from 1876 on
the accordance of administrative decisions with ordinances from 1876 on

The Imperial Court / Constitutional Court reviewed
the constitutionality of administrative decisions from 1869 on
the constitutionality and legality of ordinances from 1920 on
the constitutionality of statutes & emergency decrees from 1920 on

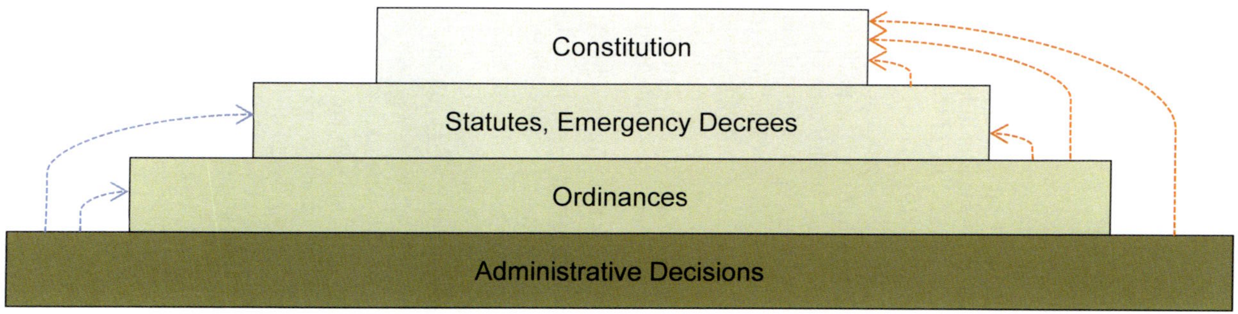

Note: Between 1867 and 1920, all courts (including the Administrative Court and the Imperial/Constitutional Court) had jurisdiction for reviewing ordinances for their legality; since then, this is the sole jurisdiction of the Constitutional Court. Since 2014, individual administrative decisions are no longer reviewed for constitutionality and legality by the Constitutional Court or (Supreme) Administrative Court, but by the administrative courts of first instance; their findings may be appealed to the Supreme Administrative or Constitutional Court.

relations. This is a consequence of the epistemological distinction between **"is" and "ought"**.

➢ Although the *substance* of the law is the product of a political process, the *validity* of legal norms cannot be derived from political factors but only from other, "higher-ranking" norms. This results in a specific structure of legal norms, which was first described by MERKL in his theory of the "hierarchical structure of the legal system".

➢ According to this view, a law is always produced in a two-tier process; first, in an "act of thought", the law-making entity needs to interpret those higher-ranking norms that authorise it to create norms and thereby provide a certain framework (for the legislator, this is the constitution; for the judge, the law in general; etc.). In a second act, which is an "act of volition" that needs to be strictly distinguished from the first, the law-making entity must choose from the elements of this framework, based on non-legal (i.e. political) considerations, to arrive at a concrete decision.

➢ The pure theory of law thus rejects the claim of conceptual jurisprudence (⇨ par. 4304) that (only) the parliament creates laws and (only) the courts enforce them. Instead, it argues that the creation and execution of laws take place at every level of the legal hierarchy.

➢ Unlike legislators, legal scholars may only interpret the law and must not attribute a new meaning to it (which would be politics); the task of jurisprudence is not the creation but merely the cognition of law. The "pure theory of law" owes its name to this effort to precisely distinguish between the two spheres of jurisprudence and politics.

6305 In contrast to natural law doctrines, the pure theory of law rejects the idea that human beings can rationally perceive supreme values (⇨ par. 8304) and therefore only studies norms that belong to positive law and that are, as a rule, effective (i.e. they emanate from an actual ruling power). However, this is not because of their effectiveness but because it seems "reasonable" from the perspective of those applying the law to *assume* that these norms are valid. This assumption is called the **basic norm**.

➢ According to KELSEN, natural law theories always presuppose the existence of absolute justice, absolute morality, etc. But there has never been a consensus on what should be called "just", "ethical", etc.; rather, there are many such norms, which always reflect only relative values. A justification of positive law in terms of natural law is therefore impossible.

➢ On the other hand, since norms always derive their validity from a higher-ranking norm, there must be a supreme norm that gives validity to the entire positive legal system and therefore cannot itself be part of positive law. This basic norm is presupposed by those applying the law. Unlike in natural law, it has no other content than to bring the positive law into force, which is why positive law can have any given content.

➢ KELSEN himself still considered a minimum of effectiveness essential for the validity of a legal system. It was MERKL's disciple ROBERT WALTER who, in his book *Der Aufbau der Rechtsordnung* (*The Structure of the Legal Order*, 1964) completely detached the concept of validity from effectiveness by explaining that it was simply reasonable (but not a must) for a lawyer to concern himself with effective law.

➢ The frequently misunderstood theory of the basic norm has merely epistemological implications. The basic norm cannot be used to classify a legal system as "good" or "evil"; this judgement is left to the subjective moral sense of the individual.

➢ One of the main criticisms directed at the pure theory of law is that its concept of law is also applicable to legal systems that are deeply in conflict with our ethical standards, such as the laws of National Socialist Germany (⇨ par. 7302). After the Second World War, positivist legal theories therefore lost ground and natural law theories experienced a revival.

Part VII

The Age of Far-Right Dictatorships

A Developments

1. Europe 1933–1939

7101 In 1932, the NSDAP won a relative majority in the German Reichstag, and on 30 January 1933, HITLER was appointed chancellor by President HINDENBURG. Step by step, he transformed the republic into a fascist dictatorship (**"Third Reich"**). After HINDENBURG's death in 1934, HITLER also took over his duties as the "*Führer und Reichskanzler*".

➢ The rise of the NSDAP had been facilitated by members of the large industrial bourgeoisie and the army, in particular, who hoped that it would provide effective protection against a Communist takeover. Great importance was therefore attached to the argument that HITLER's "seizure of power" on 30 January 1933 had occurred in accordance with the law. Even in the period that followed, the Weimar Constitution was never formally repealed, but instead undermined from within.

➢ The fire in the Reichstag building on 27 February 1933 was (against better judgement) blamed on the Communists and used as a pretext for HINDENBURG to issue (at HITLER's suggestion) an emergency decree *for the protection of the people and the state* ("Reichstag Fire Decree") on 28 February. It imposed restrictions on numerous fundamental rights (esp. the freedom of the press, of association, and of assembly) and thus allowed for the suppression of the KPD. Almost all its functionaries were arrested and their mandates in the Reichstag were cancelled.

➢ The Reichstag, weakened by this and intimidated by further National Socialist pressure (including the deployment of SA troops in the Reichstag building!), passed the *Law to Remedy the Distress of People and Reich* (the "Enabling Act") on 24 March 1933, which authorised the government to autonomously enact laws that could to some extent also deviate from the constitution. With the *Law for the Reconstruction of the Reich* of 30 January 1934, the government was eventually also granted the definitive right to pass constitutional laws.

➢ After the dissolution of all other parties and the proclamation of the NSDAP as the only remaining party (14 July 1933), the Reichstag completely lost its political significance; only in isolated instances did it continue to pass laws itself (esp. the Nuremberg Race Laws of 1935, ⇨ par. 7204). From 1942 onwards, it was no longer convened.

➢ Cabinet meetings were no longer convened from 1938, and the government instead made its decisions through circular resolutions, which further increased HITLER's power within his own government.

➢ In 1932, i.e. before the National Socialists had seized power, the (conservative) German government had already deposed the (Social Democratic) Prussian government and placed Prussia under its direct administration (*"Preußenschlag"*). In 1933, governors were also appointed for the other German states. The above-mentioned *Law for the Reconstruction of the Reich* of 1934 transferred the sovereign rights of the constituent states to the Reich (*"Gleichschaltung"*). The Reichsrat, the representation of the constituent states in the Reich, was abolished. This also eliminated the federalist principle in the Reich.

➢ The primary domestic goal of the NSDAP was the "co-ordination" of all state and social institutions with the party and their strictly hierarchical organisation according to the "Führer principle". An essential means to this end was the persecution and extermination of all kinds of minorities, especially the Jews (⇨ par. 7204, par. 7208ff).

➢ One of the NSDAP's main foreign policy goals was initially a revision of the Treaty of Versailles. In 1933, Germany withdrew from the League of Nations (its permanent seat in the Council of the League of Nations later went to the USSR) and went on to deliberately violate a number of provisions of the Versailles Treaty (invasion of the demilitarised Rhineland in 1936, etc.).

7102 Many other states, including Austria (⇨ par. 7103, par. 7215), also saw their parliamentary democratic systems decline and be replaced by **authoritarian or fascist regimes**.

➢ Similar to what happened later in Germany, MUSSOLINI had gradually dismantled Italy's democracy soon after his appointment as Prime Minister in 1922 (⇨ par. 6105); in 1926, all parties except the Partito Nazionale Fascista were banned. MUSSOLINI's dictatorship served as a model for HITLER. In terms of foreign policy, he sought to increase Italy's influence (Roman Protocols with Austria and Hungary 1934, ⇨ par. 7107). However, when he conquered Abyssinia (Ethiopia) in 1936, he became internationally isolated and subsequently dependent on Germany.

➢ In Spain (a republic since 1931), the fascist *Falange* under FRANCISCO FRANCO was able to win the civil war against the republican government (in which Communists were also represented) in 1936–39. In this war, both sides received military support from abroad (in particular from German and Soviet troops respectively).

➢ Authoritarian regimes and/or military dictatorships were also established through putsches or coups d'état: in Lithuania, Poland, and Portugal in 1926, in Estonia and Latvia in 1934, in Romania in 1938, and, for a short time, also in Bulgaria and Yugoslavia. The character of the HORTHY regime in Hungary, which had some democratic but also some dictatorial/authoritarian elements, is a difficult and controversial issue.

2. Austria 1933–1945

a) The Authoritarian Regime (1933–1938)

7103 In March 1933, the federal government took advantage of an incident in the National Council to overthrow the country's parliamentary and democratic system in a **coup d'état** (the so-called "self-elimination of the National Council") and to henceforth rule in an authoritarian manner (i.e. by means of emergency decrees). The legal basis for this was the Wartime Economy Enabling Act 1917 (*Kriegswirtschaftliches Ermächtigungsgesetz*, **KwEG**), whose narrow scope of application, however, was transgressed; hence, the federal government's activities from March 1933 onwards can only be described as pseudo-legal.

➢ The Social Democratic Party enjoyed the largest number of votes since the National Council election of 1930 but remained in opposition. The federal government, led by the Christian Social Chancellor ENGELBERT DOLLFUSS (1932–34), at times only had a majority of 83:82 votes in the National Council. The NSDAP, which came to power in Germany in 1933 (⇨ par. 6106), was also represented in several Austrian diets and, since 1932, the Federal Council. The National Council election scheduled for 1934 would very likely have resulted in the NSDAP entering the National Council as well.

➢ On 4 March 1933, during a crucial vote in the National Council relating to a railway strike, an oversight seems to have occurred, and the wrong ballot papers were used. This resulted in a tumult in which the three National Council presidents resigned one after the other, partly because they could no longer make themselves heard, but in the case of the (Social Democratic) First President RENNER and the (Christian Social) Second President RUDOLF RAMEK probably also because they wanted to be able to vote with their respective parties.

➢ The parliamentary rules of procedure made no provision for an incident of this kind (today, the oldest member would take over the presidency). It has therefore sometimes been assumed that the resignation of the third president, SEPP STRAFFNER of the Greater Germans, was in fact void. Indeed, STRAFFNER called a new meeting for 15 March.

➢ In the meantime, however, the federal government had seized the opportunity and announced that this "parliamentary crisis" was not a "state crisis". At the suggestion of the senior public servant ROBERT HECHT, the DOLLFUSS government decided to govern for an interim period by means of emergency decrees based on the KwEG, a law from the times of the monarchy.

➢ While the KwEG only provided for "government decrees to promote and re-establish economic life, to prevent economic damage and to supply the population with food and other commodities", already the first emergency decree, issued on 7 March 1933, served to impose pre-publication censorship on certain newspapers. On 30 March, the *Schutzbund* was dissolved, on 26 May, a ban was imposed on the KPÖ's activities, and on 19 June, the

NSDAP's activities on Austrian territory were made illegal. The (unconvincing) justification was that the bans were meant to "prevent damage to economic life".

➢ On 15 March, the parliament building was cordoned off by police on the chancellor's instructions. STRAFFNER managed to make a short speech to the members who had already gathered in the building, but it was evident that any attempt to reactivate the National Council would have been prevented by force.

7104 The Social Democratic Party judged the federal government's approach, quite rightly, as a breach of the constitution. Their attempts to fight this with legal means, however, only led the federal government to also eliminate the Federal Council and the Constitutional Court. With these measures, if not earlier, the rule of law was forsaken, and the coup d'état was complete. After the *Schutzbund's* military defeat in the **February Uprising ("civil war") of 1934**, the Social Democratic Party was eventually also banned.

➢ On 17 March 1933, the Federal Council, in which the Social Democrats had a majority, protested against the federal government's course of action, to which the latter replied that without a functioning National Council the Federal Council was not a legislative body and therefore its resolutions were legally irrelevant. The Federal Council continued to hold meetings until February 1934, in which the authoritarian leadership style of the Federal Government was sharply criticised, but this criticism remained ineffective.

➢ Vienna's Social Democratic provincial government made use of its right to initiate an abstract review of norms and applied to the Constitutional Court for a review of the legality of seven of the federal government's emergency decrees. However, before the Constitutional Court could act, on 23 May 1933, the federal government issued an emergency decree based on the KwEG that reorganised the decision-making capacity of the Constitutional Court. Meanwhile, HECHT, himself a substitute member of the Constitutional Court, persuaded three members and three substitute members of the court to resign. He also resigned so that the court was no longer able to pass resolutions.

➢ The remaining judges who met for the session on 22 June had to acknowledge that they could no longer review the validity of the emergency decree of 23 May 1933, because it was valid, at least for the time being, by virtue of the "error calculus" (⇨ par. 6221), and because of this validity, the Constitutional Court was unable to hand down a decision. If the constitutional judges had simply ignored the decree, i.e. found it to be absolutely void, they would have – according to their own interpretation – placed themselves above the constitution. Their appeal to Federal President WILHELM MIKLAS (1928–38) to make the court functional again had no effect.

➢ The *Schutzbund* continued its activities despite the ban. On 12 February 1934, *Schutzbund* members mounted an act of armed resistance against a house search in Linz, which was followed by several spontaneous uprisings in some Social Democratic strongholds in Upper Austria, Styria, and Vienna, but not any coordinated action on the part of the Social Democratic leaders.

➢ The *Heimwehren* and the army crushed the "February uprising", which claimed over 300 lives, by 15 February. Most Social Democratic functionaries were arrested or fled the country; nine *Schutzbund* members were executed.

7105 After the elimination of parliamentarism and the dissolution of the established party structures, the **May Constitution** of 1 May 1934 also marked the formal break with the B-VG and established an authoritarian corporative state. The newly founded *Vaterländische Front* ("Fatherland Front") became the state party.

➢ Whereas initially consideration had been given to implementing the constitutional reform of 1929 (which had not been fully realised then) and to transforming the Federal Council into a council of the Länder and corporative groups (as originally envisaged), DOLLFUSS, under pressure from the *Heimwehren*, by the autumn of 1933 had made up his mind to establish a corporative state replacing the parliamentary democracy. He first presented the concept of the new state to the public on 11 September 1933 in a speech delivered at Vienna's Trotting Racecourse, Krieau.

➢ The Fatherland Front, founded in May 1933, became the sole "bearer of the Austrian state idea". Despite its large membership, attained especially through involuntary accessions, the authoritarian regime was unable to develop it into a mass movement along the lines of the Italian or German models. The Christian Social Party dissolved and was absorbed into the Fatherland Front.

➢ The new constitution was initially enacted by way of an emergency decree (!). On 30 April 1934, the National Council, which at this stage had allegedly been dysfunctional for over a year, was again convened (without its Social Democratic members, hence as a "rump parliament") and then, in a manner that was clearly illegal under the B-VG (which was formally repealed on this occasion), authorised the government to repromulgate the new constitution.

➢ However, the abrogation of the B-VG and the enactment of a completely new constitution constituted a "total revision" as defined by Article 44 (2) B-VG and would therefore have required a referendum. To avoid this, the rump parliament abrogated this article – without a referendum, which from today's perspective would be considered inadmissible.

➢ The National Council also passed the Enabling Act 1934, which gave the government the right to pass laws (also in constitutional matters). This Act was probably intended as a transitional solution until the May Constitution came into effect. However, the May Constitution was never fully implemented; the Enabling Act and the Constitutional Transition Act 1934 concentrated all power in the government und dort wieder beim Bundeskanzler (⇨ par. 7217).

7106 The preamble of the May Constitution of 1934 invoked "God Almighty, from whom all right emanates" and described Austria as a **"Christian, German federal state on a corporative basis"**.

➢ Invoking God as the source of all law was a direct negation of Article 1 B-VG, according to which all law emanates from the people, and thus a rejection of the democratic principle. Together with the new constitution, a concordat with the Holy See (which had already been agreed on 5 June 1933) was proclaimed, which once again gave the Catholic Church great influence, particularly in the areas of marriage and education, with some parts being given the status of constitutional norms.

➢ The official name of the state was now "Federal State of Austria", which primarily served to avoid the word "republic". Nevertheless, Austria's form of government continued to be a republican one (implicitly, since it was not a monarchical one, ⇨ par. 1104).

➢ Note: The terms "First Republic" and "Second Republic" are established terms in historiography, but have no legal significance. While the term "First Republic" was previously used to refer to the entire period from 1918 to 1938, today (and in this book) it refers only to the period from 1918 to 1933, since the Second Republic did not resume where the First Republic left off in 1938, but in 1933 (⇨ par. 8111).

➢ The federal president, who was still competent to appoint the federal government, should no longer be elected by the people but by the mayors of all Austrian municipalities. The mayors should be elected by municipal congresses, comprising delegates of various interest groups, in particular such based on vocations. These complicated arrangements were intended to prevent any attempt at a popular election. Federal President MIKLAS, who had been in office since 1928, remained president until 1938.

➢ As since 1929, the most important power of the federal president was the appointment and dismissal of the federal chancellor and the other federal ministers. In practice, however, the political power lay with the federal government and here with the federal chancellor, so that the political system of the years 1933/34–38 can be described as a "chancellor dictatorship". The planned corporative state structure was only fully implemented in 1938 (⇨ par. 7217). On the (controversial) description of the political system as (Austro-)fascist, see ⇨ par. 7218.

➢ Although the federal principle was mentioned both in the name of the state and in the preamble to the constitution, it was weaker after 1934 than it had been before; for example, the federal chancellor had an absolute veto over Länder legislation. Vienna lost its status as a federal state, but as a "federal city" it had a position that was largely comparable to that of the Länder.

➢ The May Constitution comprised a catalogue of fundamental rights, but it represented a step backwards compared to the Basic Law on the General Rights of Nationals of 1867 (⇨ par. 4224). The Federal Supreme Court (*Bundesgerichtshof,* not to be confused with the Supreme Court/*Oberster Gerichtshof*) was responsible for protecting fundamental rights and also combined almost all the competencies of the two abolished public law courts, the Constitutional Court and the Administrative Court, including the right to review legislation (⇨ par. 6221). However, the Federal Supreme Court was expressly prohibited from reviewing any decrees issued under the Wartime Economy Enabling Act by 1 July 1934 (and thus the enactment of the Constitution of 1934).

7107 From the beginning, the authoritarian regime fought with the National Socialists in both Austria and Germany. To gain international support, DOLLFUSS aligned himself closely with fascist Italy ("Rome Protocols" of 17 March 1934). On 25 July 1934, DOLLFUSS was shot dead during an **attempted coup d'état by the National Socialists.** KURT SCHUSCHNIGG became the new federal chancellor.

➢ With the National Socialist seizure of power in Germany, the relationship between the two countries changed considerably: the Austrian federal government now rejected the *"Anschluss"* and tried to establish Austria as a "second German state", indeed as the "better Germany" vis-à-vis the German Reich. The German government reacted with the so-called "Thousand Marks Ban": Germans had to pay a fee of 1,000 Reichsmarks prior to travelling to Austria, which severely harmed the tourism industry.

➢ In the Rome Protocols, Italy, Austria, and Hungary agreed on political, economic, and military cooperation, including an Italian intervention in the event of domestic unrest in Austria. In terms of their European policy provisions, the Rome Protocols were not least a reaction to the "Little Entente", an alliance formed in 1920/21 by the ČSR, Yugoslavia, and Romania, which surrounded Austria and Hungary and was designed to prevent attempts at restoration by the Habsburgs or others. The Rome Protocols became practically relevant during the National Socialist July putsch of 1934 when MUSSOLINI ordered Italian troops to the Austrian border to prevent a possible intervention by National Socialist Germany.

➢ The (failed) July putsch aimed especially at detaining the federal government and occupying the building of the public broadcaster in Vienna, but fighting also broke out in some of the Länder. In total, more than 250 people died in the attempted coup and eight putschists were executed.

➢ After MUSSOLINI's rapprochement with HITLER during the Abyssinia crisis in 1936 (⇨ par. 7102), the Austrian government was left to its own devices. In July 1936, Austria had to make major concessions to National Socialist Germany. The "July Agreement" included amnesties for National Socialists and the admission of two NSDAP "persons of trust" to the Austrian federal government. Germany on the other hand guaranteed Austria's sovereignty and pledged non-interference into Austrian affairs.

b) The National Socialist era (1938–1945)

7108 On 12 March 1938, Austria was occupied by German troops. The new National Socialist Austrian federal government and the German Reich government proclaimed the "reunification of Austria with the German Reich" (the ***"Anschluss"***) on 13 March.

➢ In a meeting in Berchtesgaden on 12 February 1938, HITLER, who had made SCHUSCHNIGG completely reliant on him, demanded that the National Socialist ARTUR SEYSS-INQUART be appointed Minister of the Interior.

➢ After his return from Berchtesgaden, SCHUSCHNIGG tried to gain a stronger political base for his rule and announced a "popular consultation" for 13 March "for a free and German, independent and social, for a Christian and united Austria". Thereupon HITLER demanded SCHUSCHNIGG's immediate resignation and threatened military intervention if he did not comply. Since there was no help forthcoming from the major powers, SCHUSCHNIGG decided against putting up military resistance and resigned on 11 March, whereupon Federal President MIKLAS appointed SEYSS-INQUART as federal chancellor. When MIKLAS himself resigned on 13 March, SEYSS-INQUART took over his functions, in accordance with the May Constitution.

➢ The German troops were greeted enthusiastically by large crowds. HITLER's jubilant reception on his arrival likely led to his decision to immediately legally unify the two states.

➢ The *"Anschluss"* was legally executed by a federal constitutional law enacted by the Austrian federal government (on the basis of the Austrian Enabling Act 1934) on 13 March 1938 and by a Reich law with the same wording enacted by the German government (on the basis of the German Enabling Act 1933) on the same day ("harmonised legislation").

➢ Based on the German and Austrian Annexation acts, a referendum was subsequently held on 10 April 1938, in which more than 99 percent of those eligible voted in favour of the annexation, a result that can only be explained by massive pressure – intimidation, vote-rigging, the lifting of the obligation to maintain the secrecy of the ballot, and the exclusion of the Jewish electorate. On the other hand, both the Austrian Bishops' Conference and the Social Democrat RENNER had publicly recommended voting "yes".

7109 The immediate consequence of the *"Anschluss"* was the annexation of Austria as a province of the German Reich. The Ostmark Act of 14 April 1939 provided for the complete liquidation of Austria as a state; it was to be replaced by seven *"Reichsgaue"*, each of which was directly subordinate to the Reich government. This new structure should later also be introduced throughout the "Greater German Reich". Due to the outbreak of the Second World War, however, the implementation of this plan was delayed until 31 March 1940 and the subsequent general introduction of this structure throughout the Reich never happened.

➢ Article II of the German Annexation Act 1938 initially retained the previous Austrian legal system, with the proviso that norms (including most, but not all, of the provisions of the May Constitution of 1934) that were deemed incompatible with the National Socialist state order *ipso iure* lost their validity.

➢ The Austrian federal government under SEYSS-INQUART remained in office as a "provincial government" until 30 April 1939, retaining the legislative powers previously vested in the Austrian federal lawmaker, insofar as they had not become competences reserved for the Reich. The Austrian Bundestag (established under the May Constitution of 1934) and its preliminary advisory bodies were abolished.

➢ On 23 April 1938, JOSEF BÜRCKEL was appointed "Reich Commissioner for the Reunification of Austria with the German Reich". He organised, among other things, the fragmentation of the Austrian state into seven

"Reichsgaue" (Carinthia, Lower Danube, Upper Danube, Salzburg, Styria, Tyrol, and Vienna).

➢ The judicial authorities were transformed into authorities of the Reich; the Austrian Supreme Court was replaced by two senates at the German *Reichsgericht* (= supreme court, ⇨ par. 6220) in Leipzig that predominantly applied Austrian law.

3. The Second World War (1939–1945)

7110 National Socialist Germany pursued an imperialist foreign policy (1938 occupation of Austria and the Sudetenland, 1939 destruction of the Czechoslovak Republic), which initially met with little resistance. Only the German invasion of Poland on 1 September 1939 was answered by the UK and France (the "Allies") with declarations of war against the German Reich. In 1941, Germany invaded the Soviet Union. When Japan, which was allied with Germany and had been at war with China since 1937, also attacked the USA in 1941, all the major powers were engaged in the **Second World War**.

➢ The occupation of Austria occurred without the Great Powers objecting (⇨ par. 7108); the occupation of the Sudetenland was even legitimised by decisions taken at an international conference in Munich (29 September 1938). At this conference, Germany, Italy, France, and the UK agreed – without consulting the ČSR – to cede its German-, Hungarian-, and Polish-speaking territories to the respective neighbouring states, while the ČSR was given a guarantee of its new boundaries against unprovoked aggression.

➢ In March 1939, HITLER – in breach of the Munich Agreement – occupied the Czech part of the country and established the "Protectorate of Bohemia and Moravia". Slovakia became a formally independent state but was *de facto* dependent on Germany. Again, there was no resistance from the Great Powers.

➢ Prior to the German invasion of Poland, a non-aggression pact with the (ideologically antagonistic!) Soviet Union had been signed on 23 August 1939. In a secret protocol, Germany and the USSR divided East-Central Europe into areas of interest. On this basis, the Soviet Union conquered the eastern part of Poland and the Baltic states; the Soviet attack on Finland in 1939 led to the exclusion of the USSR from the League of Nations.

➢ Germany and its allies (the "Axis powers": Japan, Italy, and others) were initially able to take control of large parts of Europe, Asia, and Africa. France was forced to surrender in 1940. While northern France was occupied by the Germans, the authoritarian *Etat Français* (established by a constitutional law of 17 July 1940) under Marshal HENRI PÉTAIN was able to retain a certain degree of independence in the south and initially collaborated with Germany ("Vichy regime"). It was not until 1942 that the entire French territory was occupied by German troops.

7111 In 1942, the Soviet Union joined forces with the Western powers to form an "anti-HITLER coalition". The turning point in the German-

Soviet war came in 1943; in 1944, British and American troops landed in German-occupied Normandy. On 30 April 1945, HITLER committed suicide; the **surrender** of German troops became effective on 8 May 1945.

➢ In 1943, the fascist regime in Italy was overthrown, and the new government declared war on Germany. MUSSOLINI, who had tried to establish a counter-government in northern Italy ("Republic of Salò"), was shot dead on 28 April 1945.

➢ Crushing the German Wehrmacht, Allied troops had conquered almost all of Germany. On 23 May 1945, the members of the last German government were arrested. With the *Berlin Declaration* of 5 June 1945, the four Allies (USSR, USA, UK, France) assumed control over Germany and divided it into four occupation zones (on Austria ⇨ par. 8112).

➢ Under the *Potsdam Agreement* of 2 August 1945, Poland received as compensation for the territories that it had lost to the USSR the parts of Germany east of the Oder and Neisse rivers ("Westward Shift of Poland", with the exception of northern East Prussia, which fell to the USSR as the "Kaliningrad Region").

➢ While the war in Europe ended in May 1945, Japan surrendered only on 2 September 1945, after the USA had dropped atomic bombs on Hiroshima and Nagasaki. In total, well over 50 million people lost their lives during the Second World War.

➢ In 1947, a peace treaty was concluded in Paris with Germany's former allies in Europe (Italy, Finland, Hungary, Romania, Bulgaria), and another treaty in 1951 in San Francisco with Japan. The Soviet annexations from 1939 onwards (which included the Baltic states and territories in Finland, Poland, Germany, the Czechoslovak Republic, and Romania) were upheld, but otherwise, most of the territorial changes that had taken place in 1938–45 were reversed. A treaty with Germany was not concluded until 1990 (⇨ par. 8131). The measures regarding Germany were therefore widely considered to be only provisional.

7112 German and Japanese war criminals were brought before international tribunals in Nuremberg and Tokyo, respectively, in 1946. These trials, unique in the world, were of crucial importance for the development of **international criminal law**.

➢ During the war, opinions diverged on how war criminals should be punished. At the Moscow Conference of 1943 (⇨ par. 8112), it was decided that war criminals should be punished only by due process under the law of the place of the offence.

➢ With regard to the main war criminals, who had committed crimes throughout Europe, the USSR, USA, UK, and France agreed in London on 8 August 1945 to set up an International Military Tribunal, with each of the four powers nominating a judge and a prosecutor. This tribunal was competent with regard to three offences: crimes against peace, war crimes in the narrower sense (violations of the laws or customs of war) and crimes against humanity.

➤ The trial of the major war criminals took place in Nuremberg from November 1945 to October 1946 and ended with 12 death sentences (including SEYSS-INQUART, ⇨ par. 7108) and seven prison sentences; three people were acquitted. Numerous other trials were subsequently held against other war criminals on the side of the Axis powers – but not against war criminals on the side of the Allies. About the war crimes trials in Austria ⇨ par. 8114.

➤ The defendants put forward the argument, in particular, that the legal norms applied had only been created on 8 August 1945, i.e. after the offences had been committed. Against this, HANS KELSEN argued in an expert opinion for the US prosecutor that there was no prohibition of retroactive penal laws in international law and that there was no cause for moral reservations about punishing people for murder, robbery, etc.

➤ In Tokyo, the occupying powers set up an International Military Tribunal for the Far East on 19 January 1946, which was modelled on the Nuremberg trials. The tribunal sat from April to November 1946 and handed down seven death sentences and 18 prison sentences.

➤ These trials were groundbreaking for international criminal law in that it was the first time that individuals were held accountable before an international tribunal for actions taken in their capacity as state officials. The Treaty of Versailles of 1919 had already included a provision to this effect with regard to the German Emperor WILLIAM II, but he was never actually put on trial.

7113 During and after the Second World War, large-scale **forced resettlements and expulsions** took place. Academic research has proposed widely divergent estimates of how many people were affected. However, these migratory movements were certainly the largest in Europe since the migration period in the Early Middle Ages.

➤ Partly out of military considerations, but especially due to the National Socialists' racist ideology, well over fifteen million people from the territories conquered by the German Reich were forced from their homes in 1939–45, sent to concentration or labour camps, and/or murdered (⇨ par. 7204). The National Socialist regime also sought to resettle the so-called *"Volksdeutsche"* (members of the German minorities living outside the Reich) within the Reich's borders – often against their will.

➤ On 21 October 1939, HITLER and MUSSOLINI agreed that the German and Ladin-speaking South Tyroleans should be resettled in the Reich; those who did not want to emigrate were to give up their language and culture. More than 85 percent of the approximately 250,000 South Tyroleans voted for this "option", and by the end of the war approximately 75,000 "optants" had emigrated; only a small number of them returned after 1945.

➤ After the collapse of the National Socialist regime, almost all *"Volksdeutsche"* (which now also included the German populations of the countries east of the Oder-Neisse line [Silesia, East Prussia, etc.]) were expelled from their homelands. This happened partly on legal grounds, such as the decrees of Czechoslovak President EDVARD BENEŠ (1935–38, 1945–48; "BENEŠ Decrees"), and partly without such a legal foundation.

➤ Already in 1938, the United States had proposed an international solution to the refugee problem at the Évian Conference. In 1950, the office of the *United Nations High Commissioner for Refugees* (UNHCR) was created, and in 1951, the Refugee Convention was adopted in Geneva, which has since been signed by more than 140 states. Initially, it was restricted to refugees of the Second World War; this restriction was lifted in 1967.

B Structures

1. General remarks

7201 **Fascism** was the ideology underlying the dictatorships of BENITO MUSSOLINI and his *Partito Nazionale Fascista* (PNF) in Italy 1922–43, and of ADOLF HITLER and his *Nationalsozialistische Deutsche Arbeiterpartei* (NSDAP) in Germany 1933–45. The extent to which other parties or dictatorships can also be described as "fascist" is debatable.

➤ The close ideological relationship between National Socialism and Italian fascism was repeatedly emphasised by both sides; HITLER occasionally referred to his followers as "German fascists". However, there are also some considerable differences between the two movements, particularly with regard to their relationship to the law. The attempt to establish a "Fascist International" failed.

➤ Marxism in particular regarded fascism as a universal phenomenon. The Communist International (*ComIntern*) defined it in 1933 as "the openly terrorist dictatorship of the most reactionary, chauvinist, and imperialist elements of finance capital". Bourgeois political scientists, on the other hand, disputed whether one could speak of a (uniform) concept of fascism at all, given the differences between the individual "fascist" movements.

➤ In this context, "fascist" (from the Italian *fascio* = "bundle") was mainly used to describe the *Action Française*, the Spanish *Falange* (= phalanx), the Portuguese *União Nacional* (= National Union), the Hungarian *Nyilaskeresztes Párt* (= Arrow Cross Party), the Romanian *Garda de Fier* (= Iron Guard), and the Croatian *Ustaša* (= the Insurgents), as well as the Austrian *Heimwehren* ("Austrofascists", ⇨ par. 7218).

➤ However, an overly broad definition of the term – for example, by labelling Social Democrats (because of their relative proximity to the bourgeoisie) as "social fascists" or, conversely, Communists (because of their radicalism) as "left-wing fascists" (⇨ par. 5102) – would make it heuristically worthless.

➤ National Socialism saw itself as bridging the gap between the nationalism of the bourgeoisie and the Socialism of the working class; its political opponents were called "Marxists" or "Bolsheviks", while the term "Socialist" was consciously avoided. Conversely, the Marxists also preferred the term "fascist" to "National Socialist".

7202 Just as diffuse as the concept of fascism itself are its **roots**, which go back at least to the middle of the 19th century. Its **characteristic elements** are: the "leader principle" (*Führerprinzip*, ⇨ par. 7205); extreme nationalism (typically combined with racism and anti-Semitism), anti-Marxism and totalitarianism; the rejection of fundamental rights, diversity of opinion, and democracy; and the endorsement of violence as a means of achieving political goals.

➤ Due to the upheavals of the 19th and 20th centuries, broad sections of the population were affected by poverty and old regulatory systems had lost their validity. Instead of turning to the Marxist movements, like the working class did, bourgeois sections of society tended to consciously distance themselves from these movements in order to avoid descending into the proletariat themselves.

➤ Thus, the emphasis on nationalism was not least meant as a rejection of the internationalism practised by the Marxists. Under the influence of Darwinism (⇨ par. 4312), racist theories that justified nationalism became increasingly popular in the 19th century, for example through the work of JOSEPH ARTHUR DE GOBINEAU (*Essai sur l'inégalité des Races Humaines/The Inequality of Human Races*, 1853/55) or HOUSTON STEWART CHAMBERLAIN (*Die Grundlagen des 19. Jahrhunderts/Foundations of the Nineteenth Century*, 1899).

➤ This particularly affected the Jews, who had always been treated with hatred and contempt – partly for religious reasons and partly for reasons of economic envy. The pseudo-scientific doctrine that Jews were members of an inferior race was known as "anti-Semitism" from c. 1880 onwards; it made it possible for skilful demagogues (e.g. the mayor of Vienna KARL LUEGER, 1897–1910) to blame a traditionally marginalised group for the economic and social hardships suffered by the majority of the population. What was new about this concept was that the Jews could not even escape this form of hatred through assimilation and baptism, since it was now claimed that the stigma was attached to them "by nature".

➤ One of the first manifestations of fascist ideas occurred in France in 1894/1906 around the Jewish officer ALFRED DREYFUS, who had been wrongly convicted of espionage. The "DREYFUS affair" divided the French population; the Austrian journalist THEODOR HERZL, who lived in Paris at that time, considered the previous Jewish assimilation efforts to have failed and supported the establishment of a designated Jewish state, which made him the founder of modern Zionism.

➤ HITLER himself had no academic education whatsoever; his world view – outlined mainly in his two-volume work *Mein Kampf* (*My Struggle*, 1925/26) – had emerged from a wide variety of sources that are difficult to ascertain in retrospect but were mostly non-academic (e.g. illustrated magazines, pulp novels). It was only later that attempts were made to use 19th century philosophers such as FRIEDRICH NIETZSCHE and his call for a "superman" as resources for promoting fascism.

2. The National Socialist State

7203 CARL SCHMITT (⇨ par. 7301) identified three core concepts of the National Socialist order: **"state"**; **"movement"**; and **"people"**. The "state" was equated with the (static) bureaucracy, which had to be remodelled by the (dynamic) party – the "movement".

➢ The fascist state, like its Socialist counterpart, was a one-party state. E. R. HUBER (⇨ par. 7301) objected to such an equation because in his view, the NSDAP was "not an organised minority that rules [like a Communist party does] but a political selection that leads".

➢ The Reich was described as the "state of the movement"; the party led the state and effected its gradual transformation. The primacy of the party over the state was most evident in the case of the *Führer*, who was seen primarily as the party leader and only secondarily as the head of state and government.

➢ Fascism aimed at a complete integration of state and party. This became obvious in 1935, for example, when a session of the Reichstag was held as part of the Nuremberg NSDAP rally, and both gatherings were thus regarded as single event (this was the session of the Reichstag at which the Nuremberg Laws were enacted, ⇨ par. 7204).

➢ A further example of this was the reorganisation of Austria into *"Reichsgaue"* in 1939/40 (⇨ par. 7109). These were territorial administrative districts of the Reich as well as of the party (personal union of Reich governor and National Socialist *"Gauleiter"*). In the remaining territory of the Reich (*"Altreich"*), this objective was never achieved; the Gaue (as territorial subdivisions of the party) and the (largely disempowered) Länder existed side by side.

➢ Other parties were dissolved, and most of their leaders were arrested ("taken into protective custody") – mainly based on the Reichstag Fire Decree (⇨ par. 7101). Since the prisons were soon overcrowded, the construction of designated "concentration camps" began as early as 1933.

7204 The **people** were regarded as a "natural unity", and membership in this group was not determined by subjective feelings of belonging but by "objective", i.e. **racist**, **characteristics**. The two Nuremberg Race Laws of 15 September 1935 (the "Reich Citizenship Law" and the "Law for the Protection of German Blood and German Honour") were the most extreme manifestation of this ideology; under these laws, only those who were of "German or kindred blood" could be considered "citizens of the Reich".

➢ The "objective concept" of a nation was developed by the Turin jurist PASQUALE STANISLAO MANCINI at the time of the Italian unification movement and in reaction to the voluntarist concept of a "nation", according to which one's affiliation was determined by one's own allegiance.

➢ The question of who should be considered "of German blood" ("Aryan"), a "Jew", or "mixed race" (*"Mischling"*), was dealt with in a complex implementing decree that complemented the Reich Citizenship Law. The religious confession of the grandparents was the primary criterion, as it was assumed that this would provide the most reliable information about a person's racial status. People with three or four Jewish grandparents were considered "Jews". Those with one or two Jewish grandparents were considered "mixed race", unless they themselves also belonged to the Jewish religious community, in which case they were also considered "Jews" (*"Geltungsjude"*). As a result, every citizen had to prove his or her "Aryan" descent.

➢ Immediately after HITLER had seized power in 1933, Jews were subjected to repressive measures; for example, Jewish civil servants were forced to retire, and Jewish businesses were boycotted. With the Nuremberg Race Laws of 1935, these acts of discrimination became more systematic and intensified. The "Law for the Protection of German Blood and German Honour" forbid "mixed-blood" marriages. In 1938, Jews who did not bear a "typically Jewish" first name were forced to adopt "Israel" or "Sara" as their middle name to make them identifiable. In 1939/41, it became compulsory for Jews to wear a yellow badge on their clothing.

➢ The persecution of the Jews escalated on 9 November 1938 with nationwide pogroms (the so-called *"Reichskristallnacht"*), during which synagogues and Jewish businesses were destroyed and several hundred Jews were killed (⇨ par. 7208). As a direct consequence, tens of thousands of Jews were arrested. The legal basis for these arrests was again the Reichstag Fire Decree; in this case, too, there was talk of "protective custody" that was necessary to protect the Jews from the "rage of the people". They were deported to concentration camps (e.g. Dachau, Mauthausen), where they were exploited for their labour; they were maltreated, tortured, and killed.

➢ With the outbreak of the Second World War and the conquest of large parts of Europe, the persecution of the Jews intensified dramatically; deportations mainly saw them transported to concentration camps in occupied Poland (especially Auschwitz). The 11th supplementary ordinance to the Reich Citizenship Law issued in 1941 denied German citizenship to Jews who had their "habitual residence" abroad (which included both emigrants and deportees!) and declared their assets forfeited.

➢ The decision to systematically exterminate the Jews ("*Endlösung*") was taken in late 1941 and organised on 20 January 1942 at the "Wannsee Conference". For its implementation, special extermination camps (Auschwitz-Birkenau, Treblinka) were created, in which mass murder, especially by poison gas, was committed. In total, the National Socialist regime was responsible for the deaths of well over six million Jews.

7205 The "bearer of the national will" was the **Führer**, who had virtually unlimited power and considered himself bound only by the "legal essence that emanates from the nation".

➢ In establishing the "Führer principle", HITLER had borrowed from the Italian Duce MUSSOLINI, in particular, but greatly surpassed the latter, so that a veritable cult was established around HITLER's person.

➢ MUSSOLINI's position was essentially based on his functions as head of government and party; the head of state, King VICTOR EMANUEL III (1900–46), remained untouched. HITLER, on the other hand, merged the position of the NSDAP leader with the positions of the Reich chancellor and (from 1934) also the Reich president.

➢ The unlimited rule of the Führer was eventually also formally recognised by the German Reichstag at its last session on 26 April 1942, when it authorised HITLER "as leader of the nation, as supreme commander of the Wehrmacht, as head of government and supreme holder of executive power, as supreme ruler of the courts and leader of the party" to fulfil his "duties" "without being bound by existing legal provisions". Thus, not least the judiciary was also completely subject to HITLER's will.

➢ According to HUBER, the Führer's ability to ascertain the will of the people resulted from the fact that he was "devoted to the objective historical unity and wholeness of the people". With such meaningless phrases, an attempt was made to disguise the fact that the essence of fascist rule was in fact unlimited despotism.

➢ ROUSSEAU's theory of the *"volonté générale"* (⇨ par. 6202) was rejected as it represented only a common denominator of individual interests, but not the will of the people as such, which was an "objective given" and could only be ascertained by the Führer. Not even a referendum could therefore take precedence over this will.

➢ Therefore, referenda and popular consultations only served the purpose of "calling upon and engaging the entire living people for a political goal set by the Führer" (HUBER). They were held when Germany withdrew from the League of Nations (12 November 1933), when HITLER assumed the office of Reich President (19 August 1934), and when Austria was "annexed" to the German Reich (10 April 1938).

➢ Throughout the National Socialist era, the position of the Führer remained tailored to HITLER himself; provisions were in place for the installation of a deputy but not for his succession. Shortly before his suicide, HITLER decided in his will to split the functions of Reich president and Reich chancellor again; a new party leader was not appointed.

7206 Fascism was characterised by its efforts to capture every sphere of life. State-free spheres or even fundamental rights were alien to it (**totalitarianism**).

➢ However, totalitarianism is not only a characteristic feature of fascist states. Rather, totalitarian structures also developed in Socialist states.

➢ Even children were educated in the National Socialist world view and underwent military training in the "HITLER youth". Adults were organised in various subdivisions of the NSDAP or associations affiliated to it, such as the NS Lawyers' Association, NS Teachers' Association, NS Doctors' Association, etc.

➢ Typically, the fascist parties (as well as many other parties of the time) had their own (para-)military units: in Italy, these were the "*Squadre*", in Germany, the "*Sturmabteilung*" (SA) and the "*Schutzstaffel*" (SS). In other cases, the party had emerged from military associations (such as the Austrian *Heimatblock*, which had been founded by the *Heimwehren* and was represented in the Austrian National Council from 1930 onwards), or entered a close alliance with members of the army (in the case of the Spanish Falange).

➢ Economic life was fully penetrated as well; in 1925, MUSSOLINI set up corporations in which employers and workers were supposed to work together "for the good of the state". The main effect of this, of course, was that the trade unions were dissolved, and the workers were now led by fascist party functionaries; the employers were able to retain their autonomy to a somewhat greater extent and benefited substantially from the new economic model.

➢ In a similarly corporatist manner, the *"Deutsche Arbeitsfront"* (*German Labour Front*, DAF) united employers and workers in Germany from 1933 onwards, whereas the trade unions were dissolved. Membership was not officially compulsory, but the DAF eventually had more than 25 million members and could be regarded as an affiliate organisation of the NSDAP.

➢ Shortly after coming to power, in July 1933, HITLER concluded a concordat with the Holy See (still in force in Germany today), guaranteeing the Catholic Church freedom of worship. In reality, however, its activities were increasingly restricted by the totalitarian state, prompting Pope PIUS XI to clearly distance himself from National Socialism in an encyclical ("Mit brennender Sorge"/"With deep anxiety") in 1937.

➢ Some – but by no means the majority – of committed Christians (most notably, the "White Rose" resistance group) actively resisted the Nazi regime, which responded with cruel persecution and murder. Overall, however, the attitude of the Catholic and Protestant churches towards the regime remained ambivalent. Historiography after 1945 sharply criticized the Vatican's alleged silence on the persecution of the Jews; this has been somewhat retracted in recent times on the basis of newly accessible sources.

7207 The lawyer ERNST FRAENKEL, who went into exile in 1938, coined the term **"dual state"** to describe the nature of National Socialist rule (at least in its initial phase); while the rule of law and its achievements were preserved in some areas (the "normative state"), the party acted without any legal constraints when it came to seizing power or confronting its political opponents (the "prerogative state").

➢ Its commitment to the "normative state" was meant to reassure the conservative bourgeoisie, which viewed the National Socialist movement as offering protection from a possible Communist overthrow. CARL SCHMITT's essay *Der Führer schützt das Recht* (*The Führer Protects the Law*), published in 1934, served the same purpose; in his essay, SCHMITT sought to justify the assassination of SA Chief of Staff ERNST RÖHM and other senior SA members on 1 July 1934, which had been ordered by HITLER.

➢ However, as time went on, and especially after the outbreak of the Second World War, the "prerogative state" increasingly gained the upper hand over the "normative state"; the National Socialists' arbitrary rule became less and less concealed. FRAENKEL's thesis of the "dual state", developed in 1941 in American exile, therefore only applies to the initial phase of National Socialist rule.

➢ The release from the "constraints of the rule of law" was partly effected through the law itself. In Prussia, for example, it was decided that appeals to an administrative court against measures taken by the Secret State Police (*Gestapo*) would be inadmissible.

➢ In 1934, a "People's Court" was created specifically for political trials and was further expanded in 1936. Its judges were directly appointed by the Führer; trials at this court did not exhibit any of the safeguards otherwise provided by the rule of law.

➢ The decline of the rule of law was not least also the result of unsystematic legislation in response to specific events, which after a certain point did not even require promulgation in the Reich's Law Gazette. For example, the so-called "euthanasia order" of 1939 was kept secret but nevertheless considered a valid justification for acts that would otherwise have been regarded as murder (which continued to be prohibited under the German Criminal Code).

3. Excursus: Aryanization and restitutions

7208 In addition to all the personal suffering, the **racist and political persecutions** under National Socialism also had consequences in terms of property law, since those persecuted were usually deprived of all, or at least most, of their assets (in the case of Jews, their assets were "aryanized"). In some cases, this took the form of looting; in others, it was done through sovereign acts of the state (expropriations, special taxes). Mostly, however, the assets were seized under private law, especially through forced sales.

➢ Looting, by definition, only concerned movable assets. It first occurred in isolated cases immediately after the National Socialists had seized power, and then on a larger scale during the infamous pogrom against the Jews on 9 November 1938.

➢ In April 1938, Jews were forced to declare all their domestic as well as foreign assets to the authorities. Based on this, special taxes were levied on them, such as, in particular, the "Jewish Capital Levy" (*Judenvermögensabgabe*), which amounted to 20 percent of the assets declared.

➢ The exceptional financial burdens, but also professional disqualifications, boycotts, etc., soon led to the economic ruin of many Jews, who were thus forced to sell their assets and emigrate. In the case of emigration, they also had to pay a "Reich Flight Tax" (*Reichsfluchtsteuer*), which was an additional 25 percent of their assets.

➢ With the 11th supplementary ordinance to the Reich Citizenship Act of 1941, the assets of Jews who had emigrated or been deported to a concentration camp were declared forfeited. In the concentration camps, even their few remaining belongings were confiscated from the deportees before or after their death, and any dental gold was removed from the corpses.

➢ The sale of Jews' assets to non-Jewish buyers required the prior approval of the Property Transaction Office (*Vermögensverkehrsstelle*). That office also determined the price, which was as a rule far below the actual value of the assets sold. Sometimes it also ordered a sale against the declared will of the owner, which was *de facto* equivalent to expropriation.

➢ It is not even remotely possible to quantify the total value of the seized assets.

7209 After 1945, the Austrian federal government refused to accept responsibility for the National Socialist persecutions; there was initially also no public compensation for the victims (or their surviving relatives). This was justified with the **"victim theory"** (*"Opferthese"*), which stated that Austria had not been an accomplice to National Socialism, but had itself been a victim.

➢ The victim theory was mainly based on the argument (stated in the Moscow Declaration of 1943, ⇨ par. 8110) that the Anschluss in 1938 had been forced upon Austria by German military pressure. Austria's role as a "victim" therefore needs to be understood from the point of view of international law and does not describe the sentiments of a large part of the Austrian population in the period 1938–45. Nevertheless, it has often been misunderstood in this sense.

➢ The state's opposition to compensation for the victims of National Socialism must be seen in the context of Austria's difficult economic situation after 1945; however, more recent research has also pointed to the (latent) anti-Semitism present in many government bodies after 1945. The Western Allies, in particular, pushed for comprehensive reparations (*"Wiedergutmachung"*) and included a provision to this effect in the State Treaty of 1955 (Article 26). Nevertheless, the Austrian enthusiasm for reparations waned shortly after the withdrawal of the occupying forces.

7210 In Austria, reparations were therefore almost exclusively based on the principle of **in rem restitution**; if the seized assets still existed, they were returned to the persecuted individuals or their surviving relatives. This was mainly done through civil court proceedings based on the Restitution Acts. The state's contribution was thus essentially limited to providing the judicial forum.

➢ As early as 10 May 1945, the provisional state government passed a law that obligated the holders of seized assets to declare them to the authorities. Between 1946 and 1949, seven Restitution Acts were passed, which in principle reversed the various forms of asset seizures. The most significant of them was the third Restitution Act of 1947, which concerned seized assets that were now held by private individuals. It declared the seizures null and void and established a special legal setting for their reversal.

➢ Any current holder of seized assets was under a duty to return them; the previous owner's claim to restitution was therefore absolute. If the party that was obliged to effect the restitution was not him/herself the "aryaniser" but had subsequently acquired the assets from the latter, he or she could then take recourse against that person.

➢ If the persecuted individuals had sold the assets, they had to refund the price, but only to the extent that they had actually received it for their free disposal.

7211 Based on the Restitution Acts, more than 60,000 restitution proceedings took place; in addition, certain social law provisions also provided for relief for victims of National Socialism. Nevertheless, in many cases, full reparation was not realised.

➢ The large number of restitution laws as well as a complicated system of limitation periods resulted in considerable legal uncertainty. The victims of National Socialism, most of whom were still residing abroad, were provided neither assistance in returning home nor legal advice, but were instead referred to the civil courts with all their pitfalls (wilfully protracted proceedings, etc.).

➢ For certain types of seized assets, such as tenancy rights in particular, no restitution provisions were established at all. Likewise, there was no compensation for assets that no longer existed.

➢ If a victim of National Socialism was no longer alive, only a small group of family members was entitled to make a claim for restitution. Otherwise, the assets were reclaimed by special collection agencies, and the proceeds were paid out to impoverished victims of National Socialism through social security channels.

➢ Additional forms of reparation based on social law were introduced with the Victims' Welfare Act of 1947, although initially only for resistance fighters and individuals who had been persecuted for political reasons or on the basis of their ethnicity, religion, or nationality. It was only decades later that its scope was gradually expanded to also include those persecuted on the grounds of physical or mental disability, their sexual orientation, or because they had been deemed "anti-social", as well as victims of National Socialist military justice.

7212 It was not until the 1990s that Austria agreed to comprehensive compensation measures from public funds. For this purpose, the **National Fund of the Republic of Austria for Victims of National Socialism** (1995) and the **General Settlement Fund** (2001) were established.

➢ In 1991, the federal government for the first time formally declared that Austria had a moral responsibility to make reparations, since many Austrians had been involved in the National Socialist crimes. This declaration initiated a paradigm shift in Austria's reparations policies.

➢ The General Settlement Fund was tasked with providing compensation, especially in cases that had remained unresolved under previous legislation and judicature; in a few cases, in rem restitution was granted, for instance of works of art. The Fund was dissolved upon completion of its activities in 2022. The National Fund, on the other hand, continues to support a range of projects, especially those that benefit surviving victims of National Socialism.

4. The Authoritarian Corporative State

7213 The Catholic Church only belatedly began to respond to the socio-economic upheavals of the Industrial Revolution. It rejected both the unrestrained capitalism propagated by liberalism and the Socialism advocated by MARX on the grounds that both economic systems were based on a model of society that was characterised by class struggles. The Church therefore developed its own **Catholic social teaching** as a "third way" between capitalism and Socialism.

➢ The encyclical "Rerum Novarum" of Pope LEO XIII from 1891 is considered the starting point of Catholic social teaching; its tenets were carried forward exactly forty years later, in 1931, with the encyclical "Quadragesimo anno" of Pope PIUS XI.

➢ The supreme principle of Catholic social teaching is the individualistic *principle of the dignity of the human person*; it is not the individual that must serve society, but society that must serve the individual.

➢ As an *"ens sociale"*, however, each individual also bears responsibility for the right order of society as a whole (*principle of solidarity*).

➢ The third principle is the *principle of subsidiarity*, according to which entities of a higher level should only be assigned those tasks that cannot be handled by the lower-level entities on their own. This was also meant as a criticism of the all-encompassing competences of the state, which had led to other communities (e.g. families, cooperatives, and other autonomous bodies) forfeiting many of their functions. This development was seen as detrimental to the individual; however, this view failed to take into account the fact that the expansion of the state's functions in modern times had often been a reaction to the failure of precisely these other communities (⇨ par. 3209).

➢ In the 20th century, the idea of subsidiarity – inspired by Catholic social teaching – became increasingly important and, with the Maastricht Treaty, also became a principle of European Union law (⇨ par. 8221).

7214 To overcome class struggle, Catholic social teaching argued, society should not be divided horizontally into employers and employees, but vertically into corporative groups that would each include both employers and employees. However, the reference in "Quadragesimo anno" to a return to a corporative order of society is misleading in that this new concept of a corporative order differed substantially from the traditional one based on a system of estates (⇨ par. 2215), especially as it did not depend on birth rights but was built upon **vocational groups**.

➢ The corporative order of society should cover the economy, in particular, but also all other aspects of social life (science, art, etc.). In accordance with the principle of subsidiarity, the corporative groups should be able to regulate matters pertaining to their own spheres autonomously, and the state should only intervene to support them if needed. Accordingly, the corporative groups should also be independent entities that the state could neither establish nor then control.

➢ This novel concept of a corporative order had already emerged at the end of the 19th century – not without romanticising reminiscences of the old order of the estates – and was propagated in Austria by KARL VON VOGELSANG (a pioneer of the Christian Social movement), among others. It was developed further in the interwar period, especially by OTHMAR SPANN, an economist from Vienna, and found great favour with the Heimwehren.

However, these models of a corporative system did not fully match the ideas developed by PIUS XI.

7215 Although "Quadragesimo anno" had criticised the corporative model realised by the Italian fascists, which was quite similar to the Austrian one, as not corresponding to Catholic social teaching, the papal encyclical became the ideological basis of the Austrian **authoritarian corporative state** (1934–38). Since the latter, like the pope, was opposed to both National Socialism and Communism, Rome did not voice any concerns over this reinterpretation of its encyclical.

➤ The Italian model (⇨ par. 7206) was especially criticised for the excessive influence of the state on the corporative groups, which contradicted the principle of subsidiarity, and for the fact that these groups had taken the place of the trade unions instead of supplementing them. The same criticism would have also applied to the corporative groups in Austria, not least as they were corporations under public law and in some cases enjoyed compulsory membership. Hence, they cannot really be described as non-state entities.

➤ The idea of replacing the democratically elected parliament with a parliament of corporative groups was not based on "Quadragesimo anno" but on an idea of the Catholic prelate and Austrian Federal Chancellor IGNAZ SEIPEL, which he had already developed in the 1920s, and which was aimed at eliminating the "party rule" that had resulted from parliamentarism in favour of a "true democracy".

➤ In the years after 1931, PIUS XI increasingly embarked on a course of confrontation with both National Socialism (⇨ par. 7206) and Communism (⇨ par. 5204); Austria, on the other hand, which had concluded a concordat with the Holy See in 1933 that was extremely advantageous for the latter, must have appeared as a natural ally against these systems and was therefore not criticised.

➤ After Slovakia – whose prime minister was the Catholic priest JOZEF TISO – had declared its independence in 1939, a corporative state was established there as well (which also invoked "Quadragesimo anno" as its ideological basis). Nevertheless, Slovakia was a satellite state of HITLER's Germany and its ally in the Second World War.

7216 The Austrian **May Constitution** of 1934 (⇨ par. 7105) attempted to enrol the entire Austrian population in either vocational groups or cultural communities. These should be granted not only autonomy in performing their own tasks but also participation in the decision-making processes of the state (in the federal assembly, the diets, and the municipal assemblies).

➤ As early as 2 March 1934, the "Trade Union Federation of Austrian Workers and Salaried Employees" (Gewerkschaftsbund der österreichischen Arbeiter und Angestellten) was created as a public corporation. It did not have compulsory membership, but, like its Italian counterpart, it had a monopoly on the conclusion of collective bargaining agreements on behalf of the workforce. In contrast, the Austrian Trade Union Federation (Österreichischer Gewerkschaftsbund, ÖGB), founded in 1945 (⇨ par. 8111), is a private association that owes its (*de facto*) monopoly on negotiating and signing collective bargaining agreements not to any direct legal authorisation but to its large membership, which is a legal prerequisite for this role.

➢ Once the May Constitution had come into effect, laws were passed to legally assign the members of the civil service, and the self-employed in the sectors of industry and mining, commerce, financial, credit, and insurance services, trade and transport, agriculture, and forestry to their respective corporations. In reality, such corporations were only established for the civil service and for agriculture and forestry; in the other sectors, the process of setting them up did not progress beyond the planning stage.

➢ No such legal measure was taken for the independent professions, which were mostly organised in their professional associations ("chambers") anyway, which had been established in the 19th century (Austrian Medical Association, Bar Association). For employers and employees in journalism, the Austrian Press Chamber was founded in 1936, not least to exercise control over the press. The Press Chamber had the right to approve or reject the publication of a newspaper, which was tantamount to compulsory licencing.

7217 In practice, the participation of the corporative groups in federal legislation remained insignificant. This was due to the weak position of the "preliminary advisory bodies" even in the May Constitution itself, but also to the fact that the constitution was never fully implemented. The **constitutional reality** in Austria in the years 1934–38 was rather that of an authoritarian governmental dictatorship.

➢ The ordinary legislative procedure under the May Constitution of 1934 was such that new laws could be passed solely based on proposals by the federal government, i.e. parliament did not have the right of initiative.

➢ First, four "preliminary advisory bodies" (State Council, Federal Cultural Council, Federal Economic Council, Council of the Länder) would submit their opinions on these government bills, whereupon the federal government itself would be given the opportunity to make amendments. Then the bill would go to the Bundestag (a joint committee of the four preliminary advisory bodies), which could only either reject or accept the government bill (without changes). This separation of "advisory" and "decision-making" bodies deprived parliament of its political significance.

➢ The State Council was supposed to consist of "meritorious federal citizens of good character" appointed by the federal president; in the Council of the Länder, each of them was represented by its governor and another member of its government. The Federal Economic Council and the Federal Cultural Council would be made up of representatives of the corporative groups and cultural communities respectively.

➢ However, because of the transitional rules for the May Constitution, the members of the Federal Economic Council and the Federal Cultural Council were also appointed by the federal president (at the suggestion of the federal government). This arrangement was supposed to apply only provisionally until a definitive legal provision was adopted, but this never happened. Thus, the "House of Federal Legislation" *de facto* consisted entirely of confidants of the federal government and members of the Länder governments.

➢ In practice, the legislative procedure proved to be very complex and impracticable, which was exacerbated by the conduct of the federal government towards the House of Federal Legislation, when it set extremely short review deadlines, for instance.

➢ Numerous laws were therefore not even submitted to the "preliminary advisory bodies" but adopted directly by the federal government on the basis of the Enabling Act of 1934. Its right to pass legislation (which was limited in terms of neither the subject matter of the laws nor the duration of their validity) therefore became much more important than the ordinary legislative procedure at the Bundestag. For the same reason, the (very extensive) rights of the federal president and the federal government to issue emergency decrees based on the constitution of 1934 did not have any practical significance.

➢ Article 65 of the constitution also provided for the possibility of referenda, but none were ever held; note that the "popular consultation" planned for 13 March 1938 (⇨ par. 7108) was not intended to be a referendum within the meaning of Article 65 either.

7218 The nature of the authoritarian corporative state remains highly controversial. Because of the Italian fascist influence, some scholars use the term "**Austrofascism**". The main arguments in favour of this term are the regime's anti-democratic and anti-Marxist orientation and the deficits in the area of the protection of fundamental rights and the judiciary. The arguments against it are the – at least formal – commitment to the tradition of the rule of law, the anti-nationalist policies, and the fact that the totalitarianism that is typical of fascism was unable to establish itself in Austria.

➢ The May Constitution also provided for fundamental rights, the separation of powers, and administrative jurisdiction as well as constitutional jurisdiction, although some of these were promises that were never kept. For instance, the protection of judges from removal from office or relocation guaranteed in Article 102 was abolished (through transitional provisions) for the entire period of 1934–38. However, this needs to be seen in the light of the fact that many judges were members of the NSDAP or sympathised with it, which was something that the regime fought against.

➢ The powers of the police were gradually expanded at the expense of the judiciary; in some cases, law enforcement officers were even explicitly ordered to ignore administrative court rulings. Political opponents were interned in "detention camps" (most notably in Wöllersdorf in Lower Austria); however, these camps cannot be likened to the National Socialist concentration camps.

➢ In 1933, the death penalty was reintroduced in summary court-martial proceedings. From a constitutional point of view, the retroactive extension of this provision to the offence of sedition in 1934 was particularly alarming, as it made it possible to execute participants in the Social Democratic February Uprising – which was also put into practice. One of the most morally reprehensible acts was the execution of February fighter KARL MÜNICHREITER despite his severe injuries.

➢ The fascist element of the authoritarian regime came primarily from the influence of the *Heimwehren*, whose leader ERNST RÜDIGER (until 1919: Prince of) STARHEMBERG was appointed vice-chancellor in 1934. Because of his pro-Italian position, he had to resign from the federal government in May 1936, in the wake of the Abyssinia crisis; in October of the same year, the *Heimwehren* were dissolved and incorporated into the Fatherland Front.

➢ Attempts were made as early as 1935 to bring the *Heimwehren* (who were increasingly inclined towards National Socialism) under the control of the state by merging them and other paramilitary organisations by law into a single *"Schutzkorps"*. The executive was only allowed to call on this corps if the regular state forces were unable to deal with the situation. In 1936, the *Schutzkorps* – and with it the *Heimwehren* – were dissolved and in their place a *"Sturmkorps"* was created, which in 1938 had a strength of 4,000 men and served as the military wing of the Fatherland Front; their uniforms were very similar to those of the SS.

➢ Neither the May Constitution nor the laws enacted between 1934 and 1938 contained any anti-Semitic provisions; the Federal Cultural Council (⇨ par. 7217) included a representative of the Jewish communi-ty alongside representatives of the Catholic and Protestant churches. The that Jews had to endure in everyday life (social exclusion, discrimination in obtaining public office, etc.) had been steadily increasing since 1918 and had therefore reached a considerable level by the late 1930s, without this being directly attributable to the authoritarian form of government. But also in this respect, the situation in Austria was in no way comparable to that in National Socialist Germany.

➢ And also with regard to the propagated "corporatist reconstruction", parallels can be drawn to Italy, but not to Germany.

7219 One cannot overlook the fact that the Austrian authoritarian regime in many ways copied HITLER's regime in Germany, even trying to "overhitler" it (according to a dictum of the Austrian minister ODO NEUSTÄDTER-STÜRMER). However, the "copy" never reached the attractiveness and appeal of the "original", especially not among the **youth**, who defected to National Socialism in droves.

➢ This "copying" was particularly evident when DOLLFUSS or SCHUSCHNIGG appeared in uniforms like HITLER did or let themselves be addressed as *"Frontführer und Bundeskanzler"* (i.e. leader of the Fatherland Front and head of government; an analogy to the German *"Führer und Reichskanzler"*). Whether the crutch cross symbol of the corporative state was a response to (or a variation of) the National Socialist swastika is a matter of debate.

➢ Especially after the early death of DOLLFUSS, the authoritarian regime lacked a charismatic leader comparable to the Italian or German examples. And while DOLLFUSS had still pursued some ideological goals, SCHUSCHNIGG's policy was mostly limited to responding to the actions of his political opponents; he never achieved popularity.

➢ In line with the Austrian tradition of three political "camps", the authoritarian regime found itself in a "two-front war" (ILSE REITER-ZATLOUKAL), although a certain asymmetry is apparent: the fight against Marxism was waged out of ideological conviction, while that against National Socialism was fought less passionately (and therefore with less intensity).

➢ The conflict between National Socialism and the Austrian corporative state was also a generational conflict. While DOLLFUSS and SCHUSCHNIGG presented themselves as the upholders of the old order and thus tried to score points with the older generation in particular, to the younger generation, only National Socialism appeared to be a forward-looking option – a view that was deliberately strengthened by the National Socialist regime with its youth cult. This was one of the reasons why the voting age for the popular consultation planned by SCHUSCHNIGG for 13 March 1938 would have been 24, whereas that for the referendum actually held on 10 April was 20.

➢ The "corporative reconstruction" of the state propagated by DOLLFUSS did not progress beyond its initial stages; the regime was unable to offer a real alternative to the Social Democratic and National Socialist movements. Its policy was not one of acting but of reacting, and it was largely limited to the – sometimes brutal, sometimes amateurish – suppression of its opponents. Thus, the regime was never able to gain much popularity.

C Legislation and Jurisprudence

7301 From 1934 onwards, a group of young professors at the University of Kiel, in particular, attempted to develop a National Socialist jurisprudence (**Kiel School**).

➢ The programme of the Kiel School was presented in *Grundfragen der neuen Rechtswissenschaft* (*Fundamental Problems of the New Jurisprudence*, 1935), edited by the civil law scholar KARL LARENZ; other members of the school included the constitutional law scholar ERNST RUDOLF HUBER and the legal historian KARL A. ECKHARDT.

➢ Many leading jurists in Germany, such as the constitutional law scholar CARL SCHMITT in *Staat, Bewegung, Volk* (*State, Movement, People*, 1933), quickly adapted to the political climate and actively contributed to the implementation of National Socialist ideology in jurisprudence.

➢ Non-conforming jurists, such as KELSEN, who taught in Cologne from 1930–33, or the Heidelberg criminal law scholar and legal philosopher GUSTAV RADBRUCH (German Minister of Justice 1921–23) were removed from their academic positions and in many cases also persecuted on a personal level.

7302 Laws from the time before the National Socialists seized power were reinterpreted in accordance with National Socialist views and often took on a completely new meaning (**"unrestricted interpretation"**); if they clearly contradicted the National Socialist ideology, they could not be applied. Any judicial review of the Führer's decisions was forbidden.

➢ Whether a norm was considered a law or not depended on whether it was "useful to the people". Thus, every subjective right of the individual, such as the right to property, was called into question; the existence of fundamental rights was rejected altogether.

➢ Analogies were particularly significant in this context, as were general clauses, which could easily be reinterpreted. In criminal law, an amendment to the criminal code in 1935 abandoned the principle of *"nulla poena sine lege"* in favour of punishment "according to the common sense of the people" (*"gesundes Volksempfinden"*).

➢ The Kiel School rejected HECK's jurisprudence of interests because of its individualistic approach. HECK, on the other hand, sought to align himself with the Kiel School.

➢ Positivism, which was the prevailing approach to public law, often had a disastrous effect when it took the form of blind obedience to the law; at times, however, it also hindered the advance of National Socialist jurisprudence. For example, as late as 1939, the Austrian Federal Court of Justice (*Bundesgerichtshof*) refused to decide "without regard to the law in cases where there is no doubt about its correct interpretation". Later, such voices fell silent.

➢ Jurists' experiences with the National Socialist regime resulted in a growing emphasis on natural law; for instance, after 1945, RADBRUCH developed the notion of "legal injustice", which holds that while not every (alleged) case of "injustice" nullifies positive law, a normative order that does not even attempt to be just is not of a legal nature at all.

➢ This "RADBRUCH formula" was a widely noted attempt to reach a compromise between positivist and natural law approaches. It was applied after 1990, for example, in the criminal proceedings against the "*Mauerschützen*" (= soldiers of the GDR who shot at people that tried to escape to the West across the Berlin Wall, ⇨ par. 8119).

7303 After Austria's *"Anschluss"* to National Socialist Germany, individual areas of the law were harmonised, either by adopting laws from the *"Altreich"* in Austria (especially the Commercial Code) or passing new laws (especially the Marriage Act 1938). The German BGB (which National Socialist jurisprudence rejected) was not adopted in Austria; instead, the creation of a new, National Socialist **"*Volksgesetzbuch*"** (*people's code*) was initiated, which, however, was never completed. Thus, both codes remained in force during the National Socialist era; the German BGB in the so-called *"Altreich"* and the ABGB in Austria.

➢ The "Academy for German Law" in Munich, under its president HANS FRANK, was commissioned to prepare the "*Volksgesetzbuch*". It did not progress beyond consultations until 1945.

➢ The German Commercial Code 1897 (⇨ par. 4307) was introduced in Austria on 1 March 1939 and replaced the General Commercial Code from 1862. It remained in force in both states after 1945. However, the legal unity thus established eroded after 1945 due to various amendments (⇨ par. 8301).

➢ The Act on the Harmonisation of the Law of Marriage and Divorce in Austria and the Other Reich Territories (*Gesetz zur Vereinheitlichung des Rechts der Eheschließung und der Ehescheidung im Lande Österreich und im übrigen Reichsgebiet*, Marriage Act) replaced the respective provisions of the German and Austrian civil codes in 1938. This meant that the principle of compulsory civil marriage (i.e. weddings may only be performed by a state official) was now also in force in Austria, and that people of all faiths had access to divorce. The dispensation marriages concluded in the past (⇨ par. 6301) were confirmed as valid, but no further dispensations were granted.

➢ The Marriage Act 1938 was repealed in Germany in 1946 by the Allied Control Council. In Austria, only provisions that were clearly of a National Socialist nature (e.g. the prohibition of "mixed-blood" marriages) were eliminated; the remaining provisions of the Act have remained in force until today (it has however been amended several times).

➢ In Italy, a new *Codice Civile* came into effect in 1942, which was modelled on the Swiss Civil Code but was also influenced by fascist ideology. A *"defascistizzazione"* took place in 1945 as well, but otherwise the *Codice Civile* remained in force.

Part VIII

Contemporary Legal History

A Developments

1. The World in the Cold War (1945–1989)

a) The New World Order

8101 The **United Nations Organisation** (UNO) was founded on 24 October 1945 as the (*de facto*, not *de iure*) successor to the League of Nations, which was not formally dissolved until 1946. The UNO performs a wide variety of tasks under international law and is the umbrella organisation for numerous specialised organisations.

➢ The Allies and the institutions they had created were already referred to as the "United Nations" during the Second World War; the United Nations Organisation itself was founded in 1945 by 50 states that were at war with the Axis Powers. Italy and Austria were accepted as members only in 1955, Japan in 1956, and Germany in 1973 (⇨ par. 8121). Switzerland, as a neutral country, rejected UN membership as late as 1986 and only joined in 2002.

➢ The UN's character changed profoundly as more and more states were admitted. In 1960 alone, 16 African states that had recently gained sovereignty joined the UN; in the same year, the UN called for an end to colonialism in all its forms.

➢ The UN body corresponding to the former assembly of the League of Nations is the General Assembly, in which each member state has one vote.

➢ The UN Security Council replaced the League of Nations Council. The Security Council had eleven original members and has had fifteen members since 1966, ten of whom are elected for a term of two years. The USA, the USSR (from 1991: Russia, ⇨ par. 8133), the UK, France, and the Republic of China (from 1971: the People's Republic of China, ⇨ par. 8121) had/have a permanent seat on the Security Council, which includes the right to veto Security Council resolutions.

➢ As was previously the case with the League of Nations, the organisational leadership of the UN lies with a Secretary-General, who is elected by the General Assembly for a five-year term. The UN headquarters were originally in London and were moved to New York in 1952. Other main offices are in Geneva (since 1946), Vienna (since 1980), and Nairobi (since 1996).

➢ The International Court of Justice (ICJ) replaced the Permanent Court of International Justice in 1946. In addition, the International Criminal

Court (ICC) was founded in 2002 to prosecute war crimes and genocide (⇨ par. 8134); both are based in The Hague.

8102 After he Second World War, Europe was divided into spheres of influence by the two **superpowers**. An "Iron Curtain" ran right across it, separating the market economy-oriented states led by the USA ("First World") from the planned economy-oriented states under the hegemony of the USSR ("Second World"). The bloc-independent states ("Third world") were largely developing countries; their number increased steadily due to the decolonisation of Africa and Asia. In 1949, the United States, Canada and ten Western European states concluded the **North Atlantic Treaty**, thereby establishing a US-dominated defence alliance, NATO.

➢ Tensions between the ideologically hostile superpowers had already arisen during the Second World War. Immediately after the elimination of the common enemy, their conflicts erupted openly. While there was neither a direct military confrontation between them in Europe nor a deployment of nuclear weapons (hence the name "Cold War"), several local conflicts did occur outside Europe (e.g. the Korean War, ⇨ par. 8104).

➢ Already in 1947, France and the UK had concluded the Treaty of Dunkirk to cover the eventuality of renewed German aggression. One year later, they concluded the Treaty of Brussels with Belgium, the Netherlands, and Luxembourg. This treaty was also still primarily directed against Germany, but also emerged under the influence of the looming Cold War.

➢ When NATO was founded, the confrontation with the USSR already played a far greater role than the fear of a resurgent Germany. In addition to the USA and the signatories of the Treaty of Brussels, Canada, Denmark, Iceland, Norway, and Portugal were also among its founding members. Greece and Turkey joined in 1952, and other states followed (⇨ par. 8108, par. 8132).

8103 The rise of the two superpowers also meant the **end of Europe's supremacy in the world**. While Germany (⇨ par. 8105) and Italy, two of the defeated nations of the Second World War, had permanently lost their position as great powers, the UK and France struggled for much longer to regain this status (and their colonial empires), but ultimately had to come to terms with the new geopolitical situation.

➢ In Italy, the primary challenge of the post-war years was the elimination of the remnants of fascism. The royal dynasty was deposed because of its support for MUSSOLINI, and Italy became a republic in 1946. Under the Paris Peace Treaty of 1947 (⇨ par. 7111), some of its territories, among them Istria, and all colonies were lost. South Tyrol was not returned to Austria, but the German-speaking minority was granted some autonomy (GRUBER-DE GASPERI Agreement 1946, ⇨ par. 8127). In Italy, as in other countries, the economic difficulties were reflected in strong inflation (when the euro was introduced in 1999, 1,936.27 Italian lire were equivalent to 1 euro!).

➢ Following the German occupation of France in 1940, General CHARLES DE GAULLE had formed a government in exile, which took power in France after the reconquest in 1944. The Fourth French Republic was characterised by rapidly changing governments and constant inflation; their great efforts to preserve the French colonial empire were ultimately in vain (⇨ par. 8104; par. 8120).

➢ The UK had only just been able to avert being conquered by National Socialist Germany during the Second World War. It emerged from the war victoriously yet weakened. In 1947, India and Pakistan had to be granted independence; other colonies followed. Most of these states became republics but remained in the Commonwealth of Nations, which was considerably loosened (in 1949, the designation "British" was dropped). Today, the British monarch as head of the Commonwealth is therefore only the nominal head of a loose organisation of sovereign states (although in some of them, the so-called *realms*, e.g. Canada and Australia, he is also the head of state).

➢ The partition of British India into a predominantly Hindu and a predominantly Muslim state had been looming since the 1930s, even though GANDHI, among others, had tried with all his might to prevent it. After the founding of India and Pakistan in 1947, about four million Muslims left India, and seven million Hindus left Pakistan. Hundreds of thousands of people lost their lives in this population exchange. Since East Pakistan was not connected to the rest of the state, it became a separate state in 1971 as Bangladesh. The predominantly Buddhist country of Burma (since 1989 Myanmar) gained independence from the UK in 1948.

➢ The end of the British mandate over Palestine presented particular difficulties. In 1947, the UN drew up a partition plan to create a Jewish and an Arab state. Both states should be sovereign, but linked to each other in an economic union, with Jerusalem placed under international control. When the State of Israel was proclaimed on 14 May 1948, Egypt, Syria, Jordan, and Iraq immediately launched an attack against the new state, but were driven back in the Israeli War of Independence. Israel was able to expand its territory beyond that of the UN partition plan (including West Jerusalem). An Arab state in Palestine was not established; rather, East Jerusalem and the West Bank were annexed by Jordan, the Gaza Strip by Egypt.

➢ When Egypt nationalised the Suez Canal against the will of the UK in 1956, the UK, France, and Israel intervened militarily, but were forced by the USA to put an end to their intervention. This public humiliation showed that neither the UK nor France were world powers any more. While the UK now leaned all the more closely on the US, France vigorously pushed ahead with European integration in order to gain distance from the US (⇨ par. 8117).

8104 The struggle between the two systems also affected the **states of East Asia**, in some cases with lasting consequences, particularly for China, Japan, Korea, and Vietnam.

➢ In the Republic of China, which had been proclaimed in 1912, a civil war broke out in 1927 between the Nationalist Party (*Kuomintang*) under CHIANG KAI-SHEK (President of the Republic in 1928–31, in 1943–49 and, in Taiwan, in 1950–75) and the Communist Party under MAO ZEDONG (⇨

par. 5207), but was temporarily settled in 1937 due to the Japanese invasion (⇨ par. 7110). In 1946, the civil war broke out again and led to the defeat of the Kuomintang, who retreated to the island of Taiwan in 1949, while the People's Republic of China was proclaimed on the mainland. The latter was initially only recognised by the Soviet Union, however, while the Western powers (as well as the UN) only recognised the Republic of China – effectively reduced to Taiwan – as the sole representative of China until 1971 (⇨ par. 8121).

➢ Japan was occupied by US and UK troops from 1945–51 and received its present constitution in 1947, which transformed it into a Western-style democracy. The Tennō remained as a symbol of the "unity of the Japanese people", but was stripped of any political power. In Article 9 of the Japanese constitution, the country renounces the right to wage war or to establish any kind of military; however, it has, since 1953, maintained (very small) "Self-Defence Forces".

➢ In 1945, the northern part of Korea was occupied by Soviet troops, while US troops occupied the southern part. Two states emerged with political and economic systems modelled on those of their respective occupying powers. In the war waged from 1950 to 1953 over the reunification of Korea, North Korea was supported by the People's Republic of China, while South Korea was backed by the United States. Since neither side emerged victorious, both sides returned to the 1945 border.

➢ In Vietnam, which had been part of French Indochina until 1941, France tried to re-establish its colonial rule after 1945, but a communist resistance movement formed under Hồ Chí Minh, leading to a civil war. While France withdrew from the conflict in 1954, the USA became increasingly involved in the Vietnam War, but was completely defeated in 1975, after which the whole of Vietnam became communist.

b) The Formation of Two Blocs in Europe

8105 In Germany, an Allied Control Council consisting of representatives of the four occupying powers took over supreme power in 1945 but ceased its activities as early as 1948 due to differences between the Soviet Union and the Western Allies. The **division of Germany**, which had been looming for some time, was implemented in constitutional terms by the *Basic Law for the Federal Republic of Germany* (FRG) of 23 May 1949 (the German *Grundgesetz,* GG) and the *Constitution of the German Democratic Republic* (GDR) of 7 October 1949.

➢ The Allied Control Council had extensive powers but could only make its decisions unanimously. Its boycott by the Soviet representative from 1948 onwards resulted in its paralysis, but it was not formally abolished. Within the four occupation zones, the respective military administrations established *Länder* (i.e. constituent states) and their respective governments. A government for the whole of Germany could not be established. The Prussian state (which had politically already ceased to exist in 1932, ⇨

par. 6106) was formally dissolved in 1947 by a decision of the Allied Control Council.

➢ The constitutional division of Germany was preceded by a separation in economic and political terms. In the Soviet Occupied Zone, the transformation towards a Socialist social order began soon (land reform, expropriations). In addition, it was unscrupulously exploited by the USSR under the title of "reparations claims". In contrast, West Germany was thoroughly integrated into the Western market economy-oriented community of states; as early as 1947, the British and American zones were combined into a single economic area (the "Bizone"); there, as well as in the French zone, the D-Mark was introduced as the new currency and soon became a symbol of the reconstruction.

➢ The GG was passed by a parliamentary council consisting of representatives of the West German diets and approved (with certain provisions) by the military governors of the three western occupation zones. It established the FRG as a federal democracy based on the rule of law and a social market economy, but was to apply only provisionally until the German reunification. Bonn became the provisional capital. The first federal chancellor was KONRAD ADENAUER (1949–63, CDU), who was already 73 years old at the time. Due to French economic interests, in particular, the French-occupied Saarland did not join the FRG until 1957 (⇨ par. 8117).

➢ In the Soviet Occupied Zone, under Soviet pressure, the KPD and SPD merged to form the Socialist Unity Party of Germany (*Sozialistische Einheitspartei Deutschlands*, SED) in 1946, which assumed political leadership (General Secretary 1950–71: WALTER ULBRICHT, 1971–89: ERICH HONECKER). Although the constitution of the GDR of 1949 resembled the Weimar Constitution and was committed to a reunification of Germany, it was not an obstacle to the transformation of the GDR into a Socialist people's republic.

➢ The status of Berlin, which (like Germany as a whole) was politically and administratively divided into two parts from 1948 onwards, remained controversial. While the GDR claimed East Berlin as its capital, the Western Allies insisted on the four-power status for the entire city. Hence, West Berlin did not become a formal part of the FRG and was only represented in the German Bundestag by non-voting members; laws passed by the Bundestag regularly included the provision that they would only apply in (West) Berlin as well if they were adopted by the (West) Berlin Senate (the "Berlin clause").

8106 In 1947, the US Secretary of State GEORGE C. MARSHALL promised the European states financial aid for their reconstruction but also demanded the establishment of an organisation that would distribute the funds (MARSHALL Plan). In 1948, the ***Organisation for European Economic Co-operation*** (OEEC) was set up for this purpose. The states under Soviet influence did not participate in the MARSHALL Plan but established the ***Council for Mutual Economic Assistance*** (COMECON) in 1949 instead.

➢ The severe destruction caused by the Second World War could only be repaired with US financial aid, and the USA also hoped to stimulate its own economy by supporting the European states.

➢ An important preliminary stage for the OEEC was the conclusion of a world trade agreement to reduce trade restrictions (*General Agreement on Tariffs and Trade* – GATT) in 1947. The *World Trade Organization* (WTO) emerged from this agreement in 1995.

➢ All European states participated in the OEEC except those under Soviet influence and with the exception of fascist Spain. Finland, which had concluded a treaty of friendship with the USSR in 1948, and Yugoslavia were given special status. The ČSR had to withdraw its application for membership in 1947 due to Soviet pressure. However, Austria, which was partly under Soviet occupation (⇨ par. 8112), was allowed to become a member of the OEEC. The funds received were used in an organised fashion and in some cases soon led to greater prosperity than before 1939 ("economic miracle").

➢ In Albania, Bulgaria, the ČSR, Hungary, Poland, and Romania, as well as in the Soviet Occupied Zone/GDR, the respective Communist parties seized power between 1946 and 1948, largely through coups d'état and with the help of the Soviet Union, and established Socialist "people's democracies". The foreign and economic policies of these "Eastern Bloc" states closely followed those of the Soviet Union. COMECON's main task was to coordinate the individual planned economies.

➢ The only Communist-led country that was able to evade Soviet influence was Yugoslavia, which had largely liberated itself on its own account from German occupation in 1944 under JOSIP TITO. The constitution of 1946 established the Federal People's Republic of Yugoslavia, which TITO presided over as minister-president until 1953 and as president from 1953–80. However, Yugoslavia never joined COMECON or the Warsaw Pact (established in 1955, ⇨ par. 8109).

8107 On 9 May 1950, French Foreign Minister ROBERT SCHUMAN proposed placing the French and West German coal and steel production under a common "High Authority". Other states would also be able to join this community (**SCHUMAN Plan**). On 18 April 1951, the foreign ministers of Belgium, the FRG, France, Italy, Luxembourg, and the Netherlands signed the *Treaty Establishing the European Coal and Steel Community* (ECSC) in Paris. It came into effect on 23 July 1952.

➢ The production of coal and steel was of central importance for the armaments industry. By removing it from nation-state control, SCHUMAN hoped "that a war between France and Germany would become not only unthinkable but materially impossible".

➢ The most important organ of the ECSC was the High Authority, which according to Article 9 of the ECSC Treaty had a "supranational character" (*"un caractère supranational"*) and therefore had to act independently of the member states (⇨ par. 8220). The first president of the High Authority was the French civil servant JEAN MONNET (1952–55), who had been instrumental in developing the SCHUMAN Plan.

8108 Even before the ECSC came into being, its founding states agreed to complement it with a supranational **European Defence Community** (EDC). Both were to be united under the umbrella of a **European Political Community**, but in the end, neither was realised. Instead, the Western European Union (WEU) was founded in 1954.

➤ The economic rise of the FRG, which was still occupied by the three Western Allies and therefore not sovereign, was viewed with increasing scepticism in France; however, the international situation (and especially the Korean War) made the re-establishment of the German armed forces unavoidable. This gave rise to the idea of creating a supranational military alliance along the lines of the ECSC in order to integrate the West German soldiers into a European army. On 27 May 1952, the ECSC states signed the EDC Treaty.

➤ Under the new agreement, the EDC was to be a new supranational organisation with organs similar to those of the ECSC (the EDC was to have a "Commissariat" rather than a "High Authority"). With a few exceptions, the member states were not allowed to maintain their own troops alongside the common European defence forces. Close cooperation with NATO was encouraged.

➤ A political Union of the Six thus seemed within reach. At the first meeting of the ECSC Council of Ministers on 10 September 1952, it was decided that the ECSC and EDC should be brought together in an umbrella organisation. On 10 March 1953, a draft for the establishment of a European Political Community was submitted to the Council of Ministers.

➤ France in particular, which had demanded the creation of the EDC, voiced strong opposition to these plans, especially since its military autonomy was considered sacrosanct at the time (Vietnam War!). On 30 August 1954, the French National Assembly refused to consent to the EDC Treaty, hence the plans to create a European Political Community also lost their foundation. This was the first major setback for European integration (⇨ par. 8208).

➤ France was now forced to agree to the formation of a new German armed force, the *Bundeswehr*. With the *Paris Agreements* of 23 October 1954, the Western Allies revoked the occupation statute for the FRG (but not for Berlin) and granted it full sovereignty, subject only to the reservation of "rights with regard to Germany as a whole".

➤ At the same time, the FRG joined NATO. The occupying forces were largely withdrawn, but military bases of the now allied powers remained (to some extent to this day).

➤ The Paris Agreements also created the WEU as NATO's "European axis". In addition to the ECSC states, it also included the UK, but unlike the failed EDC, it had no supranational powers and was a conventional military alliance.

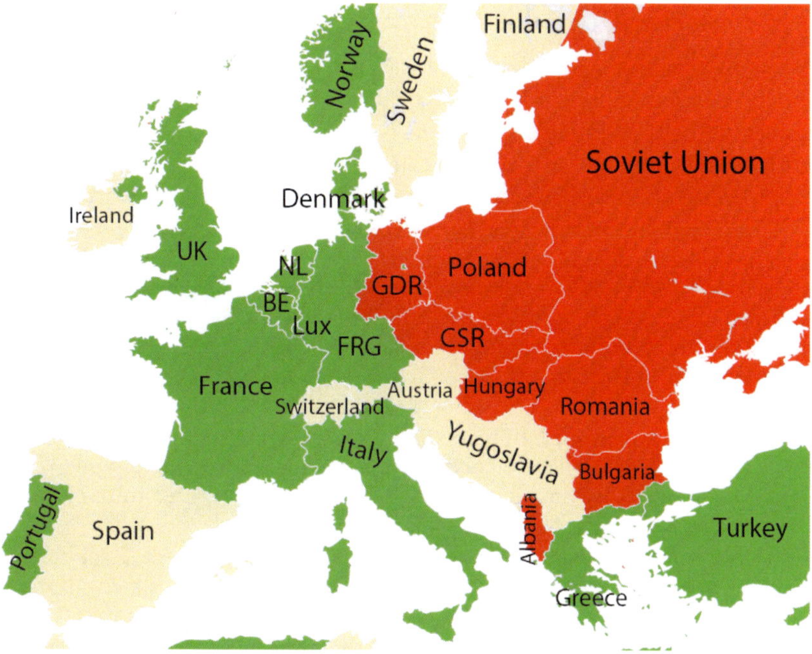

Map 13: NATO and Warsaw Pact in 1955
Source: https://commons.wikimedia.org/wiki/File:EuropaNATOWP1959.png
Text modified; green = NATO; red = Warsaw Pact

8109 In response to the Paris Agreements, on 14 May 1955, the USSR, together with Albania, Bulgaria, the ČSR, the GDR, Hungary, Poland, and Romania, concluded the **Warsaw Pact**, thereby establishing a Soviet-dominated defence alliance. One day later, on 15 May 1955, the Austrian State Treaty was signed in Vienna (⇨ par. 8115).

➢ STALIN's death in 1953 had a major impact on the USSR domestically ("de-Stalinisation") but initially had no consequences for its foreign policy. Popular uprisings in the GDR (17 June 1953) and Hungary (23 October through 11 November 1956) were put down by military force.

➢ NIKITA CHRUŠČËV became the new "First Secretary" of the CPSU (1953–64); he reacted to the declaration of the sovereignty of the FRG by the Western Allies with the declaration of the sovereignty of the GDR.

➢ Until 1955, the deployment of Soviet troops in Poland and Hungary could only be justified by the Soviet occupation zones in Germany and Austria and the need to maintain a land route to them. The Warsaw Pact created a new basis in terms of international law for the Soviet army to remain in Central Europe and in this respect was an important precondition for the Austrian State Treaty (⇨ par. 8115).

c) The Allied occupation of Austria (1945–55)

8110 The Allied victories in the Second World War (conquest of Vienna by the Soviet Army on 13 April 1945) paved the way for Austria's **declaration of independence** on 27 April 1945 (i.e. before the end of hostilities in Europe) by three "anti-fascist parties" newly founded or re-established only a few days earlier. These were:

➢ The Socialist Party of Austria (*Sozialistische Partei Österreichs,* SPÖ), which was the successor to the Social Democratic Workers' Party that had been banned in 1934. The name was changed in 1945 because of its (re-) unification on 13 April with the "Revolutionary Socialists", who had split off in 1934. The name was not changed back to "Social Democratic Party of Austria" until 1991.

➢ The Austrian People's Party (*Österreichische Volkspartei,* ÖVP) was founded on 17 April 1945. In terms of its personnel and ideology, the party was closely related to the previous Christian Social Party that had been dissolved in 1934. However, the party distanced itself from the authoritarian corporative state.

➢ The Communist Party of Austria (*Kommunistische Partei Österreichs,* KPÖ), which had continued to operate underground after its prohibition in 1933, and was now heavily supported by the Soviet occupying power.

➢ In the Declaration of Independence, the *"Anschluss"* of 1938 was described as "null and void"; the "democratic Republic of Austria" was "restored and to be organised in the spirit of the constitution of 1920". According to the National Socialist legal system that had been in force up to that point, the three parties obviously were not entitled to take such a step. As in 1918, the founding of the state in 1945 was carried out in breach of legal continuity and was thus in legal terms a revolutionary act.

➢ From this question of continuity regarding domestic constitutional law, continuity in terms of international law must be kept strictly separate: in respect of the latter, the *occupation theory* (advocated e.g. by ADOLF MERKL) gradually prevailed over the initially dominating *annexation theory* (advocated e.g. by HANS KELSEN). According to the occupation theory, Austria had not been inexistent as a subject of international law in the period of 1938–45 but had merely been incapacitated. The Second Republic thus automatically stepped into the position of the First Republic regarding its rights and obligations under international law, including the treaties that the latter had concluded, in particular the concordat with the Holy See.

➢ In contrast to the situation in 1918, Austria's independence from Germany was welcomed by most Austrians. A specifically Austrian national consciousness emerged (only now), which was also deliberately promoted by the government (celebration of the 950th anniversary of Austria in 1946; publication of the Austrian Dictionary in 1951).

8111 At STALIN's behest, RENNER, who was already 75 years old, formed a **provisional state government** in which the SPÖ, ÖVP, and KPÖ were represented. The state government decided to return to the constitutional situation of 5 March 1933; however, until the National Council was able to convene, a provisional constitution was to apply (the B-VG was not fit for the special circumstances of the time). The provisional constitution concentrated all power in the provisional state government.

➢ A characteristic feature of the republic's re-establishment, as well as of the first decades of its existence, was the parties' cooperation according to the principle of proportional representation (*"Proporz"*), designed to overcome the profound mistrust between the political factions that remained from the First Republic. The founding of the independent Austrian Trade Union Federation on 15 April 1945 needs to be understood in this context (⇨ par. 7216). Even under the chaotic conditions of the first days after the war, there was a consensus that there should not be a new constitution but rather a continuation of the democratic developments in the interwar period.

➢ While the Declaration of Independence only referred to the constitution of 1920 (i.e. did not mention its later amendments), the *First Constitutional Transition Act* of 1 May 1945 specified 5 March 1933 (the day after the so-called "self-elimination of the National Council", ⇨ par. 7103) as the cut-off date.

➢ For norms other than constitutional law, on the other hand, a general adoption of the existing legal order was stipulated in the *Transition of Legislation Act* of 1 May 1945; hence, laws taken from Germany or newly enacted between 1938 and 1945 (e.g. the Stock Corporation Act, the Marriage Act, and the Commercial Code) were also included into the body of law of the Second Republic. The only exceptions were "legal provisions that are incompatible with a free and independent state of Austria or with the principles of a genuine democracy, contradict the legal sensibilities of the Austrian people or contain typical National Socialist ideology". To further specify this rather vague general clause, the state government later issued extensive lists of the provisions that were repealed.

➢ The *Transition of Authorities Act* of 20 July 1945 abolished the German authorities still existing in Austria and assigned their responsibilities to the re-established Austrian authorities.

➢ Given that neither the National Council nor the diets existed, and the political situation in the Länder was extremely uncertain and not easily understood from Vienna, the Provisional Constitution transferred both federal and Länder legislative powers (for a limited period of six months after the first meeting of the newly elected National Council) to the provisional state government. It thereby provisionally abandoned both the principle of separation of powers and the principle of federalism inherent in the B-VG.

➢ The provisional state government comprised state secretaries from all three anti-fascist parties under the chairmanship of the state chancellor (RENNER); political decisions of "fundamental significance" were taken by a Political Cabinet Council (comprising state secretaries without portfolios and led by the state chancellor), which as a collective also performed the functions of the head of state.

8112 In the meantime, the four Allies (USSR, USA, UK, France) had occupied the entire country and divided it into four occupation zones.

With the **First Allied Control Agreement** of 4 July 1945, an Allied Council was created, which consisted of a High Commissioner from each of the four powers and assumed the supreme power in Austria. The four Allies only recognised the provisional state government in a memorandum on 20 October; however, they made its legislative power subject to their approval.

➢ During the Second World War, the Allies conducted numerous rounds of negotiation on the future fate of Austria. Austria's re-establishment as an independent state was only one of several options, which also included a merger with other former Habsburg states ("Danube Confederation") or with Bavaria ("South German Federation").

➢ In the Moscow Declaration of 30 October 1943, the Allies declared the annexation of Austria "null and void" (in 1945, this formulation was incorporated into the Declaration of Independence). The Declaration also made the restoration of Austria's independence a war goal and reminded Austria of its active participation in the war on the side of HITLER's Germany.

➢ The re-established Länder were occupied by the Allies essentially in the following manner: Lower Austria, Burgenland, and northern Upper Austria by the Soviets; southern Upper Austria and Salzburg by the Americans; Styria, Carinthia, and East Tyrol by the British; and northern Tyrol and Vorarlberg by the French. Vienna was occupied by all four powers together.

➢ The First Allied Control Agreement was an agreement between the four powers to which Austria was not a party. Initially, it was planned that the Allied Council itself would exercise the legislative function.

➢ The provisional state government was initially met with great suspicion by the Western Allies, who considered it STALIN's puppet government. Its recognition as the government of the entire country on 20 October prevented a separate government in Western Austria (which would have been based in Salzburg) and thus a division of Austria similar to that of Germany.

➢ The change of opinion among the Allies was especially encouraged by the fact that the provisional state government had been approved in September 1945 by a conference where representatives of all Austrian Länder had been present. On 12 October 1945, the Provisional Constitution was amended and the Länder were granted their own legislative and executive powers. The constitutional principle of federalism was thus restored, which also made it necessary to reintroduce constitutional jurisdiction, accomplished with the "October Amendment" (whereas the ordinary and administrative branches of the judiciary had already been restored in May 1945).

➢ The Allied Council Memorandum stated that all laws enacted by the provisional state government had to be submitted to the Allied Council for approval before they could come into effect. Also, Austria was obliged to hold elections by the end of 1945.

8113 On 25 November 1945, the **first National Council election** since 1930 was held, resulting in an absolute majority for the ÖVP (85 seats) and a crushing defeat for the KPÖ (4 seats); the SPÖ won 76 seats. With the first session of the National Council on 19 December

1945, the Provisional Constitution ceased to apply, and the B-VG was again in full force. KARL RENNER became the first federal president. He appointed LEOPOLD FIGL (ÖVP) as federal chancellor of a "concentration government" consisting of all three parties. Allied control was substantially relaxed with the *Second Allied Control Agreement* of 28 June 1946.

➢ On 13 December 1945, the provisional state government reintroduced the B-VG with the *Second Constitutional Transition Act*. The council of the Länder and corporative groups that had been envisaged in 1929 was permanently abandoned and replaced by the Federal Council according to the original concept from 1920. Also, the election of the federal president was for a last time vested in the Federal Assembly.

➢ The National Council election was an affirmation of Western democracy and a rejection of Communism; unlike in Austria's neighbouring countries Hungary and ČSR, the influence of the Communists in Austria soon dwindled into insignificance. Not least to prevent such a debacle also in East Germany, the KPD and SPD were forcibly united to form the Socialist Unity Party of Germany (*Sozialistische Einheitspartei Deutschlands*, SED, ⇨ par. 5202, par. 8105).

➢ Because of the Soviet occupying power, the KPÖ remained in government but was granted only one ministry (the ministry for energy). In 1947, the KPÖ left the government as it no longer supported its policies; the ÖVP and SPÖ remained in a "grand coalition".

➢ In October 1950, the KPÖ, with the support of the Soviet occupation forces, unleashed a strike, which today is regarded by many scholars as an attempt to overthrow the government (cf. the seizure of power by the Communists in the East-Central European Countries, ⇨ par. 8106). The Minister of the Interior, FRANZ OLAH (SPÖ), suppressed the uprising.

➢ The Second Allied Control Agreement was the Allies' reaction to the fact that conditions in Austria seemed to have stabilised. Written approval by the Allied Council was only required for constitutional laws; for other laws, Allied approval was assumed if no objection was made within 31 days.

8114 A particularly thorny problem in the post-war period was Austria's **denazification**. The Act Prohibiting the NSDAP ("Prohibition Act") of 8 May 1945 declared the NSDAP illegal, introduced compulsory registration of its former members, and set up People's Courts to punish National Socialists and war criminals. The National Socialists Act of 6 February 1947 divided former party members into "incriminated" (c. 40,000) and "less incriminated" (c. 490,000) persons and linked these categories to certain sanctions. On the question of "compensation" for victims of National Socialism, ⇨ par. 7209ff.

➢ The People's Courts, which were installed under § 24 of the Prohibition Act, comprised two professional judges and three lay judges. In practice, the three "anti-fascist parties" (SPÖ, ÖVP, KPÖ) each nominated one lay judge. Preliminary investigations took place in more than 13,000 cases, with about 10 percent ending in guilty verdicts. The courts passed 43 death sentences.

➢ The sanctions imposed on former NSDAP members included an increased tax liability, dismissal from public service, loss of their pension, forfeiture of their property, exclusion from participation in elections, etc.

➢ The initial harsh sentences were successively reduced: the death penalty was (fully) abolished in Austria in 1950, and the penalty of forfeiture of property was dropped in 1957. Several amnesty laws were passed as well. Nevertheless, convictions under the Prohibition Act still take place (the Act still has constitutional rank to this day).

➢ Those who were "less incriminated", i.e. had neither held a political leadership role nor been a member of the SS, the SA, or a similar organisation, and who had not been convicted of any war crimes, were rehabilitated across the board in 1949 and deleted from the registers of former National Socialists, which also restored their right to vote. (To put this policy into perspective, a full, blanket rehabilitation of the victims of the National Socialist judiciary did not take place until 2009!).

➢ Soon a scramble ensued for the almost half a million new voters, which was not glorious for either the ÖVP or the SPÖ. In March 1949, the Association of Independents (*Verband der Unabhängigen*, VdU) was founded as a new party and won 489,000 votes in the same year's election, gaining 16 seats, more than three times as many as the KPÖ.

8115 The Allied occupation of Austria lasted for more than ten years due to the Cold War, as it was inextricably linked to the German question. Only after the Paris Treaties of 1954 (⇨ par. 8108) could Austria's fate be detached from Germany's to embark on the "Austrian *Sonderweg*". With the **State Treaty of Vienna** of 15 May 1955, Austria was declared sovereign and the Allied Powers undertook to withdraw their troops. In a political, not a legal context, Austria declared its perpetual neutrality on 26 October 1955.

➢ Once Communist systems had been established in East-Central Europe in 1948/49, none of the Allied powers could afford to withdraw their troops from the region. Between 1949 and 1954 there was not a single meeting of the foreign ministers of the four Allies. Only the death of STALIN in 1953 led to a phase of détente in world politics. In 1954, FIGL, by then the Austrian Foreign Minister, declared that Austria, unlike the FRG and the GDR, did not want to join any military alliance.

➢ In the *Moscow Memorandum* of 15 April 1955, Federal Chancellor JULIUS RAAB (ÖVP), Vice-Chancellor ADOLF SCHÄRF (SPÖ), Foreign Minister LEOPOLD FIGL (ÖVP), and State Secretary in the Foreign Office BRUNO KREISKY (SPÖ) promised the Soviet government that Austria would maintain perpetual neutrality based on the Swiss model as the price for the withdrawal of the occupying troops. Most scholars agree that the Moscow Memorandum was not a treaty under international law but a commitment by Austria's most senior politicians to work towards the country's neutralisation.

➢ The term "perpetual neutrality" and the reference to the Swiss model denoted a special status recognised in international law. Perpetual neutrality goes far beyond simple neutrality in a concrete armed conflict. Further, perpetual neutrality also obligates the perpetually neutral party to pursue an appropriate policy in peacetime by refraining from actions that would preclude it from observing neutrality in a war, such as joining a military alliance or a customs union.

➢ The Moscow Memorandum made it possible to sign the State Treaty at Schloss Belvedere exactly one month later. The Allied Powers undertook to withdraw their troops within 90 days of the treaty coming into effect (i.e. by 25 October) and declared Austria sovereign. Austria had to guarantee to maintain its democratic system, prohibit National Socialist organisations, uphold the Habsburg Law, etc. Any political or economic union with Germany was forbidden. The Slovene and Croat minorities in Carinthia, Styria, and Burgenland were granted autonomy in schooling, language and culture.

➢ Austria consciously waited until 26 October 1955 (by which time the occupying forces had to withdraw from its territory) before it proclaimed its neutrality "of its own free will". In terms of domestic law, this was achieved through a special federal constitutional law; vis-à-vis the international community, Austria issued a unilateral declaration of its neutrality. The extent to which this declaration binds Austria under international law is disputed. Neutrality is not an end in itself but was declared "for the purpose of the permanent maintenance of [Austria's] external independence and for the purpose of the inviolability of her territory". To achieve this end, Austria undertook that it would "never in the future accede to any military alliances nor permit the establishment of military bases of foreign States on her territory".

➢ During the occupation, Austria did not have an army, only an armed gendarmerie of up to 7,000 men. On account of the regained sovereignty, it was possible to establish an Austrian army in 1955, and universal conscription was introduced. Conscientious objectors could only refuse to bear arms but not avoid military service as such; it was not until 1974 that the option of an alternative service ("civilian service") was created.

d) The economic integration of Western Europe

8116 With the Treaties of Paris, Warsaw, and Vienna in 1954/55, the division of Europe was a *fait accompli*; any further integration could only take place within one of the two "blocs". The OEEC in particular planned to create a *European Free Trade Area* that would include all non-Communist states (**"great free trade area"**). An even deeper integration in the form of a *customs union* (as already existed between the Benelux states) would have been unfeasible for many states at the time, especially the UK.

➢ In a free trade area, internal tariffs and other trade restrictions are eliminated, but only for goods from member states, which therefore require a certificate of origin. If goods are imported from other countries, they must be cleared separately under national law in each member state of the free trade area. In contrast, in a customs union, external customs duties are also centrally regulated, which means that goods, regardless of their country of origin, can move freely within the customs union.

➢ A customs union results in much tighter integration than a free trade area. Participation in a customs union seemed impossible for states such as the UK (because of its close economic ties to the Commonwealth) or Austria (because of its neutrality).

➢ The customs union between Belgium, the Netherlands, and Luxembourg was agreed upon by the governments in exile of these (at that stage German-occupied) states as early as 1944 and came into effect in 1948. With the Benelux Treaty of 3 February 1958, it was upgraded to a common market. Within it, not only goods but also people, services, and capital can move freely (the "Four Freedoms").

➢ The economic significance of the Benelux Treaty was outweighed by further European integration, but in other areas (e.g. policing) it remains important to this day. It was amended in 2008 and extended for an indefinite period.

8117 Against the plans for a free trade area (which were pursued mainly by the UK), the six member states of the ECSC agreed in 1956 on the establishment of a Common Market and, in addition, an Atomic Energy Community (SPAAK Report). On this basis, the *Treaty Establishing the European Economic Community* (EEC) and the *Treaty Establishing the European Atomic Energy Community* (Euratom, EAEC) were signed in Rome on 25 March 1957. They came into effect on 1 January 1958 (**Treaties of Rome**).

➢ At a conference in Messina in June 1955, the ECSC foreign ministers decided to set up a "committee of experts", chaired by the Belgian Foreign Minister PAUL-HENRI SPAAK, to discuss further steps towards economic integration. Initially, British representatives also took part in these consultations. However, when the committee advocated the formation of a customs union, the UK declared its withdrawal from the negotiations.

➢ The consultations were overshadowed by the Suez Crises (⇨ par. 8103) as well by simultaneous Franco-German negotiations about the Saarland, which had been placed under French administration in 1945, but joined the FRG on 1 January 1957. The resolution of the Saarland issue also facilitated the conclusion of the negotiations about European integration.

➢ The establishment of a separate Atomic Energy Community alongside the general economic union (realised by the EEC) was also a concession to France, the importance of which was overestimated (⇨ par. 8209). For as long as the EAEC had its own commission (1958–67), it was always headed by a Frenchman.

➢ With the ECSC, EAEC, and EEC, the six states were now linked in three supranational organisations with almost identical structures (High Authority resp. Commission; Council; Parliamentary Assembly; Court of Justice, ⇨ par. 8213). An agreement signed together with the Treaties of Rome stipulated that the Parliamentary Assembly and the Court of Justice of the ECSC should also act for the other two communities. There was thus always

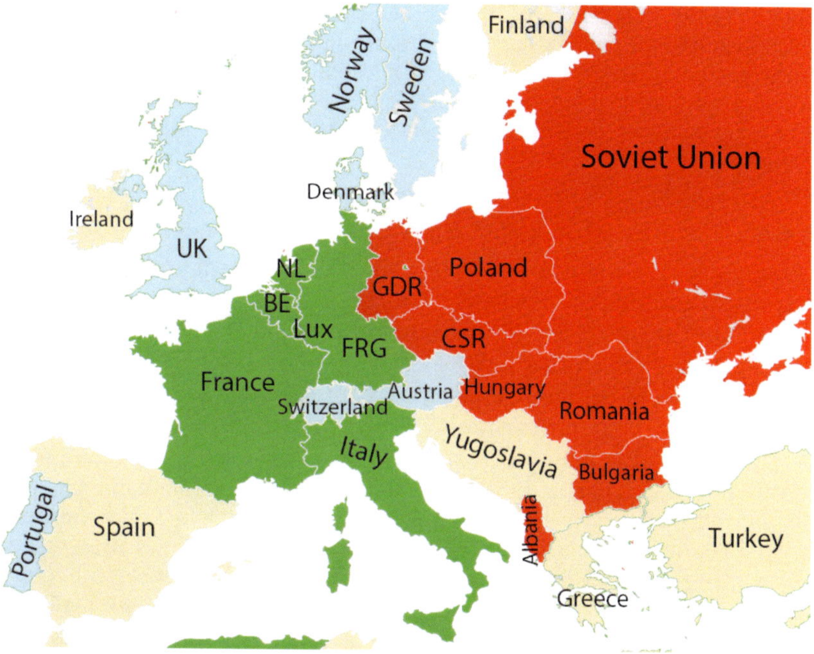

Map 14: EEC, EFTA and COMECON in 1960
Source: https://commons.wikimedia.org/wiki/File:EuropaNATOWP1959.png
Text modified; green = EEC; blue = EFTA; red = COMECON
Copyright: https://creativecommons.org/licenses/by-sa/3.0 (CC BY-SA 3.0)

only one common Parliamentary Assembly and only one common Court of Justice for the three communities.

➢ With the *Merger Treaty* of 8 April 1965, the other institutions (Commission, Council) were also merged. Although there were still three different communities, each with its own legal personality, the expression "the European Community" (in the singular) became increasingly common.

8118 With the establishment of the EEC, the plan for a "great free trade area" had failed. Under the leadership of the UK, seven OEEC states that were not members of the EEC, including Austria, joined together in 1960 to form a "small free trade area" (**European Free Trade Association,** EFTA). The OEEC was transformed into the *Organisation for Economic Co-operation and Development* (OECD).

➢ The EFTA Treaty was signed in Stockholm on 4 January 1960 by Austria, Denmark, Norway, Portugal, Sweden, Switzerland, and the UK. Finland joined EFTA as an associate member in 1961 and as a full member in 1982; in 1970, Iceland also joined as a full member. Plans to link the EEC and EFTA through an umbrella organisation failed, but individual EFTA states concluded free trade agreements with the EEC.

➢ The OEEC had accomplished its purpose with the establishment of the "Community of Six" (EEC) and the "Community of Seven" (EFTA) and was transformed into the OECD. The OECD is dedicated to European-American economic relations in particular and for this purpose also commissions extensive comparative studies, such as the *Programme for International Student Assessment* (PISA).

e) "Peaceful coexistence"?

8119 While ADENAUER continued to hold on to the distant goal of German reunification, the USSR under CHRUŠČËV strove to stabilise the status quo in Europe. The "peaceful coexistence" with the West that he propagated at the 20th Party Congress of the CPSU in 1956 stood in stark contrast to the acute danger of **nuclear war**. In 1962, the USA and the USSR began disarmament negotiations.

➢ Soviet foreign policy was especially concerned with the diplomatic recognition of the GDR as an independent state, the integration of East Berlin into the GDR, and the consolidation of the German-Polish border. ADENAUER, on the other hand, stipulated that German reunification was a prerequisite for an easing of tensions between East and West.

➢ According to the HALLSTEIN Doctrine, named after the then West German State Secretary WALTER HALLSTEIN (1951–58; EEC Commission President 1958–67), other countries could – with few exceptions – only have diplomatic relations with either the FRG or the GDR. Neither of the two German states recognised the other and each claimed the sole right of representation of the entire German nation.

➢ On 13 August 1961, the GDR erected a wall between East and West Berlin. By placing tanks at the border crossings, the Western powers ensured that their troops would continue to have access to all parts of the city, but otherwise had to accept the (literal) cementing of the division of Berlin.

➢ When the USSR stationed nuclear missiles in Cuba in 1962, a nuclear war could only narrowly be prevented; eventually, US President JOHN F. KENNEDY (1961–63) succeeded in getting the missile bases vacated through diplomatic channels. A visible sign of the policy of détente that now began was the establishment of a "red telephone" (actually a teleprinter) linking the Kremlin in Moscow and the White House in Washington.

8120 The US hegemony over Western Europe and its accommodation with the USSR increasingly met with rejection in France and the FRG. The French President CHARLES DE GAULLE (1958–69) strove for an **autonomous French policy** and also rejected the UK's accession to the EEC.

➢ After 1945, France lost almost all its colonies. In 1954, a bloody war of independence broke out in Algeria, which was not considered a colony but an integral part of France (and thus also part of the EEC), leading to severe crises in France. DE GAULLE, who had resigned in 1946, was again appointed head of government in 1958. He initiated a new constitution, which came into effect on 4 October 1958 and strengthened the role of the president. DE GAULLE himself was elected the first president of the "Fifth Republic". He subsequently succeeded in stabilising France politically and economically (which also involved a currency reform). Algeria was granted independence in 1962.

➢ The UK's aspirations to join the EEC were in line with the USA's plans for a reorganisation of Western Europe. DE GAULLE rejected the application in harsh terms in a spectacular press conference on 14 January 1963. A renewed attempt by the UK in 1967 was also rejected by France. Within the EEC, DE GAULLE rigorously enforced French interests with his "empty chair policy" aimed at boycotting the Council (⇨ par. 8216).

➢ In order to win support for his policy of self-reliance, DE GAULLE sought a close partnership with ADENAUER, who was disappointed with the American policy towards Germany (Franco-German Treaty of 22 January 1963) but could not significantly loosen the FRG's close ties to the USA.

➢ In 1966, France withdrew from the military (not the political) arm of NATO (until 2009, ⇨ par. 8132), which then moved its headquarters from Paris to Brussels. France had already begun developing its own nuclear weapons.

➢ In 1959, the European Development Fund for development cooperation in Africa was established, as provided for in the Rome Treaties. In 1963, an agreement was concluded in Yaoundé, the capital of Cameroon, between the EEC and 18 African states that had recently gained independence, which was followed by many others (including the Lomé Convention of 1975). Although the creation of a European-African free trade area was planned from the outset, it has yet to be realised.

8121 Under LEONID BREŽNEV (1965–82), the USSR continued its policy of détente with the West. Within the "Eastern Bloc", however, the Communist ideology was vigorously enforced (suppression of the **"Prague Spring"** in 1968).

➢ Especially in the ČSR (1960–90: Czechoslovak Socialist Republic – ČSSR), "de-Stalinisation" led to a certain degree of open-mindedness among intellectuals ("Prague Spring" 1968); the new First Secretary of the Czechoslovak Communist Party, ALEXANDER DUBČEK (1968–69), strove for a "Communism with a human face". His reform policy came to an abrupt end when Warsaw Pact troops invaded the ČSSR on 20/21 August; DUBČEK was deposed.

➢ The General Secretary of the CPSU, BREŽNEV, justified the invasion by arguing that the sovereignty of Socialist states ended when the Socialist world order was threatened (BREŽNEV Doctrine). In protest against the invasion, Albania, which had not participated in the intervention, withdrew from the Warsaw Pact in 1968. As a result, it became internationally isolated.

➢ In 1970, West German Chancellor WILLY BRANDT (1969–74, SPD) agreed with the USSR and Poland on a normalisation of relations and in 1972 concluded the so-called Basic Treaty with the GDR, in which the two German states granted each other *de facto* sovereignty (abandonment of the HALLSTEIN Doctrine, ⇨ par. 8119). This was also a prerequisite for both the FRG and the GDR to be admitted to the UN in 1973.

➢ The "German question" was thus resolved differently by the UN than the "Chinese question" (⇨ par. 8104): In 1971, the UN General Assembly had determined that the communist government ruling in Beijing was the only legitimate government for all of China. The People's Republic of China thus took the place in the international community that had previously been held by the Republic of China (including the permanent seat on the UN Security Council); most states, including Austria, broke off official diplomatic relations with Taiwan.

8122 At the request of both the Warsaw Pact and NATO, the **Conference on Security and Co-operation in Europe** (CSCE) was held in Helsinki and Geneva in 1972–75, bringing together all European states (except Albania) as well as the USA and Canada. Its Final Act was signed in Helsinki on 1 August 1975.

➢ In 1969, the Warsaw Pact states called for a European security conference, where the renunciation of the use of force between states should be the main priority. The NATO states, on the other hand, also included the protection of human rights in their programme for such a conference in 1970.

➢ The CSCE Final Act took both demands into account by committing the participating states to refrain from violence as well as to maintain the inviolability of borders and to respect human rights.

8123 The **Middle East** became a permanent conflict zone. The conflicts in the region were of global significance, not least due to the region's oil reserves, which is why both the USA and the USSR exerted considerable influence on the hostilities, which were ostensibly motivated by religion.

➢ In 1945, seven Arab states founded the Arab League, now consisting of 22 member states. It was particularly opposed to the immigration of Jews to Palestine and the creation of the State of Israel, but was unsuccessful in preventing either (⇨ par. 8103). In 1958, Egypt and Syria joined together to form the United Arab Republic, which, however, disintegrated already in 1961.

➢ Following the Suez Crisis of 1956 (⇨ par. 8103), the Sinai Peninsula was occupied by UN troops. When Egypt forced the withdrawal of these troops in 1967, Israel feared an imminent, concerted attack by all neighbouring states and launched a preventive strike against Egypt, Syria, and Jordan. Within a week, it had conquered the Gaza Strip and the Sinai Peninsula from Egypt, East Jerusalem and the West Bank from Jordan, and the Golan Heights from Syria (5–10 June 1967, the "Six-Day War").

➢ While Israel signed a peace treaty with Egypt in 1982 and returned the Sinai, the other aforementioned territories are still occupied by Israel today; a peace treaty has not yet been signed with either Syria or Jordan. The international status of the Occupied Palestinian Territories has yet to be clarified. The state of "Palestine" proclaimed in 1988 has been recognised by 146 states, but not by the United States or the majority of Western European states (including Germany and Austria).

➢ In 1979, the Shah of Persia (who was favourably disposed towards Western countries) was overthrown in a revolution, and the Islamic Republic of Iran was created. It is a Shiite Muslim theocracy. The political and religious leadership of Iran is vested in the Guardianship of the Islamic jurist (*Velāyat-e Fāqih*), pending the expected advent of the Mahdī (⇨ par. 2101).

f) The enlargement and consolidation of the EC

8124 After DE GAULLE's resignation in 1969, the UK, Ireland, and Denmark could be admitted to the European Communities in 1973 (**"northern enlargement"**).

➢ In 1972, accession treaties were signed with the UK, Ireland, Denmark, and Norway. However, in a referendum, the Norwegian population voted against joining the EC, especially due to the concern that Norwegian fishing waters would be opened up to the other EC member states.

➢ Due to the EEC's fisheries policy, Greenland, which had belonged to Denmark since 1380/1814 (⇨ par. 3118) also withdrew from the EC in 1985, while remaining an (autonomous) part of Denmark. It has enjoyed a special status since then.

➢ The accession of the UK and Denmark to the EC also entailed their simultaneous withdrawal from EFTA, which thus lost much of its significance. The remaining EFTA states concluded a free trade agreement with the EEC on 22 July 1972.

8125 The accession of Greece (1981) and Spain and Portugal (both in 1986) to the European Communities (**"southern enlargement"**) served to stabilise these fledgeling democracies but also placed a considerable financial burden on the EC.

➢ In Greece, a coup in 1967 led to the establishment of a military dictatorship under GEORGIOS PAPADÓPOULOS; King CONSTANTINE II went into exile. The military regime was overthrown in 1974, when the planned annexation of Cyprus to Greece failed (⇨ par. 8139). A referendum in the same year brought a vote in favour of a republic.

➢ Spain had remained neutral in the Second World War, meaning the fascist regime could remain in place after 1945. After FRANCO's death in 1975, and in accordance with his wishes, a grandson of the king who had abdicated in 1931, JUAN CARLOS I (1975–2014), became the new king of Spain. He initiated a cautious process of democratisation. An attempted coup in 1981 failed due to the king's resistance; one year later, Spain was admitted to NATO.

➢ In Portugal, the authoritarian regime established in 1926 (Prime Minister ANTÓNIO DE OLIVEIRA SALAZAR, 1932–68) also remained in place after the Second World War and was only removed in a military coup in 1974 ("Carnation Revolution"). In this context, the last Portuguese provinces in Africa also gained their independence in 1975. The influence of the military over the slowly emerging democratic structures continued to have an impact for a long time.

8126 Despite efforts to deepen European integration, the 1970s saw a certain standstill and the initial "europhoria" gave way to "eurosclerosis". In the 1980s, however, integration was pushed forward again and efforts were made to develop the EC into a political community. The **Single European Act** (SEA) of 17/28 February 1986 declared the creation of a "European Union" an explicit goal. It came into effect on 1 July 1987.

➢ The initiative to reform the EC came from the foreign ministers of Italy and the FRG, EMILIO COLOMBO and HANS DIETRICH GENSCHER, on the one hand and the new Commission President JACQUES DELORS (1985–94) on the other.

➢ The SEA did not replace the three founding treaties of 1951 and 1957 but comprehensively amended them, linking them to the – until then only informal – European Political Cooperation (EPC, ⇨ par. 8211). The SEA also institutionalised the previously informal summit meetings of the heads of state and government of the EC states, which had already been called the "European Council" since 1974.

g) Austria as a Neutral State

8127 Despite its neutrality, Austria subsequently pursued an **active foreign policy** and joined the UN in 1955 (⇨ par. 8101), the Council of Europe in 1956 (⇨ par. 8206), and EFTA in 1960 (⇨ par. 8118). The grand coalition of ÖVP and SPÖ continued until 1966, but also after this period, domestic politics was characterised by the **"social partnership"** and the *"Proporz"* system of proportional distribution of public offices among representatives of the two parties. This approach resulted in a weak political position of the National Council, a situation that was increasingly criticised.

➢ Although the ÖVP lost its absolute majority in 1949, it remained the party with the largest number of votes, and the federal chancellors continued to come from its ranks (LEOPOLD FIGL 1945–53, JULIUS RAAB 1953–61, ALFONS GORBACH 1961–64, JOSEF KLAUS 1964–70). The ÖVP and SPÖ together held well over two thirds of the seats in the National Council and were, therefore, able to pass constitutional laws, of which they made extensive use – mostly, however, not for major structural reforms, but for enshrining ever more details in the constitution. Subsequent National Council elections up to 1966 did not significantly change this situation.

➢ The VdU disintegrated due to internal disputes. In 1955, the *Freiheitliche Partei Österreichs* (FPÖ, usually translated as "Freedom Party", literally the "Liberal Party of Austria") emerged from the VdU. The first party leader of the FPÖ was ANTON REINTHALLER who had been Minister of Agriculture under Nazi chancellor SEYSS-INQUART in 1938. Until 1986, the FPÖ never won more than twelve of the (initially 165, from 1971) 183 National Council seats. The KPÖ left the National Council in 1959.

➢ One consequence of the grand coalition was that the highest offices, but also other positions in the civil service, were almost always awarded based on "black or red" (i.e. ÖVP or SPÖ) proportional representation. For the

Länder governments, the system of proportional representation was even enshrined in the constitution, since all parties represented in the diet also had to nominate a proportional number of members for the government, which usually resulted in a distribution of posts between the ÖVP and the SPÖ. Until 1964 (and again in 1991–99), in seven of the nine Länder, the governor was an ÖVP politician.

➢ The core of the social partnership was the "Joint Commission for Wage and Price Issues", in which representatives of the Chamber of Labour, the Trade Union Federation, the Chamber of Commerce, and the Chambers of Agriculture agreed (without a legal basis) on essential social and economic policy issues, which were then only "rubber-stamped" in the National Council.

➢ A major foreign policy problem was the "South Tyrolean question". Italy had only partially implemented the autonomy promised to South Tyrol in 1948 (⇨ par. 8103), which provoked a series of terrorist acts from 1956 onwards. Austria brought the issue before the UN in 1960, whereupon Italy issued a new, improved Statute of Autonomy in 1971. Under Austrian law, South Tyroleans were granted almost the same rights as Austrian citizens.

➢ In the 1960s, the differences between the ÖVP and the SPÖ became increasingly noticeable, especially on the issue of entry permits for OTTO HABSBURG-LOTHRINGEN, the son of the last emperor, who in 1961 had submitted the waiver of privileges required by the Habsburgs Act 1919 (⇨ par. 6108). Since the coalition government failed to reach an amicable solution, the issue was decided in favour of HABSBURG-LOTHRINGEN by the Administrative Court in 1962/63 following a default complaint.

➢ In 1966, the ÖVP won an absolute majority in the National Council; Chancellor KLAUS formed an ÖVP-led government and the SPÖ went into opposition.

➢ In 1970, this was reversed: the SPÖ was the party with the largest number of votes and BRUNO KREISKY (1970–83) formed an SPÖ minority government tolerated by the FPÖ. In 1971, the SPÖ won an absolute majority, which it was able to maintain and even increase in the National Council elections of 1975 and 1979. During this period, far-reaching reforms of family law (⇨ par. 8301) and criminal law (⇨ par. 8303) were enacted.

➢ In 1983, the SPÖ lost its absolute majority but remained the party with the largest number of votes; KREISKY's successor, FRED SINOWATZ (1983–86), formed a "small coalition" with the FPÖ.

8128 The year 1986 ushered in a new phase in Austrian domestic politics: the traditional "limping two-party system" was broken up and replaced with genuine **party pluralism**. The new party system meant that the National Council also regained some of its significance. The social partnership, on the other hand, lost in importance.

➢ The election of JÖRG HAIDER as FPÖ party leader in 1986 ended the SPÖ/FPÖ coalition and led to an early parliamentary election. It brought a strong gain in votes for the FPÖ; the Greens entered the National Council for the first time. The SPÖ again formed a grand coalition with the ÖVP, now under SPÖ leadership (Federal Chancellors FRANZ VRANITZKY 1986–97, VIKTOR KLIMA 1997–2000).

➢ In subsequent National Council elections, the FPÖ won an increasing number of seats at the expense of the SPÖ and ÖVP, which lost their joint two-thirds majority in the National Council for the first time in 1994 (which they regained in 1995–99 and 2002–08). In 1993, the Liberal Forum split from the FPÖ and was subsequently represented in the National Council until 1999.

2. Developments since 1989

a) Overcoming the division of Europe

8129 In the 1980s, the "Eastern Bloc" gradually began to disintegrate. In Poland in particular, the **Communist regime** fell into a **deep crisis**. The new head of the Soviet Communist party, MIKHAIL GORBAČËV (1985–91), announced a series of reforms in the USSR.

➢ The resistance to the Polish Communist party found support in the Catholic Church in particular, which was considerably strengthened by the election of the Archbishop of Cracow, KAROL WOJTYŁA, as pope (JOHN PAUL II, 1978–2005). The independent trade union *Solidarność*, founded in 1980 by the Gdansk shipyard worker LECH WAŁĘSA, became a *de facto* opposition party. In 1981, the Communist government imposed martial law in Poland and banned *Solidarność* but could not break the increasingly strong resistance.

➢ After BREŽNEV's death in 1982, the CPSU leadership oscillated between rigidity and reform. In 1985, GORBAČËV became the new General Secretary of the CPSU. He embarked on an economic transformation ("*perestroika*") and the opening up of the Soviet Union ("*glasnost*").

8130 In 1989, the Communist regimes in Poland, Hungary, the GDR, the ČSSR, Romania, and Bulgaria collapsed within a few months ("**Velvet revolution**").

➢ The surprisingly rapid disintegration of the Eastern bloc occurred largely without bloodshed. It was essentially the result of the economic problems of the Socialist states. The Communist regimes no longer had the support of the USSR, as they did not want to support GORBAČËV's reform policies. The USSR, for its part, abandoned the BREŽNEV Doctrine, thereby leaving the Communist regimes of East-Central Europe to their fate.

➢ As early as January 1989, the Hungarian Communist party renounced its claim to leadership and allowed the formation of other political parties. In February, the Polish Communist party leadership entered into reform talks with the WAŁĘSA-led opposition. On 24 August 1989, Poland's first non-Communist government since the Second World War was formed, and WAŁĘSA was elected president of Poland in 1990 (until 1995).

➢ When Hungary opened its border with Austria to GDR citizens on 11 September 1989, a mass exodus began. Demonstrations (e.g. the weekly "Leipzig Monday Demonstrations") led to the fall of SED leader ERICH HONECKER. On 9 November, the borders to West Berlin and the FRG were opened (fall of the "Berlin Wall"). The first (and only) free elections in the GDR took place on 18 March 1990.

➢ The uprising in the GDR triggered a revolt in the CSSR, whose Communist party renounced its claim to leadership on 29 November 1989; the poet and dissident VÁCLAV HAVEL, who had coined the term "Velvet Revolution", became the new Czechoslovak president (1989–92, Czech president 1993–2003).

➢ There were also uprisings in Romania and Bulgaria that toppled their respective Communist regimes; the Romanian Communist leader NICOLAE CEAUŞESCU was executed on 25 December 1989.

➢ On 3 December 1989, GORBAČËV and US President GEORGE H. W. BUSH (1989–93) proclaimed the end of the Cold War at a summit meeting held on the high seas off Malta.

8131 Under German Chancellor HELMUT KOHL (1982–98, CDU), **Germany was reunified** within a year (3 October 1990). The four Allied powers renounced their prerogatives with regard to Germany and Berlin as a whole and released Germany into full sovereignty.

➢ After the fall of Communism in the GDR, the future of the country was initially controversial; KOHL advocated its unification with the FRG in the shortest possible time. As early as 18 May 1990, an economic and monetary union was created, and the D-Mark was introduced as the common currency (replacing the GDR mark).

➢ The "2+4 Treaty" signed in Moscow on 12 September 1990 between the FRG and the GDR on the one hand and the USSR, the USA, the UK, and France on the other lifted all restrictions on the sovereignty of the unified Germany. It was to consist of the territories of the FRG, the GDR and Berlin, which also entailed the definitive relinquishment of the territories beyond the Oder-Neisse line (⇨ par. 7111). Germany agreed not to possess nuclear weapons and also to reduce its conventional armed forces. The Soviet Union undertook to withdraw its troops from Germany by 1994, which it did.

➢ The FRG and the GDR agreed on 31 August that the GDR would accede to the FRG based on Article 23 GG, as the Saarland had already done in 1957 (⇨ par. 8117). When the accession came into effect on 3 October, the territory of the GDR was divided into five Länder, so that the united Germany consisted of sixteen Länder (ten West German and five East German, plus the reunited Berlin).

➢ This procedure also had the effect that the unified Germany was identical with the FRG established in Bonn in 1949 (and therefore also a member of the EC and NATO), whereas the GDR ceased to exist. The laws that had previously only applied in the West (e.g. the German Civil Code) were, with few exceptions, also made applicable in the new Länder. In 1999, the parliament and government moved from Bonn to the new capital, Berlin.

8132 **COMECON was dissolved** on 28 June 1991; the **Warsaw Pact** followed suit on 1 July 1991. The Eastern and Central European states joined the Council of Europe and, from 1999, successively also NATO. In 1995, the CSCE was transformed into the Organisation for

Security and Cooperation in Europe (OSCE), an international organisation based in Vienna.

➢ The follow-up meetings of the CSCE (⇨ par. 8122) in Stockholm (1984–86) and especially in Vienna (1986–89) contributed significantly to overcoming the division of Europe. In 1992, the decision was made to institutionalise the conference, which was realised in 1995 with the establishment of the OSCE.

➢ In 1999, the Czech Republic, Hungary, and Poland joined NATO, followed by Bulgaria, Estonia, Latvia, Lithuania, Romania, Slovenia, and Slovakia in 2004, Albania and Croatia in 2009, Montenegro in 2017, and Northern Macedonia in 2020. These expansions led to tensions with Russia, also because of its region Kaliningrad (⇨ par. 7111), which now constitutes a Russian enclave surrounded by NATO member states.

➢ For NATO, which had not experienced a single combat mission during the Cold War, a transformation process began in 1989. Its military missions, which it has carried out since 1999 (Kosovo, ⇨ par. 8134) within and outside of Europe, are in tension with the EU's efforts to establish an independent European security policy without US involvement (⇨ par. 8211).

➢ France's return to the military structures of NATO in 2009 (⇨ par. 8120) was therefore also interpreted as indicating that, even after the end of the Cold War, a European security policy only seemed realistic if the USA was involved as well.

b) The disintegration of the multi-ethnic states in Central and Eastern Europe

8133 The disintegration of the Eastern bloc led to serious crises and eventually to the **disintegration of the Soviet Union**. On 8 December 1991, the presidents of Russia, Belarus, and Ukraine founded the *Commonwealth of Independent States*, which most of the other former Soviet republics also joined. On 25 December 1991, GORBAČËV stepped down.

➢ His reform course had increasingly encountered difficulties domestically and was to some extent also sabotaged. The disintegration of the Eastern bloc meant the loss of the Soviet Union's position as a superpower, which added to the discontent.

➢ In 1990, GORBAČËV had the constitution amended and was elected president (following the US model), but this did not halt his loss of power. In February/March 1991, referenda in the union republics of Estonia, Latvia, and Lithuania each resulted in majorities in favour of leaving the USSR.

➢ In August 1991, the opponents of the reforms attempted a coup, detained GORBAČËV, and declared him deposed. The coup failed due to the resistance of the president of the union republic of Russia, BORIS ELCIN (1991–99), who became the new "strong man" in the disintegrating Soviet Union and proclaimed a ban on the CPSU on 24 August.

➢ With the collapse of the Soviet Union, Russia, Ukraine, Belarus, Estonia, Latvia, Lithuania, Moldova, Georgia, Armenia and Azerbaijan, Kazakhstan, Kyrgyzstan, Turkmenistan, Tajikistan, and Uzbekistan became sovereign states. They are all multi-ethnic in their composition; the Caucasus region in particular has subsequently been the scene of repeated wars.

➢ The Commonwealth of Independent States, which all former union republics except the Baltic states (which have been part of the EU since 2004) joined, is a loose association under international law. Georgia, which only acceded to the commonwealth in 1993, withdrew from it in 2009 due to a military conflict with Russia, as did Ukraine in 2018 (⇨ par. 8143).

8134 In the context of the decline of the Communist regimes, **Czechoslovakia and Yugoslavia collapsed** as well. While the Czech Republic and Slovakia gained their independence peacefully on 1 January 1993, the disintegration of Yugoslavia led to a bloody civil war in 1991/92.

➢ In Yugoslavia, ethnic conflicts broke out soon after the death of TITO, the figurehead of integration in the country, in 1980. When the Serbian President SLOBODAN MILOŠEVIĆ (1989–97) opposed the election of the Croat STJEPAN MESIĆ as President of Yugoslavia in 1991, conflict erupted.

➢ In 1991, Slovenia and Croatia declared their independence; violent conflict broke out mainly because of the presence of a Serb minority in Croatia (1991–95).

➢ In 1992, the Bosniak and Croat parts of the population of Bosnia-Herzegovina advocated independence, while the Bosnian Serbs wanted to join Serbia. The resulting civil war ended with the Dayton Agreement of 21 November 1995, which divided the country into a Bosniak-Croat and a Serb part, while nominally preserving state unity. Compliance with the treaty was initially monitored by NATO troops (IFOR, SFOR), and has been monitored since 2004 by an EU force (EUFOR).

➢ Macedonia also declared its independence in 1991. In this context, armed conflicts with the Albanian minority broke out. In 2003, Macedonia was occupied by EUFOR soldiers for a few months. In 2019, under Greek pressure, in particular, it changed its name to "Northern Macedonia".

➢ In 1989, unrest had broken out in the Serbian province of Kosovo (inhabited mainly by Albanians), which escalated into war and could only be ended by NATO military intervention in 1999. Kosovo has been occupied by NATO troops (KFOR) ever since; in 2008, it declared its independence.

➢ The remaining constituent republics of Serbia and Montenegro merged in 1992 to form the Federal Republic of Yugoslavia, where MILOŠEVIĆ was president from 1997 to 2000. In 2003, the Federal Republic of Yugoslavia was transformed into a mere confederation of states and dissolved altogether in 2006.

➢ In 1993, an international tribunal was established to deal with crimes committed in connection with the Yugoslav war. MILOŠEVIĆ was one of those extradited to appear before the tribunal, but he died in 2006, while still on trial. The tribunal was one of the forerunners of the International Criminal Court, which was established in 2002 (⇨ par. 8101).

c) The European Union during the era of the "three pillars"

8135 The efforts to create a European Union (EU), which had already begun before 1989, gained new momentum with the collapse of the Eastern Bloc and German reunification (⇨ par. 8131). The negotiations, which officially began in 1990, resulted in the **Treaty of Maastricht** (*Treaty on European Union*, TEU) of 7 February 1992. It added two additional "pillars", namely the Common Foreign and Security Policy (CFSP) and cooperation in the areas of justice and home affairs, to the three existing supranational communities (the "first pillar" of the European Union). The EEC was renamed the "European Community" (EC) and had its competences considerably extended. The European Union came into being as a result of the Maastricht Treaty on 1 November 1993.

➤ The German Chancellor KOHL and Foreign Minister GENSCHER, in particular, pressed ahead with the establishment of the EU, as they wanted to overcome fears of a stronger unified Germany by firmly anchoring Germany in Europe. They received substantial support from the French President FRANÇOIS MITTERAND (1981–95) and Commission President DELORS.

➤ Just like the SEA in 1986, the TEU was a mantle treaty that did not replace the founding treaties of 1951/57 but amended them substantially and supplemented them with additional provisions.

➤ The renaming of the EEC as the EC demonstrated that European integration had already substantially transcended the realm of economic policy. The EC remained the "core" of the EU; the terms "EC" and "EU" were often used interchangeably. The EAEC and the ECSC (which later expired in 2002, ⇨ par. 8207), on the other hand, increasingly receded into the background.

➤ The three "pillars" of the EU were not of the same nature; while the first pillar was made up of three supranational organisations, the second and third pillars represented areas of intergovernmental cooperation where the general rules of international law applied (in particular the principle of unanimity). However, they were able to make use of the organs of the first pillar.

➤ The EU itself could be viewed as an umbrella organisation for the three pillars; its own legal nature remained controversial until 2009. The only organ directly attached to it was the European Council (⇨ par. 8217); otherwise, it acted through the organs of the first pillar.

➤ The entry into effect of the TEU was delayed because a referendum in Denmark initially rejected the treaty. After special arrangements for Denmark regarding the CFSP were agreed upon in further negotiations (⇨ par. 8143), a second referendum resulted in a vote in favour of the TEU.

Table 9: The European Union

Organisation before the Treaty of Lisbon 2009

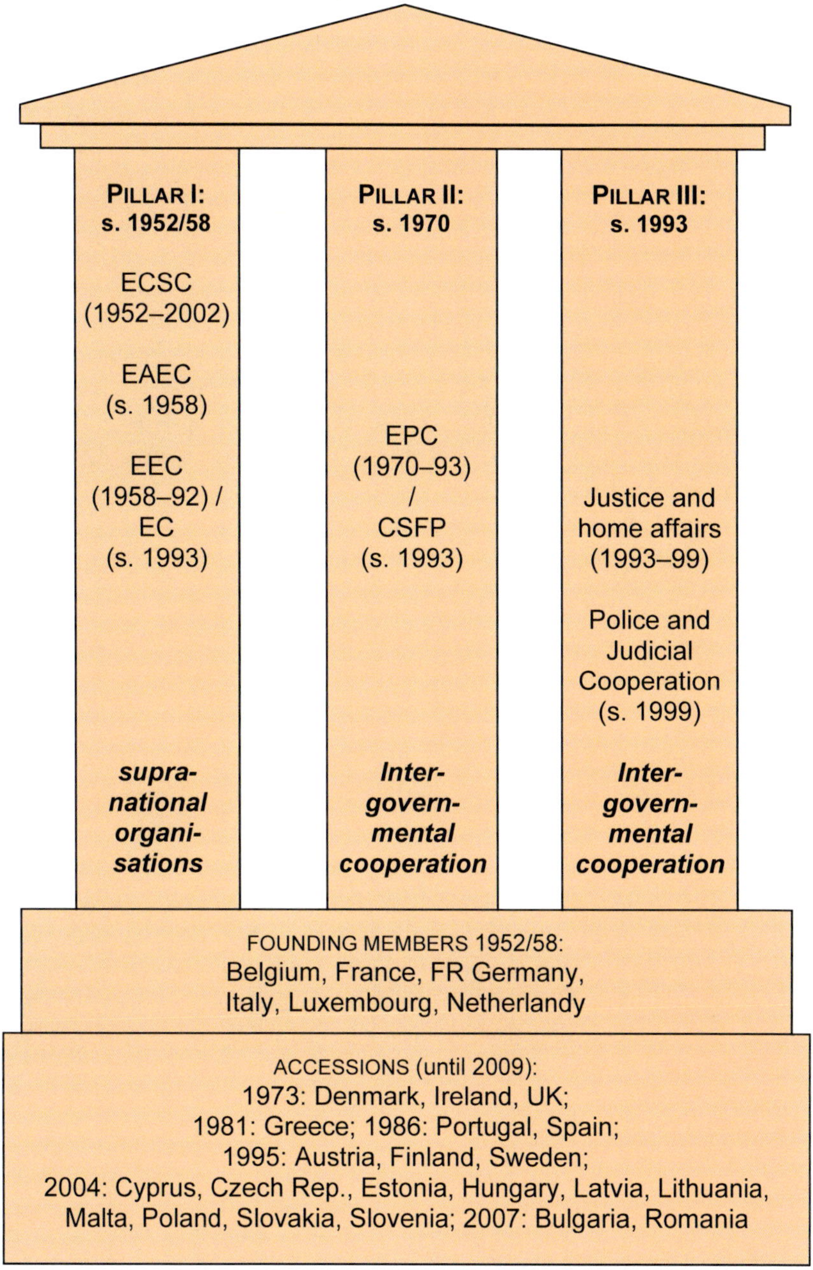

Note: In 2013, Croatia joined the EU. In 2020, the UK left the EU.

8136 Parallel to establishing the EU, Commission President DELORS, in particular, pursued the formation of a **European Economic Area** (EEA), which was to bring the EU and EFTA states together. The EEA Treaty was concluded in Porto on 2 May 1992 and came into effect on 1 January 1994.

➢ When the internal market of the EC/EU states was realised in 1992, this raised concerns in the EFTA states about possible economic disadvantages. The EEA was meant to enable them to participate in the internal market without formally joining the EC/EU.

➢ The EC, for its part, did not want to lose its autonomy in policy matters to a superordinate organisation. Any legislation in the EEA therefore had to emanate from the EC institutions, which led to an imbalance of power between the EC and EFTA.

➢ Switzerland was the only EFTA country not to participate in the EEA, following the outcome of a referendum. In Austria, a referendum according to Article 44 (3) B-VG (⇨ par. 6206) was not considered necessary, despite the far-reaching legal consequences of accession to the EEA.

8137 For most EFTA states, the EEA was only a transitional arrangement until their full integration into the EU. **Austria, Sweden, and Finland joined the EU** on 1 January 1995.

➢ Austria had already applied for membership in 1989 (⇨ par. 8144); Sweden and Finland as well as Norway and Switzerland followed suit. Referenda in Austria, Sweden, and Finland in 1994 approved the accession of these countries to the EU.

➢ In Norway, a referendum in 1994 resulted in another rejection of EU membership (as in 1972); again, fishing rights were the decisive issue, this time especially regarding competition from Spanish fishermen. In Switzerland, the negative outcome of the EEA referendum had already made its accession to the EU virtually impossible; instead, the Swiss concluded a number of bilateral agreements with the EU.

8138 The continued development of the European Union was especially characterised by efforts to thoroughly reform its institutions in order for it to be equipped for additional accessions (especially of the East-Central European states). The **treaty revisions in Amsterdam** in 1997 and **Nice** in 2001 did not achieve this goal, however, but only led to changes in some details.

➢ The Maastricht Treaty provided for its own revision ("Maastricht II") with a view to maintaining the momentum of the integration process. However, the subsequent consultations showed that national interests outweighed the ambitions to deepen the Union.

➢ The Treaty of Amsterdam of 2 October 1997, which came into effect on 1 May 1999, brought some changes to the TEU and the EC Treaty; in particular, competences of the third pillar were transferred to the supranational first pillar and thus reinforced. The third pillar, which thereby lost some of its relevance, was given the name "Police and Judicial Cooperation in Criminal Matters".

➢ The Treaty of Amsterdam also recognised the principle of "enhanced co-operation", whereby not all EU states are required to participate in certain areas of integration, but those that do can draw on EU institutions, procedures, and mechanisms. Examples of this are the Schengen Agreement or the introduction of the euro, which do not apply to all EU member states; hence, at present, some member states participate more fully in the European integration process than others. This integration at different speeds, which the founding fathers of the EEC had rejected, is likely to become even more relevant in the future.

➢ At the Nice Summit, the modalities for the forthcoming "eastern enlargement" (⇨ par. 8139) as well as a Charter of Fundamental Rights (CFR) were agreed upon. The Treaty of Nice was signed on 26 February 2001; due to an initially negative referendum in Ireland, its implementation was delayed until 1 February 2003.

8139 On 1 May 2004, Cyprus, the Czech Republic, Estonia, Hungary, Latvia, Lithuania, Malta, Poland, Slovakia, and Slovenia joined the EU; Bulgaria and Romania followed on 1 January 2007. This **"eastern enlargement"** presented the EU with its greatest challenge to that date.

➢ All the candidate countries, with the exception of Cyprus and Malta, had been run by Communist parties until 1989. Their accession to the EU was only possible after radical economic reforms; still, it placed a heavy financial burden on the EU, even more so than the "southern enlargement" in 1981/86 (⇨ par. 8125).

➢ Germany and Austria in particular were concerned that the opening of their borders to the east might entail economic disadvantages, for example in regard to the labour market. These concerns were addressed by severely restricting the "four freedoms" for a transitional period. Initially, the new member states joined neither the Schengen Area nor the eurozone (⇨ par. 8210, par. 8212), so that the effects of their accession came or will come to fruition only gradually.

➢ Since the failed Greek annexation attempt in 1974 (⇨ par. 8125), Cyprus has *de facto* been divided into two states, with northern Cyprus occupied by Turkey and not recognised internationally. The dividing line is monitored by the UN. A plan for the reunification of Cyprus devised by the UN failed due to the resistance of the Greek-speaking southern part (referendum on 24 April 2004), with the result that on 1 May 2004, EU law only became effective in the south.

d) Europe since the Treaty of Lisbon

8140 A constitutional convention established by the European Council in 2001 drew up a draft constitution for the EU by 2003; on this basis, the *Treaty establishing a Constitution for Europe* was signed in Rome on 29 October 2004. Negative referenda in France and the Netherlands, however, prevented its implementation. With the **Treaty of Lisbon**, signed on 13 December 2007, only another reform (though far-reaching) of the founding treaties of 1957/92 was adopted, instead of a formal constitution. This "Reform Treaty" came into effect on 1 December 2009.

➢ The CFR adopted in Nice had been drafted by a convention chaired by the former German Federal President ROMAN HERZOG (1994–99) and aimed at reducing the impact of individual national interests. Following this model, the European Constitutional Convention was set up in 2001. It consisted of representatives of the existing EU member states as well as those states that only joined the EU in 2004, plus representatives of the European Parliament and the Commission. It was chaired by the former French President VALÉRY GISCARD D'ESTAING (1974–81).

➢ The Constitutional Treaty was intended to adapt the structures developed for the original community of six members to apply to a community of 27, as well as to remedy the democratic deficits and codify the primary law (⇨ par. 8220), which was scattered across numerous treaties, in a single document. However, the terms "constitution", "federation", etc. used in the process gave rise to concerns among the public that a "European superstate" was being established.

➢ As part of the ratification procedure, referenda were held in four EU states (⇨ par. 6205). Those in Spain and Luxembourg led to an affirmative vote, whereas those in France and the Netherlands led to a rejection of the treaty. The ratification procedure was then discontinued.

➢ Only after a lengthy "reflection period" did the German Council presidency succeed in getting the other states to agree to a "reform treaty" in July 2007. Like the Treaties of Amsterdam and Nice, the Treaty of Lisbon did not replace the treaties of 1957 and 1992 but amended them profoundly; the EC Treaty was renamed "Treaty on the Functioning of the European Union" (TFEU).

➢ The Lisbon Treaty eliminated the "pillar structure" (⇨ par. 8135) of the EU, which now acquired legal personality in its own right and was fully merged with the EC, while the EAEC remained a separate supranational organisation. The CFR was not integrated into the treaty but was declared binding on all EU states except Poland and the UK.

➢ The omission of terms such as "constitution" or "minister" as well as provisions on EU symbols (flag, anthem) was intended to avoid the impression that the EU had become a state. Nevertheless, the Treaty of Lisbon also met with resistance in certain countries, in some cases substantially so. A referendum in Ireland in 2008 initially produced a negative result, whereupon a second referendum was held in 2009 that came out in favour of the treaty (even though it had not been amended at all!).

➢ With the Lisbon Treaty, the EU member states (including the previously neutral ones) committed themselves to a common security and defence framework, which also includes a reciprocal obligation to provide military assistance. The WEU, created in 1954 (⇨ par. 8108), had thus become unnecessary and was dissolved on 30 June 2011.

8141 The **financial crisis** that began in 2007, the **refugee crisis** that reached its (first) climax in 2015, and the **Covid pandemic** that broke out in 2019 are not only heavy burdens on two of the most "visible" elements of the EU – the eurozone (⇨ par. 8210) and the Schengen Area (⇨ par. 8212) – but also on the European Union as a whole. The markedly nationalistic approach of individual EU member states to these crises is increasingly jeopardising the European idea.

➢ The global financial crisis sparked by the collapse of the US real estate market in 2007 led to a recession throughout Europe in 2009 (after decades of economic growth), and several states were on the brink of national bankruptcy. Since the TEU explicitly precludes aid for over-indebted member states, 17 EU member states, including Austria, founded the *European Stability Mechanism* (ESM) in 2012, an international organisation independent of the EU that grants loans to states and provides guarantees (subject to strict conditions). Greece, which was dependent on this aid, lost its financial sovereignty for years (similar to Austria in 1922 as a result of the Geneva Protocols, ⇨ par. 6115). It was only in 2022 that the European Commission fully concluded its monitoring of Greece's public finances.

➢ In 2015, the civil war in Syria (2011–2024), in particular, resulted in refugee movements of hitherto unseen proportions, which overburdened the EU mechanisms for months. The willingness of European states to help varied greatly; attempts by the EU to organise a distribution of the refugees according to rational criteria failed. Thousands of refugees still live under inhumane conditions in refugee camps on EU territory.

➢ Likewise, the European states reacted in different ways to the Covid pandemic, also because the EU has very little authority in the area of public health. As during the refugee crisis in 2015, many borders were shut down, this time to prevent the spread of the disease. The EU and the ESM took far-reaching measures to address the severe economic consequences of the pandemic.

➢ In 2017, the European Commission initiated a procedure to suspend Poland's membership rights because, in the Commission's view, Poland had violated the principles on which the EU is based (Article 7 TEU, ⇨ par. 8144). The procedure was discontinued in 2024 following the (possibly only temporary) political change in Poland in 2023. A similar procedure against Hungary, initiated in 2018, is currently (spring 2025) still pending.

8142 In 2013, Croatia was the latest country to join the EU; currently, Albania, Bosnia-Herzegovina, Montenegro, Northern Macedonia, Serbia, Turkey, and, since 2022, Ukraine and Moldova (⇨ par. 8143), are officially candidates for membership. On the other hand, the UK exited the EU in 2020 ("Brexit"). The EU maintains a number of association and partnership agreements with neighbouring states. In addition, the EU and its predecessor, the European Communities, have since the Treaties of Rome pursued plans that extend well **beyond Europe**.

➢ In a referendum in the UK on 24 June 2016, almost 52 percent of those who cast their votes opted to leave the EU, but due to protracted negotiations, "Brexit" did not take place until 31 January 2020. Great Britain remained in the EU's single market until the end of 2020, with a free trade agreement negotiated for the period after that. Northern Ireland continues to be part of the EU single market (with certain restrictions), so that customs borders now exist within the UK.

➤ Turkey applied for membership in the then EEC as early as 1959 and concluded an association agreement in 1963 and a customs union with the EU in 1996. Its aspirations for full membership, however, met with vehement resistance from parts of the European, and especially also the Austrian, population – partly for economic and partly for religious and cultural reasons. With its constitutional reform, which happened in 2017, and its turn towards an authoritarian path, Turkey has made closer ties with Europe an impossible prospect.

➤ In 2020, an agreement was signed in Cotonou (Benin) between the EU and a total of 79 African, Caribbean, and Pacific states, which replaced the previous Lomé Conventions (⇨ par. 8120) and governs the EU's development policies; unlike previous agreements, it also addresses the human rights situation in the ACP states. The European Development Fund was replaced in 2021 by the Global Europe instrument, which is funded directly from the EU budget.

➤ In order to ensure close cooperation with the states neighbouring the EU, the "Union for the Mediterranean", which includes the states of North Africa and the Middle East, was founded in 2008, followed by the "Eastern Partnership" with Ukraine, Belarus, Moldova, and the Caucasus states in 2009. The latter met with considerable Russian protest.

8143 In 1989, the US came out of the Cold War as the only remaining superpower, but is gradually growing tired of its role as "global policeman". Russia experienced its defeat as humiliating and, since 2000 at the latest, has been pursuing new imperialist ambitions, as demonstrated above all, but not only, by its attack on Ukraine. However, both powers may soon be surpassed by the People's Republic of China in economic and military terms. The **world order is undergoing its greatest upheaval since 1945**, and Europe's future role in this new world order is unclear.

➤ Since the mid-19th century, the view had been emerged in the United States that it was its "Manifest Destiny" to spread its culture across the American continent, which in the 20th century developed into a belief in a global mission. Military setbacks, particularly in Vietnam (⇨ par. 8104), but also in the unsuccessful fight against terrorism, increasingly called this idea into question. Nevertheless, until recently, European NATO member states placed full trust in the superior military strength of the US – a stance that may soon change in light of the 2024 US elections, in the wake of which the USA is increasingly questioning the transatlantic alliance.

➤ In the ongoing Middle East conflict, the US has been the main opponent of Islamism since at least the 1979 revolution in Iran, culminating in the terrorist attacks in the USA on 11 September 2001, which left nearly 3,000 people dead. The USA responded with the military occupation of Afghanistan in 2001–21 and Iraq in 2003–11, without succeeding in solving any of the pressing problems. On 7 October 2023, an Islamist terrorist group murdered more than 1,000 Israelis, to which Israel responded with a military strike against Gaza, but this has also failed until now to resolve the underlying problems. Moreover, this also brought Israel and its ally, the US, into direct military confrontation with Iran for the first time in 2025.

➢ In 2000, Russia, together with four other successor states of the USSR, founded a *Eurasian Economic Community*, which most other former Soviet republics joined, while the Commonwealth of Independent States (⇨ par. 8133) lost importance. In 2010, Russia, Belarus, and Kazakhstan formed a customs union. It evolved into the *Eurasian Economic Union* in 2015, which also includes Armenia and Kyrgyzstan. Modelled on the EU, it is led by a Eurasian Commission and also aims to implement the "four freedoms" (⇨ par. 8116).

➢ After the pro-Russian government of Ukraine was overthrown by revolutionary means in 2014, the new government sought closer ties with the EU. In response to this, two regions with a substantial Russian population seceded from Ukraine to form the People's Republics of Donetsk and Lugansk, while Russia annexed the Crimean Peninsula. On 24 February 2022, Russia launched a full-scale attack on Ukraine, annexing Donetsk, Lugansk, and other Ukrainian territories it had conquered on 30 September. These events have never been recognized by Ukraine, the EU, or the US. Instead these countries, and other states, responded with aid and arms deliveries for Ukraine and economic sanctions against Russia, but did not intervene with their own troops. The Russian invasion led to the largest mass refugee exodus in Europe since 1945. Ukraine and Moldova were granted EU candidate status, while Ukraine's application for NATO membership was rejected.

➢ In the face of Russian aggression, the founding meeting of the *European Political Community* – a platform for the informal exchange of 47 heads of state and government, including the UK and Ukraine, but excluding Russia and its ally Belarus – took place in Prague on 6 October 2022 at the initiative of France. Denmark lifted its reservations regarding the CFSP (made in 1992, ⇨ par. 8135). In 2023, Finland joined NATO, followed by Sweden in 2024.

e) Austria since 1989

8144 For a long time, **Austrian membership in the European Communities** (EC) was considered incompatible with its neutrality. Not until 1989, shortly before the fall of Communism in East-Central Europe, did Austria officially apply for membership. On 12 June 1994, a referendum resulted in a clear vote in favour of EU membership, which became effective on 1 January 1995 (⇨ par. 8137). A comprehensive reform of the federal state that was planned in this context was shelved.

➢ Austria's accession to the EC constituted a major interference in the principles of democracy, federalism, and legality enshrined in the federal constitution, and thus a total revision of the constitution as defined in Article 44 (3) B-VG. Whether such an amendment could be effected through a state treaty or only through a federal constitutional law was a matter of dispute. In legal terms, the problem was solved by holding a referendum in which the people adopted a federal constitutional law authorising the competent bodies to conclude the accession treaty.

➢ A long debate ensued over Austria's neutrality, which was finally settled for the time being in 1993 with its "reinterpretation" by the federal government, according to which neutrality contained three "core elements" (non-participation in wars, non-participation in military alliances, and prohibition of foreign military bases in Austria), which were compatible with EU membership. Nevertheless, accession to the CFSP necessitated the inclusion of appropriate provisions in the B-VG (Article 23f), which in part resulted in a substantive derogation of the Neutrality Act. These provisions were extended in 2003 as a consequence of the Treaty of Nice (⇨ par. 8138).

➢ Austria's federal structure was also a major problem, as European integration affects both federal and Länder competences, yet the Länder are not adequately represented in the European institutions. The German model, which allows the Federal Council to predetermine the actions of the German representative in the Council (revised Article 23 GG), was rejected in Austria because the Austrian Federal Council only represents the interests of the Länder in a very inadequate manner (an argument that also put the existence of the Federal Council itself into question).

➢ Instead, the *Perchtoldsdorf Agreement* of 1992 created a new body, the Integration Conference of the Länder, which consists of the governors and the presidents of the diets and can issue resolutions that are binding on the Austrian representative in the Council. However, the practical significance of this conference is limited.

➢ A comprehensive reform of the federal state structure, which was also envisaged in 1992, failed in December 1994 due to the governors' veto, which was formally justified by the costs that would accumulate. The amendment of the B-VG in 1994 therefore only adjusted the federal constitution to bring it in line with the new legal situation created by the accession to the EC.

➢ Following the National Council election in 1999, the SPÖ/ÖVP coalition broke apart. The ÖVP, although it had dropped to third place, formed a coalition with the FPÖ as its junior partner and forced the SPÖ, which was still the strongest party, into opposition. For the first time since 1929, the government (Federal Chancellor WOLFGANG SCHÜSSEL, ÖVP, 2000–07) was constituted without a mandate, indeed against the will, of the federal president (THOMAS KLESTIL), who swore in the government only after tough negotiations on 4 February 2000 (⇨ par. 6211).

➢ In reaction to the FPÖ's involvement in the government, the other EU states imposed sanctions on Austria (in particular, restrictions on bilateral relations; this was not an EU measure as such). These sanctions were only lifted on 12 September 2000 after HAIDER's withdrawal from all party offices and an international observers' report on the political situation in Austria.

➢ At the same time, HAIDER's resignation sent the FPÖ into a deep crisis which, following massive electoral losses in 2005, led to the secession of the Alliance for the Future of Austria (*Bündnis Zukunft Österreich,* BZÖ), in which HAIDER (governor of Carinthia 1989–91 and 1999–2008) again had a leading role (until his death in 2008). The coalition with the ÖVP continued as an ÖVP/BZÖ coalition (2005–07).

➢ Following these events, the EU decided in 2009 to introduce measures to deal with situations when individual member states violate the Union's values, including the suspension of membership (cf. now Article 7 TEU).

8145 As early as 1980, the former Minister of Justice HANS KLECATSKY (1966–70) described the federal constitution as **"in ruins"** both "on the inside and on the outside". Thirty years later, this observation has lost none of its pertinence, on the contrary. The completely fossilised federal structure proved resistant to attempts at major reform, which was made even more difficult by the erosion of the two former major parties. Only in the area of administrative jurisdiction did a significant reform take place in 2012.

➢ In 1999, a stocktaking revealed that the body of federal constitutional law was scattered among more than 1,300 (!) constitutional laws, state treaties with constitutional rank, and constitutional provisions incorporated in simple laws and state treaties. This fragmentation and level of detail of a constitution, which is unique in the world, is due on the one hand to the deep mutual distrust between the ÖVP and the SPÖ, and on the other hand to the continually increasing number of Constitutional Court decisions, and severely restricts the freedom of the (simple, i.e. non-constitutional) legislator.

➢ The most ambitious project for a total reform of the constitution so far was the "Österreich-Konvent" (2003–05), which was established on the model of the European Constitutional Convention (⇨ par. 8140) and should draw up a draft for a new federal constitution. As in 1920, the distribution of competences between the federal level and the Länder, and the reform of the fundamental rights were the most controversial issues. The Convention was unable to reach a consensus; a draft prepared unilaterally by its president, FRANZ FIEDLER, failed to win a majority at the Convention's final session on 28 January 2005.

➢ In 2007–17, an SPÖ/ÖVP coalition was in office again (Federal Chancellors ALFRED GUSENBAUER 2007–08; WERNER FAYMANN 2008–16; CHRISTIAN KERN 2016–17; all SPÖ). As of 2008, neither party had more than one third of the seats in the National Council. Hence, neither could prevent constitutional amendments from being passed, nor could they alone, without opposition parties, pass one themselves.

➢ In 2012, a reform of administrative jurisdiction, an urgent demand for many decades, eliminated more than one hundred separate authorities. With the new administrative courts of the Länder, the constituent states, which until then only had their own legislative and administrative bodies, also gained their own judicial authorities. Above all, however, the relationship between the judiciary and the administration was changed significantly, leading legal scholars to debate (but ultimately reject) the idea that this reform amounted to a total revision of the constitution. In any case, the reform of administrative jurisdiction in 2012 constitutes the most significant administrative reform in Austria since 1925.

8146 Despite this "ruinous" state of affairs, the B-VG has been remarkably successful, especially in view of the **domestic and international crises** of the recent past, and has even gained integrative power. Although the B-VG is the oldest republican constitution still in existence in Europe, a fundamental reform was not in sight – at least not until the 2024 National Council elections.

➢ The financial, refugee, and Covid crises (⇨ par. 8141) have each had a direct impact on Austria's social and economic conditions and the political climate. The political party and interest group power structure has been undergoing significant changes for several years, and it is impossible at present to predict what these changes will lead to.

➢ With the National Council election of 2017, the ÖVP once again (after 1945–70 and 2002–06) became the party with the largest number of votes and regained its blocking minority regarding constitutional legislation (until 2024). Under Federal Chancellor SEBASTIAN KURZ (ÖVP), an ÖVP/FPÖ constitution was established. Unlike in 2000, the other EU states did not react with sanctions.

➢ When the ÖVP/FPÖ coalition collapsed in May 2019, KURZ attempted to continue his government with ministers nominated by him alone, whereupon the National Council passed a vote of no confidence against the entire federal government on 27 May 2019 (⇨ par. 6209). Federal President ALEXANDER VAN DER BELLEN therefore dismissed the Federal Chancellor immediately, and the other ministers six days later. He appointed an "expert government" for the transitional period until the next election, consisting mainly of senior civil servants and headed by the former president of the Constitutional Court (2018–19), BRIGITTE BIERLEIN, who thus became Austria's first female federal chancellor.

➢ The ÖVP emerged even stronger from the National Council election of September 2019 and formed a coalition with the Greens in January 2020. SEBASTIAN KURZ again became federal chancellor, but had to resign already in 2021. He was succeeded by ALEXANDER SCHALLENBERG (ÖVP) and, in the same year, KARL NEHAMMER (ÖVP, until 2025).

➢ As previously during the presidential election of 2016 (which extended over seven months due to a successful challenge of the election results before the Constitutional Court), also during the government crisis of 2019, all political "players" adhered to the "rules of the game" laid down in the federal constitution. Thus, in neither of these situations the temporarily limited functioning of individual organs developed into a constitutional crisis. This outcome testifies to a certain democratic maturity of politics and society in Austria, the extent of which can probably only be adequately assessed by way of international comparison. Take, for example, the 2020 presidential election in the US, the results of which were not recognized by the incumbent, prompting a mob to storm Congress, an event that resulted in several deaths.

➢ It is all the more worrying that in 2021, the Constitutional Court – for the first time since it was founded over 100 years ago – had to request the federal president to execute one of its findings directed against a federal minister. This happened in accordance with Article 146 B-VG, because the minister had not complied with the finding up to that point. Should the disregard of constitutional court decisions set an example, this would have dramatic effects on the rule of law in Austria.

8147 In the federal elections in September 2024, the **FPÖ** won a relative **majority** for the first time, but failed to form a government under its leadership.

➢ Already in June 2024, in the European Parliament election in Austria, the FPÖ won the largest number of seats; it joined forces with the French *Rassemblement National*, the Hungarian *Fidesz* and other right-wing parties to form a new European Parliament group, the "Patriots for Europe".

➢ The FPÖ's victory in the 2024 National Council elections led to the longest government negotiations since 1945. After six months, in March 2025, a coalition was formed under Chancellor CHRISTIAN STOCKER (ÖVP) consisting of the ÖVP, SPÖ, and the liberal NEOS party (which was founded in 2012). The FPÖ remained in opposition.

B Structures

1. The return to democracy

8201 The democracies of the interwar period collapsed not least because they no longer had the support of significant parts of the population. KELSEN had warned of this development as late as 1932, at the same time emphasising the idea that "a democracy that tries to assert itself against the will of the majority, perhaps even by force, has ceased to be a democracy". Nevertheless, since its return to democracy, Germany, in particular, has sought to protect its democratic tradition against anti-democratic forces (**"defensive democracy"**).

➢ Article 79 (3) GG stipulates that certain core provisions (the federalist and democratic principles, human dignity) may not be compromised by any constitutional amendments. Such an "eternity clause" is not found in the Austrian B-VG, whose Article 44 (3) also allows quite radical constitutional amendments. However, the Austrian State Treaty of 1955 entails an obligation under international law to uphold the democratic principle. The extent to which such provisions might indeed help to effectively safeguard democracy is debatable.

➢ The term "defensive democracy" was coined by the Federal Constitutional Court in Germany; political parties may be declared unconstitutional if they, "by reason of their aims or the behaviour of their adherents, seek to undermine or abolish the free democratic basic order or to endanger the existence of the Federal Republic of Germany" (Article 21 GG). Two parties have so far been banned on these grounds: a neo-Nazi party in 1952; and the German Communist Party (KPD) in 1956. The former GDR state party, the SED, on the other hand, was not banned after German reunification; its successor party, "Die Linke" (The Left), is represented in the Bundestag and several state parliaments and is even part of two German state governments.

➤ An increasingly pressing problem is the Alternative for Germany party, which has been classified as far right by many political scientists since its founding in 2013 and, since 2025, also by the Federal Office for the Protection of the Constitution. In both the 2024 European elections in Germany and the 2025 German federal elections, it came in second place with 15.9 % and 20.8 % of the vote, respectively. It has never been part of the federal government or any state government, and even the Rassemblement National refused to accept it into "Patriots for Europe" (⇨ par. 8147).

➤ In Austria, the formation of National Socialist parties is prohibited under criminal law (§ 3a of the Prohibition Act). A party that has been lawfully established can only be dissolved by a federal constitutional law, in accordance with § 1 (3) of the Political Parties Act, which has never happened so far. An obligation under international law to take such measures with regard to National Socialist or fascist organisations derives from the State Treaty of 1955 (Article 9).

8202 Today, in the 21st century, the word "democracy" as such has become less meaningful because it is used by a wide variety of political systems. "Modern democracy of the western type" (a **democracy of fundamental rights**, *isonomy*) is characterised by the fact that the democratic principle is combined with certain other principles, such as the rule of law and the liberal principle, in particular, to ensure the *freedom and equality of all humans*.

➤ The word "democracy" is not only found in the Austrian B-VG and the German GG, but also, for example, in the name of the Democratic People's Republic of Korea (i.e. North Korea); fascism was also called "true democracy" by many of its supporters. In practically all existing political systems, political leaders call themselves representatives of the people and refer to an alleged "will of the people" that they are supposedly carrying out.

➤ Dictatorial systems tend to view the people as a more or less homogeneous mass (which may partly explain the persecution of minorities); the will of the people is often viewed as an actual mass-psychological phenomenon that can be identified using more or less rational methods. Democracies based on fundamental rights, on the other hand, acknowledge the diversity in pluralistic societies; the "will of the people" is then merely a metaphor for democratic decisions, e.g. in elections.

➤ In democracies that are based on fundamental rights, even the rule of democratically legitimised leaders is not without limits; it is constrained, in particular, by the separation of powers (whether by function or because of a federal structure, ⇨ par. 6203), by the temporal limitation of their rule, and by the fundamental rights themselves. Thus, the self-limiting character of democracy is one of its most important features.

8203 The years after 1945 saw a massive **expansion of the rule of law**, not least under the influence of the ECtHR (⇨ par. 8222). This was achieved partly through legislative measures with regard to the public law courts, and partly through their own judicature. The increasingly frequent use of the Constitutional Court's power to repeal laws is problematic from the point of view of democratic theory. The attempt by parliament to render the findings of the Constitutional Court ineffective through ad hoc constitutional provisions constitutes a serious problem for the rule of law. Overall, the relationship between the Constitutional Court and parliament is therefore characterised by considerable tension.

➢ The Austrian model of constitutional jurisdiction, which before 1938 had only been adopted in Spain, and had a "twin" in Czechoslovakia in 1920–1939, was widely adopted after 1945, for example in Germany, Italy, and France, but also in Colombia and Indonesia, among others.

➢ In Austria itself, far-reaching reforms of the constitutional jurisdiction were carried out in 1975. In particular, individuals who maintain that their rights have been directly violated by an unconstitutional law can submit an application for review to the Constitutional Court. Since 2015, individuals can also file a complaint with the Constitutional Court against the application of an unconstitutional law by a civil or criminal court (with some exceptions).

➢ For a long time, the Austrian Constitutional Court was strongly influenced by the Pure Theory of Law (⇨ par. 6303) and therefore rarely reviewed political value judgements by the legislator. In contrast, under the influence of the jurisprudence of values (⇨ par. 8304), the German Federal Constitutional Court developed a "material understanding of the rule of law", according to which the constitution stipulates certain values (such as human dignity, peace, freedom, equality, and security), against which laws can be evaluated in terms of their content.

➢ Around 1980, the Austrian Constitutional Court also increasingly began to repeal laws on the grounds of "non-objective differentiation". As the ÖVP and SPÖ still had a joint constitutional majority at the time, they repeatedly responded to such repeals by elevating disputed provisions to constitutional status – even if they concerned a mere detail within the legal order – and thus shielding them from review by the Constitutional Court.

➢ From the point of view of the Constitutional Court, this tactic of the National Council was an attempt to undermine its power of judicial review, contradicting the overall structure of the federal constitution (in particular the basic principle of the rule of law). This is how it arrived at the thesis of "unconstitutional constitutional law": constitutional law is graded in itself, and "simple constitutional law" must not contradict the basic principles of the constitution. The latter, however, may only be changed by a referendum in accordance with Article 44 (3) B-VG (⇨ par. 6206).

➢ In 2001, the Constitutional Court ruled for the first time in a particularly blatant case that a constitutional provision contained in an ordinary law (the 2000 amendment to the Federal Procurement Act) violated the fundamental principles of the constitution and must therefore be repealed.

2. The European Integration

a) The Beginnings

8204 Where we may find the beginnings of European integration is a contentious issue. The answer to this question depends primarily on how one wants to view the **nature of the European Union** in its present form – is it an economic area? A nascent federal state? A Christian community based on shared values? It is therefore a political rather than a legal-historical question.

➢ Efforts to trace its development back to its earliest precursors result mainly from the desire to create a "European identity" among the population – something that is still lacking in many ways.

➢ In this context, visions of a united Europe that date back to the Middle Ages, for example, with the intention to ward off Islam (PIERRE DUBOIS, 1306), are sometimes cited as the precursors of European integration. The American statesman WILLIAM PENN developed a model that already appears very modern – and also includes "the Turks" – in his essay *Towards the Present and Future Peaces of Europe* from 1693.

➢ The Holy Roman Empire and the Austro-Hungarian dual monarchy are also described as resembling a "European monarchy" because of their supranational (rather: non-national) conceptions of the state.

8205 The thesis that the **Pan-European movement** of the Austrian RICHARD (until 1919: Count of) COUDENHOVE-KALERGI as well as the efforts of the French Foreign Minister ARISTIDE BRIAND to unify Europe were direct precursors of the European unification movements after 1945 has been widely accepted.

➢ In his "Pan-European Manifesto", which he published in 1923 without any official mandate, RICHARD COUDENHOVE-KALERGI called for the unification of the European states. This "Pan-Europe" was to encompass all European states (including their colonies in Asia, Africa, and America) except the Soviet Union and the British Empire. It was meant to be a response to "Soviet Russian imperialism" in particular, but also to the rising economic power of the USA. The Pan-European movement led by COUDENHOVE-KALERGI attracted considerable public interest, even though it did not achieve an immediate success.

➢ ARISTIDE BRIAND (several times prime minister and/or foreign minister of France between 1909 and 1932) first put forward the idea of a federation of the European states before the League of Nations in 1929. A memorandum of the French government "on the organisation of a regime of European federal union" suggested to retain the sovereignty of the nation states. This initiative also initially remained unsuccessful.

8206 While there were thus already some efforts in this direction before 1945, European integration in its modern shape primarily arose from the experiences of the Second World War, the division of Europe, and the Cold War, as well as the decline of the major European powers, which forced them to join together but also made this process easier (⇨ par. 8101). As early as 1949, the **Council of Europe** was founded, an international organisation to which almost all European states today belong and which is tasked with safeguarding and realising the ideals and principles that are the common heritage of the member states, especially focusing on the maintenance and further realisation of human rights and fundamental freedoms. To this end, several international agreements have been concluded, the most important of which is the *European Convention on Human Rights* (ECHR) of 4 November 1950.

➢ In addition to the still existing Pan-European movement, numerous initiatives for the political unification of Europe emerged after 1945. A speech held by CHURCHILL in Zurich in 1946, in which he called for the establishment of the "United States of Europe", attracted considerable attention. However, these initiatives always remained confined to the non-Communist part of the continent.

➢ The founding members of the Council of Europe in 1949 were Belgium, Denmark, France, Greece, Ireland, Italy, Luxembourg, the Netherlands, Norway, Sweden, and the UK. In the following years, the other Western European states joined as well (Austria in 1956); the Eastern European states only joined after 1989. Belarus is the only European state that has never been a member of the Council of Europe. Russia, which did not join the Council of Europe until 1996, was expelled in 2022 because of its invasion of Ukraine.

➢ In addition to the ECHR, other important agreements adopted by the Council of Europe include the European Social Charter of 18 October 1961, which contains fundamental social rights (as state objectives), and the Biomedicine Convention of 4 April 1997.

b) The politics

8207 The roots of today's European Union do not lie in the universal approach of the Council of Europe but in the **European Coal and Steel Community,** established in 1952 (⇨ par. 8107). This is despite the fact that initially only six states (the Federal Republic of Germany, France, Italy, Belgium, the Netherlands, and Luxembourg) participated in it; it also was not intended to give rise to a general political union but was limited to a rather narrow sector, namely the production, trade, and consumption of coal and steel.

➢ The general task of the Coal and Steel Community was to "contribute to economic expansion, the development of employment and the improvement of the standard of living in the participating countries through the institution, in harmony with the general economy of the member States, of a common market" (Article 2 of the ECSC Treaty).

➢ Therefore, import and export duties or quantitative restrictions on trade in coal and steel, discrimination against foreign producers or buyers, and state subsidies that could distort competition, as well as other practices that could run counter to a common market were prohibited.

➢ Since the ECSC Treaty – unlike the EEC and EAEC Treaties – was concluded for 50 years rather than for an indefinite period, it expired on 23 July 2002. The previous responsibilities of the ECSC are now carried out by the EU.

8208 The failure of the European Defence Community and the European Political Community (⇨ par. 8108) meant that European integration remained for more than 30 years focused on economic aspects. However, it was hoped that there would be a **spill-over effect**. According to MONNET, successful economic integration should not only facilitate subsequent political integration. Indeed, it was foreseeable that a harmonisation of economic policy would also entail harmonisation in other policy areas. How Europe's economic integration would evolve was initially not quite clear.

➢ MONNET proposed an extension of the ECSC's competences to other economic sectors. He was particularly interested in nuclear energy; the FRG had been allowed to use nuclear energy (for non-military purposes) since 1954. In France, this evoked a desire for regulatory supervision similar to that of coal and steel production, as it was another important factor in potential military conflicts.

➢ The Dutch Foreign Minister JOHAN BEYEN, on the other hand, rejected this "sectoral integration" and advocated a more general approach to economic integration. This, however, was initially rejected in France out of fear of a "national sell-out".

➢ An expert committee established at the Messina Conference (⇨ par. 8117) was initially to advise on the Common Market, conventional energy, nuclear energy, and transport and traffic. As the discussions progressed, the decision was made to also pursue the concept of general economic integration, with nuclear energy treated separately. This resulted in the parallel establishment of the European Atomic Energy Community (EAEC) and the European Economic Community (EEC) through the *Treaties of Rome* of 25 March 1957.

8209 The EEC took up its work on 1 January 1958 and was supposed to establish a **common market** between the member states within a transitional period of twelve years, i.e. until 1970. For this purpose, not only a customs union (⇨ par. 8116) was to be established, but also more generally, all obstacles to the free movement of goods, persons, services, and capital should be removed. Whereas the customs union could be achieved before the deadline expired, the realisation of the **four fundamental freedoms** became increasingly difficult.

➢ The EAEC, which was founded at the same time, was (like the ECSC) also only concerned with sectoral integration, namely the creation of terms and conditions for the production and development of nuclear energy. The relevant legal instruments were regulated in detail in the EAEC Treaty, i.e. the emphasis there was on *primary law* (⇨ par. 8220).

➢ The EEC, on the other hand, had rather broadly defined competences that required a more detailed definition through legal acts passed by the EEC organs (emphasis on *secondary law*, ⇨ par. 8220). This also explains the dynamic character of the EEC compared to the rather static character of the EAEC and ECSC.

➢ As early as 1959, internal tariffs were reduced by 10 percent, and in 1968, they were abolished altogether. However, the free movement of goods was still impeded by other barriers to trade than tariffs; this had apparently not been taken into consideration when the Treaties of Rome were signed.

➢ The Commission initially tried to counter these barriers with very detailed trade regulations, for which it was rightly criticised (cf., for instance, the "European Banana Regulation" of 1994, according to which bananas must have a length of 14 centimetres and a thickness of 27 millimetres!). Trade regulations of this kind were regularly vetoed by individual member states.

➢ The principle developed by the ECJ (most notably in the Cassis de Dijon decision of 1979) that restrictions to the free movement of goods by individual member states are inadmissible, unless they are necessary to satisfy mandatory requirements in the general interest, proved to be more effective. From this decision, legal scholarship has developed the principle of *mutual recognition*, according to which goods that may be sold in one member state can usually also be introduced in the other member states.

8210 Since the Single Market could not be realised by 1970, as originally envisaged, demands were voiced for a comprehensive reform of the Communities as well as an **Economic and Monetary Union** (EMU) to complement them. Following the DELORS Report of 12 April 1989, provisions on an EMU were inserted into the E(E)C Treaty by the Treaty of Maastricht. The EMU was realised with the introduction of a common currency – the euro – on 1 January 1999; however, not all EU member states also participate in the "eurozone".

➢ In 1970, a committee headed by the then prime minister of Luxembourg, CHRISTIAN WERNER, had already presented a plan for the establishment of an Economic and Monetary Union ("WERNER Plan").

➢ After initial efforts to limit the fluctuations between member state currencies had failed, a European Monetary System (EMS) was introduced in 1979, and an artificial currency unit, the ECU (*European Currency Unit*; also the name of old French gold and silver coins) was created as a single unit of account.

➢ The subsequent realisation of the Single Market and the creation of the EMU were mainly the achievements of the president of the European Commission from 1985 to 1995, JACQUES DELORS, who, shortly after taking office, presented a White Paper that specified concrete measures to achieve these objectives, most of which were then also implemented.

➢ According to DELORS' plans, the monetary union was created in three stages; the first began on 1 January 1990 with the complete liberalisation of the movement of capital and financial services.

➢ The entry into effect of the Maastricht Treaty was a prerequisite for the second stage; as of 1 January 1994, the monetary, economic, and financial policies of the EU member states were harmonised, and four convergence criteria were agreed upon, the fulfilment of which was to be a condition for participation in the third stage. According to these criteria, the *inflation rate, government deficit and debt*, and *long-term interest rates* in the participating states could not exceed a certain level, and the exchange rates between their currencies needed to have remained stable over the previous two years.

➢ The third stage was the introduction of the euro on 1 January 1999, initially in eleven EU member states and only in non-physical form. Although Greece did not meet the convergence criteria, it was admitted to the eurozone in 2000 based on incorrect information. Hence, when euro cash was introduced in 2002, only the UK, Denmark, and Sweden held on to their national currencies. Of the states that joined the EU after this date (⇨ par. 8139), Slovenia adopted the euro in 2007, Malta and Cyprus in 2008, Slovakia in 2009, Estonia in 2011, Latvia in 2014, Lithuania in 2015, and Croatia in 2023. Bulgaria is expected to join in 2026. The eurozone then will comprise 21 states.

8211 Despite the primarily economic character of European integration, the idea of a general/political union was never abandoned. In 1993, the *European Political Cooperation* (EPC), founded in 1970, developed into the **Common Foreign and Security Policy** (CFSP), which now constituted the "second pillar" of the European Union alongside the supranational communities. With the Treaty of Lisbon, it was incorporated into the supranational structures of the EU, yet special rules and procedures remained in place.

➢ The economic power of the European Communities almost automatically made them a "global player", which resulted in a need to coordinate the foreign policies of the member states.

➢ A Treaty of Friendship signed by DE GAULLE and ADENAUER on 22 January 1963 sought to intensify political cooperation between France and the FRG; it was thought that the other EEC states would join this alliance under Franco-German leadership, but this did not materialise.

➢ After DE GAULLE's resignation in 1969, the EEC member states set up a working group under Belgian Foreign Minister ETIENNE DAVIGNON (1959–77). Its report was the basis for the creation of the EPC in 1970. The EPC should not become part of the Communities but instead remain rooted in traditional international law. This meant that the EC institutions were not involved; instead, the EPC remained a matter for the member states, and the principle of unanimity continued to apply to their resolutions. But as early as 1974, the EPC became *de facto* linked to the European Council, albeit on an informal basis.

➢ It was only with the Single European Act (SEA) of 1986 that a legal basis for the EPC was created. Together with the European Communities, it was supposed to contribute to "making concrete progress towards European unity". The European Commission and the European Parliament were henceforth involved in the EPC, and the foreign ministers together with a member of the Commission were to meet at least four times per year within the framework of the EPC.

➢ With the Maastricht Treaty, the EPC was expanded and transformed into the CFSP. The latter has not just foreign and security policy objectives, but also clear defence policy aims, which were further developed with the Treaties of Nice and Lisbon.

➢ The CFSP was initially an area of "intergovernmental cooperation" without legal personality or its own organs, and therefore made use of the organs of the first pillar (except the ECJ). The Treaty of Amsterdam of 1997 created a separate organ, the "High Representative for the CFSP", who also acted as the secretary-general of the Council. The (failed) Constitutional Treaty would have provided for the elevation of this post to that of a "foreign minister" of the EU. Since the Lisbon Treaty, he or she has been called the "High Representative of the EU for Foreign Affairs and Security Policy" and also acted as the vice-president of the European Commission. The elimination of the "pillar architecture" in 2009 introduced, among other things, a competence of the ECJ also in CFSP matters.

➢ The CFSP has engaged in military operations from 2003 onwards by deploying troops of the European Union Force (EUFOR), initially in Macedonia and Congo, in Bosnia-Herzegovina in 2004, and in Chad in 2007 (⇨ par. 8132, par. 8134).

8212 *Cooperation in justice and home affairs* was established as the third pillar of the EU in 1993. With the Treaty of Amsterdam, some of its areas were transferred to the first pillar, and with the Treaty of Lisbon, the third pillar as such was eliminated altogether. The relevant provisions are now found primarily in the TFEU's Articles 67–89 (**"area of freedom, security and justice"**).

➢ An important impetus for cooperation in the areas of justice and home affairs came from the implementation of the free movement of persons and the freedom to establish and provide services respectively, but this initially took place outside the framework of the EU.

➢ In particular, the Schengen Agreement on the gradual abolition of checks at common borders of 14 June 1985 was originally not part of Community law but was signed as a separate agreement by France, the FRG, and the Benelux countries; other states joined later (Austria with effect from 1 December 1997).

➢ The cooperation in the fields of justice and home affairs established by the Maastricht Treaty was, like the CFSP, a case of intergovernmental cooperation without a supranational character.

➢ With the Treaty of Amsterdam of 1997, the Schengen Agreement was incorporated into Community law; it was replaced by an EU regulation in

2006 (the "Schengen Borders Code"). Currently, the "Schengen area" includes all EU and EFTA countries except Ireland and Cyprus.

➢ The Treaty of Amsterdam also transferred several areas of the third pillar (e.g. matters of asylum) to the first, thus placing them under the jurisdiction of the ECJ; the remainder (e.g. the Europe-wide fight against crime) constituted the "Police and Judicial Cooperation in Criminal Matters". With the Lisbon Treaty, these matters were incorporated into the supranational structure of the EU.

c) The institutions

8213 The significance of the Coal and Steel Community for the development of the Union as we know it today lies especially in the fact that the ECSC Treaty already established the types of organisation and law-making that were later adopted in a modified form in the EEC and EAEC Treaties, and which have not changed a lot since then. Almost all of **the EU's main organs** can be traced back to the corresponding organs of the ECSC:

➢ the *European Commission* (referred to in the ECSC Treaty as the High Authority);

➢ the *Council of the European Union* (in the ECSC Treaty the Special Council of Ministers);

➢ the *European Parliament* (in the ECSC Treaty the Common Assembly); and

➢ the *European Court of Justice* (in the ECSC Treaty the Court of Justice).

➢ The ECSC Treaty did not include the *European Council*, which was only established in 1974 and was legally linked to the European Communities in 1986.

➢ Other organs include: the Economic and Social Committee, created in 1958, and the Committee of the Regions, established in 1993, which both have advisory functions; the European Court of Auditors, established in 1975; etc.

8214 According to the original conception, the *High Authority* was the main law-making body of the ECSC. With the Treaties of Rome of 1957, commissions for the EEC and the EAEC respectively were established alongside it; only when the Merger Treaty came into effect in 1967 were the two commissions merged with the High Authority to form the **European Commission**. It is a collegial organ whose members "shall perform their duties in the general interest of the Community with complete independence" (Article 157 of the EEC Treaty; cf. now Article 17 TEU, and previously also Article 9 of the ECSC Treaty). Their responsibilities include, in particular, initiating the provisions to be adopted by the Council, as well as implementing them, and also ensuring the general application of Community law.

➢ The independence of its members entails the freedom from instructions from their national governments, which must refrain from influencing them in any way. However, this is in contrast to the political reality, which is such that the national governments view the individuals whom they have nominated as "their" commissioners.

➢ The High Authority consisted of nine members, eight of whom were elected by the member states, with a maximum of two members coming from the same country. These eight members then elected a ninth member. Every two years, two members retired and were replaced. This helped to ensure continuity within the High Authority.

➢ The Merger Treaty of 1967 stipulated that the Commission should include at least one national of each member state, hence the number of commissioners gradually increased with subsequent enlargements. In the Treaty of Nice, the larger member states refrained from nominating two commissioners, as they had done until then; since 2005, each country has only nominated one commissioner. A further reduction in the number of members as envisaged in the Treaty of Lisbon has not yet been realised.

➢ Since 1995, the members no longer need to be replaced or reappointed on an ongoing basis. Instead, all commissioners are elected once every five years, in line with the legislative term of the European Parliament. Their election is subject to the latter's approval.

➢ The president of the Commission (High Authority) was initially elected by the member states from among the Commission members; since 1995, his or her election has taken place prior to that of the other Commission members, for whose selection his or her approval has been required since 1999.

➢ The founding treaties of 1952/57 already included provisions requiring the Commission to resign upon a two-thirds decision of the European Parliament. To date, this has never happened, but in 1999, the entire Commission resigned due to a corruption scandal, to avoid its dismissal.

8215 To safeguard national interests, the ECSC Treaty established a Council of Ministers alongside the High Authority. The Treaties of Rome of 1957 made the **Council** rather than the High Authority (Commission) the main legislative body. Each member state sends a representative at the ministerial level to the Council; every six months, the presidency rotates among the member states. Whether unanimity or a simple or qualified majority is required for a decision is not uniformly regulated but subject to casuistic rules. As integration progressed, the areas for which unanimous decisions were needed, and in which each member state therefore had a right of objection ("veto"), were increasingly reduced.

➢ Depending on the subject matters that will be discussed, the Council will be composed of different members (e.g. the foreign ministers or the ministers for economic affairs of the member states); still, it is a single organ.

➢ The ECSC Treaty required an absolute majority of the member states' representatives, and at least either France or the FRG needed to support the decision. Unanimity was required in certain cases.

➢ The EEC Treaty also required an absolute (simple) majority for most votes but did not stipulate blocking rights for individual countries. Instead, a qualified majority (12 out of 17 votes) was introduced for certain other votes; in such cases, the FRG, France, and Italy each had four votes, Belgium and the Netherlands two each, and Luxembourg one. The votes were thus weighted according to the number of inhabitants, but with a bias in favour of the smaller member states.

➢ With the subsequent accessions, the votes in the Council were redistributed each time, yet the equal number of votes of Germany, France, Italy, and (from 1973) the UK was maintained – even after Germany's reunification, which caused it to have far more inhabitants than the other large member states.

➢ The redistribution of votes in the Council was one of the main points of contention during the negotiations on the Treaty of Nice (in the run-up to the eastern enlargement), which resulted in extremely complex provisions (⇨ par. 8216), some of which remained relevant until 2017. Eventually, it was agreed in the Treaty of Lisbon that in future, a qualified majority should require a minimum of 55 percent of the votes, which needed to represent at least 65 percent of the population (*double majority*).

8216 The introduction of simple or qualified majorities instead of unanimous decisions (which are otherwise required in international law) is probably the most profound interference in the member states' sovereignty and has therefore been repeatedly contested by individual member states. The **compromises of Luxembourg in 1966 and Ioannina in 1994** sought to avoid such conflicts through informal arrangements. This, as well as the solution found in Nice, clearly illustrates the EU's complex entanglement of law and diplomacy.

➢ On 1 July 1965, France left the table due to a dispute over agricultural matters and did not send a representative to the Council meetings for a period of six months, thus rendering the Council unable to take decisions ("empty chair policy"). It was not until 29 January 1966 that the French boycott was resolved in the Luxembourg Compromise, a legally non-binding agreement that stipulated that in cases in which "very important interests" of member states were under negotiation, the Council was not allowed to majoritise them but had to find solutions that could be adopted unanimously ("consensus").

➢ When the UK invoked the Luxembourg Compromise in 1982 – again in negotiations on agricultural matters, but really to push through other, unrelated issues – France interpreted the Luxembourg Compromise narrowly, arguing that it should not be misused to block community procedures altogether. Henceforth, the Luxembourg Compromise was no longer relevant.

➢ With the EU enlargement of 1995, the number of votes required to prevent a qualified majority decision increased from 23 to 26, which further reduced the influence of the individual member states and gave rise to resistance on the part of the UK, in particular. The Ioannina Compromise of 30 March 1994 stipulated that if Council members with 23–25 votes opposed a decision, discussions would have to continue until the minority had fallen to a maximum of 19 votes. This regulation also remained legally non-binding.

➢ The Treaty of Nice enshrined "soft law" in EU primary law with the provision that a certain voting requirement (namely the fact that a majority decision should be carried by states with at least 62 percent of the EU's population) could only be reviewed if this was demanded by a member state.

8217 The Council of the European Union must be distinguished from the **European Council**, which was only established with the SEA of 1986. It consists of the heads of state or government of the member states, the president of the Commission, and, since 2009, the president of the European Council. According to Article 15 TEU, it "shall provide the Union with the necessary impetus for its development and shall define the general political directions and priorities thereof".

➢ The decision as to whether the head of state or the head of government will represent the member state depends on the constitutional law of the respective country (and can be taken as an indication of whether it is a presidential or a parliamentary democracy).

➢ Informal meetings of the heads of state or government of the EEC states took place at irregular intervals from an early date; in 1974, it was agreed in Paris that these meetings would take place regularly and would be called the "European Council". With the Maastricht Treaty, the European Council became the only organ directly assigned to the EU (instead of the EC); since 2009, its activities have also been subject to the jurisdiction of the ECJ.

➢ Until 2009, the European Council was chaired by the head of state or government of the country that also presided over the Council. The Treaty of Lisbon established the position of President of the European Council, who is elected by the Council for a term of two and a half years.

8218 The **European Parliament**, which has its origins in the Common Assembly of the ECSC, is the only directly democratically legitimised organ of the EU. However, compared to national parliaments, it initially had only limited powers. These have been steadily expanded since the SEA of 1986.

➢ An agreement concluded at the same time as the Treaties of Rome stipulated that the Common Assembly of the ECSC should also have this role for the EAEC and EEC. There was thus always only one parliament. The name "European Parliament" was unofficially introduced in 1958 and became official in 1986.

➢ The European Parliament originally consisted of delegates from the individual national parliaments. Direct election was first adopted in 1979; the electoral rules vary from country to country, but always follow the principle of proportional representation (⇨ par. 6214). As in the Council, the number of representatives per state is based on the number of inhabitants, with a bias in favour of the smaller member states.

➢ Originally, the European Parliament was to have almost only advisory functions. Its role was significantly strengthened in 1986 by the SEA, which stipulated that the Council could only act on certain matters "in co-operation with the European Parliament". If the Parliament rejected the Council's position, the Council could only uphold it by unanimous decision.

➢ The Maastricht Treaty of 1992 introduced the "co-decision procedure" for certain policy areas, which enables the European Parliament to block Council decisions. If the Parliament makes amendments, these must be approved by the Council. With the Lisbon Treaty, this modality was declared the "ordinary legislative procedure" that should be applied as a rule; still, other procedures also to exist for certain policy areas.

8219 The **European Court of Justice** (ECJ) gained great significance, as its case law established many key concepts of European law in the first place (⇨ par. 8209, par. 8221). In 1988, a European Court of First Instance was introduced to alleviate its workload.

➢ The ECJ, too, was originally only competent for the ECSC, and only from 1957 also for the EEC and EAEC; until 2009, it had no competences in the second and third pillars of the EU. It has its seat in Luxembourg.

➢ With the Treaty of Nice of 2001, a specialist court was created to adjudicate in disputes between the European Union and its civil servants but dissolved again in 2016.

➢ Since the Treaty of Lisbon, the ECJ, the European Court of First Instance (and 2004–16 the EU Civil Service Tribunal) have been collectively referred to as the "Court of Justice of the European Union"; however, they continue to be independent courts.

➢ The judges are appointed by the governments of the member states for six years; there are no limitations on their reappointment.

d) The law

8220 Even without a Constitutional Treaty, the EU has constitutional law in the formal and substantive sense, which is called its **primary law**. It consists of the founding treaties of the Communities, the accession treaties, and certain other sources of public international law. **Secondary law**, the law created by the EU institutions themselves, is based on them.

➢ The EU's primary law can be regarded as its constitution in the substantive sense, as it lays down the conditions under which secondary law can be created (*principle of conferral*). It is also constitutional law in the formal sense, since it is created under more restrictive conditions than secondary law, and violations of primary law can be challenged before the ECJ by way of an action for annulment. An annulment according to Article 264 TFEU leads to only a relative nullity of the challenged legal act (in this respect, the procedure is similar to the Austrian review procedure before the Constitutional Court).

➢ In contrast to the law of other international organisations, EU law (both primary and secondary) addresses not only the member states but also the natural and legal persons belonging to them. This direct effect transcends the traditional dualism of state law and international law and is – together with the majority principle, which has replaced the unanimity principle otherwise applicable in international law – one of the main reasons why the European Communities are regarded as *"supranational"*.

➢ Legal acts that are binding in all their parts were called "decisions" in the ECSC Treaty; in the EEC Treaty, this term was only used if the decision only applied to a specific group of addressees. If, on the other hand, it was to have a general (i.e. law-like) effect, the EEC Treaty (or now Article 288 TFEU) used the term "regulation". The renaming of "regulations" as "European laws", which was envisaged in the (failed) Constitutional Treaty of 2004, was not realised.

➢ The ECSC Treaty designated as "recommendations" those legal acts that were binding only with regard to the objectives that they defined but left it to the addressees to choose the appropriate means for achieving them. In the EEC Treaty, these legal acts, if they were to have general application, were called "directives". The Constitutional Treaty would have renamed them "European framework laws"; here too, the Lisbon Treaty reverted to the terms "directive" and "recommendation".

8221 Since the primary law of the EU is rooted in general international law and can only be amended by unanimous decisions of the member states, only the latter, not the Union itself, have the competence-competence and are thus, according to a pronouncement of the German Federal Constitutional Court of 12 October 1993, the **"masters of the treaties"** ("Maastricht decision"). However, the judgments of the European Court of Justice have contributed to a dynamic development of Community law, which increasingly restricts the sovereignty of the member states. The principle of subsidiarity laid down in the Maastricht Treaty provides some protection against an excessive expansion of Community law.

➢ The ECJ has always pursued a very liberal interpretation of Community law. In doing so, historical methods of interpretation take second place to teleological approaches, with the declared aim of interpreting Community law in such a way as to ensure its practical effectiveness (*effet utile*).

➢ Thus, for example, the above-mentioned principle of conferral was substantially modified when the ECJ, in its AETR decision of 31 March 1971, confirmed that the EEC was competent to conclude international transport policy agreements, even though such a competence was not explicitly mentioned in the EEC Treaty; it was implicitly derived from other competences (*theory of implied powers*).

➢ Of fundamental importance for the development of European law was the ECJ's decision in COSTA v. E.N.E.L. of 15 July 1964, in which it held that the EEC Treaty had created an independent legal order that was directly applicable in the member states and could not be overridden by domestic legal provisions (*principle of the primacy of Community law*).

➢ The principle of subsidiarity (which has its roots in Catholic social teaching, ⇨ par. 7213) holds that the Community may take action in areas that do not fall under its exclusive competence “only if and in so far as the objectives of the proposed action cannot be sufficiently achieved by the member states”.

➢ The subsidiarity principle was introduced into European law by the Maastricht Treaty (cf. now Article 5 TEU) and extended in 2007 by a special protocol supplementing the Lisbon Treaty. According to this protocol, national and regional parliaments shall be involved in the EU’s law-making process and may bring actions regarding violations of the principle of subsidiarity before the ECJ.

3. International Human Rights Protection

8222 The experience of National Socialist terror led to a worldwide strengthening of the concept of human rights and to the internationalisation of *fundamental rights*. On the basis of the Universal Declaration of Human Rights by the United Nations in 1948, the Council of Europe adopted the **European Convention on Human Rights (ECHR)** in 1950, which Austria joined in 1958 and which has since then supplemented the Basic Law on the General Rights of Nationals of 1867, which had come into force again in 1945.

➢ Already at the Paris Peace Conference in 1919/20 (⇨ par. 6102), it was recognised that ethnic and religious minorities in the individual states would have to be protected by the international community itself, leading to the inclusion of corresponding provisions in the treaties. The relevant Articles 62–69 of the Treaty of Saint Germain continue to have constitutional status in Austria today. The State Treaty of Vienna-Belvedere of 1955 (⇨ par. 8115) also protects ethnic minorities in Austria.

➢ From the outset, the UN made the protection of human rights one of its key tasks. A commission headed by ELEANOR ROOSEVELT drafted the Universal Declaration of Human Rights, which was proclaimed on 10 December 1948 but is not legally binding. Two UN human rights conventions agreed in 1966 are of relatively limited practical significance.

➢ The ECHR of 1950, on the other hand, was endowed with its own protective mechanism from its inception, with the aim of enforcing the human rights it guaranteed. The procedure was very complicated and envisaged that a *European Commission of Human Rights* should initially seek to achieve an out-of-court settlement. Only if this proved unsuccessful, and after the matter had also been dealt with by the Committee of Ministers of the Council of Europe, was the *European Court of Human Rights* (ECtHR) entrusted with the final decision. The 11th Protocol to the ECHR, which came into force in 1998, significantly simplified the procedure and abolished the European Commission of Human Rights. Since then, the ECtHR can be invoked directly by individuals.

➢ Note that the ECtHR (based in Strasbourg) is different from the ECJ (based in Luxembourg). The ECtHR is a body of the Council of Europe, while the ECJ is a body of the EU.

➢ Whether the ECHR has constitutional status in Austria was initially disputed; this status was eventually confirmed in 1964 by a federal constitutional law. Since then, the ECHR and the Basic Law on the General Rights of Nationals have complemented each other on the basis of the principle of favourability: the Constitutional Court always applies the one of the two fundamental rights catalogues that provides more comprehensive protection in the specific case.

➢ In a parallel development, a reform of the Basic Law on the General Rights of Nationals was initiated, but this only led to the inclusion of the protection of telecommunications privacy in 1973 and the freedom of artistic expression in 1982. Other important rights granted after 1945 include, in particular, the fundamental right to data protection and the fundamental right to alternative civilian service. They are enshrined as constitutional provisions in the Data Protection Act and the Alternative Civilian Service Act respectively.

➢ Note that the Universal Declaration of Human Rights – formulated mainly by representatives of Western states – was not unanimously approved around the world. In 1990, the Organisation of Islamic Cooperation adopted the Cairo Declaration on Human Rights in Islam, which affirmed human rights but always with the reservation that they must be in accordance with Sharīʿa. In 2020, this declaration was significantly revised and the reservations were substantially reduced.

8223 Although the ECHR was not adopted by the EC/EU but by the Council of Europe, it was also applied by the ECJ. It was only at the Nice summit in 2000-01 (⇨ par. 8138) that a separate **Charter of Fundamental Rights (CFR)** was adopted. Since the Lisbon Treaty came into force, it has been enforceable in most EU states. The Austrian Constitutional Court recognises the provisions contained in the CFR as constitutionally guaranteed rights, which it applies in the same way as the ECHR.

➢ The European Political Community project of 1953 (⇨ par. 8108) envisaged the incorporation of the ECHR, but this did not materialise due to the failure of the project. In 1974, the German Federal Constitutional Court declared that, "as long as" (in German: *"solange"*) the EC did not have its own catalogue of fundamental rights, the Court would also examine legal acts in EC matters for their conformity with the fundamental rights enshrined in the German Basic Law ("Solange I").

➢ However, already in the 1960s, the ECJ began to apply the ECHR by analogy, on the grounds that it was one of the general principles of Community law. This was explicitly recognised in the Maastricht Treaty in 1992. In 1986, the German Federal Constitutional Court also declared, in a departure from its previous position, that it would not exercise its own jurisdiction in this area "as long as" the ECJ guaranteed effective protection of fundamental rights ("Solange II").

➢ The CFR is closely modelled on the ECHR and also grants some social fundamental rights; it was amended in 2007. However, it could not be enforced by the courts until the Lisbon Treaty came into force in 2009.

➢ The inclusion of fundamental rights in the European Constitution was one of the most controversial points during its creation, not least because of fears that the EU would use this as a means to expand its competences to new areas. In the end, they were not incorporated into the text; rather, the Treaty of Lisbon refers to the CFR and declares them binding, but also states that this does not extend the scope of Union law. Furthermore, individual member states (the UK, Poland, and the Czech Republic) were granted the option of not recognising the legally binding nature of the agreement for their respective jurisdictions; the first two countries mentioned have exercised this option.

➢ The Lisbon Treaty also authorised the EU itself to join the ECHR. However, in 2014, the ECJ issued an opinion against an accession because it would have put the ECJ in a weaker position vis-à-vis the ECtHR.

8224 The provisions of the ECHR and CFR regarding the **"fair trial"** were particularly consequential. They led to a comprehensive reform of public law jurisdiction in Austria in 1988/2012.

➢ Article 6 ECHR guarantees everybody a "fair and public hearing by an independent tribunal in the determination of his civil rights and obligations or of any criminal charge against him." A similar provision is contained in Article 47 CFR.

➢ According to the judicature of the ECtHR, the term "civil right" has a much broader meaning than the German term *"Zivilrecht"* and also encompasses large areas of administrative law. On the other hand, the ECtHR does not place the same high demands on a "tribunal" as the Austrian Constitutional Court does on a "*Gericht* (court)".

➢ In order to guarantee compliance with Article 6 ECHR in administrative matters, the Austrian constitutional legislator established "Independent Administrative Tribunals" for each of the Länder in 1988-91. They were set up in a court-like manner and acted mainly as an instance of appeal; their decisions were subject to review by the Administrative Court. In 1997, a special Federal Tribunal for Asylum Matters was added, followed in 2002 by a Federal Tribunal for Financial Matters. In 2007, the Asylum Tribunal was expanded into an Asylum Court.

➢ In 2012, after decades of discussions, nine Administrative Courts at the provicial level (*Landesverwaltungsgerichte*) were established to replace the Administrative Tribunals of the Länder. A Federal Financial Court (*Bundesfinanzgericht*) was established to replace the Financial Tribunal, and a Federal Administrative Court (*Bundesverwaltungsgericht*) was replaced the Asylum Court. They enjoy the same independence as the civil and criminal courts. An appeal against their decisions may be lodged with the (now Supreme) Administrative Court (in German still referred to as *"Verwaltungsgerichtshof"*). If a violation of a fundamental right is alleged, an appeal may be lodged with the Constitutional Court.

C Legislation and Jurisprudence

8301 In the Western democracies, the idea of codification lost ground in the 20th century, and individual acts of legislation, mainly in reaction to specific needs, became more important. This resulted in a process of **decodification**. The evolution of Austrian private law, in particular, occurred mostly outside of the ABGB. Only since the 1970s has the text of the codification been increasingly amended again.

➢ This needs-based, unsystematic approach to enacting statutory law is a negative side effect of modern democracy, in which politicians dependent on fluctuating votes are looking for easily exploitable accomplishments, which makes it increasingly difficult to enact more complex legislation.

➢ Significant areas of private law that have been regulated outside of the ABGB include labour law, tenancy law, marriage law, and consumer protection law. The ABGB is now only a "torso" but has retained its central role in private law.

➢ The current Austrian Commercial Code (*Unternehmensgesetzbuch*, UGB), which came into effect on 1 January 2007, is not a completely new codification but merely an, albeit extensive, amendment of the previous commercial code (*Handelsgesetzbuch*) from 1897 (⇨ par. 7303). The code also needed to be renamed because it replaced the central concept of the merchant *("Händler")* with that of the entrepreneur (*"Unternehmer"*). In English, the UGB is nevertheless commonly referred to as the "Commercial Code".

➢ The idea of codification gained new momentum when the European Parliament proposed the creation of a European Civil Code in 1989. A draft presented in 2011, however, only provided for a uniform sales law, which the contracting parties could choose as an alternative to national sales laws – similar to what the UN had already done with moderate success in 1980 (UN Convention on Contracts for the International Sale of Goods, also called the *Vienna Convention* after the place where it was signed).

8302 In some European states, especially in Eastern and East-Central Europe, major **codifications** continued to be enacted. To deal with the problem of getting extensive bills through parliament, they were often not enacted in a single legislative act, but in a step-by-step process.

➢ In 1947, the Netherlands was one of the few Western European states to adopt a new codification, which was to be more independent of French law than the old *Burgerlijk Wetboek* of 1838 and would encompass not only general civil law but also some specialised areas of private law. The ten parts of the Dutch Civil Code were deliberated individually and progressively enacted from 1970 onwards; the most important parts were enacted in 1992.

➢ A remarkable recodification took place in Germany, where a marriage law issued by the Allied Control Council had been in force since 1946. The law could be repealed, and the marriage law was incorporated into the BGB when the Allies gave up their reservations in 1990 (⇨ par. 8131). Another significant amendment of the BGB took place in 2002, regarding the law of obligations. In the same year, the BGB was repromulgated, and the occasion was used to incorporate numerous subsidiary statutes into the codification.

➤ Many codifications were passed in the former Socialist states after the fall of Communism in 1989; for example, a new Russian Civil Code was enacted in three parts in 1995, 1996, and 2002, and a Czech and a Hungarian Civil Code were adopted in 2014. While the Hungarian Civil Code is primarily modelled on its Dutch counterpart, the Czech legislator made use of earlier drafts from the interwar period, which in turn were based on the ABGB. Thus, the new Czech Civil Code is markedly similar to the Austrian one.

➤ In the 19th century, the desire for a modern codification that would replace the existing compilation of the *Corpus Iuris Canonici* was expressed in canon law circles as well. On 27 May 1917, Pope BENEDICT XV promulgated the *Codex Iuris Canonici*, which provided the Roman Catholic Church with a comprehensive legal system formulated in abstract legal principles, but introduced only relatively few substantial innovations. As a result of the far-reaching reforms of the Catholic Church by the Second Vatican Council (1962–65), a new *Codex Iuris Canonici* was devised, and it was promulgated by Pope JOHN PAUL II on 25 January 1983.

8303 The most recent large-scale codification project in Austria took place in the field of criminal law with the **Criminal Code** (*Strafgesetzbuch*, StGB) of 23 January 1974, marking the conclusion of more than 150 years of efforts to reform criminal law. A major reform of criminal procedure in 2004, on the other hand, did not take the form of a new codification but was passed as a partial amendment to the existing Code of Criminal Procedure.

➤ The Criminal Code of 1852 had not been a new codification but only a renewed version of the previous Criminal Code of 1803 (⇨ par. 3312), which had become necessary mainly because of the extension of its scope to Hungary (⇨ par. 4106); its main redactor was ANTON HYE VON GLUNEK (⇨ par. 4310). In 1861, HYE was commissioned to draft a completely new criminal code, but his reform proposal, like numerous subsequent drafts, did not progress beyond the parliamentary consultation stage.

➤ After 1871, the Austrian drafts were oriented towards the German Criminal Code of 1871, but it soon became apparent that the latter was also in need of reform. Therefore, in 1927, a joint Austrian-German draft was prepared (with contributions from the Austrian jurist FERDINAND KADEČKA), but it too was unsuccessful (⇨ par. 6119). After 1945, the ministers of justice CHRISTIAN BRODA (1960–66, 1970–83, SPÖ) and HANS KLECATSKY (1966–70, ÖVP) were particularly engaged in efforts to implement a large-scale reform of criminal law.

➤ Overall, the final draft attracted broad parliamentary approval; nevertheless, the bill was passed only by the National Council in 1973 with the votes of the SPÖ, due to its provisions on abortion, which protected women who terminated their pregnancy during its first three months from criminal prosecution. When the Federal Council objected to the National Council's decision, the latter passed a vote of persistence in 1974, which allowed the new criminal code to enter into effect in 1975. Salzburg (then ruled by the ÖVP) referred the matter to the Constitutional Court (based on the constitutional provisions on abstract judicial review, ⇨ par. 6221), but the Court upheld the new abortion rules.

➢ The Code of Criminal Procedure 1873 was amended to adapt it to the new criminal code and then repromulgated in 1975 (hence its current title, Code of Criminal Procedure 1975). The reform of the Code of Criminal Procedure in 2004, which came into effect in 2008 and eliminated the last inquisitorial elements from the pre-trial stage, affected more than a third of its text; still, the code was neither formally recodified nor repromulgated.

8304 After 1945, the doctrine of civil and criminal law was able to build on the teachings of the interwar period. The jurisprudence of interests (⇨ par. 6302) developed into the **jurisprudence of values**. It, too, understands the work of the courts as a weighing of different interests (as does the jurisprudence of interests). The judiciary identifies the legislator's value attributions and makes them the benchmark for its decisions. For each individual case, these value attributions are to be considered as a "flexible system", depending on their intensity and significance.

➢ Whether the years 1933–1945 represented a break in this development or whether there were continuities across all breaks is a matter of debate. Note, for example, that Karl Larenz, a member of the Kiel School, became a pioneer of the jurisprudence of values (*Methodenlehre der Rechtswissenschaft/Methods of Jurisprudence*, 1960).

➢ The jurisprudence of values sees itself as an improved continuation of the jurisprudence of interests that merely corrects the weaknesses of the latter. What was criticised in particular was the concept of "interests", which was used by the jurisprudence of interests to describe both the intentions of the persons involved and the value attributions of the legislator. The jurisprudence of values restricts the concept of interests to the former in order to better distinguish "interests" from "value attributions".

➢ The need to recognise the highest-ranking value attributions (especially *justice*, but also *legal certainty*, for example) became particularly evident after the experiences during the National Socialist regime (⇨ par. 7302). It was expressed, for example, in the *Oberste Grundsätze des Rechts* (*Supreme Principles of Law*, 1947), a treatise by the Frankfurt civil law scholar and legal historian Helmut Coing. This aligns the jurisprudence of values with natural law theories.

➢ Karl Engisch, a criminal law scholar from Heidelberg, recognised that the highest principles do not stand in isolation but are linked to each other in a system. Building on this, the civil law scholar Walter Wilburg from Graz developed (around 1950) the theory of the "flexible system", which his disciple, the Viennese civil law scholar Franz Bydlinski substantially elaborated in his *System und Prinzipien des Privatrechts* (*System and Principles of Private Law*, 1996). According to Bydlinski, the highest principles are "optimisation imperatives", which can only be followed incrementally and in consideration of the other principles. For example, the pursuit of absolute *justice* would endlessly delay trials; in the interest of *legal certainty*, they must be completed within a reasonable period, which may result in unjust verdicts that will have to be accepted.

➢ The jurisprudence of values can be considered predominant in civil and criminal law in Germany and Austria today, but it is also increasingly influential in public law (⇨ par. 8203).

8305 At the beginning of the second quarter of the 21st century, jurisprudence is facing a range of problems. The following are some of the most pressing topics: Europeanisation of the law; globalisation of the world economy; an excessive volume of new legislation; electronic legal databases; and artificial intelligence. All this also has a significant influence on the organisation of **legal education**.

➢ The legal education system introduced with THUN's reform (⇨ par. 4306) remained for the most part in place until 1978, after which it was fundamentally reorganised. Since then, law students have had to follow a *diploma programme* to obtain the academic degree of *Magister/Magistra*; only this qualification, and not the *doctoral programme* that builds upon it, is a prerequisite for the "traditional" legal professions. Recently, three-tier programmes (Bachelor/Master/Doctorate) have been introduced – initially, in 2006, in Business Law, and also in International Legal Studies since 2021.

➢ Since 2004, the universities – after a hiatus of some 250 years (⇨ par. 3316) – have once again become corporations with full legal capacity and regained full control over their own curricula. Nevertheless, the legislator prescribes certain minimum requirements for legal curricula that prepare their alumni for professional roles in the judiciary, as attorneys or notaries.

➢ While the doctoral programme is meant to have a more academic character, the demand for more "practical relevance" has been at the forefront of all reforms of the diploma programme since 1978. In effect, this led to a significant reduction in the teaching of legal philosophy and legal history; however, some of the economic subjects were also greatly reduced, which ran counter to the demand for more "practical" content.

➢ The explosion in student numbers since around 1968 in particular, but also a new understanding of academia, have resulted in the degree programmes becoming increasingly organised like secondary school studies (e.g. compulsory attendance, standardised learning materials, prescribed order of examinations), so that today they bear more resemblance to the programmes of the Pre-March period than to those of the time after 1848, which were characterised by the freedom of teaching and learning.

Bibliographical remarks

I.

This book is largely an English translation of parts of my textbook *Rechtsgeschichte. Einführung in die historischen Grundlagen des Rechts* ([6]2023). On pages 458–482, it contains an extensive bibliography of legal historical literature (mainly in German).

The bibliography mentioned above also includes several textbooks, of which the manual commonly used in Vienna is particularly noteworthy: *Rechts- und Verfassungsgeschichte* ([7]2024), a joint publication of the "Arbeitsgemeinschaft Österreichische Rechtsgeschichte" ("Working Group Austrian Legal History": G. KOHL, CH. NESCHWARA, TH. OLECHOWSKI, I. REITER-ZATLOUKAL, M. P. SCHENNACH). For more in-depth information and reference, consult the *Studienwörterbuch Rechtsgeschichte und Römisches Recht*, edited by TH. OLECHOWSKI and R. GAMAUF ([4]2020). A good textbook in English, similar in structure to the present one but giving more space to earlier (and less to modern) periods, is R. LESAFFER, *European Legal History* (2009); for contemporary legal history, see also F. BERMEJO BATANERO (ed.), *The Legal History of European Integration* (2021).

II.

The following authors are cited in this textbook with these books and articles: Par. 0001: H. MITTEIS / H. LIEBERICH, *Deutsche Rechtsgeschichte* ([19]1992) 1; W. OGRIS, *Rechtsgeschichte und Juristenausbildung*, in: idem, Elemente Europäischer Rechtskultur (2003) 3–9, 7; M. STOLLEIS, *Rechtsgeschichte, Verfassungsgeschichte*, in: H.-J. Goertz (Hg), Geschichte ([3]2007) 391–412, 392. Par. 0002: R. WALTER / H. MAYER / G. KUCSKO-STADLMAYER, *Grundriss des österreichischen Bundesverfassungsrechts* ([10]2007) 1; M. Weber, *Wirtschaft und Gesellschaft* (1920, reprint 1976) 17. Par. 0002: H. KELSEN, *Reine Rechtslehre* ([2]1960, reprint 2020) 289. Par. 0006: K. BRUNNER, *Einführung in den Umgang mit Geschichte* ([4]2004) 91. Par. 0007: C. JABLONER, *Vergangenes Recht*, in: Festschrift W. Barfuß (2002) 113–126, 125. Par. 1202: TH. MOMMSEN, *Römische Geschichte I* (1854) 54. Par. 4210: W. BRAUNEDER, Austria's Bicameralism 1861–1873: Two "First Chambers", in: idem, Studien I (1994) 127–139. Par. 6110: E. ZÖLLNER, *Geschichte Österreichs* ([8]1990) 504.

III.

In addition, the following works, which are **not included** in the bibliography quoted above, were used for this book: A comprehensive, general reference book is ST. N. KATZ, *The Oxford International Encyclopedia of Legal History*, 6 vol. (2009). For ancient legal history see H. CANCIK (ed.), *Der neue Pauly. Enzyklopädie der Antike*, 16 vol. (1996–2003); W. SELB, *Antike Rechte im Mittelmeerraum* (1993); ST. HODKINSON/M. KLEIJWEGT/K. VLASSOPOULOS (ed.), *The Oxford Handbook of Greek and Roman Slaveries* (2016). On the three Abrahamic religions and their significance for global legal development: J. WITTE jr./R. DOMINGO (eds.), *The Oxford Handbook of Christianity and Law* (2024); H. KÜNG, *Das Judentum* (1991); IDEM, *Das Christentum* (1994); IDEM, *Der Islam* ([4]2006); R. BHALA, *Understanding Islamic Law (Sharīʿa)* ([2]2016); N. J. SMELSER/P. B. BALTES (eds.), *International Encyclopedia of the Social & Behavioral Sciences* (2001). On modern developments in international law: S. KOCH/J. SUNDE (eds.), *Comparing legal cultures* ([2]2020); Th. BENJAMIN (ed.), *Encyclopedia of Western Colonialism since 1450* (2007); St. PRESS, *Rogue Empires. Contracts and Conmen in Europe's Scramble for Africa* (2017);

J. BOYER, *Austria 1867–1955* (2022): Z. STEINER, *The Lights that failed. European International History 1919–1933* (2005); H. PAUER STUDER, *Justifying Injustice. Legal Theory in Nazi Germany* (2020); D. TWITCHETT et al (eds.), *The Cambridge History of China*, 15 vol. (1978–91, several reprints).

Index of Persons

Index of Subjects